AFRICA
EXPLORED

EUROPEANS IN THE DARK CONTINENT, 1769–1889

By the same author

The Court at Windsor
The Days of The French Revolution
The Great Mutiny: India 1857
London: The Biography of a City
The Rise and Fall of the House of Medici
Edward VII: A Portrait

CHRISTOPHER HIBBERT

AFRICA
EXPLORED

EUROPEANS IN THE DARK CONTINENT, 1769–1889

W · W · NORTON & COMPANY
New York   London

First American Edition 1983

Library of Congress Cataloging in Publication Data
Hibbert, Christopher, 1924–
    Africa explored.
    1. Africa, Sub-Saharan—Discovery and exploration.
I. Title.
DT351.H5   1983   967   83–2462

ISBN 0-393-01760-5

W. W. Norton & Company, Inc., 500 Fifth Avenue, New York, N.Y. 10110
W. W. Norton & Company Ltd., 37 Great Russell Street, London WC1B 3NU

1 2 3 4 5 6 7 8 9 0

CONTENTS

ACKNOWLEDGEMENTS

The author and the publishers are grateful for permission to reproduce illustrations from the following sources:
Barth, H., *Travels and Discoveries in North and Central Africa* (1857): Plates 26, 27, 28, 29; B.B.C. Hulton Picture Library: Plates 10, 15, 16, 24, 34, 38, 39, 46; Bruce, J., *Travels to Discover the Source of the Nile* (1790): Plates 1, 2, 3, 4, 5; Burton, R. F., *Lake Regions of Central Africa* (1860): Plates 31, 32; Burton, R. F., *A Mission to Gelehele, King of Dahome* (1864): Plate 41; Caillié, R., *Travels through Central Africa to Timbuctoo* (1830): Plates 21, 22; Cameron, V. L., *Across Africa* (1885): Plates 49, 50; Clapperton, H., *Journal of a Second Expedition into the Interior of Africa* (1829): Plate 14; Denham, D., *Narrative of Travels and Discoveries in Northern and Central Africa* (1826): Plates 11, 12, 13; Junker, W. J., *Travels in Africa* (1892): Plate 45; Laing, A. G., *Travels in Timannee and West Africa* (1825): Plate 19; Lander, R. and J., *The Niger* (1832): Plates 17, 18; Livingstone, D., *Missionary Travels and Researches in South Africa* (1857): Plates 47, 48; Park, M., *Travels in the Interior Districts of Africa* (1799): Plates 7, 8, 9; Richardson, J., *Travels in the Great Desert of Sahara* (1848): Plates 23, 25; Royal Geographical Society: Plates 20, 30, 33, 39, 40, 51, 52; Royal Library, Windsor Castle, Courtesy H. M. the Queen: Plate 6; Schweinfurth, G., *The Heart of Africa* (1873): Plates 42, 43, 44; Speke, J. H., *Journal of the Discovery of the Source of the Nile* (1863): Plates 35, 36, 37; Stanley, H. M., *In Darkest Africa* (1890): Plate 53; Stanley, H. M., *Through the Dark Continent* (1878): Plate 54.

LIST OF MAPS

For James and Sharon

AUTHOR'S NOTE

This is a narrative of the principal explorations of Africa undertaken by Europeans from the days of James Bruce and Mungo Park to those of Livingstone and Stanley, Cameron, Schweinfurth and Junker. It is based largely upon the diaries, letters and published works of the explorers themselves and is intended to convey an impression of how Africa and Africans appeared to these eighteenth- and nineteenth-century travellers and how both land and people were represented to their readers.

I am, once again, deeply indebted to the staffs of the British Library and the London Library, and to Mr G. S. Dugdale, Librarian of the Royal Geographical Society, Mr David Wileman, Deputy Librarian, and their staff. I am also most grateful for their help in a variety of ways to Mrs John Rae, Mrs John Street, Mrs Francis Pollen, Mrs Martin Goodier, and to my wife for compiling the index. Sir Patrick Turnbull, Dr James Bull and Mr Christopher Hawker have been kind enough to let me keep their books for the two years during which I have been engaged upon my own. And Mr Anthony Kirk-Greene, Fellow of St Antony's College, Oxford, has been kind enough to read the book in proof and has given me much useful advice for its improvement. He has also helped me with the glossary.

Contemporary spellings have been used for most place and tribal names in the text, but alternative and modern spellings have also been given on some of the maps and in the index. Because so many African towns, even large towns, have disappeared without trace, it has not been possible to mark on all the maps all the places mentioned in the text.

C.H.

Tangier
Rabat. Fez
Algiers
Tunis
TUNISIA
Tripoli
Alexandria
Cairo
Mediterranean Sea

MOROCCO
ALGERIA
LIBYA
EGYPT
Aswan

S A H A R A   D E S E R T
R. Nile
Red Sea

MAURITANIA
Nouakchott
MALI
NIGER
CHAD
Khartoum
SUDAN
DJIBOUTI

SENE-
Dakar GAMBIA
Bamako
R. Niger
Niamey
Ouagadougou
UPPER
VOLTA
L. Chad
Ndjamena
Addis Ababa
ETHIOPIA

Bissau
GUINEA
Conakry
Freetown
IVORY
COAST
GHANA
BENIN
NIGERIA
R. Benue
CAMEROUN
CENTRAL
AFRICAN REP.
Bangui
SOMALI
REP.
Mogadishu

Monrovia
LIBERIA
Accra
Lagos
Bight of Benin
Yaoundé
R. Zaïre
UGANDA
Kampala
KENYA
Nairobi
Abidjan
Porto Novo

Libreville
Cape St Catherine
GABON
CONGO REP.
ZAÏRE
L. Victoria

A T L A N T I C
Brazzaville
Kinshasa
L. Tanganyika
TANZANIA
Dar es Salaam
Zanzibar
INDIAN

O C E A N
Luanda
ANGOLA
ZAMBIA
Lusaka
Lilongwe
L. Malawi
(L. Nyasa)
MALAWI
O C E A N
Mozambique

Zambezi R.
NAMIBIA
Cape Cross
Windhoek
BOTSWANA
Gaborone
Harare
ZIMBABWE
Sofala
MOZAMBIQUE
Tananarive
MADAGASCAR
(Malagasy Rep.)
Limpopo R.
Pretoria
Maputo

Alexander Bay
Orange R.
Vaal R.
SOUTH
AFRICA
Cape Town
Cape of Good Hope
Port Elizabeth

Key to map areas

1. GUINEA-BISSAU   5. RWANDA
2. SIERRA LEONE   6. BURUNDI
3. TOGO   7. SWAZILAND
4. EQUATORIAL GUINEA   8. LESOTHO

PROLOGUE

Near the eastern end of Pall Mall there once stood a fashionable tavern known as the St Alban's. Early one summer evening in 1788 nine rich and distinguished members of a small dining club met here to enjoy one of the excellent meals provided by the establishment. During the course of the evening the conversation turned to Africa, that mysterious continent of which so little was then known; and before the club members parted they had decided to form 'an Association for promoting the Discovery of the Interior parts of Africa' in the belief that 'so long as men continued ignorant of so large a portion of the globe, that ignorance must be considered as a degree of reproach on the present age'.

Africa had always been the dark continent, reluctant to reveal its secrets. In the great days of Rome, when the Empire on the southern shores of the Mediterranean stretched all the way along the African coast from the Nile to the Atlantic, the vast expanses of the hinterland were largely *terra incognita*. Expeditions were occasionally made into strange lands to punish unruly tribes, to cement alliances, to trade, or to expand the empire, but none seems to have reached further south than Tibesti west of the Nile valley; and when the Emperor Nero sent an expedition into the Nubian desert under the command of two brave centurions they returned to report that beyond the wastes of sand lay impenetrable swamps. Five hundred years earlier, the Greek historian and traveller, Herodotus, had journeyed up the Nile as far as the first cataract at Aswan; but the course of the river further south was impossible to determine. 'Of the sources of the Nile no one can give any account,' he wrote. 'It enters Egypt from parts beyond.' These parts he called 'the wild beast region'.

From time to time the reports of adventurous merchants would enable geographers to draw tentative lines on maps. In about A.D. 140 Claudius Ptolemaeus, who spent much of his working life in Alexandria and became known to posterity as Ptolemy, prepared a map of Africa from such reports. It showed the continent as a vast land mass merging into what is now Antarctica, and depicted the sources of the Nile far south of the equator in two huge inland seas beyond which a long range of mountains, reaching almost to the coast north of Madagascar, were marked *Lunae Montes*, the Mountains of the Moon. At right angles to the Nile, Ptolemy drew another river, the Niger,

13

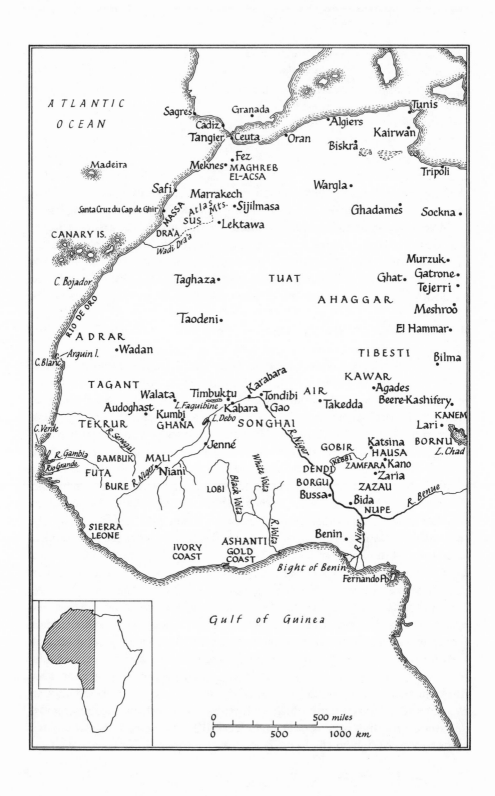

ATLANTIC
OCEAN

Sagres
Granada
Cadiz
Algiers
Tunis
Tangier Ceuta
Oran Kairwan
Biskra
Madeira
Fez
Meknes• MAGHREB
EL-ACSA
Tripoli
Safi
Wargla•
Santa Cruz du Cap de Ghir Marrakech
Ghadames• Sockna •
Atlas Mts. •Sijilmasa
SUS •Lektawa
CANARY IS. DRA'A
Wadi Dra'a Murzuk•
Gatrone•
C. Bojador Taghaza• TUAT Ghat. Tejerri •
AHAGGAR Meshroo•
Taodeni•
El Hammar•
ADRAR •Wadan TIBESTI Bilma•
Arguin I.
C. Blanc KAWAR
TAGANT Karabara •Agades
Walata Timbuktu •Tondibi AIR Beere-Kashifery•
Audoghast L.Faguibine Kabara Gao •Takedda KANEM
Kumbi L.Debo SONGHAI Lari• BORNU
TEKRUR GHANA Katsina L.Chad
C. Verde GOBIR HAUSA
R. Gambia Jenné ZAMFARA •Kano
BAMBUK MALI DENDI •Zaria
Rio Grande BURE Niani BORGU ZAZAU
FUTA LOBI Bussa• •Bida
NUPE R. Benue
SIERRA Benin
LEONE IVORY ASHANTI
COAST GOLD
COAST Bight of Benin
Fernando Po

Gulf of Guinea

0   500 miles
0   500   1000 km

which was shown as flowing almost the whole way across the continent between Ethiopia and the Western Ocean. In subsequent generations the reliability of Ptolemy's map was constantly questioned in Europe, though no one knew for sure in what ways it was inaccurate, for no one had returned from the interior of Africa to prove it so.

After the Arab invasions of northern Africa in the seventh century and the introduction of the indispensable camel as a beast of burden on long journeys, parts of the hinterland began to be revealed. An interest in geography – fostered by the obligation upon those Muslims who could do so to travel to Mecca – combined with a desire to discover new lands in which to trade, led to Arabs penetrating down the east coast beyond Zanzibar to Sofala and ever deeper into the interior of the continent both as merchants and as explorers in search of knowledge. In the course of time, caravan routes were established across the vast expanses of the Sahara Desert and trading agreements were made with the black tribes beyond the edges of the desert to the south, several of which – the Hausa, the Bornu, the Songhai and Mandingo among them – were converted to Islam. Ivory, gold, nuts, leather-work, palm oil and peacock feathers were carried north; salt and cloth and beads were taken south.

Two Arab explorers whose works have survived were Ibn Haukal, a tenth-century native of Baghdad, and Ibn Battuta who was born in a Berber family in Algiers in 1304. Ibn Haukal reached as far south as Kumbi, the capital of Ghana, and stood on the banks of the Niger which he reported as flowing to the east in confirmation of Herodotus. Ibn Battuta, who had also travelled widely in Asia, ventured into the Sudan, visited Timbuktu and spent eight months in Mali at Niani where, so he recorded, the Sultan received with honour some cannibals from Wangara, and 'gave them as his hospitality gift, a servant, a negress. They killed her and ate her, and having smeared their faces and hands with her blood came to the Sultan to thank him.'

Following in Ibn Battuta's footsteps, Leo Africanus also visited Timbuktu and Niani. A Moor from a Granada family who had settled in Fez, he had been captured by Christian corsairs off Jerber in 1518 and, because he was obviously intelligent and widely travelled, instead of being sold into slavery, he was sent to Pope Leo X who granted him his freedom, had him baptized and gave him his own name. Leo Africanus went to Gao, Hausaland and Bornu as well as Timbuktu and Niani, and he also saw the Niger but, unlike Ibn Haukal and Ibn Battuta, he declared that it flowed to the west, confirming the view of the celebrated Spanish Arab geographer, El-Edrisi, who had, however, never seen it. Other confusions arose when Leo's *History and Descriptions of Africa* was printed and translated, and when cartographers, misreading and misinterpreting it, drew maps which, while perpetuating mistakes, added new errors of their own. As Swift observed:

15

So Geographers in Afric-Maps,
With Savage-Pictures fill their Gaps,
And o'er unhabitable Downs
Place Elephants for want of Towns.

One famous map depicted Mansa Musa, the incalculably rich King of Mali and 'Lord of the Negroes of Guinea', sitting enthroned in the midst of his kingdom. Above him is 'a region of people who veil their mouths [Tuaregs] ... who live in tents and have caravans of camels', and north of that is a gap in a mountain range through which 'pass the merchants who travel' to his lands.

Guinea, which probably took its name from *aguinaou*, the Berber for Negro, and certainly gave its name to the English coin first minted in 1662, had long fascinated Europe as the source of the gold that flowed out of Africa in a seemingly endless stream. A few brave European merchants had attempted to find this source in the fifteenth century by the overland route from the north. A Genoese merchant, Antonio Malfante, for instance, had reached Tuat in the middle of the Sahara but he was able to discover nothing of the fabulous gold fields to the south-west; while Benedetto Dei, a representative of the Florentine banking house of Portinari, who was in Timbuktu a few years later, was no more successful. It was not, indeed, until Prince Henry the Navigator, fourth son of King Jão I of Portugal, determined to seek the gold fields of Guinea by way of the sea that the first real triumphs of European exploration began to be realized.

Prince Henry had distinguished himself in the capture of Ceuta, the Moroccan citadel on the Barbary shore, in 1415; and, having thus helped to establish the first European settlement in Africa since Roman times, he turned his mind to the gold of Guinea. Other reasons were later given for the voyages which he directed – the conversion of the pagans to Christianity, the discovery of a sea route to India, the search for the legendary Prester John who was said to reign over a Christian kingdom in the heart of Africa. But gold was the real lure. He was repeatedly warned of the dangers: the Green Sea of Darkness, as the Arabs called the Atlantic, was beset with unimaginable terrors for the seaman. Monsters lurked here; islands suddenly loomed out of the suffocating mist, vomiting fire and blood; ships were pulled down into the deep by the forces of evil.

Yet Henry had faith in his Portuguese ships. He felt sure that the Green Sea of Darkness could be conquered. Herodotus had written of Phoenician sailors, under orders from Pharaoh Necho II, circumnavigating Africa in about 600 B.C. And certainly in about 480 B.C. a Carthaginian naval expedition under Hanno had explored the Atlantic coast as far as Rio de Oro and brought back with them the skins of three man-like animals which their interpreters called 'gorillas'. Pliny had told of a Carthaginian admiral who in 450 B.C. had sailed

16

down the West African coast to a point where savages had attacked his ships with stones. In about 130 B.C., according to Strabo, a Greek sailor had found on the East African coast the prow of a boat which he believed had sailed all the way round the continent from Cadiz. And in the end Prince Henry was proved right. At first his captains returned, one after another, having failed to get by Cape Bojador, maintaining that beyond the Cape the land was barren and deserted, that there was no water to be had, and that the tides were so strong that once their ships sailed on they would never be able to return. But Prince Henry persisted, sending them back with the promise of greater rewards, dispatching others after them, impressing upon them the importance of their mission; and in 1414 one of them, Gil Eanes, 'disdaining all peril', succeeded in passing the cape and bringing his *barcha* back again. Seven years later another *barcha*, commanded by Antão Gonçalves, passed beyond the Cape as far as Rio de Oro. Then, in the early 1430s, Nuno Tristão, in one of the caravels recently constructed at Sagres, got past Cape Blanco to discover the Arguin archipelago; and in 1445 Dinis Dias took another caravel past the mouth of the Senegal River and doubled Cape Verde. After Prince Henry's death in 1460 the voyages continued. In 1462 Pero de Sintra sailed beyond the mouth of the Gambia to discover a coast which he called Sierra Leone because, so it was said, he had heard lions roaring in the mountains beyond the shore. Subsequent expeditions sailed further and further into unknown waters, passing the Ivory Coast and the Gold Coast into the Bight of Benin and the Bight of Biafra, moving east all the time so that their commanders thought that they were rounding the southern shores of the continent and were discovering a sea route to India until, in 1473, by the island in the Bight of Biafra that was to bear his name, Fernando Po saw that the shore line here turned south again and supposed, correctly, that there were thousands more miles to sail before the southern tip of Africa was reached. In the years that lay ahead these coasts beyond the equator were gradually charted. Rui de Sequiera reached Cape St Catherine; and in 1482 Diogo Cão discovered the mouth of a river whose muddy waters were discharged with such force into the sea that tree trunks and floating islands were carried in the rushing torrent far past his ship into the depths of the ocean to the west. He asked the people, the Bakongo, who lived by its estuary, what this powerful river was called. They told him it was the *nzere*, 'the river that swallows all others'. In Cão's mouth this became the Zaire, and by this name it was known until, two centuries later, it was more usually called the Congo.

Diogo Cão sailed on past the Congo, down the coast of what is now Angola, and reached as far as Cape St Mary. Then, on a second voyage, in the name of King John II of Portugal, he planted a stone pillar at Cape Cross on the coast of the Namib Desert in Namibia.

17

Although so close to turning the continent, Cão did not succeed in doing so. But shortly after his death one of his captains, Bartholomeu Dias de Novais, returned to Cape Cross, sailed south to Alexander Bay in what is now South Africa and, passing the Cape of Good Hope, reached Port Elizabeth where he saw the shore line extending north to the horizon and knew that he had proved Ptolemy wrong: he had sailed past the southern shores of Africa. Ten years later, in 1497, Vasco da Gama set out on his momentous journey round the Cape to India.

The opening of this route to the east and the almost simultaneous discovery of America in the west turned men's minds to other distant lands, and the interest in African exploration thereafter began to wane. By then exploration had in any case long ceased to be the main purpose of European voyages. Antão Gonçalves had taken captive ten Sanhaja Tuaregs when he had landed on the coast at Rio de Oro, and ever since then slaves had been brought back in such numbers in the caravels that by 1448 it was estimated that almost a thousand had been landed in Portugal. And, although the Pope had forbidden all other nations to trade along the west African coast without Portugal's permission, many of them had begun to ship out slaves, too. The Spanish, the French and the Dutch, the Danes, the Swedes, the Prussians and, predominantly, the British, drawn by the lure of gold, ivory and gum, were soon all deeply engaged in the slave trade; and by the middle of the eighteenth century thousands of slaves were being sold every year in the numerous markets along the Atlantic seaboard and were being carried away, usually to colonies of European powers. This inordinately profitable trade, far from helping to reveal the continent's secrets, tended to conceal them more darkly than ever, for not only were merchants sufficiently satisfied with their profits from human cargoes so easily picked up on the coast that they had little inclination to search deeper inland for other African goods, but those Africans who were themselves engaged in the trade, as suppliers and middlemen, were determined to prevent white men discovering the territories where the best slaves were to be found. So, to difficult and often inaccessible terrain of rain forest and swamp, unnavigable rivers, a forbidding climate, dangerous beasts, strange and frequently fatal fevers and hostile tribes was added a new disincentive to the exploration of Africa's interior. When the African Association was formed in 1788 it could, indeed, be fairly said that the continent was little better known, and in some respects far less well known, than it had been in the days of the Caesars.

Soon after the formation of the Association its Secretary, Henry Beaufoy, the son of a Quaker wine merchant, Member of Parliament for Great Yarmouth and later Secretary to the Board of Control, had drawn up a *Plan* in which he had written that the map of the interior of Africa was 'still but a wide extended blank, on which the geographer, on the authority of Leo Africanus and of the

Xeriff Edrissi, the Nubian Author [had] traced, with a hesitating hand, a few names of unexplored rivers and of uncertain nations'. The African Association had, accordingly, resolved to cast light upon darkness. Their work would be in the national interest. 'Gold is there so plentiful,' a member of the Association's Committee wrote of Timbuktu, 'as to adorn even the slaves ... If we could get our manufactures into that country we should soon have gold enough.' The Association's work would also be in the interests of learning. And 'in the pursuit of these advantages', Beaufoy emphasized, benefits would at the same time be 'imparted to nations hitherto consigned to hopeless barbarism and uniform contempt'.

Since the sixteenth century all the countries north of the Sahara, with the exception of Morocco, had been nominally part of the Turkish Ottoman Empire, though over the centuries Ottoman power had declined so far that local rulers acted in virtual independence of the Sultan in Constantinople. These countries, which the Arabs knew collectively as the Maghreb, the West, were well enough known; but of the lands that lay to the south of the desert scarcely anything was known at all. And to the African Association it seemed that no better start could be made in unravelling the mystery of Africa than by sending an expedition up the Niger to the city of Timbuktu which was believed to stand on its banks and was reputed to contain treasures of unparalleled richness. Money was soon raised and John Ledyard, an American adventurer who claimed to have lived for several years among Red Indian tribes, who had certainly sailed with Captain Cook and who had been arrested while attempting to walk across Russia, was instructed to make his way to Timbuktu and the Niger from Cairo. At the same time Simon Lucas, a former wine merchant who had been vice-consul in Morocco for many years after having been captured and enslaved by Moorish pirates, was asked to travel to the Niger across the desert from Tripoli. Neither attempt was successful. Before his journey had begun Ledyard poisoned himself in Cairo with excessive doses of acid of vitriol and tartar emetic taken to combat dysentery; while Lucas felt obliged to turn back when warfare in the Fezzan made further progress hazardous. The African Association then decided to make an approach upon the Niger from the west African coast. But before this mission could be undertaken a book by a Scottish explorer, whose arrival in London some years previously had aroused the liveliest curiosity, reawakened interest in another part of the continent.

1

'ETHIOPIAN BRUCE'

JAMES BRUCE · HIS EARLY LIFE AND ADVENTURES · HIS
ARRIVAL AT MASSAWA, 1769 · ADVENTUROUS
JOURNEY THROUGH DIGSA, ADOWA AND AXUM TO
GONDAR, THE ETHIOPIAN CAPITAL · THE IMPERIAL
FAMILY AND ABYSSINIAN CUSTOMS · A SAVAGE BANQUET ·
ENCOUNTERS WITH A REBEL CHIEF · SOUTH TO LAKE
TANA · THE TISISAT FALLS · RETURN TO GONDAR ·
DISCOVERY OF THE SOURCE OF THE BLUE NILE · THE
NILE WORSHIPPERS · RESIDENCE AT SENNAR · A
'CITY OF THE DEAD' · THE KING'S HAREM · THE
FEARFUL CROSSING OF THE NUBIAN DESERT · BRUCE'S
RECEPTION IN LONDON, 1774

'Africa is, indeed, coming into fashion,' Horace Walpole told Sir Horace
Mann in 1774. 'There is just returned a Mr Bruce, who has lived three years in
the court of Abyssinia, and breakfasted every morning with the Maids of
Honour on live oxen.'

This Mr Bruce, whose stories of his strange adventures in Abyssinia were
listened to with amused scepticism in London drawing-rooms, was an extremely tall Scotsman of forty-four, gruff, quarrelsome and touchy, whose
response to those who presumed to doubt his veracity was to flare up in
sudden anger or to lapse into an equally intimidating silence, a silence rendered
all the more menacing by a complaint of the lungs, the result of exposure to
the suffocating winds of the Nubian desert, which made his whole stomach
'heave like an organ-bellows'. He was a proud man, proud of his ancestry which
he traced back to King Robert, conqueror of the English at Bannockburn,
and proud of his achievements which included, he insisted, that of being the
first European to reach the source of the Nile. He had certainly led an adventurous life. After leaving Harrow he had been sent to Edinburgh to study
for the Scottish Bar for which he had no taste. He had abandoned his studies
and had made up his mind to seek a fortune in India, but before his ship

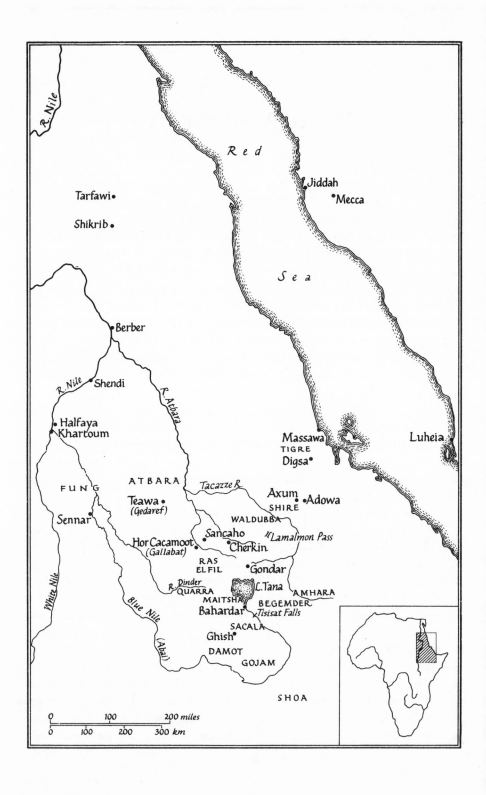

R. Nile

Red

Tarfawi•

Shikrib•

Jiddah•
•Mecca

Sea

•Berber

R. Nile•Shendi

R. Atbara

•Halfaya
•Khartoum

Massawa
TIGRE
Digsa•

Luheia

FUNG

ATBARA

Tacazze R.

Axum•Adowa
SHIRE

Teawa•
(Gedaref)

WALDUBBA

Sennar

Lamalmon Pass

Hor Cacamoot•Sancaho
(Gallabat)•Cherkin

RAS
ELFIL

•Gondar

White Nile

R. Dinder
QUARRA

L. Tana

AMHARA

MAITSHA

Blue Nile

Bahardar

BEGEMDER

Tisisat Falls

SACALA

(Abaï)

Ghish•

DAMOT

GOJAM

SHOA

0   100   200 miles
0   100   200   300 km

sailed he had fallen in love with a wine merchant's daughter. He married her and was taken as partner into her family's business. Soon afterwards, to his unutterable grief, she had died in Paris while they were on their way to the south of France; and what he took to be the meddlesome interference of 'many Roman Catholic clergy, hovering about the doors' of her sick-room in the hope of a death-bed conversion, had confirmed him in that dislike of the Popish religion which he ever afterwards held and frequently expressed.

Returning home he decided that the wine trade was not a business to which he could happily devote his life; and, since he was well enough off to keep himself without it, he made up his mind to travel widely, to see the far corners of the world, and to make a name for himself on a wider stage. He studied languages; he learned to draw; he carefully examined books about ancient architecture. He went to Portugal, then to Spain where he developed a deep interest in the Moors and the language and culture of the Arabs. He travelled through France, in the Netherlands, Holland and Germany. Recommended to the Government by an influential Scottish friend, he was offered the appointment of British Consul-General at Algiers on the understanding that he would use the opportunities provided by that office to make drawings of the remains of Roman architecture in the area for the King's collection. Eager to pursue his Arabic studies, Bruce accepted the post and – having rushed north to settle his affairs on the estate which he had inherited upon his father's death and fallen in love with a sixteen-year-old girl, Margaret Murray, who promised to wait for him until he returned – he set off for North Africa by way of Italy and Malta.

He was, however, far too masterful and independent a man to be a successful diplomat; he was saved from ignominious dismissal only by his offer of resignation from the Consul-Generalship. But his time in Algiers was by no means wasted. He took lessons in medicine from the Consulate's doctor; he taught himself Greek with the help of an old Cypriot priest; he became an extremely adept horseman; and to help him improve his skill as a draughtsman he employed a talented and hard-working young Italian, Luigi Balugani, a member of the academy of fine arts at Bologna, who was to accompany him on his travels. Later, after he had left Algiers for Tunis, Tripoli and Syria and had fallen seriously ill in Aleppo, Bruce greatly increased his medical knowledge with the help of the English doctor, a specialist in Eastern diseases, who was called in to treat him. He was by then, indeed, well equipped for the exploration into the heart of Ethiopia about which he had long been thinking. Knowing of this ambition, and hearing of the loss of his instruments in a shipwreck on his way to Crete, various French savants whom he had met in Paris offered to help him. They wrote to him to say that King Louis

XV had agreed to send him a quadrant which he could pick up at Alexandria. Replacing his other lost instruments, his books and weapons himself, Bruce reached Alexandria at the end of the third week in June 1768, wearing Arab clothes and styling himself in the Arabic manner El Hakim Jagoube, Doctor James. He moved on to Cairo, collecting letters of credit and of recommendation wherever he could and from everyone whose name or rank might grant him some protection in Ethiopia.

He had originally intended to make his way to the source of the Nile, which he expected to find south of Gondar, by an overland route. But fighting had broken out in the area and so he decided instead to sail down the Red Sea to Massawa, which had been Ethiopia's main port before the Turks had assumed control of it in the middle of the sixteenth century, calling on the way at Jiddah on the eastern shore of the sea. Here he hoped to obtain letters of recommendation from its ruler, the Sherif of Mecca, and from the Sherif's chief adviser, Metical Aga, an Ethiopian by birth and a friend of Ras Michael, the principal minister of the Christian Emperor of Ethiopia. On his arrival at Jiddah, Bruce received the letters he required from the helpful Metical Aga; he was also provided with the services of an agent who was to help him in his negotiations with the authorities at Massawa, the gateway to Ethiopia.

Little about Ethiopia was known in the Western world, other than that it was a tropical land whose desolate and rugged plateaux rose so high in the north that the climate was quite temperate, that it was ruled by a dynasty claiming descent from Solomon and the Queen of Sheba, that it had its own strange kind of Christianity and its own written languages and records of a distant past. Europeans had, indeed, been there before Bruce and had written of their travels. A Portuguese embassy had landed at Massawa in 1520 and its chaplain, Francisco Alvarez, had given some account of the country. At the beginning of the next century two other Portuguese, Pedro Paez and Jeronimo Lobo, both Jesuit priests, had travelled in Ethiopia and written of their experiences. Lobo had seen the Tisisat Falls and Paez the source of the Blue Nile, neither of which achievements Bruce cared to acknowledge. Since their day, in 1660, Balthazar Tellez had published an abridgement of Almeida's *History of High Ethiopia*; the German scholar, Job Ludolf, had, with the help of a native informant, written books on the history and languages of the country; a French doctor, Charles-Jacques Poncet, 'an adventurer, a great talker and a great drinker', had been up the Nile to Gondar where, as representative of Louis XIV, he had treated the Emperor and had afterwards set down a description of his experiences. But none of these books was widely read and all had been written a long time before. Bruce was determined to overshadow them, not only to reach the source of the Nile but to provide as detailed an account as he could of the country through which it flowed and of the peoples who lived by its banks.

'Very much tired of the sea and desirous to land', Bruce arrived at Massawa, 'a small island immediately on the Abyssinian shore', on 17 September 1769. But eager though he was to get ashore, he decided to remain on board that night as he did not trust the local ruler, the Naib, who was known to extort money from unprotected travellers and even to murder them. Prudently Bruce sent a representative into the port to make his arrival known to Achmet, the Naib's nephew, a friend of the influential Ethiopian, Metical Aga, who had shown himself accommodating enough at Jiddah. The next morning Bruce was taken to meet Achmet in the market place. An unprepossessing little figure of a man, dressed all in white, he was sitting in one of two armchairs placed in the middle of the square, supervising the inspection of the bales and packages which had been unloaded from Bruce's ship and upon which customs duties were to be paid. He stood up as Bruce approached him, carried his fingers to his lips, then laid his arm across his chest. When Bruce pronounced the salutation of the inferior, '*Salam Alicum!* Peace be between us!' he answered immediately, '*Alicum Salam!* There is peace between us!' He then ordered coffee which Bruce took to be a reassuring sign, 'as the immediate offering of meat or drink is an assurance that your life is not in danger'. Over coffee he read the letters which Bruce presented to him, commenting, 'You will give these to the Naib tomorrow.' As Bruce stood up to take his leave he was immediately drenched by deluges of orange-flower water, showered upon him from left and right by two of Achmet's attendants carrying silver bottles.

Further favours were soon to follow. Bruce was provided with a 'very decent house' to which Achmet sent a 'large dinner ... with a profusion of melons and good fresh water'. Then all the baggage arrived intact, much to the relief of Bruce who feared that his clock, telescopes and quadrant might all have been broken by the violent manner in which the customs officers had satisfied their curiosity about him. And, late at night, Achmet himself came to the house. He took Bruce's hand and they sat down on cushions together. Bruce told him that he had a present for the Naib. 'But I was taught, in a particular manner, to repose upon you as my friend,' Bruce continued, producing a pair of English pistols of 'excellent workmanship'; 'and a small, but separate acknowledgement is due to you ...' Achmet hastily interrupted him, 'I understand everything you say, and everything you would say ... Let the pistols remain with you and show them to nobody till I send you a man ... The person that brings you dry dates in an Indian handkerchief, and an earthen bottle to drink your water out of, give him the pistols.'

When Bruce met the Naib the following day he realized how well advised these precautions were. 'He was very tall and lean; his colour black; he had a large mouth and nose, dull and heavy eyes; a kind of malicious, contemptuous smile on his countenance; he was altogether of a most stupid and brutal appearance ... He had nothing upon him but a coarse cotton shirt, so dirty that it seemed all pains to clean it would be thrown away, and so short that it scarcely reached his knees. He was sitting in a large wooden arm-chair, at the head of two files of naked savages who made an avenue from his chair to the door.' Bruce presented to him his firman which, he thought, would have brought the greatest pasha in the Turkish Empire to his feet in reverence. But the Naib did not even take it into his hands, pushing it back to Bruce and commanding him to read it aloud. Bruce replied that he could not do so, as it was in Turkish and he had never learned that language. 'Nor I either,' said the Naib. 'And I believe I never shall.'

Bruce then handed him the other letters which were brushed aside with equal disdain. 'You should have brought a mullah along with you,' the Naib said. 'Do you think I could read all these letters? Why, it would take me a month!' He spoke through an interpreter in the dialect of the country, affecting not to be familiar with Arabic of which, in fact, he had an easy mastery. He accepted his presents without thanks; and Bruce left him 'very little pleased' with his reception, and beginning to doubt that he would receive the permission he needed to proceed upon his journey.

Determined not to give him this permission until he had received more valuable presents, the Naib threatened to have Bruce thrown into a dark and airless dungeon 'till the bones came through his skin for want'. On the morning of 6 November, however, the Naib was forced to give way when two emissaries arrived from the Emperor of Ethiopia. They were both wearing the imperial livery, 'a red short cloak lined and turned up with mazarine-blue', and they carried with them a letter from the chief minister, Ras Michael, who wrote to say that his master's health was bad, and that he was astonished to learn that the European physician 'was not forwarded instantly to him at Gondar as he had heard of his being arrived at Massawa some time before'. Evidently frightened by this letter, the Naib immediately granted Bruce permission to depart and provided him with a guide and bearers for his baggage, though he could not forbear warning him, 'with a considerable degree of eloquence', of the difficulties of the journey, the 'rivers, precipices, mountains and woods', 'the number of wild beasts everywhere to be found; as also the wild savage people that inhabited those places'.

Bruce was soon himself made aware of the hardships that faced him. As he took the track that led to the south, the mountains of Ethiopia loomed above him in three ridges, the first ridge 'full of gullies and broken ground, thinly covered with shrubs; the second, higher and steeper, still more rugged and bare; the third a row of sharp, uneven-edged mountains which would be counted high in any country in Europe'.

Far higher even than this last range towered that 'stupendous mass, the mountain of Taranta ... the point of which is buried in the clouds, and very rarely seen but in the clearest weather; at other times abandoned to perpetual mist and darkness, the seat of lightning, thunder and of storm'. And it was across this forbidding mountain that Bruce was directed to go towards Digsa; for Achmet, riding after him, warned him that to travel inland by the easier route would take him through territories belonging to the Naib and he could not answer for the orders given to the people there. Bruce took the advice, allowed Achmet to remove four of the bearers whom his uncle had provided and to put others more reliable in their place, and accepted from him 'a narrow web of muslin which, with his own hands he wrapped round [Bruce's] head in the manner the better sort of Mahometans wear it in Digsa. He then parted, saying, "He that is your enemy is mine also." '

Bruce's column, a long line of asses and men, Luigi Balugani, the Italian, among them, moved off again across the plain. Soon the dry grass underfoot, bright with yellow flowers and shaded by acacia trees, gave way to gravel. Then, after the first day, the travellers turned west along the bed of a ravine down which, in the rainy season, torrential waters rushed in raging violence to the sea. The dry sandy bed of the torrent was now covered with vegetation, its banks lined with tamansks, and with capers and tamarinds heavy with fruit. Large numbers of dark-skinned Saho nomads wandered down the ravine towards him, descending from the mountains with their wives and naked children, taking their flocks to pasture on the plains below which were soon to be watered by the imminent rains. Bruce saluted the man whom he took to be their leader and asked him if he would sell a goat. The man returned the salute but 'either could not speak Arabic, or declined further conversation'. Some of the bearers, 'nearer in colour to the Sahos', managed, however, to obtain a lame goat in exchange for some antimony, four large needles and some beads.

Late in the afternoon it began to threaten rain; there were long peals of thunder; and the lightning, very frequent, was deeply tinged with blue. Suddenly Bruce heard a roar on the mountains above, 'louder than the loudest thunder'. The guides flew to the baggage and removed it to the highest ground as the river gushed down upon them 'in a stream about the height of a man and the breadth of the whole bed it used to occupy'.

While the waters cascaded past them, the straggling file of men and animals continued on their way beneath mountains of bleak, bare black rock, 'almost calcined by the violent heat of the sun', through dense forests of acacia, whose thorny branches scratched hands and face, past trees thrown down from the roots by herds of elephants whose dung, Bruce noticed, was full of pieces of undigested wood. So they passed out of the land of the Saho and into that of the Hazorta who lived in caves or in huts like cages, just large enough to hold two people and covered with the hides of oxen. Under the eyes of some of these people, Bruce went to bathe in a pool of water. He took his firelock with him. But they did not stir from their huts, displaying as little curiosity in the white man as though he had lived amongst them all their lives.

That night the travellers pitched their tents at a place called Sadoon which, after a bitterly cold night, they left at half past six on the morning of 19 November. Passing through Tubbo – where the sycamore trees were full of birds, some brilliantly coloured but silent, others plainer but singing 'with a variety of wild notes in a stile of music distinct and peculiar to Africa' – they moved on to Lilla and began to ascend the foothills of Taranta, passing on their way immense herds of antelope and flocks of partridge, neither of which seemed to regard them as enemies. The climb up the steep mountainside was a fearful ordeal. The carriers, laden with baggage and arms, found it difficult enough to clamber up the 'huge monstrous fragments of rock' which, loosened by the water, had been tumbled down in their path; they protested that it was quite impossible to carry up the heavier pieces of equipment, in particular the instruments and, above all, the quadrant which it had taken four men to carry on even less precipitous ground. So Bruce and an Ethiopian named Yasin, who had joined his party and had been appointed supervisor of the servants, undertook to carry this heavy load themselves; and, to 'the wonder of all', so Bruce proudly declared, they succeeded in hoisting both the quadrant and its iron stand 'above the stoney parts of the mountain'. Their hands and knees were 'all cut, mangled and bleeding, with sliding down and clambering over the sharp rocks'; their 'clothes were torn to pieces'; yet they declared their ability 'to carry the two telescopes and the time-keeper also'. This so much humbled the rest of their companions 'that one and all put their hands so briskly to work that, with infinite toil', they managed to place all 'the instruments and baggage, about two o'clock in the afternoon, near half way up this terrible mountain of Taranta'.

Having rounded up the asses which had bolted in protest while being beaten up the mountain, and which were now threatened by hordes of hyenas, the men were too exhausted to pitch tents, even had there been earth into which to drive the pegs; so that night was spent in caves.

Early the next morning the journey up the mountain was resumed. The climb was even harder than it had been the day before, the rock 'steeper, more craggy, rugged and slippery'. 'Our knees and hands were cut to pieces by frequent falls,' Bruce wrote, 'and our faces torn by the multitude of thorny bushes.' Yet, as he encouraged his 'company with good words, increase of wages and hopes of reward', he was pleased to notice that 'the baggage moved much more briskly than the preceding day'. And before nightfall they had reached the summit and entered a village which was surrounded by wild olives and cedar trees and occupied by people with dark yellowish skin and hair curled round wooden sticks. They seemed very poor but their white cows were of an exquisite beauty, and the fleece of their black sheep was 'remarkable for its lustre and softness'. The travellers spent another cold night among these people; and in the early afternoon of the next day they came to the small hill-town of Digsa where the Christians lived on the lower slopes, the Muslims on the higher and both made their living by selling slaves, mainly children. Here they rested for two days, then moved on again, crossing the river that marked the boundary of the land controlled by the Naib, marching through plains sown with wheat and barley and Indian corn and beneath small, silent villages perched on the tops of hills. They were joined by several traders who, with their heavily laden donkeys, kept close to them for the sake of protection; and, by way of Hadawi, where Bruce acquired a black horse from a friendly provincial governor, the enlarged caravan entered Kella where they were detained for three days by customs collectors demanding payment of the most exorbitant dues, and by the reluctance of the inhabitants to accept money for provisions. They wanted goods in exchange, they protested, particularly antimony which the women used to darken their eyelids, also coloured beads of a particular kind. But 'the person employed to buy our beads at Jiddah,' as Bruce put it, 'had not received the last list of fashions from this country. He had bought us a quantity beautifully flowered with red and green, and as big as a large pea; also some large oval, green and yellow ones; whereas the *ton* now among the beauties here were [small blue beads and large yellow ones] ... All our beads were consequently rejected by six or seven dozen of the shrillest tongues I ever heard.' Fortunately a Muslim merchant, whom Bruce had favoured by contributing towards the cost of a new ass after his own creature had been badly wounded by a hyena, came to the party's rescue by producing just such beads as the women wanted. A great shout was set up by the women purchasers and a violent scramble followed. 'Twenty or thirty threw themselves upon the parcel, tearing and breaking all the strings ... Whips and sticks were laid unmercifully upon their hands and arms till each dropped her booty. The Abyssinian men that came with them seemed to be perfectly unconcerned at the fray, and stood laughing, without the least sign of wishing to interfere in favour of either side.' Despite the sound whipping the women received, the beads would not have been entirely recovered, Bruce thought, had not Yasin, who knew the country well, fired a blunderbuss into the air behind their backs. At hearing 'so unexpectedly this dreadful noise, both men and women fell flat on their faces; and the women were immediately dragged off the cloth'. The bargaining was then resumed in a more orderly fashion until the strangers were plentifully supplied with honey, butter, flour and a quantity of delicious pumpkins that tasted like melons. Delighted by these acquisitions, Bruce gave some of the prettier girls a present of a few beads, asking how many kisses they would give for each. 'Poo!' they replied. 'We don't sell kisses in this country. Who would buy them? We will give you as many as you wish for nothing.' And, in that bargain, Bruce commented, they were 'very fair and liberal dealers'.

On 4 December, Bruce's caravan set out once more; and the next day the strange high perpendicular rocks of the mountains of Adowa came into view, looking like steeples or obelisks. Adowa, although then a small place of about three hundred houses, each with an enclosure of hedges and trees, was an important stronghold, the capital of Tigre. It was also the residence of Ras Michael whose house, occupied in his absence by his deputy, was more like a prison than a palace since it contained, manacled in cages, some three hundred prisoners, a number of whom had been there for twenty years, waiting in vain for the ransom to be paid for their release.

Bruce was greeted with the utmost friendliness by Ras Michael's Greek steward, Janni, a benign old man clothed in an Abyssinian costume of white cotton with a red, gold-embroidered sash. Attended by various servants and slaves, both male and female, he conducted Bruce and Balugani through a courtyard planted with jasmine to a large room furnished with a silk-covered sofa, its floor strewn with Persian carpets and cushions and its walls and windows decorated with evergreens for the approaching Christmas season. Seeing his visitors' dirty and lacerated feet and learning with horror that they had come most of the way from Massawa on foot, Janni sent for bowls of water, then had them served with 'a great dinner' while standing attentively over them, a towel in his hand.

Refreshed and cheered by such treatment, Bruce travelled on to Axum, the ancient capital of Abyssinia, a place of extensive ruins. In a square which he took to have once been the centre of the town were forty obelisks, and, by a long flight of granite steps leading to a long-since vanished temple, the stone thrones on which the emperors of Ethiopia were still crowned as their predecessors had been long before the Christian era.

Shortly after leaving the ruins, Bruce came upon three men driving a cow before them. They had black goatskins upon their shoulders, lances and shields in their hands and appeared to be soldiers. Suddenly they tripped up the cow which fell heavily to the ground. One of the men sat across her neck, holding her head down by the horns; another twisted a halter about her forefeet; while a third, with a knife in his hand, jumped astride her belly and then, to Bruce's 'utter astonishment', cut out two huge hunks of flesh from her flank which were placed upon a shield. While the cow was still held down, the flap of skin was replaced over the gaping wound and fixed in place by small skewers. 'Whether they had put anything under the skin, I know not,' wrote Bruce; 'but at the river side they prepared a cataplasm of clay with which they covered the wound. Then they forced the animal to rise, and drove it before them to furnish them with a further meal.'

Disappointed in his hopes of acquiring some beef for himself, Bruce was further disgruntled when, having shot a wild boar with his pistol, he realized that to eat it now that he was close to the Emperor's court would give deep offence to the Ethiopians who, though Christians, held pork of all kinds in the utmost detestation. So, contenting himself with some onions, garlic and pumpkins which he bought from a peasant, he went on through Mai-Shum into the plain called Selech-lecha. Bruce, like Poncet who had been that way before him, compared it to the most beautiful parts of Provence. The hedgerows were full of honeysuckle and the fine trees were festooned with vines bearing juicy black grapes. Across this lovely plain Bruce's path led to Sire, a town of clay houses with thatched roofs in the shape of cones, thence to Maisbinni, Dagashaha and the River Tacazze. Much of the way was as beautiful as the plain of Selech-lecha, the banks of the Tacazze being covered with tamarisks and its waters full of fish. The women who came forward to offer food in return for antimony, beads and incense were of a lighter colour, taller and more beautiful than those who had bartered at Kella. They were equally free with their favours, agreeing that 'these favours ought to be given, and not sold; and that all coyness and courtship was but loss of time, which always might be employed better to the satisfaction of both'. But pleasant as was the countryside and complaisant as were the women, the travellers could not but be aware that their journey was now becoming more dangerous. Crocodiles in great numbers slithered among the hippopotami upon the banks of the river, and the camp at night was surrounded by lions and hyenas. The lions were kept at bay by fear of the white tent ropes, the canvas trembling in the wind, and by the jangling of the brass bells tied to the storm-strings; but their roaring and perhaps their smell so terrified the mules that the poor animals were drenched with sweat in the morning, looking as though they had spent the hours of darkness struggling with heavy loads through the mountain passes. And the hyenas, not to be deterred as the lions were, stalked about the camp, even occasionally attacking it. Bruce fired his gun at one which, with a snarl and a kind of bark, advanced directly upon him before being laid low by a second shot. Yasin and his men killed another with a pike. Less dangerous, but an even more constant trial, were the huge black ants, almost an inch in length, that came out from under the ground, demolishing carpets and the lining of the tents with astonishing voracity and eating their way into every

31

bag and sack they could find. Also distressing to Bruce were the rumours that constantly reached him of the defeat of Ras Michael's forces by rebels who had risen against the rule of the Emperor. One day Bruce came across a deserter from Ras Michael's army 'driving before him two miserable girls, about ten years old, stark naked, and almost famished to death, the part of the booty which had fallen to his share in laying waste the country'. Bruce asked him to confirm the truth of a rumour that Ras Michael had fought a savage battle with Fasil, a rebel chief leading a revolt of the pagan people, the Gallas, and that thousands of men had been killed. The deserter, obviously afraid that an unwelcome answer might cost him his booty, was evasive in his replies, sometimes saying 'there had been a battle, sometimes none'. Bruce thought he had not 'the air of a conqueror, but rather a coward who had sneaked away and stolen these two miserable wretches he had with him'. And it was not until he reached Gondar that he was able to discover the outcome of the civil war.

Addis Ababa had not then been built and Gondar was the capital of Ethiopia. Here, rising above the clay huts of the populace, was the Emperor's palace, a large stone building surrounded by a high wall and flanked by towers, some crenellated, others domed. But when Bruce arrived in the town the Emperor was not there, nor was Ras Michael, nor were any of those other important Christians to whom he had letters of introduction. He thought it best, therefore, to remain with Yasin in the Muslim part of the town and to continue for the moment to wear the Arab clothes in which he had been travelling. His first notable visitor was one Ato Aylo, the chief adviser of the Iteghe, the formidable grandmother of a previous Emperor, Joas, who had been strangled in 1769. To the consternation of the Muslim in whose house Bruce was staying, Aylo arrived accompanied by several armed men. But it was soon clear that this visit, the first, so it was believed, that Aylo had ever made to the Muslim town, was a compliment rather than a threat. He descended from his mule and uncovered his head and shoulders 'as if he had been approaching a person of the first distinction'. He found Bruce studying an Ethiopian book and, having expressed gratified astonishment at this, complimented him on his mastery of the Tigre tongue which he spoke as well as he did Arabic. 'Come, come, he'll do,' Aylo said to his companions. 'There is no fear of him. He'll make his way.' Aylo went on to say that Ras Michael's son, Welled Harwaryat, had returned from the army and was lying ill in the Iteghe's palace at Kusquam. It was feared that he had smallpox. Would Bruce come to treat him? Bruce readily agreed; and so the next day the two men rode over to the palace after sharing a breakfast of bread, melted butter and honey. Aylo once again congratulated the European visitor, this time upon his horsemanship, for the Ethiopian was, so Bruce said, 'an absolute stranger to the great advantage of bridles, spurs and stirrups, in the management of a violent, strong, high-mettled horse'. When they arrived at the palace, Welled Harwaryat was reported to be better: a holy man had inscribed some characters in ink on a tin plate, 'which characters were washed off by a medicinal liquor, and then given him to drink'. Having swallowed this medicine, his appetite had returned and he 'had ate heartily of raw beef'. The beef, however, appeared not to suit him as well as the medicine, and he was soon as ill as ever. Other holy men, one of whom 'had neither ate nor drank for twenty years', now came forward to offer a cure. This consisted in the laying of a large and heavy cross upon the patient's chest together with a picture of the Virgin in a 'very dirty gilt frame'. While Welled Harwaryat was being subjected to this miraculous treatment, Bruce was advised by Aylo not to interfere. He had no intention of interfering, he replied; a miracle was certainly the easiest kind of cure; but it would undoubtedly be a miracle if the patient was not dead by tomorrow night. Aylo then went to see the Iteghe who agreed to receive the European doctor. She was a remarkable old woman, once beautiful, the daughter of a noble from the mountain province of Quara. She had Portuguese blood and her skin was paler, Bruce thought, than that of most Portuguese. She was gracious and amiable, though she took Bruce to task for being sceptical about miracles. 'Is there any harm in believing too much?' she asked him. Surely that was better than believing too little? There was 'nothing impossible with God'. On a later occasion, after she had discovered the reason for Bruce's journey to Gondar, she said to him, 'See! See! How every day our life furnishes us with proofs of the perverseness and contradictions of human nature. You have been to Jerusalem, and have come here through vile Turkish governments, and hot, unwholesome climates, to see a river and a bog, no part of which can you carry away were it ever so valuable, and of which you have in your own country a thousand larger, better and cleaner ... While I, on the other hand, the mother of Emperors, who have sat upon the throne of this country more than thirty years, have for my only wish, night and day, that, after giving up everything in the world, I could be conveyed to the Church of the Holy Sepulchre in Jerusalem, and beg alms for my subsistence all the rest of my life, if I could only be buried at last in the street within sight of the gate of that temple where our blessed Saviour once lay.'

Bruce proved right about the treatment of Welled Harwaryat. There was no miracle. He died the next day, as did his daughter. By then an epidemic of smallpox was raging at Kusquam, and several members of the Empress Dowager's family were amongst those afflicted. These included three children of her daughter, Princess Esther, an intelligent and beautiful young woman who had married, as her third husband, Ras Michael. Her second husband had been murdered by the pagan Gallas; and, though a kind and affectionate woman, she hated the Gallas so virulently in consequence that she was as relentless in demanding their cruel punishment as any of Ras Michael's most violent followers. Bruce found her enchanting. One could not talk to her, he wrote, without being 'attached to her forever'. Having readily agreed to take over as physician at the palace from the unsuccessful holy men, he saw much of her over the next few days and grew to admire her more and more. 'She did not eat, or sleep, herself; and the ends of her fingers broke out into pustules from touching the several sick persons.' Immediately upon his appearance as royal physician, wearing Abyssinian clothes procured for him in Gondar, his hair 'cut round, curled and perfumed in the Amharic fashion', he had insisted upon all the windows of the palace being thrown open, the rooms being fumigated with incense and vinegar. And gradually his patients, who had been languishing in the suffocating heat of their germ-laden apartments, began to revive. 'If I am not as good a friend to Yagoube who has saved my children, as I am a steady enemy to the Gallas, who murdered my husband,' Esther declared when they were out of danger, 'say then Esther is not a Christian.' One of the children for whose salvation she thanked him was her baby son by Ras Michael.

Bruce saw Ras Michael for the first time in the second week of March. 'He was lean, old, and apparently much fatigued,' Bruce wrote. 'He was dressed in a coarse, dirty cloth, wrapt about him like a blanket, and another like a tablecloth folded about his head ... He had also sore eyes.' Bruce had heard much of his ruthlessness: a Galla chief whom he had captured had been flayed and the stuffed skin had been displayed outside his tent; twelve other chiefs, their eyes torn out, were later driven into the fields at night to be eaten by hyenas. Bruce had heard, too, that he was a man whom it was not at all easy to approach. And certainly on this occasion Ras Michael took scarcely any notice of his visitor who went away 'very little pleased with the reception' which was accorded to him.

The next time Bruce saw Ras Michael was on the occasion of the army's triumphal procession into Gondar. He rode bareheaded in front of his troops, a black velvet coat with a silver fringe over his shoulders, attended by a page carrying a long silver wand. Behind him rode the governors of provinces wearing gilt or silver horns attached to bands tied round their heads; the young Emperor, surrounded by the officers of state; the Executioner of the Camp and his attendants; the household troops; a man bearing upon a pole the stuffed skin of a Galla chieftain; and then thousands of ordinary soldiers whose custom it was to attach to their lances and firelocks shreds of scarlet cloth, representing the number of enemies they had slain, and the testicles of their victims.

There was no opportunity to talk to Ras Michael that day, and it was not until 14 March that an interview was at last arranged. On this occasion Bruce found the minister much more impressive than he had done at their first meeting. He appeared to be 'thoughtful but not displeased'; his 'air was perfectly free from constraint'. Tall, lean, white-haired, with sharp, clear eyes, he bore an astonishing resemblance to Bruce's friend, the great French naturalist, the Comte de Buffon. Bruce made as if to kiss the ground before him. But he held out his hand to shake his visitor's.

'Yagoube, I think that is your name,' Ras Michael began gravely, his words echoed by a voice which Bruce took to be that of a priest in a far corner of the room. 'Hear what I say to you, and mark what I recommend to you. You are a man, I am told, who makes it your business to wander in the fields in search after trees and grass in solitary places, and to sit up all night alone looking at the stars of the heavens. Other countries are not like this, though this was never so bad as it is now. The wretched people here are enemies to strangers; even if they knew they were to get nothing by it, they would murder you for mere mischief ... Therefore, so that you may safely follow your own designs, I have appointed you Baalomaal [a kind of Lord of the Bedchamber] and commander of the Kaccob horse [the cavalry in the guards] ... Go then to the Emperor and kiss the ground upon your appointment.'

The young Emperor, Takla Haymanot II, was a less imposing figure than Ras Michael. He asked Bruce an interminable series of 'idle and tiresome questions', such as where his country was, an understandable reply to which it was impossible to give as he knew no countries other than his own. Some of the people in the room fell asleep; others stole away to bed; Bruce, 'tired to death with standing', leaned against the wall. But still the interrogation continued until Bruce was 'absolutely in despair, scarcely able to speak a word, and sincerely praying that this might be [his] last promotion at that court'. Later, when he grew to know the Emperor better, he formed a higher opinion of him. He was more intelligent than he had at first appeared, tall, good-looking, 'not so dark in complexion as a Neapolitan'; 'his features, even in Europe, would have been thought fine'. There was no doubt, however, that Ras Michael, who had had the young man's incompetent father murdered, was the real ruler of the country.

Once the way had been made clear for him to do so, Bruce longed to escape from Gondar and to continue on his journey. But he was not yet permitted to depart. A great wedding was to be celebrated. The bridegroom was the powerful Governor of Begemder, the bride the daughter of Ras Michael's dead son, Welled Harwaryat, who had been married to Princess Esther's sister. And during the protracted ceremonies which accompanied this important match the Ras required Bruce's presence every day at his dinner table; and Bruce invariably suffered a headache from the quantities of honey wine which he was forced to swallow. 'After dinner we slipt away to parties of ladies, where anarchy prevailed as completely as at the house of the Ras,' Bruce confessed. 'All the married women ate, drank and smoked, like the men; and it is impossible to convey to the reader any idea of this bacchanalian scene in terms of common decency.'

Bruce's description of an Ethiopian banquet does, however, give a clear impression of what some of these parties must have been like. A long table was set in the middle of a large room with benches beside it for the guests. A cow was then brought to the door and its feet tied. Its throat was then cut slightly to let a few drops of blood fall upon the ground in satisfaction of the Mosaic law. Two butchers then cut the skin along the spine and, placing their fingers between the skin and flesh of the animal, flayed it alive. All the flesh of the buttocks was first cut off in solid, square pieces; and the prodigious noise the animal made was the signal for the company to take their places.

Each guest was provided with three or four pancakes of unleavened bread to serve as plates, and several pieces of ordinary, blackish bread for use first as napkins and afterwards as supper for the servants. When the hunks of meat were brought in, 'the motion of the fibres yet perfectly distinct', the men cut it up into steaks while the women sliced it into smaller pieces which, wrapped round the bread and strongly flavoured with salt and black pepper, they stuffed into the men's mouths. Other wads of bread and flesh so quickly followed the first mouthfuls that the men, leaning over the table, were in constant danger of being choked. Their hunger at last satisfied, they performed the same service for the women who ate quite as ravenously. Men and women all drank together out of big handsome horns, while the last remaining slabs of tender flesh were being hacked from the cow outside, still alive and bellowing in agony.

After quantities of drink had been consumed the guests fell to the floor where 'everything' was permitted with absolute freedom. There was, Bruce said, 'no coyness, no delays, no need of appointments or retirement to gratify their wishes; and, if one may judge by sound, they seem to think it as great a shame to make love in silence as to eat ... All this passes without remark ... The ladies are ... women of family and character.'

While the marriage celebrations were still in progress, news came to Gondar of more troubles in the south: the rebel chief, Fasil, was up in arms again; and, although the rainy season was not far away, Ras Michael decided that no time must be lost in attacking him once more. So, in the middle of May, the advance guard of the army marched out of the town to the continuous tapping of kettle drums whose sound spread terror throughout the districts which they traversed, since Ras Michael, 'strict and just as he was in time of peace ... was most licentious and cruel the moment he took the field'.

Bruce was delighted to receive permission to accompany the expedition, as their objective was the countryside around Lake Tana and this was the very area he wanted to explore. He was not required to go in his capacity as commander of the horse guards, so he would be able to follow in the wake of the army, to reach the Tisisat Falls and then go on to the swamp known as Ghish Abbai where, at the source of the stream known as the Little Abbai, he would, he convinced himself, discover the source of the Nile. Before leaving, he was invited to breakfast by Princess Esther who, although pregnant, was to accompany her husband on the campaign. Her servants placed before her guest stewed fowls so inflamed with cayenne pepper as almost to blister the mouth; guinea hens as tough as leather; huge chunks of raw beef; and, what was much more agreeable, 'a large quantity of wheat-bread, equal in all its quality to the best in London or Paris'. To drink, there was a kind of beer fermented with herbs or the leaves of trees, an equally intoxicating honey wine, and a red wine so extremely strong and pressed so insistently upon Bruce by Esther, who warned him that their time was short and the signal would soon be given for striking the tents, that he was quite drunk and almost fell over when he went to make his farewell obeisance to the Emperor.

Bruce was within less than twenty miles of the Tisisat Falls when news reached him that there had been treachery in Ras Michael's army: two of his leading commanders had gone over to the enemy and the imperial forces were con-sequently withdrawing to Gondar, leaving the countryside through which Bruce had intended to pass in the hands of rebels who would murder him without a second's hesitation. Having got so far, however, Bruce was determined to see the Tisisat Falls at least; so he pressed on until the distant roar of the great cataract reached his ears. The sight of it was as awe-inspiring as the sound. It was, indeed, the 'most magnificent sight' that Bruce had ever seen. 'The river had been considerably increased by rains and fell in one sheet of water, without any interval, above half an English mile in breadth, and with a force and noise that was truly terrible, and which stunned and made me, for a time, perfectly dizzy. A thick fume, or haze, covered the fall all round, and hung over the course of the stream both above and below, marking its track, though the water was not seen.'

It was one of the 'most magnificent, stupendous sights in the creation'. Un-fortunately, it was, as he knew, a sight that had been witnessed by European eyes before. The seventeenth-century Portuguese priest, Pedro Paez, who had travelled widely in Ethiopia and had persuaded the Emperor Susenyos publicly to accept Roman Catholicism both for himself and for his people, had not only seen the falls but had built a large church at Gorgora, at the northern end of Lake Tana. Paez had been followed by Father Jeronimo Lobo, whose account of his travels had been translated by Samuel Johnson from a French version into English. Lobo had described the Tisisat Falls in some detail and Bruce's jealous resentment that this foreigner, a Roman Catholic to boot, had been there before him, led him to attempt to discredit the missionary's description.

First he measured the height of the falls with poles and calculated that it was forty feet, whereas Lobo had said it was about fifty. Then he considered Father Lobo's claim to have climbed out on to a ledge below the falls and, with his back to the rock, to have looked through 'the curve of the stream, as it was falling', at 'a number of rainbows of inconceivable beauty in this extraordinary prism'. Bruce, 'without hesitation', declared this to be 'a downright falsehood'. It was quite impossible to reach such a position. The whole story was the invention of 'a grovelling fanatic priest'.

In fact, Bruce was wrong. He was there when the falls were in flood, whereas Father Lobo had seen them in the dry season. It was perfectly possible to get under them then, as later explorers were to discover. Also Bruce's measurements are even less accurate than the Jesuit's: the falls are not nearly half a mile wide, as he said they were, and they are more than three times as high as he calculated. But Bruce was more concerned to prove his predecessors wrong than to make accurate measurements himself. He could not tolerate rivals. Luigi Balugani was probably with him that day, though Bruce does not mention him. Indeed, Balugani is scarcely mentioned at all in any of the seven volumes in which Bruce was to describe his adventures and discoveries. And when Bruce returned home he was to insist that his companion, who was to die at Gondar in 1771, had perished a year earlier. Bruce was not a man willingly to share his glory with anyone.

Soon after the exhilaration which the roaring splendour of the Tisisat Falls had inspired in him, Bruce found himself 'more than ordinarily depressed'. His spirits were 'sunk almost to a degree of despondency' as he made his way back to Gondar. He began to fear that he would never see the source of the Little Abbai, and that, even if he did, he would never get home to report his triumph, that the many dangers he had encountered so far had all been survived in vain. The countryside through which he passed on his return lowered his spirits still further. 'Not a living creature appeared in those once well inhabited plains ... The houses were all reduced to ruins and smoking like so many kilns; even the grass, or wild oats, which were grown very high, were burnt in large plots of a hundred acres together; everything bore the marks that Ras Michael had gone before ... An awful silence reigned everywhere, interrupted only at times by thunder.' The sky darkened and then the rains began to fall. Bruce caught up with some parties of straggling soldiers, dragging with them women and girls whom, though Christians like themselves, they intended sell as slaves to the Turks. Then he came upon the main army and joined his black guards with whom he struggled through the swollen streams as Fasil's horsemen pursued them, threatening to attack.

Emissaries from Fasil rode into the camp. Their master had decided to retire to the south, they announced; he wished only to live as the Emperor's loyal subject; he would marry one of Ras Michael's granddaughters; he regretted his alliance with the chiefs who had deserted the Ras and would never trust them again. To Bruce's amazement these overtures were not merely welcomed, but a proclamation was issued at the door of the Emperor's tent making Fasil governor of four of the most opulent provinces of Ethiopia. One of these provinces was that in which the swamp of Ghish Abbai lay; so when Fasil's envoys approached Bruce for medicine for one of the Galla chiefs, he saw an opportunity to achieve his ambition. In return for the medicine he asked Fasil, 'without fee or reward and without excuse or evasion', to help him to reach Ghish when it was possible to move south again, and to confirm the grant of the governorship of the village and the area around it which the Emperor was prepared to bestow upon him. Under instructions from the Emperor, the envoys swore to confirm the grant in Fasil's name.

Bruce then sought permission to stay behind in Gondar when the Emperor moved on to Tigre with Ras Michael who was anxious to re-establish his authority in his own provinces in the north. He needed to recover his health, he said; and he must be ready to go south again as soon as he could, to find the source of the Nile, otherwise he would return to his own country in disgrace. Permission was granted him: he could in the meantime live with the Empress at Kusquam. So Bruce remained there until the rains were over. Then on 27 October 1770 he set out again for the south. He was accompanied by Balugani and by Strates, a Greek, who had succeeded Yasin in the supervision of the other servants.

Bruce found Fasil, the powerful chieftain whose protection he would need for his journey, in camp near the northern shores of Lake Tana. He was sitting in his tent on a cushion over which had been thrown a lion's skin. Another lion's skin was spread at his feet. 'There were no carpets or cushions in the tent,' Bruce recalled, 'and only a little straw, as if accidentally thrown thinly about it. I sat down upon the ground ... He looked steadfastly at me, saying, half under his breath, "How do you do? Are you very well?" I made the usual answer, "Well, thank God." He again stopt, as if for me to speak; there was only one man present, who was sitting on the floor mending a mule's bridle. I took him at first for an attendant, but observing that a servant, uncovered, held a candle to him, I thought he was one of his Galla; but then I saw a blue silk thread which he had about his neck, which is a badge of Christianity all over Abyssinia, and which a Galla would not wear. What he was I could not make out; he seemed, however, to be a very bad cobbler and took no notice of us. [A] servant who stood behind me, pushed me with his knee as a sign that I should speak.'

'I am come by your invitation and the King's leave,' said Bruce, 'to pay my respects to you in your own government, begging that you would favour my curiosity so far as to suffer me to see ... the source of the Nile.'

'The source of the Nile?' Fasil repeated in feigned astonishment when reminded of the object of Bruce's quest. 'The source of the Nile? Why it is God knows where in the country of the Galla, wild, terrible people. Are you mad? It might take you a year to get back ... A boy of the Galla would think nothing of killing a man of your country. You white people are all effeminate; you are not fit to go into a province where all is war and the men are warriors from their cradles.'

The exchanges between the two men grew more and more heated until Bruce, accused by Fasil of being 'a Frank', that was to say a Roman Catholic, lost his temper. He vehemently denied being of 'the Romish religion'; he contended that the 'worst and lowest individual among the most uncivilized people' had never treated him as Fasil had treated him that day under his own roof; he claimed that on horseback and armed in the fashion of his own country he would willingly challenge two of the best warriors in Fasil's army. So furious did he become, indeed, that his nose, as it often did at such moments, started streaming with blood. He was obliged to allow himself to be conducted from the tent. Upon his return he found Fasil in an apparently more amenable mood: the traveller would be permitted to continue his journey; Fasil's Galla soldiers were about to be sent home south; Bruce would be well advised to leave before them so that they would not molest him on his way; he could have a present of a horse as a token of godspeed. Bruce chose a pony which Fasil's groom pressed upon him as being one of the best of his master's mounts though too quiet for his taste. He accepted it; but no sooner was he astride it than the animal kicked, reared and leapt so violently that he realized it had not been broken. The skill with which he brought it under control, however, and the easy manner in which, so he claimed, he brought down two kites with his double-barrelled shotgun from the saddle, so impressed Fasil and his attendant Gallas that he was immediately offered another horse and the head of the groom for whose reprehensible actions Fasil disclaimed responsibility. Accepting the horse but declining the execution of the groom, Bruce gave Fasil some obviously welcome silk sashes, Egyptian blue glass bowls and a Persian pipe in order to cement their new-found friendship. He was then ritually clothed in garments, worthy of his status as Governor of

Ghish, in the presence of seven ferocious-looking witnesses. 'You see those seven men,' Fasil said to him. 'They are all leaders and chiefs of the Gallas – you may think them savages, but they are all your brethren. You may go through their country as if it were your own. You will soon be related to them all, for it is their custom that a stranger of distinction like yourself, when he is their guest, should sleep with the sister, daughter, or near relation of the chief man among them ... Now, go in peace. You are a Galla; there is a curse on them and their children, their corn, grass and cattle, if they ever lift a hand against you or yours.'

So, Bruce left Fasil's camp confirmed as Governor of Ghish and accompanied by an Agau guide, Shalaka Woldo, a bushy-haired, shabbily dressed man who walked barefoot beside his mule, sometimes carrying a pipe in his hand, at others a long stick 'with which he dealt about him very liberally, either to man, woman or beast, upon the slightest provocation'. Cantankerous and slovenly, Woldo was also extremely shrewd, 'exceedingly sagacious and cunning', in Bruce's opinion, seeming to penetrate the meaning of conversations in languages of which he did not understand a syllable. They had not proceeded far when, by the banks of the Kelti river, Woldo announced that they would seek the protection of a robber known as 'the Jumper', the greatest thief and murderer in all the country of the Galla. Bruce ironically complimented him upon the choice of protector he had made. 'To which he answered laughing, "The better, the better; you shall see how it is the better."'

They came upon 'the Jumper' just as he had emerged from washing himself in the river. He was rubbing his skin with melted tallow while a servant was plaiting his hair with the guts of an ox. Ox guts were also placed around his neck as a necklace from which a dangling pendant reached the pit of his stomach. 'Our conversation was neither long nor interesting,' Bruce recorded. 'I was overcome with the disagreeable smell of blood and carrion.' It was clear, however, that 'the Jumper' regarded Fasil with some respect, for he handed a bull over to the strangers as he had been requested to do; and, having accepted a present 'with great indifference', he sent them on their way, informing them that they would soon come under the protection of a party of Galla horsemen commanded by his brother who was known as 'the Lamb' because of his merciful kindness in never killing female enemies, even when they were pregnant. He was, however, 'the Jumper' contended with evident pride, otherwise 'just such a murderer and robber as himself'.

They were on the point of departure when a group of men from Gondar came into 'the Jumper's' camp. Among them was a messenger from Princess Esther who claimed to be desperately ill and in urgent need of Bruce's advice. Knowing well that if he did not respond to her call he would be accused of ingratitude to a faithful friend, 'the foulest and basest of all sins', Bruce was also only too well aware that, if he did turn back, the quiescent war might well erupt again and destroy his hopes for ever. He could not bear *that* prospect, and so was soon once more on his way south.

He was close to the Little Abbai by now. The countryside was extraordinarily beautiful: acacia trees, crowded with strange birds of the most vivid plumage, grew on every side; the ground was covered with jasmine, roses and lupins. They passed the camp of 'the Lamb' who accepted Bruce's presents, including a large quantity of tobacco, with even greater indifference than had been displayed by his brother but seemed pleased enough with a tablecloth on which the traveller's breakfast had been served and which, readily given to him when he asked for it, he 'spread upon his head till it covered half his face'. And at two o'clock on the afternoon of 2 November 1770 Bruce reached the banks of the Nile.

He discovered it to be venerated as a sacred river. The people who lived there 'protested immediately with much vehemence, against any man's riding across the stream mounted either upon horse or mule'. They therefore unloaded the mules, laid the baggage upon the grass, insisted that the travellers take off their shoes, and threatened to stone any of them who attempted to wash the dirt off their cloaks and trousers in the water. Eventually Bruce, Balugani and Strates, the Greek supervisor, were permitted to wade across in bare feet, cutting their soles upon the sharp rocks; the mules too were driven to the far bank; but Woldo, the guide, with bearers, servants and baggage, were left on the other side. And the natives insisted that they must be paid before the baggage was taken across. For some time Woldo discussed the matter with them, sitting on a green hillock by the ford, calmly smoking his pipe. But then he suddenly leapt to his feet, apparently in a most violent passion, threw down his pipe, picked up his stick and ran into his fellow-Agaus, shouting, 'You want payment, do you? Here is your payment!' as he lashed about him, striking them on their heads and faces. He wrested a lance from one of them who fled away, followed headlong by the others while Woldo called out loudly for a gun. He then picked up his pipe and, as though nothing had happened, led the porters and servants through the ford, leaving the baggage on the far side and advising Bruce and Balugani to mount their horses and ride away. Immediately the Agau dashed back to the baggage and, while one crossed the river to beg the travellers to wait, the others brought the baggage across, beseeching Woldo not to report them to Fasil for fear lest heavy chastisement fall upon their villages.

Beyond the river, acacia trees still abounded but here they were all pollarded, the twigs from their tops being used for making large baskets which, hung from the branches like bird-cages, all contained bee-hives. During the day the bees proved an 'excessive plague' to Bruce and his companions, who were frequently stung. They were also plagued by the heat of the sun which beat down mercilessly upon the plain through which the river wound backwards and forwards, making, so Bruce calculated, more than a hundred turns within the space of four miles. But, to Bruce himself at least, this was an easily supportable inconvenience, for he could now clearly hear the noise of what – numbering them from the source, instead of from north to south – he called the First Cataract; and looming in the distance were ranges of high mountains which he took to be the Mountains of the Moon, described by Ptolemy as the guardians of the Nile's source. Bruce's servants and bearers now also seemed in better spirits, realizing that they were approaching the end of their journey. Woldo, on the contrary, seemed utterly depressed. He complained first of sickness, then of lameness; he fell behind and eventually disappeared. A variety of suggestions were made as to what had become of him. Some thought he had resolved to betray and rob the rest of the party. Others supposed he was slain by wild beasts, probably by apes or baboons, 'whose voracity, size and fierce appearance were exceedingly magnified, especially by Strates, who had not the least doubt that Woldo would be so entirely devoured that we might seek in vain without discovering even a fragment of him'. When Woldo reappeared he at first accounted for his behaviour by explaining that he was afraid of falling into the hands of hostile villagers who would not hesitate to slay him as a servant of Fasil. But later, when the travellers had climbed to an abandoned church 9,500 feet above sea level, he declared that he would tell the truth; he had been promised a reward at the end of the journey; and he coveted beyond all things the splendid crimson silk sash which Bruce wore round his waist and into which were tucked his pistols. He was afraid that the white man would be so disappointed when he reached the object of his long journey that he would be denied the present upon which he had set his heart. Hearing this story, Bruce handed over the sash; and Woldo promptly pointed to a green hillock in the middle of a nearby marsh. It was there, he said, that the fountains of the Nile were to be found. If you go down there, Woldo warned him, 'pull off your shoes, as you did the other day, for these people are all pagans, worse than those that were at the ford; and they believe in nothing that you believe, but only in this river, to which they pray every day, as if it were a God. But this, perhaps,' he added, 'you may do likewise.'

Half undressed as I was by the loss of my sash and throwing my shoes off [Bruce wrote in the fifth volume of his *Travels*] I ran down the hill, towards the little island of green sods, which was about two hundred yards distant; the whole side of the hill was thick grown over with flowers, the large bulbous roots of which appearing above the surface of the ground occasioned me two very severe falls before I reached the brink of the marsh. I after this came to the island of green turf, which was in form of an altar and I stood in rapture over the principal fountain which rises in the middle of it.

It is easier to guess than to describe the situation of my mind at that moment – standing in the spot whicn had baffled the genius, industry, and inquiry of both ancients and moderns, for the course of near three thousand years. Kings had attempted this discovery at the head of armies, and each expedition was distinguished from the last, only by the difference of the numbers which had perished ... Though a mere private Briton, I triumphed here, in my own mind, over kings and armies.

Bruce's elation, however, was immediately followed by despondency as his thoughts turned from his present success to the dangers of the future journey home. And in an attempt, so he said, to divert this despondency until he could overcome it, he called out to Strates, 'Faithful squire! Come and triumph with your Don Quixote! ... Come and triumph with me over all the kings of the earth, all their armies, all their philosophers, and all their heroes!'

'Sir,' replied Strates deflatingly, 'I do not understand a word of what you say ... But you had much better leave that bog.'

In his excitement, Bruce picked up a half coconut shell which he had procured in Arabia as a drinking vessel and proposed a toast to King George III. Indulgently responding, Strates joined in the toast, threw his cap in the air with a loud huzza, and added, 'And confusion to his enemies!' Thinking of the girl whom he hoped was waiting for him at home, Bruce then proposed a toast to Maria. Was that the Virgin Mary? Strates asked him. 'In faith, I believe so, Strates,' replied Bruce. Strates did not answer, 'but only gave a humph of disapprobation'. He declined also to drink to their safe return, maintaining that the water was too cold, and that it had been bewitched by the people who prayed over it every morning. But when Bruce asked him to toast Catherine, Empress of all the Russias, whose fleet had recently defeated the Greeks' enemies, the Turks, Strates declared he would drink *that* health even if it killed him. 'Huzza!' he shouted, tossing his cap in the air, 'Huzza! Catherine and victory!'

Drawn by these loud cries, several Agaus came down the hill and asked Woldo what was happening. Woldo replied that Strates had gone out of his mind. He had been bitten by a mad dog. The Agaus assured Woldo that the waters of the source of the Nile would cure him.

These were not, though, the waters of the source of the Nile. The true source, the origins of the White Nile, lay far away to the south in Lake Victoria. Bruce was, geographers would argue, not even at the source of the Blue Nile which may more accurately be said to be in Lake Tana near Bahardar. Furthermore, he was not the first person to have been there: Pedro Paez, whose claims Bruce disingenuously dismissed as mere hearsay, had been at Ghish in 1608.

Bruce, however, was confirmed in his belief that he was at the source of the Nile by the ancient, white-bearded headman of the village of Ghish whose family had, 'from the beginning of the world, so he imagined', held the office of 'servant of the Father of Waters'. This dignified old man, the father of fifty-six children, offered three of them as housekeepers to the travellers. He also offered them some of the village's clay and straw houses for as long as they cared to stay. They accepted his offer and stayed for five days while Bruce studied and measured the river, explored the surrounding countryside, made drawings of the plants and animals, and listened to strange stories of the rites of the Nile worshippers. Every year, he was told, a black heifer was sacrificed upon the principal fountain; its head was cut off and wrapped in its hide which had previously been meticulously washed in the river's waters. The carcass, washed with equal care, was then eaten raw, Nile water being drunk with it 'to the exclusion of any other liquor'. After they had finished eating the animal the priests carried the head into the cavern which reached below the fountains, and there performed their rites, the particulars of which Bruce was never able to discover. He was told that the Devil appeared to the worshippers and that they ate the head of the heifer with him, swearing obedience to him on certain conditions, that of sending rain and a good season for their bees and cattle. Whether or not they made these contracts with the Devil, they certainly prayed to the spirit residing in the river, whom they called the Everlasting God, Light of the World, Eye of the World, God of Peace, Saviour and Father of the Universe.

Having discovered as much as he could about this spirit and the people who worshipped it, Bruce set out on the return journey to Gondar. All the men in the village, carrying lances and shields, attended him to the borders of their territory and there wished him well.

On his return to Gondar, Bruce found himself plunged into new dangers and tribulations. In the absence of Ras Michael and the Emperor, the throne had been usurped by a drunken profligate who claimed to be a son of the Emperor Jesus II and had taken the name of Susenyos. This man summoned Bruce to his presence and, squirting tobacco juice on to a floor already awash in spittle, demanded gold from him on pain of death. Bruce was saved from Susenyos by the intervention of the usurper's adviser, a nephew of the Empress Dowager; and soon afterwards, when news reached Gondar of the imminent return of Ras Michael and Takla Haymanot II, Susenyos fled from the capital. But, although propitiously received by the Ras and the Emperor, Bruce's troubles were not yet over. For, sickened as he was by the savage vengeance which both men wreaked upon their enemies, he also had to bear the loss of Balugani who died at this time of dysentery. He longed to escape from the 'bloody country', yet was instead forced not only to remain but also to pay for horses and weapons for his guards whom he had occasionally to lead into battle in one of the indecisive campaigns of the protracted civil war. Whenever he could, he went out on scientific and botanical expeditions, collecting plants and minerals, making meteorological recordings, gathering documents, sketching, studying the history of the country. The months he was forced to remain in Ethiopia were not, therefore, wasted. But he grew daily more depressed until, on 26 December 1771, after Ras Michael had been deposed and the country was temporarily more quiet, he was allowed to leave with the permission of the Emperor and the Iteghe. He set out with three Greeks, a Copt, a gang of porters, and with horses and other animals to carry the baggage, which included the presents with which he hoped to appease the local chieftains. He was accompanied also by an old Turkish janissary, Hadji Ismail, who was to perform the same functions as Yasin and Strates had done on previous expeditions.

Reluctant to place himself again at the mercy of the predators at Massawa and anxious to see the country to the north, Bruce had decided to take the inland route which would take him across the mountains to the deserts of the Sudan, through Cherkin, Sancaho and Ras el Fil to the Nile at Sennar, the capital of the Fung, a people of uncertain origin whose lands had been frequently invaded by black men from the south.

It was an adventurous and perilous journey. Near Cherkin he paused to hunt boar, buffalo and rhinoceros and was charged by a young elephant which came to the rescue of its mother whose Achilles tendon had been cut by two members of a forest tribe; in their customary way, they had ridden up to her 'absolutely naked' on a horse, one holding the reins of the animal, the other wielding a huge broadsword the sharp blade of which was slashed at the elephant's heel. At Sancaho, Bruce was insulted by the Negro chieftain, the largest man he had ever seen, 'perfectly black, flat-nosed, thick-lipped and woolly-haired', who received him in a tent 'all hung round' with elephants' trunks, giraffes' heads and rhinoceros' skulls. At Hor Cacamoot, now known as Gallabat, where the temperature rose to 114° in the shade, he almost died of dysentery and took two months to recover. Beyond the border town of Ras el Fil, the watering-places in the Sudan were almost dry; the villages had been destroyed by nomad raiders and were littered with the skeletons of their former inhabitants who had died of starvation when their crops had failed; between the trees prowled hyenas and lions whose hunger drove them to attack men as well as mules. The *simoom*, the burning wind of the desert, obliged the travellers to lie down with their faces pressed against the ground to avoid its suffocating blast. They were able to cover scarcely more than nine miles a day. At Teawa, now Gedaref, Sheikh Fadl, the Governor of the Fung province of Atbara, demanded fifty ounces of gold and threatened to murder Bruce if he did not receive them. He was not allowed to depart until messengers from the Fung king arrived in Teawa to escort him to Sennar.

At the end of April 1772 Bruce's bedraggled party crossed the Dinder River and arrived at last in Sennar. This was the capital of the Fung kingdom but it was not a welcome sight. It seemed a city of the dead: men did not live long in the appallingly hot climate; diseases of all kinds were common, 'epilepsies, apoplexies, violent fevers, obstinate agues and lingering painful dysenteries'. Animals fared no better: 'no horse, mule, ass, or any beast of burden, will breed, or even live at Sennar or many miles around it. Poultry does not live there. Neither dog nor cat, sheep nor bullock, can be preserved a season there.'

The king, Ismail, a weak young man controlled by his viziers, was no more prepossessing than his capital of flat-roofed mud houses. Brown-skinned – his mother was an Arab – and wearing nothing but a loose blue cotton shirt, he received Bruce in a small room in his bare and crumbling palace where it was his habit to have himself regularly rubbed with foul-smelling elephant grease which, he contended, 'made people strong, and preserved the skin very smooth'. He read the letters which Bruce presented to him, looking puzzled as though he could not fully understand them, then asked Bruce – as he had so often been asked – why he travelled abroad in such discomfort when he could live in pleasure in his own country. The king did not appear to find much enjoyment in life himself. On a subsequent visit Bruce discovered him in a characteristically ill-humoured mood. He asked Bruce 'in a very peevish manner' why he was not yet gone. Bruce said that it was impossible for him to leave Sennar without the king's assistance in providing him with safe conduct through his dominions. The king made no reply, but indicated by a petulant gesture that his visitor should depart. But at about four o'clock that same afternoon Bruce was again sent for to the palace where the king told him that several of his wives were ill, and desired that he would give them his advice.

Bruce entered the harem where about fifty women, 'all perfectly black' and naked but for a narrow piece of cotton about their waists, sat in a gloomy, ill-lit apartment. One of the women took his hand to lead him, 'rudely enough', into another, brighter room where three women, wearing the long blue cotton shirts which were the usual costume of the people of Sennar, sat together on a long bench. The largest of these women was, apart from elephants and rhinoceroses, the 'largest living creature' Bruce had ever seen, a huge accumulation of flesh, six feet tall and 'corpulent beyond all proportion'. 'Her features were perfectly like those of a Negro; a ring of gold passed through her underlip, and weighed it down, till, like a flap, it covered her chin, and left her teeth bare ... The inside of her lip she had made black with antimony. Her ears reached down to her shoulders, and had the appearance of wings; she had in each of them a large ring of gold ... The weight of these had drawn down the hole where her ear was pierced so much that three fingers might easily pass above the ring. She had a gold necklace ... of several rows [and] on her ankles two manacles of gold larger than [those placed] upon the feet of felons ... The others were dressed pretty much in the same manner; only there was one that had chains, which came from her ears to the outside of each nostril, where they were fastened ... There was also a ring put through the gristle of her nose, and which hung down to the opening of her mouth.'

These grotesque queens insisted first on being blooded, then on being given ipecacuanha which made them copiously sick all over the floor. They took off all their clothes, showing Bruce their breasts which hung down below their knees, and they desired him to undress, too, calling in the whole court of female attendants to see the whiteness of his skin which made them all cry out in horror, believing the colour to be the effects of some disease.

Obtaining no satisfaction from the king, despite the care with which he treated the manifold ailments of his women, Bruce went to see one of his viziers, Sheikh Adelan, who lived on the edge of the desert surrounded by the quarters of his personal cavalrymen whose fine horses, gleaming shirts of mail, copper helmets and enormous broadswords made a most impressive display of strength and order. Adelan, too, was an impressive figure, tall, masterful, splendidly arrayed in a camel-hair cloak trimmed with silk and lined with yellow satin, with a gold-mounted dagger in his sash and a vast amethyst on his finger. But he was preoccupied with the problems of taxation of the nomadic tribes whose chiefs were outside his door and, having informed Bruce that his brother could do more for strangers than he could, he contented himself with advising his visitor not to go into the town without a black companion. But Bruce had little need of the warning: he had already been taunted as a foreigner, threatened with the same fate as had overtaken a French envoy, Du Roule, who had been murdered in 1705; and now, on his return to Sennar, he was menaced by people who followed him, demanding gold and tobacco.

While waiting for his passes and guides, Bruce made the same kind of detailed observations in Sennar which he had made in Gondar, consulting the Master of the Royal Household, a helpful and kindly man whose inappropriate duty it was to kill the king, should a council of his advisers decide that he was an unsuitable person to occupy the throne, and whose office had already obliged him to cut the throat of the previous king, Ismail's brother, Nasser, as well as that of Nasser's son.

It was September before Bruce was able to escape from Sennar; and by then he had been forced to part with all but six of the links of the massive gold chain which the Emperor Takla Haymanot had presented to him as a reward for his services in commanding the imperial guards. He had no means, other than this gold, to pay his way across the desert; and he was accompanied only by the old Turk, Hadji Ismail, and the three Greeks who had come with him from Gondar. But he left in good spirits, with five sound camels, and soon reached the junction of the Blue and White Niles at Halfaya. He noticed that the White Nile was very deep and had a more powerful flow than the Blue Nile; but he said no more about it. It was as though he refused to recognize that the Blue Nile, whose source he had investigated, was not the main stream: he referred to the other Nile only by its native name, the Abbai.

At the beginning of October Bruce reached Shendi, and went to pay court to the widowed Queen Mother of the province who received him from behind a screen through which, though he could not see her, she apparently observed him quite clearly. On his next visit, however, Bruce was favoured with the sight of her. She appeared before him, magnificently dressed in a purple silk robe, a cap of solid gold upon her head, her hair in plaits hanging down below her waist. 'She was a woman, scarcely forty, taller than the middle size' with the finest teeth Bruce had ever seen and small square black specks of kohl at the top of her nose, between her eyebrows and in the middle of her chin. He kissed her hand. She told him that this had never happened to her before. But she seemed pleased rather than offended. She told him that he must on no account consider continuing his journey without a guide, and when one was found, an Arab named Idris, she examined him closely before assuring Bruce of his reliability.

With Idris, another young Arab, two Nubians who were placed in charge of the camels, Hadji Ismail and the three Greeks, Bruce embarked on the last stages of his homeward journey across the Nubian desert. It was to be the most hazardous of all the journeys he had made. Filling goat-skins with dried and powdered durra bread, which, soaked and swelled in water from their *gerbas*,* was to be their only food, the travellers set out for Aswan on 11 November 1772 after Bruce had taken a farewell bathe in the Nile, 'very doubtful' that he would ever meet his 'old acquaintance' again. He almost did not. Already weakened by the painful ravages of a guinea worm in his leg, he was soon in agony from inflamed and bleeding feet; his neck was covered with blisters and his face so swollen that he could hardly open his eyes. The water in the wells was so brackish that it was drinkable only after it had been filtered through a cloth; before the journey was over the bread had begun to run out. There was danger of dying a violent death as well as of starvation: 'prodigious pillars of sand ... at times moving with great celerity' suddenly appeared and threatened to overwhelm the travellers. These sand-pillars retreated almost out of sight, 'their tops reaching to the very clouds', before sweeping menacingly forward again. When they had disappeared, the appalling heat of the simoom forced the exhausted men to lie down and cover their

* A glossary of unfamiliar African words will be found on page 318.

faces. Near the well at Tarfawi a Bisharin tribesman made an attempt to steal their camels. Later one of the camels died; another refused to rise to his legs and had to be abandoned; a third perished that same day. Despite the blows that were rained upon them, the remainder could not be forced to their feet after one particularly cold night and were killed; and the water, fresh and tasteless, was drained from their bodies. Strips of flesh were cut from their sides and dried in the sun; but the smell was so repugnant that Bruce could not eat it. Without means of transporting them, his specimens, seeds, manuscripts and drawings had to be left in the sand.

After almost three weeks of dreadful suffering, the caravan slowly approached the Nile. Kites were seen overhead; then trees were glimpsed in the distance; then the sound of the cataract above Aswan could be heard. Bruce arrived in Aswan painfully thin, his clothes in rags, his red and swollen face partly concealed by a long beard. For some days he could not move; but then, having managed to borrow a camel in order to retrieve his precious possessions from the desert, he began to recover his spirits. He sailed down the Nile to Cairo, and moved on from there to Alexandria. Here he found a French boat willing to take him to Marseilles where he landed on 25 March 1773.

In France, Bruce was respectfully received. His friend the Comte de Buffon, who was to write highly of his achievements in the third volume of his *Histoire des Oiseaux*, came to meet him and to accompany him to Paris where he was introduced to several prominent savants, presented some of his seeds to the royal botanical gardens and a copy of the apocryphal Book of Enoch to the King's Library. From France he went to Italy to seek a cure for his still troublesome leg at the baths of Poretta; and while in Italy he heard to his dismay that Margaret Murray, whom he had, with sublime confidence, expected to wait for him for over ten years, had married an Italian nobleman in his absence. Bruce challenged the poor Marchese to a duel which he was persuaded not to insist upon only when he was apologetically informed that the husband had not been told of any previous engagement. His ruffled feelings were somewhat soothed in Rome where he was received as respectfully as he had been in Paris, and where the Pope presented him with several gold medals.

When he reached London, however, on 21 June 1774 his reception was a bitter disappointment to him. The big, vain, self-confident Scotsman who treated idle, ill-informed questions with the utmost brusqueness and from whom, in James Boswell's words, information was as difficult to get as 'from a flinty rock with pick-axes', was at first treated with scepticism then as a downright impostor. The King received him politely enough and accepted various drawings for the royal collection. Bruce, claiming credit for Balugani's as well as his own, received some remuneration for these, but that was almost his last token of official recognition. He was elected a Fellow of the Royal Society, but the Society's President confided to Boswell that their new Fellow was a 'brute' whose tales were not fully to be credited. This also was the opinion of Samuel Johnson, recognized as an authority on Abyssinia since his translation of Father Lobo's travels and the publication of his novel, *Rasselas*. On meeting the man whom Fanny Burney's friend, Mrs Strange, called 'His Abyssinian Majesty', Johnson had expressed the justified opinion that he was 'not a distinct relater'. Since then he had come to the opinion that Bruce had not been in Abyssinia at all. It was an opinion widely shared. When Bruce, in answer to a question at a dinner party, replied that he had, indeed, seen a musical instrument in Abyssinia – a lyre – a fellow guest, George Selwyn, murmured to his neighbour, 'I am sure there is one less since *he* came out of the country.'

Bruce had not expected all this; and, more proud and taciturn, more over-bearing than ever, he returned to Scotland. There he fell in love again, with a girl twenty-four years younger than himself, and married her. He settled down to country life and the business of his estate, occasionally wearing Ethiopian costume, translating Ethiopian documents, looking into his journals but refusing to publish anything. And it was not until his wife died after some nine years of marriage that he was persuaded to take his journals out again and to begin the book for which his few remaining friends had long been waiting. Most of it he dictated, employing as amanuensis a Moravian pastor without whose painstaking help the volumes would doubtless have been even more muddled in composition than they are. When the laborious work was finished the pastor asked for some recompense; and Bruce, protesting that he had never thought of his assistant 'on the footing of payment', begrudgingly sent him five guineas.

Travels to discover the Sources of the Nile in the Years 1768, 1769, 1770, 1771, 1772, and 1773 by James Bruce of Kinnaird Esq. F.R.S. appeared in five volumes in 1790. The book was immediately and highly successful. But it aroused all the familiar prejudice against the Scotsman's boastfulness and aggressive self-satisfaction, his refusal to give any credit to his predecessors and companions. Walpole wrote that he was 'sick of his vanity' and what he supposed to be his 'want of veracity'. Another, more expert critic, Edward Wortley Montagu, who had spent several years in the Middle East, supported Johnson's contention that Bruce had never been to Ethiopia at all, that he had spent the years when he was supposed to have been there in some out-of-the-way place like Armenia.

Such disbelief enraged Bruce in his tetchy last years. When a visitor to Kinnaird had the temerity to suggest that beef could not be eaten raw, Bruce sent off to his kitchen for a steak which he salted and peppered in the Ethiopian way and slapped down before him with the challenge that unless he ate it there and then he would be hurled downstairs 'from the top step to the bottom'. 'Now, Sir,' said Bruce, when the visitor had avoided this fate by munching through the beef, 'you will never again say it is impossible.'

Yet people continued to say that such things as Bruce had described in his *Travels* were impossible. And it was not until after his death in 1794, when he fell down a flight of steps at Kinnaird, that the reports of other travellers proved that, faulted as they could be in minor details, his tales were essentially true. He was recognized posthumously not only as a very brave man, but as an explorer of great originality and importance, one who had 'put Africa on the map'.

2

DEATH ON THE NIGER

While Bruce was working on his *Travels* in Scotland, the African Association, undeterred by the failures of the missions of Ledyard and Lucas, had continued with their plans to solve the riddle of the Niger. They had instructed a retired army major, Daniel Houghton, who had served in the consulate in Morocco and in the British fort at Goree off the coast of Senegal, to approach the river from the west African seaboard and to make a report upon the rise, course and termination of the Niger and upon the 'various nations that inhabit its borders'. Houghton, an impoverished, good-natured Irishman, seems to have been drawn to African exploration as a means of supporting his large family, to have accepted with alacrity the meagre pay offered him, and to have had every confidence in the success of his mission. The instructions of the African Association certainly indicated that the mission was expected to be one of no great hardship. Houghton, however, had found it impossible to carry out. He had reached the Gambia safely, had penetrated further inland than any European was previously known to have done and had announced his intention of going on to Timbuktu; but after numerous misadventures, including a fire that destroyed much of his baggage, an accident with a gun that badly injured his arms and face, an attack of fever, and the desertion of his interpreter who went off with his horse and three of his five asses, he met his death in mysterious circumstances in the middle of 1791.

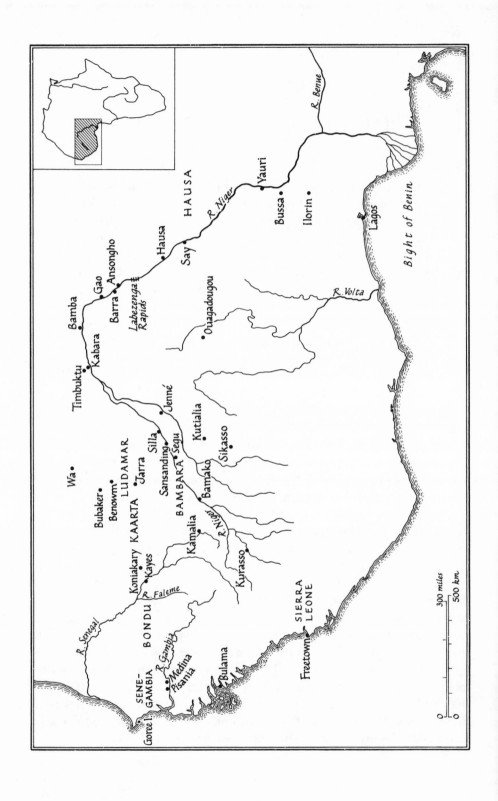

When news of Houghton's probable death reached London the African Association had already been approached by an eager Scotsman, Mungo Park, who also had expressed his willingness to go 'to Timbucktoo and back'.

Park was then twenty-two years old. The son of a thrifty tenant farmer also named Mungo after the patron saint of Glasgow, he had been born at Foulshiels four miles from Selkirk, the seventh of twelve or perhaps thirteen children. Theirs was a humble but not a poor family: their house was small and inevitably cramped but there was enough money for a maidservant and a tutor. One of Mungo's brothers became a successful lawyer, another a ship's surgeon. Mungo himself, after attending Selkirk's grammar school, also made his mind up to become a surgeon, though his father had wanted him to go into the church. He was accordingly apprenticed at the age of fourteen to a doctor in Selkirk and three years later went to Edinburgh University where his studies were completed in 1792. He then went to London where he stayed in Bloomsbury with the family of his brother-in-law, James Dickson, who, formerly a gardener, then a seedsman at Covent Garden, had become an authority on botany and had accordingly attracted the attention and regard of the great botanist, Joseph Banks, the extremely rich and energetic President of the Royal Society, companion of Captain Cook in his circumnavigation of the globe and one of the founders of the African Association. Banks took an interest in Park as he had done in his brother-in-law, Dickson, and after the promising young man had passed his examinations at the Company of Surgeons, had obtained employment as a surgeon's mate on the East India-man, the *Worcester*, and had sailed to Sumatra and the island of St Helena, Banks promised to support him in his application to the African Association.

Park professed himself to be not in the least discouraged by the news of Houghton's death. On the contrary, he wrote, this intelligence 'animated me to persist in the offer of my services with the greater solicitude. I had a passionate desire to examine into the productions of a country so little known, and to become experimentally acquainted with the modes of life and character of the natives. I knew that I was able to bear fatigue, and I relied on my youth and the strength of my constitution to preserve me from the effects of the climate. The salary which the committee allowed me was sufficiently large, and I made no stipulation for future reward. If I should perish in my journey, I was willing that my hopes and expectations should perish with me; and if I should succeed in rendering the geography of Africa more familiar to my countrymen, and in opening to their ambition and industry new sources of wealth and new channels of commerce, I knew that I was in the hands of men of honour, who would not fail to bestow that remuneration which my successful services should appear to them to merit.'

The bargain, then, was a satisfactory one for both parties. The African

Association had hopes of fulfilling some of those aims which it had declared to be its *raison d'être*; and Park was given the opportunity of achieving that fame upon which, as he openly admitted to his brother, Alexander, he had set his heart. The salary, which he considered 'sufficiently large', was to be 7s.6d. a day from 1 August 1794 until he departed for the interior, then 15s. a day for the next two years of exploration. It was not an extravagant sum but it was considerably more than he would have been paid had he continued as a surgeon's mate; and he was to receive in addition a capital sum of £200 for equipment.

His instructions, as he put it himself, were 'very plain and concise'. He was to go out to Fattetenda with James Willis, a young man who had recently been appointed Consul-General in Senegambia. He was then to 'pass on to the river Niger, either by way of Bambouk or by such other route as should be found most convenient ... to ascertain the course and, if possible, the rise and termination of that river ... to use [his] utmost exertions to visit the principal towns or cities in its neighbourhood ... and afterwards to be at liberty to return to Europe, either by way of the Gambia or by such other route as ... should appear to be most advisable'.

Although he expected to be away for more than two years he had neither the inclination nor the means to take with him anything like the amount of baggage with which Bruce had sailed to Ethiopia. Nor did he trouble to equip himself, as Bruce had done, with native costume. Contenting himself with just such clothes as he might have packed had he been going on a prolonged holiday in England, and leaving James Willis to follow him later, he sailed from Portsmouth on 22 May 1795 in the brig *Endeavour*, a small vessel trading to the Gambia for bees-wax and ivory; and, 'after a pleasant journey of thirty days', he landed at Jillifree in the kingdom of Barra, 'a town on the northern bank of the river Gambia, opposite to James's Island, where the English had formerly a small fort'.

Park was still not yet twenty-four, a tall good-looking man, reserved, serious and rather diffident, though fully conscious of his abilities and determined to make the best use of them. As soon as he set foot on the African coast he began making those observations which he was later to set down in his *Travels*. And as he made his way upriver from Jillifree to Vintang in the kingdom of Fogny, through Jonkakonda to Pisania, where he arrived on 5 July, he made notes on native customs and trade, on the appearance of the countryside, and on the Jola, 'a wild and unsociable race of people' who collected bees-wax from the woods to sell to the Europeans through their agents, the wilier people of the Mandingo nation, who, with the connivance of the white traders, cheated the Jola in their transactions. At Pisania where he stayed for five months with a slave trader, Dr John Laidley, Park learned the Mandingo language and as much as he could about the people through whose lands the Gambia flowed. He found that their domestic animals were much the same as in Europe, but that the flesh of swine was not esteemed, probably because the 'marked abhorrence in which this animal is held by the votaries of Mohammed' had 'spread itself among the pagans'. The Mandingos far preferred the flesh of elephants which they slaughtered in great numbers principally for the sake of the teeth, never considering the possibility that these powerful and docile creatures might be trained to serve them and laughing to scorn as a 'white man's lie' Park's assertion that elephants were thus trained in the East. The gloomy Jola, Park was told, never forgave an injury: 'If a man loses his life in one of those sudden quarrels which perpetually occur at their feasts, when the whole party is intoxicated with mead, his son, or the eldest of his sons, endeavours to procure his father's sandals, which he wears *once a year*, on the anniversary of his father's death, until a fit opportunity offers of revenging his fate.' The Woloffs, a neighbouring tribe, were an 'active, powerful and warlike race, inhabiting great parts of that tract which lies between the river Senegal and the Mandingo states on the Gambia'. Their noses were not so depressed, nor their lips so protuberant as those of most Africans, so, although their skin was 'of the deepest black', they were considered by the white slave traders as the 'most sightly negroes in this part of the Continent'. The Fulani were 'chiefly of a tawny complexion with soft silky hair and pleasing features'. They were 'much attached to a pastoral life' and had 'introduced themselves into all the Kingdoms on the windward coast as herdsmen and husbandmen', paying a tribute to the sovereign of the country for the lands they occupied. Most of these people of the Gambia wore clothes of cotton which they dyed an 'excellent blue colour' with indigo, the women winding a kind of narrow bandage many times around their foreheads. They lived in 'small and incommodious hovels' with circular mud walls about four feet high and bamboo cane roofs thatched with grass. Their household furniture was 'equally simple': 'A hurdle of canes placed upon upright sticks, about two feet from the ground, upon which is spread a mat or bullock's hide, answers the purpose of a bed; a water jar, some earthen pots for dressing their food, a few wooden bowls and calabaches, and one or two low stools compose the rest.' But small and crowded though they were, these huts were kept sweet-smelling by bags of fragrant gums which, thrown on to hot embers, produced 'a very pleasant odour'. In each town there was a large platform erected in the shade of a tree. This was the *bentang* which served the purpose of a public hall. It was here that the lazy met to smoke their pipes and discuss the business of the day, where trials were conducted and public affairs transacted.

Park's observation of the natives' way of life was interrupted by a severe bout of fever from which he was slow to recover. It was appallingly hot, the rain poured down ceaselessly upon the roof above his head, hyenas and jackals howled in the bush, and frogs croaked interminably. As the rains began to lighten, however, his strength gradually returned; and within a few weeks he felt well enough to continue his sketches of botanical specimens and to make plans for his onward journey into the interior. James Willis, the Consul-General designate, had still not arrived; so Park decided to go on without him.

The hospitable Dr Laidley had found him a Mandingo interpreter, a sprightly slave named Demba who spoke the language of the Serahuli as well as his own tongue and who was promised his freedom should Park give a satisfactory report of his services on their return. Laidley had found him a servant also, a native of that part of Africa who had been shipped as a slave to Jamaica and, granted his freedom there, had been taken back by his master to England where he had lived for several years before returning home. He answered to the name of Johnson. Both he and Demba were provided with an ass; Park was furnished with a horse. Their baggage was light, consisting chiefly of provisions for two days and a collection of beads, amber and tobacco with which to pay for further supplies as they proceeded. Apart from a few changes of linen, Park's personal equipment was limited to a pocket sextant, a magnetic compass, a thermometer, two fowling pieces, two pairs of pistols and an umbrella. He kept his notes in the crown of his tall, wide-brimmed beaver hat.

On 2 December 1795 he set out from Pisania at last, accompanied by his interpreter and servant, as well as a freed slave who was making for Segu, two Serahuli slave merchants on their way to Bondu and a man from Khasso named Tami who had been employed as a blacksmith by Laidley and who was returning home with his savings.

Dr Laidley and two other English slave traders kindly accompanied the caravan for the first two days of their journey, bidding Park farewell on the afternoon of 3 December and leaving him with the gloomy thought that, having now parted 'from the last European [he] might probably behold and having quitted the comforts of Christian society perhaps for ever', he faced 'a boundless forest and a country, the inhabitants of which were strangers to civilized life, and to most of whom a white man was the object of curiosity or plunder'. He had not, indeed, ridden a further three miles when the first plunderers were upon him, demanding that he go with them to their king who required presents from all travellers passing through his domains. Arguing in vain that he was not an ordinary merchant and was therefore exempt from taxation, Park was obliged to hand over a large proportion of his tobacco in order to get rid of them. It was the first of many such exactions.

At Medina, however, capital of the kingdom of the Wuli, which Park reached the following day, he was treated with the utmost respect. It was a town of about one thousand houses, fortified in the usual African manner by a surrounding high clay wall with an outward fence of prickly bushes and pointed stakes which had suffered much 'from the active hands of busy housewives who had plucked up the stakes for firewood'. Park was offered accommodation by one of the king's relations who warned him on no account to shake his majesty's hand, a liberty not usually allowed to strangers.

Thus instructed [Park recalled], I went in the afternoon to pay my respects to the sovereign, and ask permission to pass through his territories to Bondou. The king's name was Jatta ... I found him seated upon a mat before the door of his hut; a number of men and women were arranged on each side, who were singing and clapping their hands. I saluted him respectfully, and informed him of the purport of my visit. The king graciously replied, that he not only gave me leave to pass through his country, but would offer up his prayers for my safety. On this, one of my attendants, seemingly in return for the king's condescension, began to sing, or rather to roar, an Arabic song; at every pause of which the king himself, and all the people present, struck their hands against their foreheads, and exclaimed, with devout and affecting solemnity, *Amen, amen!* The king told me furthermore, that I should have a guide the following day, who would conduct me safely to the frontier of his kingdom. I then took my leave, and in the evening sent the king an order upon Dr Laidley for three gallons of rum, and received in return great store of provisions.

Early the next morning Park went again to the king whom he found on this occasion sitting on a bullock's hide and warming himself before a large fire, since Africans, so Park had discovered, were 'sensible of the smallest variation in the temperature and frequently complained of cold when a European was oppressed with heat'. With 'a benevolent countenance' the king warned Park against proceeding any further, for beyond the boundaries of his domains lived a people who had never seen a white man and would probably kill him as Major Houghton had been killed. But when Park replied that, 'notwithstanding all dangers', he was determined to proceed, the 'good old king' sadly shook his head and said that a guide to take him to Konjour would be ready that afternoon.

It was at Konjour that the first quarrel erupted amongst Park's companions. For their evening meal they had enjoyed a sheep which Park had purchased in exchange for some beads. One of the Serahuli slave traders, who had performed the duties of butcher, demanded the horns of the sheep as his perquisite. His claim was strongly contested by Johnson. Park settled the dispute by awarding one horn to each, but the incident made him realize the important part which superstition played in these people's lives. For sheep horns were valued highly by pagans as well as Muslims since they were easily convertible into portable sheaths for containing and keeping secure the pieces of paper inscribed with sentences from the Koran which were worn as magical charms against disease, hostile weapons, hunger and thirst, snake- and alligator-bites and all other dangers that man had to face in his journey through this world.

The next day Park's Christian susceptibilities were further offended by the sight of 'a sort of masquerade habit, made of the bark of trees, which [he] was told, on inquiry, belonged to *Mumbo Jumbo*'. This was 'a strange bug-bear, common to all the Mandingo towns, and much employed by the pagan natives in keeping their women in subjection'. When a husband found the quarrels of his women insupportable he would clothe himself in this strange costume, or ask a friend to do so, then, as darkness fell, the presence of *Mumbo Jumbo* would be announced in the woods by 'loud and dismal screams'. As soon as it was dark the figure appeared, armed with a rod, and would make all the women dance and sing until, at midnight, the one selected for punishment was stripped and beaten while the others were required to jeer at her. This custom Park condemned as 'indecent and unmanly'; but another he subsequently came upon rather appealed to him. This was that of hanging to a large tree, 'called by the natives *neema taba*', scraps of cloth and rags. 'The custom has been so greatly sanctioned by time,' he commented, 'that nobody now presumes to pass without hanging up something. I followed the example, and suspended a handsome piece of cloth on one of the boughs.'

Park was by now growing quite used to African ways. The 'mode of living was at first unpleasant' to him; but he had, after several days' travelling, found that 'custom surmounted trifling inconveniences, and made everything palatable and easy'. Provisions were cheap: one day he managed to exchange a bullock for six small amber stones. The local beer was excellent, almost indistinguishable from the strong beer of Scotland and brewed in much the same way. The people were friendly. At Koojar, for instance, though 'not wholly unaccustomed to the sight of Europeans', they greeted him with 'a mixture of curiosity and reverence', invited him to a wrestling match at the *bentang*, followed by a dance at which the performers, regulating their movements to the tapping of a drum, had little bells fixed to their legs and arms. Some of the women were, indeed, too friendly for the modest Park's taste. In a large village near the banks of the river Faleme in the country of the Bondu crowds of them, dressed in thin gauze 'well calculated to display the shape of their persons', surrounded him, begging for amber and beads in a way that he found most embarrassing and troublesome. They tore his cloak, cut the buttons from his servant's clothes and 'were proceeding to other outrages' when he mounted his horse and rode off to escape them. Later, at Joag, the women entertained him with a dance during which their movements 'consisted more in wanton gestures' than in graceful attitudes as they vied with each other 'in displaying the most voluptuous movements imaginable'.

In Fatteconda, the capital of the Bondu, he waited at the *bentang*, as had become his usual custom, for someone to approach him with an offer of hospitality. On this occasion he was befriended by a 'respectable' native slave trader who conducted him to his hut where, soon after his arrival, a royal messenger arrived with a request that he should go to the king immediately if he were 'not too much fatigued'.

The king, sitting under a tree on the edge of a cornfield outside the town, asked him if he wished to purchase any slaves or gold and seemed surprised when Park replied that he did not. Knowing that Major Houghton had fallen foul of him, Park decided that it would be advisable to be generous with his presents; and so that evening, when he was summoned to the palace for a second interview, he arrived with a bag full of gunpowder, tobacco, amber, and his umbrella. The palace, a collection of huts and courtyards, was surrounded by a high mud wall in an opening in which a sentinel stood with a musket on his shoulder. Other sentinels stood on guard at different doors and gates within the maze-like interior. Outside the king's own hut Park's interpreter and guide removed their sandals. The guide then pronounced in a loud voice the name of the king and repeated it until he was answered from within.

Park found the king sitting on a mat with two attendants by his side. He seemed at first suspicious of Park's motives in passing through his country, since he had supposed that every white man must necessarily be a trader. But when he saw the presents his attitude changed. He was particularly delighted with the umbrella which he repeatedly furled and unfurled 'to the great admiration of himself and his attendants who could not for some time comprehend the use of this wonderful machine'. Then after a long preamble in favour of the whites, their immense wealth and generous dispositions, the king bestowed high praise upon his visitor's blue coat and its yellow buttons which he suggested might with propriety be added to the other presents. He assured Park that he would wear it upon all public occasions in future and inform everyone who saw it of the donor's liberality. Since the request of an African prince in his own domains, particularly when made to a stranger, was 'little short of a command', Park obediently took off his coat and laid it on the ground at the king's feet.

In return Park was presented with a great variety of provisions and invited to come back to the palace the next morning. Upon his return the king, protesting he was ill, asked to have a little blood taken from him; but, as soon as Park had tied up his arm and produced his lancet, the king changed his mind and asked Park to go to see his wives instead. The women surrounded him with great enthusiasm, some asking for medicine, others for amber and all of them 'desirous of trying that great African specific, *blood-letting*. They were ten or twelve in number, most of them young and handsome, and wearing on their heads ornaments of gold and beads of amber.'

They teased Park, 'with a good deal of gaiety', upon the whiteness of his skin and the prominency of his nose, insisting both were artificial, the skin the result of being dipped in milk as a baby, the nose the product of daily pinching 'until it had acquired its present unsightly and unnatural conformation'. With characteristic compliance Park did not dispute his own deformity, instead paying compliments to African beauty, praising the lovely shapes of their own flattened noses and the glossy jet-black of their skins. But they cut him short with protests that flattery, or as they called it 'honey-mouth', was not esteemed in Bondu. To show they were not altogether displeased, however, they presented him with some fish and a jar of honey.

When Park took his final leave of him the king was equally gracious, presenting his guest with some pieces of gold, informing him that although it was customary to examine the baggage of every traveller, this rule would be waived in his case, and assuring him that he was free to leave whenever he wished.

Park accordingly left Fatteconda the next morning and set out across eastern Bondu for the neighbouring kingdom of Kajaaga. His fellow-travellers warned him that in Kajaaga his reception might well prove less welcoming. The boundary between the two countries in particular was dangerous and it was advisable to cross it by night. Park took the advice and by the light of a bright moon, as wild beasts howled in the woods, and wolves and hyenas glided like shadows from one thicket to another, he passed into Kajaaga, the country of the Serahuli.

The next day, Christmas Day, Park found the warnings of his companions only too well justified. He was resting in the evening at a *bentang* when one of a party of horsemen who had gathered round him tried to steal his musket, thinking him asleep. The man desisted when Park stirred, but he and his companions remained all night watching over him and were joined in the morning by ten more horsemen, all of whom were armed with muskets. At length one of them informed Park that he was travelling in their country without permission of their king, that all his people and baggage were therefore forfeited and that he must accompany them to the royal huts immediately. Park saved himself from this interview by offering the horsemen the gold he had been given in Fatteconda. The horsemen accepted it, but before moving off they ransacked Park's belongings and took everything that caught their fancy, leaving him with only those few articles which he had managed to hide and which he dared not offer in exchange for food lest these, too, were taken from him.

Two people then came to his rescue, first an old female slave who, hearing that the king's men had taken all his possessions, offered him some groundnuts from the basket which she was carrying on her head, then the nephew of Demba Sego Jalla, ruler of the neighbouring Khasso, who had been on an embassy to Kajaaga on his uncle's behalf and who offered to escort Park home with him to the royal court at Tessee. Park thankfully accepted the offer and set out with his protector for the river Senegal, the boundary between Kajaaga and Khasso, his servant Johnson pausing on the way to tie a white chicken to the branch of a tree with the announcement that, thanks to this sacrifice, the party might now proceed in safety and that the journey would be prosperous.

No sooner had Park arrived in Khasso, however, than Demba Sego demanded 'a handsome present' for his services. Anxious as always to avoid any unnecessary trouble and unpleasantness, Park dipped into the rapidly dwindling remains of the stores he had managed to salvage from the plunderers of Kajaaga and gave the importunate young man some amber and tobacco. Fortunately, the ordinary people of Khasso were less rapacious. They attended Park everywhere as he walked about the town of Tessee, treating him with 'great kindness' as well as curiosity and supplying him with milk, eggs and other provisions 'on very easy terms'. They themselves, though possessed of both cattle and corn in abundance, were 'not over nice in articles of diet', rats, moles, squirrels, snakes and locusts being eaten 'without scruple by the highest and lowest'. The kinds of food preferred by the white man were accordingly not so much prized by them; and eggs in particular were cheap and plentiful since women, for some reason which Park was unable to discover, were forbidden to eat them. Despite the friendliness of the natives, however, Park was anxious to leave Khasso, for war was expected to break out soon with Kajaaga and when that happened the Moors to the north were sure to ride down to profit from the troubles. But as soon as he made his wishes known Demba Sego declared that duties would have to be paid and further presents given. Again Park offered him amber and tobacco. This time, though, these gifts were considered inadequate and Demba Sego and his attendants began to open Park's bundles, spread their contents on the ground and take what they pleased. When they had finished Park calculated that, having been plundered of half his possessions in Kajaaga, he had now lost half the remainder. He was able to raise some money from a native trader who owed Dr Laidley for five slaves and who handed over their value in exchange for a receipt that Park carried with him. But immediately upon hearing of this transaction, a cousin of Demba Sego's swooped down upon Park with a party of horsemen and demanded the lion's share of the money. Park was as usual 'prepared to submit'; but the trader interposed and eventually persuaded the predators to accept a smaller proportion, thus enabling Park to continue his journey.

He left Tessee on 10 January 1796 for Koniakary, the capital of Khasso, calling on the way at Jumbo, the home town of Tami, the blacksmith, who had accompanied him all the way from Pisania. Here there was such excitement at the blacksmith's return that Park remained unnoticed until, in recounting his adventures, Tami made mention of the white man's kindness towards him. 'In a moment,' Park recounted, 'all eyes were turned upon me; I appeared like a being dropped from the clouds; every one was surprised that they had not observed me before; and a few women and children expressed great uneasiness at being so near a man of such an uncommon appearance. By degrees, however, their apprehensions subsided, and when the blacksmith assured them that I was perfectly inoffensive, and would hurt nobody, some of them ventured so far as to examine the texture of my clothes. But many of them were still very suspicious; and when by accident I happened to move myself, or look at the young children, their mothers would scamper off with them with the greatest precipitation. In a few hours, however, they all became reconciled to me.'

Their ruler at Koniakary was as helpful as the king of the Wuli had been. He discouraged Park from proceeding farther, warning him of the troubled times that were to come, for his country, too, was threatened with invasion. But when Park insisted he must continue his journey, he was provided with two guides to take him into the neighbouring territory of the Kaartans. In Guemou, the capital of Kaarta, he was also kindly treated by the king, though to most of the people in these regions a white man was a phenomenon which they had never seen before and it proved impossible to keep the inquisitive out of the hut with which he was provided near the royal compound. He was surrounded by as many staring faces as the hut would contain; and when the first party of visitors had satisfied their curiosity and had left, another took their place until the hut had been filled and emptied thirteen times.

The king, Desse Koulibali, to whose presence he was admitted shortly before sunset, sat upon a leopard skin on a bank of earth surrounded by his court, his warriors on his right hand, his women and children on his left. He was perfectly affable, but pointed out, as the ruler of Khasso had done, that in the present state of unrest he could do little to afford his guest protection, even in his own country. He advised him to go back to Khasso and wait until the imminent war was over. 'This advice was certainly well meant on the part of the king, and perhaps I was to blame in not following it,' Park wrote later. 'But I reflected that the hot months were approaching, and I dreaded the thought of spending the rainy season in the interior of Africa. These considerations, and the aversion I felt at the idea of returning without having made a greater progress in discovery, made me determine to go forward ... Finding that I was determined to proceed, the king told me that one route

1. James Bruce, 'His Abyssinian Majesty', a 'tiger', in James Boswell's words, 'that growled whenever you approached him'.

2. *Cusso di Banksia Abissinica*. Named after Sir Joseph Banks, one of the founders of the African Association, and drawn by James Bruce for his *Travels to Discover the Source of the Nile*.

3. A hyena, also drawn by James Bruce for his *Travels*.

4. Kefla Yasous, a general in the army of Ras Michael Suhul, the Governor of Tigre and Chief Minister in the Ethiopian Empire.

5. Princess Esther, wife of Ras Michael and daughter of the Empress of Ethiopia.

6. Entrance to the hieron at Suffetula by James Bruce and Luigi Balugani, who made an archaeological tour of north Africa before embarking for Ethiopia.

7. Mungo Park, 'a tall, good-looking man, reserved, serious and rather diffident'.

8. Mungo Park watches porters carrying goods across the Ba-fing or Black River on his way towards the mouth of the Niger.

9. A view of Kamalia from Mungo
   Park's *Travels in the Interior
   Districts of Africa*. The bearded
   Park sits in the shade of a tree in
   his white straw hat.

10. Dixon Denham, 'an extremely
brave and talented officer, although
opinionated and excessively
managing'.

11. Shuwa Arab women of Bornu as depicted by Dixon Denham in his *Narrative of Travels and Discoveries*: 'The Shouaas Arabs are a very extraordinary race and have scarcely any resemblance to the Arabs of the north: they have fine open countenances with aquiline noses and large eyes; their complexion is a light copper colour . . . and they resemble some of our best-favoured gypsies in England, particularly the women.'

12. Denham's sketch of the British travellers' reception by the chief of Bornu: 'He received us in an open space in front of the royal residence . . . His people took their places on the ground in front, but with their backs to the royal personage which is the custom. He was seated in a sort of cage of cane or wood.'

13. Denham's drawing of the arrival
of the raiding party at Mora, the
capital of Mandara: 'The Arabs
were all eagerness; they eyed the
Kerdy huts which were now visible
on the sides of the mountains before
us, with longing eyes . . . "We'll eat
the dogs quickly . . . Why, they are
all just niggers!"'

14. Hugh Clapperton, 'a man with a
ready laugh, commanding and self-
assured'.

15. Richard Lander, Clapperton's servant, a young Cornishman 'of rambling inclinations' recommended to the Colonial Office as the 'fittest person' to send to Africa to settle the problem of the Niger.

16. John Lander, Richard's younger brother, 'of a more reflective and studious turn of mind'.

17. Homage paid to a fetish-man in a village by the banks of the Niger from the Landers' *Journal*.

18. Native pirates in the Lower Niger. 'A great number of Canoes were lying near the bank,' the Landers wrote. 'They had flags flying on long bamboo canes . . . with figures of a man's leg, chairs, tables, decanters, glasses and all kinds of such devices.'

19. Witch-doctors of West Africa as depicted in Laing's *Travels*.

still remained, but that, he said, was by no means free from danger – which was to go from Kaarta into the Moorish kingdom of Ludamar from whence I might pass, by a circuitous route, into Bambarra. If I wished to follow this route, he would appoint people to conduct me to Jarra, the frontier town of Ludamar.'

While this interview was in progress news came that the invading army from Segu had already been sighted. The discussion, therefore, came to an immediate halt. And next morning, having presented the king with his pistols and holsters, and received in return an escort of eight horsemen, Park set out for Jarra. Five days later, on 18 February, he entered Ludamar. In the eleven weeks since he had left Pisania, he had travelled 560 miles.

Ludamar, a country of nomadic Muslim people living on the fringes of the desert and speaking Arabic, had been ruled by one Ali since 1762. His camp was at Benowm and it was to Benowm that Park was summoned by a party of horsemen on 7 March: Ali's wife, Fatima, so he was told, had set her heart on seeing a Christian.

Park's experiences up till then in Ludamar had not been propitious. He had managed to obtain some more money from another trader who owed Dr Laidley for some slaves; but of much of this he was soon to be robbed. He had already lost the services of Johnson who, terrified of Moors, had begged to be allowed to go home to the Gambia with his master's letters and papers. And Park had begun to fear that he might well meet the same fate as Major Houghton who had perished in these parts, having been either murdered or left to die of starvation by the Moors. Certainly the Moors whom Park had so far encountered had treated him with the utmost contempt, shouting at him, hissing at and abusing him, and spitting in his face. One party 'had recourse to the final and decisive argument' that Park was a Christian and consequently his property 'was lawful plunder to the followers of Mahomet'. They accordingly opened his bundles and robbed him of 'everything they fancied'.

When he arrived in Benowm with his faithful interpreter Demba, Park was treated with equal contempt by Ali who received him in his tent where he sat clipping hairs from his upper lip while a female attendant held up a glass. Not deigning to address him directly, Ali asked his attendants if the man spoke Arabic. When told that he did not he affected to lose all interest in him. His attendants, however, 'especially the ladies', were much more curious. They asked him innumerable questions; they inspected his clothes and searched his pockets; they made him undo his buttons, so that they could examine the whiteness of his skin; they even counted his fingers and toes. When they at last desisted in order to answer the call to evening prayers, the man who had acted as interpreter informed him that Ali was about to present him with something to eat. This turned out to be a wild hog which, as suitable fodder for a despicable Christian, some boys brought into the tent and tethered. Ali made signs to Park to kill it and cook it for his supper; but Park, though very hungry, considered it imprudent 'to eat any part of an animal so much detested by the Moors and therefore told him that [he] never ate such food'. The hog was then untied, apparently in the hopes that it would charge the Christian as its natural enemy; and, since it declined to do so, attacking instead everyone else indiscriminately, Ali gave orders that it should be taken to Park's hut, there to live with him. Back as a prisoner in the hut, Park was subjected to the same kind of inspection he had had to undergo in Ali's tent; he was obliged to undress and dress again to show his inquisitive visitors how these opera-tions were performed and the use that was made of buttons. He was kept em-ployed in this manner, he said, from noon until nightfall when he was given a little couscous and salt, the only food he tasted that day.

Throughout his enforced stay at Benowm, Park was constantly insulted and derided, accused of being a spy, and robbed of most of his few remaining possessions, apart from his compass which was returned to him as though it were feared that there 'was something of magic in it' and that it might be dangerous to retain possession of so strange an instrument. He was told that he was to be executed, then that he would be set free with the loss of his right hand, finally that it had been decided to put out his eyes which 'resembled those of a cat'.

While waiting for one or other of these punishments, Park was visited by various women of the court who indicated by gestures that they wished to satisfy themselves whether or not Christians were circumcised. Park gamely replied that it was not customary in his country 'to give ocular demonstration of such cases before so many beautiful women, but that if all of them would retire', except one particularly good-looking young woman to whom he pointed, he would satisfy her curiosity. The joke apparently went down well and the young woman afterwards sent him something to eat and some milk. This was a rare indulgence. For most of the time Park was left without food and drink, and Demba was forced to go out to a nearby Negro village to fetch handfuls of groundnuts. Yet all the time Park, in his own words, 'patiently bore every insult' and 'readily complied with every command' in order to 'conciliate favour, and, if possible, to afford the Moors' no further excuse for ill treating him. 'But never,' he added, 'did any period of my life pass away so heavily: from sunrise to sunset was I obliged to suffer, with an unruffled countenance, the insults of the rudest savages on earth.'

At the end of April he was taken north to Bubaker where he was shown to Fatima, a grossly corpulent woman who seems to have taken pity on him, for occasionally she sent him water. When she did not he and Demba had to go out begging in the dreadful heat. 'The heat was now almost insufferable,' he wrote, 'all nature seemed sinking under it. The distant country presented to the eye a dreary expanse of sand, with a few stunted trees and prickly bushes, in the shade of which the hungry cattle licked up the withered grass, while the camels and goats picked off the scanty foliage.' One night, 'having solicited in vain for water at the camp', he stole out to try his fortune at the wells from which, however, he was driven away as soon as he asked permission to drink. Passing from one to the other he eventually found a well where an old man drew him up a bucket of water but as he was about to take hold of it the man, evidently possessed of a sudden fear that the bucket might be polluted by a Christian's lips, dashed the water into a narrow trough into which Park thrust his head between two cows.

Almost a month was spent at Bubaker. Then, on 26 May, Ali returned to Jarra, taking Park with him but insisting that Demba stay behind as a slave. Park for once lost his temper, furiously upbraiding Ali for depriving him of so good and faithful a servant. But Ali merely replied that if he did not mount his horse immediately he would be kept at Bubaker as well. So Park and Demba had to say good-bye, both of them in tears at their parting. They were never to see each other again.

Park was forced to spend most of June at Jarra; but on 1 July, when he overheard some of Ali's men talking about taking him back to their master, he made up his mind to try to escape to Segu. Shortly before dawn he crept out into the darkness, leading a stolen horse. 'I proceeded with great caution,' he recorded, 'surveying each bush, and frequently listening and looking behind me for the Moorish horsemen, until I was about a mile from the town ... [Here some] shepherds followed me for about a mile, hooting and throwing stones after me; and when I was out of their reach, and had begun to indulge the pleasing hopes of escaping, I was again greatly alarmed to hear somebody holloa behind me, and looking back, I saw three Moors on horseback coming after me at full speed, brandishing their double-barrelled guns. I knew it was in vain to think of escaping, and therefore turned back and met them. Two of them caught hold of my bridle, one on each side, and the third, presenting his musket, told me I must go back to Ali.'

They were, however, intent on plundering rather than capturing him; and, having made a disappointing search of his belongings, they took his cloak and rode off. Free at last, Park was overwhelmed by a sudden elation. He felt 'like one recovered from sickness' and found 'unusual lightness' in his limbs. 'Even the desert looked pleasant.' But this exhilaration soon subsided as Park considered how 'very deplorable' his situation was. The horse was at the end of its tether; his gold and money and presents were all gone; his scanty clothes were in rags; he was parched with thirst; the 'burning heat of the sun was reflected with double violence from the hot sand, and the distant ridges seen through the ascending vapour, seemed to wave and fluctuate like the unsettled sea'. Feeling faint with thirst he climbed a tree in the hope of seeing some sign of habitation but there was 'nothing all around but ... the same dismal uniformity ... of thick underwood and hillocks of white sand'. He chewed the leaves of various shrubs to relieve the burning pain in his mouth and throat; but they were bitter to the tongue. At sunset he climbed another tree, only to see once more the barren wilderness stretching away to the distant horizon. Descending, he found his weak and exhausted horse hungrily devouring brushwood and, considering that it might be the last act of humanity in his power to perform, he took off its bridle and set it free to shift for itself. Then, overcome with giddiness, he fell upon the sand, believing that the hour of death was fast approaching.

Slightly revived by the cool of the evening, however, he rose to his feet, replaced his horse's bridle and struggled on, resolving to travel as far as his strength allowed in hopes of reaching a watering-place. After about an hour he was encouraged by a flash of lightning, then by a strong wind roaring through the bushes. He opened his mouth to receive the refreshing rain but was instantly covered with a cloud of sand, driven with such force by the wind that he was obliged to mount his horse and take shelter behind some brushwood to prevent himself being suffocated. For almost an hour the sand whirled around him. Then at last came the rain. He spread his clothes upon the ground and quenched his thirst by wringing and sucking them. Refreshed, he moved on, and towards daybreak he was drawn by the sound of croaking to some shallow muddy pools so full of frogs that he had to beat the water with a branch before his horse, frightened by the noise they made, could be induced to drink. Having drunk plentifully himself, he climbed a tree again and this time caught sight of a plume of smoke about twelve or fourteen miles away.

Arriving at the Fulani village from which this smoke arose, Park made his way to the headman's hut where he was denied admittance and refused even a handful of corn. As he rode slowly out of the town, however, an old motherly-looking woman spinning cotton by one of the low, scattered huts beyond the walls looked with compassion upon his dejected and bedraggled appearance and asked him in Arabic to come inside. She placed before him a dish of couscous that had apparently been left over from a meal she had prepared the previous evening and, rewarded with one of Park's handkerchiefs, readily supplied corn for his horse. It was the first of several acts of kindness which were to save his life.

The next day, having crossed a hilly terrain where wild hogs, antelope and ostriches abounded, he was welcomed by a Fulani shepherd into a low tent pitched beside a watering-place. Crawling in on his hands and knees, he found a woman and three children huddled in the cramped space. Nervously they watched him eat the boiled corn and dates which were set before him, and when the shepherd explained to them that their visitor was a Christian the children burst into tears, then ran outside after their mother who had sprung from the tent like a terrified greyhound. Nor could they be persuaded to re-enter until, having bought some more corn for his horse with a few of his last brass buttons, Park moved off in the direction of Segu.

He reached Oussebou on 7 July 1796 and remained there four days while waiting for a guide to lead him on to Satile which he learned was 'distant a very long day's journey, through woods without any beaten path'. He occupied the time by helping the headman's family to plant corn in the fields, working alongside slaves who, so he calculated, made up about three-quarters of the population. These slaves seemed contented enough, but others he encountered when he had found guides to take him to Satile were far less fortunate. There were about seventy of them in the coffle, bound together in groups of seven with thongs around their necks, making their long way through Bambarra and Ludamar, across the desert to Morocco.

A week after leaving Oussebou, Park reached Doolinkeabo beyond which he fell in with 'two negroes who were going from thence to Sego'.

I was happy to have their company and we set out immediately [Park recorded]. About four o'clock we stopped at a small village, where one of the negroes met with an acquaintance, who invited us to a sort of public entertainment, which was conducted with more than common propriety. A dish, made of sour milk and meal, called sinkatoo, and beer made from their corn, was distributed with great liberality, and the women were admitted into the society – a circumstance I had never before observed in Africa. There was no compulsion – everyone was at liberty to drink as he pleased – they nodded to each other when about to drink, and on setting down the calabash commonly said *Berka*. ('Thank you.') Both men and women appeared to be somewhat intoxicated, but they were far from being quarrelsome.

Park was approaching the Niger now and, excited by the prospect of reaching the great river which the natives called Joliba (the Great Water), he bore without complaint the laughter and derision of the people who, pointing to his bedraggled appearance and mistaking him for a Moor, told each other that he had obviously just been to Mecca: you could tell that by his clothes.

'We passed four large villages,' Park recalled, 'and at eight o'clock saw the smoke over Sego ... And looking forwards, I saw with infinite pleasure the object of my mission – the long-sought-for majestic Niger, glittering in the morning sun, as broad as the Thames at Westminster, and flowing slowly to the eastward. I hastened to the brink, and having drunk the water, lifted up my fervent thanks in prayer to the Great Ruler of all things, for having thus far crowned my endeavours with success.'

The river was full of long canoes made out of hollowed-out tree trunks passing continually from bank to bank between the four separate towns of which Segu consisted. Each of these towns was surrounded by a high mud wall behind which the clay, whitewashed houses were clustered in narrow streets and overshadowed by Moorish mosques which were to be seen in every quarter. Park estimated that the population was about 30,000, and the size and appearance of the place 'formed a prospect of civilization and magnificence' which he had little expected to find in the heart of Africa.

His hopes of crossing the river and getting into the town on the south bank were, however, disappointed; for the Negro ruler, Mansong, who, Park believed, would have liked to welcome him, doubted that he could protect him from the Moors who, as slave traders in Segu, were determined to crush any European competition. So Park was required to wait in a village on the northern bank where a woman, whose fellow-villagers were too frightened to help him, invited him into her hut and gave him a broiled fish for his supper. The woman's daughters, spinning cotton, at first gazed upon him 'in fixed astonishment', then as he lay down to sleep on the mat their mother provided for him, one of them sang him a song, with 'a sweet and plaintive air', the words of which she composed for his benefit, her sisters joining in the chorus:

> The winds roared, and the rains fell,
> The poor white man, faint and weary,
> Came and sat under our tree.
> He has no mother to bring him milk
> No wife to grind his corn.
>
> *Chorus:*
> Let us pity the white man
> No mother has he to bring him milk
> No wife to grind his corn.

Park felt deeply moved and could not sleep. In the morning he gave the girls' mother two of the four brass buttons that remained on his waistcoat, the only recompense he could make her.

After waiting in the village for three days, Park was told that he must move on but that if he wished to go to Jenné he might do so. He would be provided with a guide as far as Sansanding and given a present of 5,000 cowries to enable him to buy food and shelter on his journey. Angry with the Moors, whose 'blind and inveterate malice' prevented him from entering Segu, but thankful for Mansong's help, Park accepted the offer and departed for Sansanding, a town of some eight to ten thousand inhabitants 'much resorted to by the Moors, who bring salt from Beeroo, and beads and coral from the Mediterranean, to exchange here for gold-dust and cotton cloth'. These Moorish traders were as antagonistic towards him as Mansong had feared they would be in Segu. 'They assembled in great number, with their usual arrogance, compelling the negroes to stand at a distance', and immediately began to question him concerning his religion. They made him ascend a high seat by the door of the mosque so that everyone might see him; they demanded that he eat raw eggs in their presence, convinced that Europeans subsisted 'almost entirely on this diet'; and they would no doubt have subjected him to further indignities and perhaps physical assault had not the headman of the town told them that the white man was 'the king's stranger' and under royal protection.

Park rose the next morning before the Moors were about and, obliging the headman's request for a *saphie* – which, as a white man's, must necessarily be better than a Moor's – by writing out the Lord's Prayer on a thin board, he set out for Jenné by way of Silla. Silla, though, was as far as he reached. His horse was so weary that he had to leave it behind. He was exhausted himself after a succession of sleepless nights during which he had to walk about, beating off the mosquitoes that rose in dense swarms from the creeks and swamps. Suffering also from fever, he was forced to conclude that he would certainly die if he tried to struggle on to Jenné and thence to Timbuktu. So, on 30 July 1796, he turned back.

It was a terrible journey. The rain poured down in torrents. Suspected of being a spy sent by some Christian power to make plans of the country with a view to conquering it, he was turned away from several villages and pursued by the hollow roar of lions; food was scarce as the harvest was not yet in and for three days he 'subsisted entirely upon raw corn'; his way was blocked by streams in flood across which he was obliged to swim; he was attacked by robbers who cut off the final metal button from his waistcoat then stripped him naked, minutely inspected his boots, the sole of one of which was tied to the instep with a broken bridle-rein, then returned to him his shirt, his trousers, and his hat with his notes still stuffed into its crown, before making off with everything else, including his compass.

Worn out by fever he arrived on 16 September at Kamalia whose inhabitants did not at first believe that this tattered figure with yellow skin and long beard could possibly be European. He was befriended there by one Karfa Taura, a slave-dealer who was collecting a coffle to take up to sell to the Europeans on the Gambia when the dry season came and who offered to take Park with him. The offer was accepted and Park promised to reward Karfa with the value of one slave when he was in a position to do so. 'Thus was I delivered, by the friendly care of this benevolent negro, from a situation truly deplorable,' Park wrote. 'In the hut which was appropriated for me, I was provided with a mat to sleep on, an earthern jar for holding water, and a small calabash to drink out of – and Karfa sent me, from his own dwelling, two meals a day, and ordered his slaves to supply me with firewood and water.'

Despite these attentions Park's fever grew worse; but as the rains became less frequent he began slowly to recover. He was able to carry his mat out to the shade of a tamarind tree 'to enjoy the refreshing smell of the corn fields and to delight [his] eyes with a prospect of the country'. At length he found himself 'in a state of convalescence, towards which the benevolent and simple manners of the negroes ... greatly contributed'.

While gathering his strength and waiting for Karfa to assemble his coffle of slaves, Park made a study of Kamalia and of the people who lived in the two quarters, Muslim and pagan, into which it was divided. He watched them at work on the land and collected specimens of their crops to dry and press; he watched them fishing, hunting elephant, panning for gold dust, spinning, weaving, dyeing cloth and working in leather and iron. He admired their skill as surgeons, which he judged far superior to their skill as physicians, and considered it fortunate that their diseases were few in number since the medicines prescribed were hardly ever efficacious. He noted that the practice of circumcision was common to both Muslims and pagans and to both sexes, it being believed by all that the operation rendered 'the marriage state prolific'. He described a wedding at which the bride was conducted into a hut when night had fallen, arrayed in a white cotton dress, and surrounded by old women who told her how to behave as a wife while young girls interrupted these lessons with songs and dances 'more remarkable for their gaiety than delicacy'. At about midnight the bride was taken to another hut where she was joined by her husband who had been eating and celebrating with his family and friends. In the morning the couple were disturbed by women who came to inspect the nuptial sheet and to dance around it.

Park had hoped to get away from Kamalia soon after Karfa's return to the town on 24 January 1797 with thirteen slaves and a young bride, his fourth wife. But it was not until 19 April after Ramadan, a fast which Park himself tactfully observed for three days, that the coffle at last set off, the slaves, over thirty in number, roped together at the neck during the march and fettered in irons at night. Living for the most part on bamboo seeds and a paste made from the pods of the locust bean tree, they covered the five-hundred-odd miles to Pisenia in just over eight weeks.

At Pisania, Park, reunited with Dr Laidley who welcomed him 'as one risen from the dead', was able to settle his debts both to him and to Karfa with a bill drawn on the African Association. And on 17 June he went aboard an American ship, the *Charlestown*, which by a happy chance had just arrived in the Gambia with a cargo of rum and tobacco. It was a rotten ship, incapable of making the Atlantic crossing; and, with twenty of its cargo of a hundred and thirty slaves dead and the rest close to death, it was forced to make for Antigua in the West Indies where the survivors were sold. Ten days after his arrival, Park obtained a passage for England aboard the *Chesterfield Packet* and arrived at Falmouth on 22 December 1797.

Park went from Falmouth by coach to London, arriving early on Christmas morning, too early to go to the Dicksons' house in Bloomsbury and so going instead to the British Museum to pass the time by walking in the gardens where, to their mutual astonishment and pleasure, he met James Dickson who had been called there upon some matter of 'trifling business'.

In London the adventures and achievements of this hitherto unknown young man, who had been deep into the interior of Africa and had seen that almost legendary river the Niger, were widely reported and discussed. Articles appeared in the newspapers; Bryan Edwards, Beaufoy's successor as Secretary of the African Association, published a short work, *Abstract from the Travels into the Interior of Africa* based on Park's notes and on interviews with him; Major James Rennell, an acknowledged authority on African geography and compiler of the *Construction of the Map of Africa* which had been included in the African Association's 1790 report, produced his *Geographical Illustrations of Mr Park's Journey*. Park himself, however, was a disappointment. As uncommunicative as Bruce, he had none of the 'Abyssinian Emperor's' commanding presence. With strangers in society his shyness and reticence made him appear unfriendly and aloof. At Holland House the formidable châtelaine found him extremely uninteresting. 'A person who was sent about two years ago to explore the interior parts of Africa is just returned,' she recorded in her journal. 'He is a Scotchman of the name of Mr Park, very much protected by Sir Joseph Banks, and esteemed a man of veracity. He has neither fancy or genius, and if he does fib it is dully.'

His sponsors also now found Park rather difficult. In June he went back to Scotland after an absence of three years to work on a more extended version of his *Travels* for which Edwards's brief account had helped to create an eager market. While there he proposed to Alison, the eldest daughter of Dr Anderson to whom he had been apprenticed as a boy, and the sister of his closest friend, Alexander. And it was her acceptance of this proposal which, in Banks's opinion, was largely responsible for Park's decision to withdraw from a mission he had at first enthusiastically agreed to undertake. This was a journey of discovery in Australia. Park himself professed that his enthusiasm for the journey had been dampened not by his engagement but by the financial inducements offered him which indicated that the proposers of the voyage considered it in a 'very different light' from that in which his own fancy had painted it. At the conclusion of his correspondence with Park, which grew more and more irritable, Banks felt obliged to apologize for 'having put confidence in this fickle Scotsman'; and Edwards, in a letter to Banks, agreed that Park's conduct had, indeed, been 'fickle and perverse'. Yet the African Association were anxious not to lose the services of a man who had, unlike his predecessors, come home alive from a perilous journey which had enabled them to trace with some confidence the course of the Niger as far east as Timbuktu and to relate it more or less accurately to the Gambia and the Senegal. They continued to finance him while he wrote his book, which was published in April 1799 and was an immediate success; and at their General Meeting in May the Treasurer praised Park's 'strength, courage, patience and judgement which had opened a gate into the Interior of Africa, into which it is easy for every Nation to enter and to extend its commerce and Discovery'. How best to use the man's talents in the service of their own nation was a problem to which the Government as well as the African Association directed much thought.

While they deliberated Park married his 'lovely Allie' in August 1799; and the next year, having passed the examination of the Royal College of Surgeons, he set up in practice at Peebles. His heart, though, was not in his profession. 'A country surgeon is at best a laborious employment,' he told Banks to whom he was by then reconciled; 'and I will gladly hang up the lancet and plaister ladle whenever I can obtain a more eligible situation.' His *Travels* had brought him some fame as well as money; but as the months passed he felt himself sinking back into that obscurity from which, ambitious for renown as ever, he was determined to emerge. Besides, his work in Africa was not finished, nor could it be until he had reached the mouth of the Niger. He thought of that challenge constantly, and thought, too, of Africa itself, that vast continent to which, for all his terrible experiences there, he felt irresistibly drawn.

The months passed into years; his wife bore him children; and, although he loved his family, his dissatisfaction with his life as an ill-paid and overworked country doctor became more pronounced, his silences more prolonged. And then in September 1803 he was summoned to London by the Secretary of State for War and the Colonies who wished him, as Park put it, 'to take another trip into the Centre of Africa, with a view to discover the termination of the Niger'. He told Banks that it would be a crime 'to engage in an expedition of such magnitude without first acquainting Mrs Park'; but there could be no doubt that he had made up his mind to go.

The original proposals, however, were changed, then changed again as the war with France followed its erratic course and the Government tottered and fell. And it was not until January 1805, when Park had learned Arabic in preparation for his journey, that he at last received his formal instructions from the new Secretary of State, Lord Camden:

74

Sir,

It being judged expedient that a small expedition should be sent into the interior of Africa, with a view to discover and ascertain whether any, and what commercial intercourse can be opened there for the mutual benefit of the natives and of His Majesty's subjects, I am commanded by the King to acquaint you, that on account of the knowledge you have acquired of the nations of Africa, and from the indefatigable exertions and perseverance you displayed in your travels among them, His Majesty has selected you for conducting this undertaking ...

The great object of your journey will be to pursue the course of this river to the utmost possible distance to which it can be traced; to establish communication and intercourse with the different nations on the banks; to obtain all the local knowledge in your power respecting them ...

He was to be paid £3,000 on his producing a chart of the river and £1,000 was to be paid to his wife for her use during his absence. He was, in addition, authorized to draw up to £5,000 for expenses. He was to be accompanied by his friend and brother-in-law, Alexander Anderson, who was to receive £1,000 if the mission succeeded and he survived, the money to be paid to his father if he did not. He was also to have the services of another young man from Selkirk, George Scott, who had been apprenticed to an engraver in London and was to act as the expedition's draughtsman.

By the time all the arrangements had been made weeks had passed. It was not until the last day of January 1805 that Park's party set sail; and, because of contrary winds and storms at sea, not until the end of March that they came within sight of the West African coast. And when at last they left Pisania on 4 May there were only a few weeks in which to reach the Niger before the rains came. There were those who considered it folly to proceed on so hazardous a journey at such a time and in the hottest season of the year. But Park was determined not to miss his opportunity now he had come so far; and he set off with the feeling, expressed to Lord Camden, that if he succeeded in his mission he would reckon himself 'the happiest man on Earth'. In addition to himself, Alexander Anderson, and the draughtsman, George Scott, there were now in the party Isaaco, an African trader, who agreed to act as guide as far as the Niger and was accompanied by some members of his family and various attendants, two British sailors who had been at Goree aboard the *Squirrel* and had been induced to join the expedition by the offer of double pay and future freedom from the press-gang, four carpenters who had been specially released from prison hulks at Portsmouth and would be required to build the boats in which the party intended sailing down the Niger, and thirty-five non-commissioned officers and men from the Royal African Corps garrison at Goree who, like the sailors, had been offered double pay to volunteer as well as a free discharge if they carried out their duties satisfactorily. These British soldiers, most of whom had chosen to serve in the Royal African Corps as an alternative to a severe flogging in their own regiments, were commanded by Lieutenant John Martyn, an energetic, tough, hard-drinking and rather heartless young Irishman.

There were severe difficulties and troubles from the beginning. Stubborn asses became intractable, shed their loads, could not be pulled from the cloying mud of rice-fields, and died after being stung by swarms of bees. The temperature rose to 135°F. by day and the airless nights seemed quite as suffocating. The soldiers, armed with loaded muskets, panted and grew faint in their thick clothes and the flannel vests which had been issued to them in the general belief that such was suitable wear for tropical climates. Local chiefs were importunate in their demands for presents, and one of them captured Isaaco, the guide, held him hostage and flogged him when exorbitant demands for customs were not met. Diversions had to be made to avoid suspected ambushes by bandits.

At the end of the first week in June the rains began, and at the same time the soldiers, one of whom had already died after an epileptic fit, fell ill with food poisoning or fevers. It was, as Park recorded in his journal, 'the *beginning of sorrow*. I had proudly flattered myself that we should reach the Niger with a very moderate loss ... But now the rain had set in, and I trembled to think that we were only half way through our journey. The rain had not commenced three minutes before many of the soldiers were affected with vomiting; others fell asleep, and seemed as if half intoxicated.' By 19 August over thirty men had perished. Park and Martyn, both of whom contracted fever themselves, encouraged the survivors to continue, Park holding those who could not walk in the saddles of their mounts as they sloshed through the mud and the sodden undergrowth. Villagers followed the bedraggled caravan, watching for opportunities to plunder men too weak to resist them, rushing forward to snatch clothes and baggage, muskets and asses. Lions came charging by day through the camp after asses, and wild dogs attacked them by night. While wading across a swollen stream, driving before him the few asses that had survived, Isaaco was bitten in the leg by a crocodile that would have killed him had he not opened the creature's jaws by driving his finger into its eyes.

This was on 4 July. By the 30th the last ass had either died or been stolen; on 15 August Scott died at Koomikoomi; four days later, after a journey of fourteen appalling weeks, when Park at last saw the Niger once more near

Bamako, there were only twelve Europeans left out of the forty-five who had started. From Bamako they travelled upstream to Samee near Segu, another soldier dying on the way, and waited for permission to proceed from the local ruler, Mansong, who had been so generous with his cowrie shells on Park's previous journey. Again, Mansong, interested by Park's promise that Europeans could supply his people with goods more cheaply than the Moors, undertook to grant them his protection and to find them canoes in which to sail downstream to the mouth of the great river. When the first canoe arrived, however, it was half rotten; and another which came later was in a similar condition. But Park, helped by one of the soldiers, four more of whose companions had died within the last few days, worked hard to make these two defective boats into a sound one. And by sawing and planing, binding with ropes and caulking holes, a serviceable craft had been constructed by the end of the second week in November. It was flat-bottomed and not, therefore, easily manoeuvrable; but Park comforted himself with the thought that shallow waters and rocks concealed below the surface would be less of a hazard than they would have been to a boat with a keel. There were white sails, a cabin at the stern and a screen of bullock hides as a protection against the spears and arrows of the Tuaregs, the light-skinned, probably hostile people through whose country they were to pass. Park named the boat, with touching pride, 'H.M. Schooner Joliba'.

There were now, besides himself, only four men left to sail in her, Lieutenant Martyn and three of his soldiers, all the other soldiers as well as Alexander Anderson now being dead. There were also two slaves and a guide named Amadi Fatouma, a native of Khasso, who agreed to conduct them on the first stage of their journey.

We departed from Sansanding in a canoe the 27th day of the moon, and went in two days to Sellee [Silla] where Mr Park ended his first voyage [Amadi afterwards recounted]. Mr Park bought a slave to help him in the navigation of the canoe ... We went in two days to Sinne [Jenné].

From Jenné they sped on past Lake Debo to Kabara, the river port of Timbuktu, apparently on the way firing upon a boat whose occupants, armed with bows and arrows, Park took, perhaps mistakenly, to be hostile. At Kabara the 'Joliba' seems to have moored for some time amidst the marshes; but Park evidently did not enter the town. It is impossible to write with certainty of these events for Amadi is not a reliable witness, and others who saw Park and his companions in the later stage of their journey gave conflicting reports, some of them long afterwards and not always willingly. But there can be no doubt that Park, occasionally fighting off approaching Tuaregs and once a troublesome hippopotamus, was paddled downstream from Kabara, past Bamba, Gao and Ansongho, over the Labezenga rapids and out of the Tuaregs' country into that of the Hausa where the river, in places a mile wide in its flood, flowed more quietly between green and silent banks. The strange boat was often sighted, its tall commander standing on the rough planks which served as a deck, wearing, so a German explorer was told many years later, 'his long coat, his straw hat and large gloves'. 'He was a very tall and powerful man,' another explorer learned, 'with long arms and large hands, on which he wore leather gloves reaching above the elbows. Wore a white straw hat, long coat, full white trousers, and red leather boots. Had black hair and eyes, with a bushy beard and mustachies of the same colour.'

From time to time Amadi was sent ashore to buy provisions. But at Yauri, after provisions had been purchased and presents given to the local chief, Amadi said, 'I agreed to carry you into the kingdom of Hausa; we are now in Hausa. I have fulfilled my engagements with you. I am therefore going to leave you here.'

The chief offered Park another guide to take them overland to their destination since, so he said, the river people were unfriendly and might not let them pass. Besides, there were 'many rocks in the belly of the river, all pointed'. Park, however, declined the offer. Either disbelieving the reports or supposing himself so near the river's mouth that, having risked so much, he might as well risk all, he went on his way towards Bussa. Here, many years later, Richard Lander, who was to complete the exploration which Park had so bravely begun, was able to gather information which allowed him to offer a credible account of Park's and Martyn's end:

Their strange-looking canoe was observed by one or two of the inhabitants, whose shouts brought numbers of their companions, armed with bows and arrows, to the spot. At that time the usurpations of the [Fulani] had begun to be the general talk of the black population of the country, so that the people of Bussa, who had only heard of that warlike nation, fancied Mr Park and his associations to be some of them, coming with the intention of taking their town, and subjugating its inhabitants. Under this impression, they saluted the unfortunate Englishmen from the beach with showers of missiles and poisoned arrows, which were returned by the latter with a discharge of musketry. A small white flag had been previously waved by our countrymen, in token of their peaceable intentions; but this symbol not being understood by the people of Bussa, they continued firing arrows. In the meantime the Englishmen, with the blacks they had with them, kept firing unceasingly amongst the multitude on shore, killing many, and wounding a still greater number, till their ammunition being expended, and seeing every hope of life cut off, they threw their goods overboard and desiring their assistants to swim towards the beach, locked themselves in each other's arms, and springing into the water, instantly sank, and were never seen again.

3

SOUTH TO LAKE CHAD

OUDNEY, CLAPPERTON AND DENHAM · THEIR CHARACTERS
AND QUARRELS · ARRIVAL AT MURZUK, 1822 · SOUTH
ACROSS THE DESERT TO BILMA · THEY REACH LAKE CHAD ·
WELCOME AT KOUKA BY THE CHIEF · DENHAM
ACCOMPANIES A SLAVING EXPEDITION INTO MANDARA ·
RAID UPON A FULANI TOWN · THE RAIDERS DEFEATED ·
'DISGRACEFUL PROCEEDINGS' · RETURN TO KOUKA AND
EXPEDITION TO BORNU AND GAMBARON · THE SHORES
OF LAKE CHAD· DENHAM GOES SOUTH TO THE SHARY AND
THEN EXPLORES THE EASTERN SIDE OF LAKE CHAD · HE
CROSSES THE DESERT ONCE MORE TO MURZUK AND SOCKNA ·
HE RETURNS TO ENGLAND IN 1825

When Mungo Park's *Journal of a Mission to the Interior of Africa* was published the long war with Napoleon was over and it was possible to plan new explorations to continue the work Park had begun. In 1815, the year of victory, two important expeditions were planned. One, an army expedition, was to be sent to the Niger by the overland route from Gambia; the other, led by naval officers, was to sail up the Congo. Both set out but neither succeeded. The military expedition was prevented from reaching the Niger by the jealousy and hostility of the local chiefs. The leaders of the naval expedition all died of fevers, having failed to get their boats across the rapids of the lower Congo.

In 1817 it was decided to make an attempt to reach Central Africa by a different route. Some twenty years before, under the auspices of the African Association, a German clergyman's son, Frederick Hornemann, who had been recommended by one of Sir Joseph Banks's correspondents, Professor Blumenbach of Göttingen University, had travelled in the guise of a Muslim from Cairo to Murzuk in Fezzan where he fell seriously ill with fever and his servant, Joseph Frendenburgh, died, 'led astray', so Hornemann said, 'by wine and women'. Brave, adventurous, industrious and unassuming, with an easy command of Arabic and a deep knowledge of Islamic law, Hornemann had

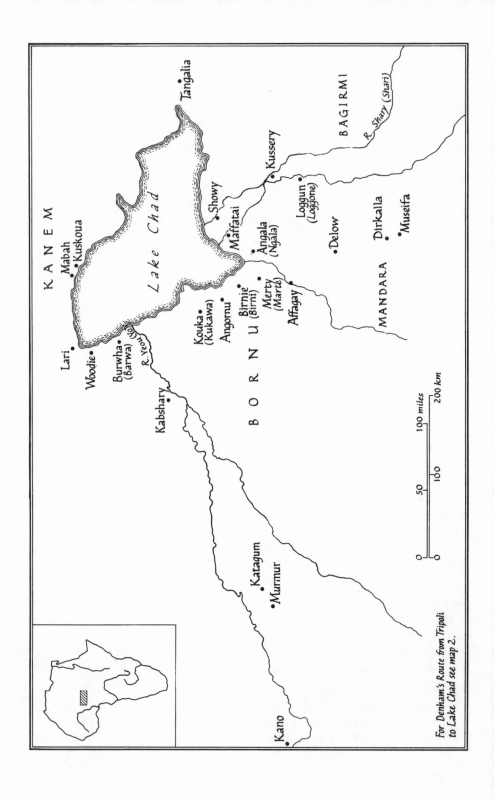

KANEM

Tangalia

BAGIRMI

R. Shary (Shari)

Lake Chad

Showy

Kussery

Maffatai

Loggun
(Loggone)

Mabah
Kuskoua

Angala
(Ngala)

Dirkalla

Museifa

Delow

Lari

Woodie

Burwha
(Barwa)

Kouka
(Kukawa)

Birnie
(Birni)

Merty
(Marte)

MANDARA

Angornu

Affagay

R. Yeou (Yo)

B O R N U

Kabshary

Katagum

Murmur

Kano

0   50   100 miles

0   100   200 km

For Denham's Route from Tripoli
to Lake Chad see map 2.

been able, after his recovery, to cross the desert to Bornu. From Bornu he had passed on to Katsina, but he had died of dysentery before being able to report upon the later stages of his explorations.

Now, with the agreement of the Pasha of Tripoli, suzerain of Fezzan, Joseph Ritchie and George Francis Lyon were to be sent by Hornemann's route into Fezzan. But Ritchie, ill-supplied with funds and burdened with unsaleable merchandise, died at Murzuk; while Lyon, after visiting Tejerri, went back to Tripoli where, in March 1820, he arrived 'more dead than alive', though still capable of singing 'God save the King' and 'Rule Britannia' as he entered the town.

In October 1821 two other British explorers, Walter Oudney and Hugh Clapperton, arrived in Tripoli, intent upon reaching the Niger by the same route through Fezzan. A third, Major Dixon Denham, was soon to follow them.

Oudney, aged thirty-one, came from a humble family in Edinburgh where he had acquired enough knowledge of medicine to obtain a post as surgeon's mate aboard a man-of-war. When peace came he had returned to Edinburgh and, having graduated at the university, had set himself up in a private practice in the town. He was a slight, small, rather pedantic man 'with a pale, grave face, pleasing manners, and possessed of much enterprise and perseverance'. Clapperton, also a Scotsman, was two years older and had come from a scarcely less poor family. His father, a surgeon, had twenty-one children and Hugh, the youngest son of his first wife, was given little education. At the age of thirteen he was taken on as a cabin-boy in a ship trading between Liverpool and America and was remembered on board as a spirited boy who refused to demean himself by blacking the captain's shoes. He later became a cook's mate, and after service in a frigate, then in a privateer, was made a midshipman. Following brave service in the West Indies, he had been promoted lieutenant and given command of a schooner. He had afterwards served in Canada, and in 1817 had returned to Scotland on half pay. In Edinburgh he met Oudney who fired his interest in African exploration, and when Oudney was appointed British consul at Bornu, Clapperton agreed to accompany him on his journey to Central Africa. He was a tall, strong, good-looking man, with a ready laugh, commanding and self-assured. Although the servant in whose arms he was to die thought of him as a dear, kind master, there were others who found him arrogant, vulgar and excitable. Among these was Dixon Denham.

Denham was a major in the 3rd Buffs. Educated at Merchant Taylors' School, he had been articled to a solicitor before joining the Army as a volunteer to fight in the Peninsular War. Recognized as an extremely brave and talented officer, although opinionated and excessively managing, he had been accepted into the senior department of the Royal Military College in 1817;

and after the death of Joseph Ritchie he had offered to continue Ritchie's work. Oudney and Clapperton had already been sent out to Tripoli, but since Denham demanded no payment for his services, merely promotion in his profession, his offer was accepted by Lord Bathurst, Secretary for War and the Colonies, and he, too, left for Tripoli to join the expedition.

No sooner had he arrived there than he took charge of the mission and began to issue peremptory orders in so high-handed a manner that both Clapperton and Oudney found him intolerable. He, in turn, regarded them as the 'most tiresome companions imaginable'. Clapperton, he told his brother, was 'vulgar, conceited and quarrelsome'. Oudney, he complained to Lord Bathurst, was utterly unqualified for his duties, incapable of speaking a word of any language other than his own, incompetent as a horseman, and so inexperienced as a traveller that never before, except by water, had he been more than thirty miles from Edinburgh.

Denham was relieved beyond measure when his two unwanted colleagues departed for Murzuk. He set out himself on 5 March 1822 accompanied by William Hillman, a shipwright and expert carpenter, who had agreed to accompany the mission for a salary of £120 a year. They passed through Sockna, the first English travellers, Denham believed, to do so in European clothes; then, travelling for two or three days at a stretch without finding a supply of water, and undergoing the torture of sand storms which left them with a parching thirst and obliterated their camels and the sun from sight, they arrived at Murzuk on 7 April. The Sultan, however, refused them an escort to take them on to Bornu, so Denham decided to return to London in the hope of arranging his promotion to lieutenant-colonel. At Marseilles, however, a letter reached him promising the escort previously denied; and so he went back to Tripoli where he employed three freed slaves as servants, a Gibraltarian Jew as a kind of store-keeper, four men to look after the camels and a native of the island of St Vincent who had travelled widely in a merchant vessel and spoke three European languages as well as fluent Arabic. Denham also encountered several Arab merchants who 'gladly embraced' the protection of his escort 'to proceed to the interior with their merchandise'. Prominent among these was one Boo-Khaloom, 'a merchant of very considerable riches and influence in the interior'.

At Murzuk, which they entered again on 30 October, Denham found that Oudney and Hillman had both been delirious with fever and were not yet fully recovered, while Clapperton was still in bed, having been lying there in a sorry state for fifteen days. They greeted Denham without enthusiasm and soon the old quarrels were resumed. So, ill as they were, Clapperton and Oudney were thankful to escape from Murzuk on 19 November and to set out for Gatrone. Ten days later Denham and Boo-Khaloom followed them.

The first part of their journey was across a burning desert with no living thing to be seen, no birds nor even those insects which had been the plague of their existence in the valley of Murzuk. But the nights were cool and refreshing, lit by brilliant stars beneath which they went to sleep in hollows scooped out of the soft sand as a gentle breeze brushed their faces. When Denham and Boo-Khaloom arrived at Gatrone they found Clapperton, Oudney and Hillman were all still ill but anxious to proceed on their journey in the belief that 'a change of scene would bring them round'. So they all went on grumpily together through El-Bahhi to Tejerri, the native women following the caravan with songs for several miles. At Tejerri they halted for two days to buy more dates and provisions and to allow a rest both for Oudney, whose cough was now so bad that a walk of even a few hundred yards exhausted him, and for Hillman, now so weak he had to be lifted on and off his mule. Denham was also feeling unwell. He had had a horrible meal of couscous and rancid oil cooked by a Negro woman, all his own servants being ill, and he was woken from an uneasy sleep on his first night at Tejerri by Boo-Khaloom who asked him to share a meal of camel's heart, a most unwelcome invitation which he thought it politic not to refuse.

After their brief rest, they continued their journey on 13 December over a plain without the least appearance of vegetation and strewn with coarse opal, petrified wood, sandstone and the skeletons of slaves who had perished on their way to Fezzan where they were to have been fattened up for the Tripoli market. Around the well outside Meshroo there were over a hundred of these skeletons, some of them with the skin still attached to the bones; and when Denham expressed his horror his Arab companions laughed at his squeamishness. They were only blacks, they said, as they knocked the bones about with the butt-ends of their firelocks, pointing out which were women and which young men and cursing them all: 'Damn their fathers!'

Day after day the caravan came upon these scattered skeletons, 'mangled in a shocking manner', in Dr Oudney's words: 'here a leg, there an arm, fixed with their ligaments at considerable distances from the trunk. What could have done this? Man forced by hunger, or the camels? The latter are very fond of chewing dried bones, but whether they ever do so to those with dried flesh on them I cannot say.' At El Hammar the number of skeletons was countless.

Those of two women, whose perfect and regular teeth bespoke them young, were particularly shocking [Denham recorded]. Their arms still remained clasped round each other as they had expired, although the flesh had long since perished by being exposed to the burning rays of the sun, and the blackened bones only left: the nails of the fingers, and some of the sinews of the hand, also remained; and part of the tongue of one of them still appeared in the teeth. While I was dozing on my horse about noon, overcome by the heat of the sun, which at that time of the day always shone with great power, I was suddenly awakened by a crashing under his feet, which startled me excessively. I found that my steed had, without any sensation of shame or alarm, stepped upon the perfect skeletons of two human beings, cracking their brittle bones under his feet, and, by one trip of his foot, separating a skull from the trunk which rolled on like a ball before him.

The horses and camels were now as weary as the men whom Denham described on 26 December as nearly falling from their saddles with fatigue. For as long as eight days on end the camels were without water, and often when a well was reached the animals had to wait for hours while cartloads of sand were removed from the surface before the water was uncovered. Then, having eaten dates after slaking their thirst, the camels would stagger about and fall over in a state of evident intoxication, induced, so Oudney thought, by the 'spirituous fermentation in their stomachs'.

On New Year's Day 1823 a camel died from exhaustion and a few days later four others collapsed. On such occasions, so Denham said, the Arabs waited 'in savage impatience, with the knives in their hands, ready on the signal of the owner to plunge them into the animal, and tear off a portion of the flesh for their evening meal ... A knife is struck in the camel's heart while his head is turned to the east, and he dies almost in an instant. But before that instant expires, a dozen knives are thrust into different parts of the carcass, in order to carry off the choicest part of the flesh. The heart, considered as the greatest delicacy, is torn out, the skin stripped from the breast and haunches, part of the meat cut, or rather torn, from the bones, and thrust into bags, which they carry for the purpose; and the remainder of the carcass is left for the crows, vultures and hyenas.'

A hyena was once caught and tied to a tree by the Arabs who amused themselves by shooting at it 'until the poor animal was literally knocked to pieces'. From now on other animals also were occasionally to be seen in the less barren countryside. A herd of oxen was glimpsed on 8 January; and soon afterwards a young gazelle was shot by an Arab who lay down in the grass imitating its cry and then killed the mother, too, as she came bounding towards the spot.

By this time the incompatible leaders of the expedition were scarcely on speaking terms. The aggressively authoritarian Denham told Clapperton to use his sextant at regular intervals so that their latitude could be recorded in the official report. Clapperton declined to do so on the grounds that the observations were his own work and he did not see why anyone else should take the credit for them. When Denham repeated his request, Clapperton replied in writing:

> Sir, I thought my previous refusal would have prevented a repetition of your orders. You take upon yourself a great deal to issue orders which could not be more imperative were they from the Horse Guards or the Admiralty. You must not introduce Martial

System into what is civil and scientific; neither must you expect from me what it is your duty to execute . . .

I have the honour to be Sir

Your most Obt. humble servant, Hugh Clapperton.

While Clapperton complained of Denham's conduct, Denham protested even more forcibly about Clapperton's, accusing him of losing his temper at the least provocation, threatening to knock down an argumentative Arab and to shoot a servant whom he did knock down. Far worse than this, so Denham reported, there were rumours that Clapperton was having homosexual relations with one of the other servants. Oudney, whom Denham instructed to investigate these rumours, could find no evidence to support them and Lord Bathurst eventually decided that they were unfounded. But Denham, while assuring everyone that he had never himself supposed them to be true, did not apologize to Clapperton for having made them public.

As the weeks passed and the journey south continued, the Scotsmen and the Englishman took care to have as little to do with each other as possible.

On 12 August they reached Bilma, the capital of the Tibboo. They were not a prepossessing race, Denham thought. Some of the men were indeed 'really hideous' with long yellow teeth, noses resembling nothing so much as round lumps of flesh stuck on their faces and nostrils so large that when they took snuff, which they did in large quantities, their fingers 'went up as far as they would reach in order to ensure the snuff an admission into the head'. The women of Bilma, though, were far from unattractive. They accompanied the white men into the town, 'dancing and throwing themselves about with screams and songs in a manner quite original. The pearly white of their regular teeth was beautifully contrasted with the glossy black of their skin, and the triangular flaps of plaited hair, which hung down on each side of their faces streaming with oil, with the addition of the coral in the nose and large amber necklaces, gave them a very seducing appearance.' They carried fans made of grass, branches of trees or ostrich feathers to keep away the flies, and wore loose gowns over their shoulders which left their right breasts bare. They danced to the rhythm of an instrument formed out of a calabash covered with a goat's skin, at first slowly, moving their head, hands and body only, then gradually with increased violence until, gnashing their teeth, shaking their hands at each other and leaping about in every direction, they fell exhausted to the ground.

After leaving Bilma the travellers had to 'bid adieu to every appearance of vegetable production' and enter desert again. The camels sank nearly knee-deep into the fine sand which, in these wilds, drifted into unfamiliar shapes overnight and formed hills as high as sixty feet with nearly perpendicular sides. All traces of the passage, even of a large party, might disappear within a few hours and the caravan was obliged to steer its course by the dark sandstone ridges which rose above the dry ocean of sand. 'The greatest care is taken by the drivers in descending these banks,' Denham noticed. 'The Arabs hang with all their weight on the animal's tail, by which means they steady him in his descent. Without this precaution the camel generally falls forward, and, of course, all he carries goes over his head.'

By 27 January, after thirteen days' slow march, the arid desert was crossed, vegetation began to appear once more, stunted trees spread out their branches, gazelle and the footprints of ostrich were seen, and the camels, which had had to exist on the small branches of the *suag* for the past few days, 'now found abundance of food'. Beere-Kashifery was reached on 28 January and here the sheikh, who usually demanded heavy exactions from all caravans passing through his territories, was placated with a scarlet burnous of coarse cloth, a tawdry silk kaftan which he considered 'a superb present', and a looking-glass 'into which he gazed with a satisfaction which burst from his lips in frequent exclamations of joy and which he also occasionally testified by sundry high jumps and springs into the air'. The male Tibboos here were quite as ugly as those of Bilma but 'small active fellows, mounted on small horses, of great swiftness'. They promised the strangers fine sheep, oxen, honey and butter, but actually produced nothing other than camel's milk, full of dirt and sand, and rancid fat. Denham was thankful, therefore, to be able to buy a lean sheep which 'was indeed a treat'. He was also thankful that, as at Bilma, the girls made up for the extreme ugliness of the men. And although the irritation caused by the violent wind and drifting sand 'produced a soreness almost intolerable', he found that 'a little oil or fat from the hands of a negress (all of whom are taught the art of shampooing [massaging] to perfection), rubbed well round the neck, loins and back, is the best cure, in cases of this kind'. He regretted that his Christian beliefs deprived him of the 'luxury of possessing half a dozen of these shampooing beauties', yet, by marrying his Negro servant to one of them, she became 'to a certain degree' his servant also ... and she was of the greatest comfort to him. 'It is an undoubted fact,' he commented, 'and in no case probably better exemplified than in my own, that man naturally longs for attention and support from female hands, of whatever colour or country, as soon as debility or sickness comes upon him.'

Denham and his companions moved off from Beere-Kashifery on 1 February through wild corn up to their horses' knees, killing on the way one of the largest serpents they had ever seen. They found it impossible to prevent the Arabs of the caravan plundering the Tibboos, stealing their sheep and goats, the loads from their camels' back and even the clothes from the women's bodies. On

3 February, as they approached Lari on the shores of Lake Chad, Denham witnessed the distressing sight of 'all the female, and most of the male inhabitants, with their families – who had been plundered by the Tuaregs only the year before and hundreds of their people butchered – flying across the plain in all directions, alarmed at the strength of our *kafila*'. But his shame at being connected with such dreaded marauders was soon replaced by a 'sensation so gratifying and inspiring that it would be difficult for language to convey an idea of its force and pleasure'. These feelings of delight were occasioned by the sight of the great lake, which he believed to be 'the key to the great object of their search', glowing in the golden rays of the sun below him.

In Lari the terrified people were eventually calmed by Boo-Khaloom's assurances that the white men meant them no harm, and the women then shyly came out, 'good-looking, laughing negresses, all but naked', to sell *gussub*, *gafooly*, fowls and honey at absurdly low prices. One merchant bought a fine lamb for two bits of amber worth about tuppence each in Europe; another, a fowl for two needles; a third, four or five good-sized fish from the lake for a handful of salt.

The sweet and pleasant waters of the lake abounded in fish which the women caught by wading in and then, having formed a line facing the shore, charging through the shallows, grabbing them as they tried to swim away or leapt upon the shore. Birds, too, were astonishingly plentiful, spoonbills, widgeon, teal, plovers, pelicans, cranes four or five feet in height, birds resembling both snipe and woodcock but larger than either, flocks of geese and wild ducks. They were not in the least alarmed by Denham's appearance amongst them, merely changing their places a little to the right or left, and it was some time before he could bring himself to use his gun. When he did so, however, he killed more birds than he could carry.

Unlike the birds, the Tibboos were terrified by the white men's guns. They would go round a tree against which one of the guns had been laid, stepping on tiptoe as if afraid of disturbing it, talking to each other in a whisper. When Denham, curious to see inside, went into one of their huts carrying his gun, the owner followed closely and warily at his heels, spear and dagger in hand, as the uninvited guest inspected the bed, a couch of rushes lashed together, covered with the skins of tiger-cats and wild bulls. 'Round the sides,' Denham recorded, 'were hung wooden bowls, used for water and milk; the man's tall shield rested against the wall. The hut had a division of network, one half being allotted to the female part of the family. My host, however, continued to look at me with so much suspicion, and seemed so little pleased with my visit ... that I hurried from the inhospitable door, and resumed my walk through the town.'

The travellers did not stay long in Lari but soon plunged on through high undergrowth and a thick forest of acacias along the banks of the Chad towards Kouka. Here they came upon the footprints of elephants, heaps of their dung three and four feet high, and marks of their passage through the forest in which whole trees had been broken down and young trees and shrubs crushed beneath their weight. They also saw wild red cattle, gazelle, guinea fowl in flocks of a hundred, numerous chattering monkeys, and an enormous snake eighteen feet long which, surviving the impact of five musket balls, was killed by two Arabs with swords and then opened up by the native guides who prized its fat as a sovereign remedy for sick cattle. Later they killed a wild hog, but failed to destroy a lion which fell upon a camel and partly devoured its body, leaving the unwanted portions to be entirely consumed by the hyenas who howled round the camp at nights.

Having passed Burwha, a town with walls thirteen or fourteen feet high and surrounded by a ditch as a protection against Tuareg raiders, they approached Kouka on 17 February, wondering whether they would find its chief 'at the head of thousands, or be received by him under a tree, surrounded by just a few naked slaves', but entirely unprepared for their reception which Denham described:

I had ridden a short distance in front of Boo-Khaloom, with his train of Arabs, all mounted, and dressed out in their best apparel; and, from the thickness of the trees, soon lost sight of them, fancying that the road could not be mistaken. I rode still on-wards, and on approaching a spot less thickly planted, was not a little surprised to see in front of me a body of several thousand cavalry drawn up in a line, and extending right and left quite as far as I could see; and, checking my horse, I awaited the arrival of my party, under the shade of a wide-spreading acacia. The Bornou troops re-mained quite steady, without noise or confusion; and a few horsemen, who were moving about in front giving directions, were the only persons out of the ranks. On the Arabs appearing in sight, a shout, or yell rent the air: a blast was blown from rude instruments of music equally loud, and the horsemen moved on to meet Boo-Khaloom and his Arabs. There was an appearance of tact and management in their movements which astonished me: three separate small bodies, from the centre and each flank, kept charging rapidly towards us, to within a few feet of our horses' heads, without checking the speed of their own until the moment of their halt.

The commanders of this intimidating throng were clothed in coats of iron mail which covered them from the head to the knee; some had skull-caps of the same metal; their horses' heads were also protected by plates of iron, brass and silver. Spearmen under their orders lined the way to the chief's house into which the four white men were invited after Boo-Khaloom had been admitted on his own. One by one they were allowed to mount a staircase at the top of which they were brought to a halt by black guards with crossed spears who placed their open hands upon the strangers' breasts as an indication that they were to proceed no further. They were then shown into a small dark room where the ruler sat on a carpet, plainly dressed in a blue gown and a shawl turban. Two

Negroes were on each side of him armed with pistols. What was the purpose of their visit to his country? he asked them. 'To see the country merely,' his visitors assured him, 'and to give an account of its inhabitants, produce and appearance, as our king is desirous of knowing every part of the globe.'

The ruler assured them that they were welcome; he would show them whatever they desired; and had already ordered huts to be prepared for their accommodation. He accepted with pleasure various presents, including a pair of pistols and a double-barrelled gun, and sent to their huts in exchange vast quantities of provisions, bullocks, barley flour and rice, butter, curds and honey, as well as two camel-loads of bream from the lake.

During their two-months' stay at Kouka, Denham took the opportunity to visit the nearby towns. He went to Birnie where the chief, attended by courtiers 'tottering under the weight and magnitude of their turbans and their bellies', received him sitting behind the cane bars of a little pavilion as though in a cage. He visited Angornu, which he supposed to be the largest town of Bornu with a population of 'at least thirty thousand inhabitants'. He made an expedition to the shores of Lake Chad where he saw herds of elephant and buffalo and thousands of cattle belonging to the ruler, the rewards of a recent raid upon Begharmi. And everywhere he went, his 'excessive whiteness' was a cause of 'both pity and astonishment, if not disgust', as crowds followed him through the markets and women upset their wares in their anxiety to get out of the way. On his return to Kouka, Denham 'became better friends' with the ruler than he had 'ever been before' by presenting him with a Swiss musical-box and by revealing, in his answers to the questions put to him, that he spoke quite good Arabic. When he sought permission to make more extensive explorations than he had so far been able to do the chief was, however, unhelpful. But Denham persisted, arguing that the orders of his own king must be obeyed, and protesting that if he was not allowed to accompany Boo-Khaloom, who was to take his Arabs on a slaving expedition into Mandara to the south, he would have to be forcibly restrained by the irons used upon refractory slaves, for he would 'certainly go'; he 'dare not lose such an opportunity of seeing the country'. The chief thereupon gave way. He did not grant his formal permission but he instructed one of his most trusted soldiers, a man named Maramy, a former slave in the family of a cousin who was on a pilgrimage to Mecca, to follow the white man wherever he might go. So, on 15 April, when Denham set out for Merty, where Boo-Khaloom's men and a force of Bornu cavalry under the command of one Barca Gana had assembled, Maramy went with him. Barca Gana received him 'with a great deal of civility' and invited him to put up his tent near his own; while Boo-Khaloom's Arabs were so pleased to see him again that they all cheered loudly as he shook their leader's hand.

Before dawn next morning the tents were struck; and, to the beat of drums, the shrill notes of a reed pipe and the deep-toned blasts of a buffalo's horn, Barca Gana led the combined party of Arabs and Bornu cavalry off towards Affagay. They were preceded by twelve running footmen who carried long forked poles with which, most dexterously, they kept back the branches of the trees to open up a path through the woods, constantly crying out warnings and singing the praises of their commander: 'Take care of the branches! Mind the holes! Watch the thorns! They are like spears! Worse than spears! Who in battle is like the rolling thunder? Barca Gana! Barca Gana! Now for Mandara! Now for the battle of the spears! Who in battle spreads terror around him like a buffalo in his rage? Barca Gana! Barca Gana! God be praised!'

This litany was kept up until they reached Affagay where Denham joined Barca Gana and five or six of the Bornu chiefs for a meal of roasted sheep. 'The black chiefs stripped off the dark blue shirt, their only covering,' Denham wrote; 'the sharpest dagger in the party was called for, and being given to one who acted as carver, large slices of the flesh were cut, distributed about and quickly devoured without either bread or salt ... Our repast closed with huge draughts from a large bowl of rice water, honey, tamarinds and red pepper.' The meal was a perfectly convivial one, but when the chiefs later learned that the white man was not a Muslim there was a 'general groan'. Boo-Khaloom, who was 'extremely liberal in his religious opinions for a Musselman', attempted to excuse Denham's reprehensible lack of faith by declaring that the English were the best of Christians, they worshipped no images, they believed in one God, they were, in fact, 'almost Moslems'. But 'these bigoted followers of the prophet' and particularly Barca Gana's influential *fighi*, or charm writer, thereafter regarded Denham with suspicion and distaste. And later, when Denham astonished some of the chief's sons by the use of an india-rubber while sketching, and allowed them to make marks on the paper with his pencil and then rub them out, the *fighi* wrote a sentence from the Koran making so deep an impression that the words still appeared legible after the rubber had been used. 'These are the words of God, delivered to our Prophet,' declared the *fighi* exultingly. 'I defy you to erase them.' He displayed the paper with great satisfaction to all around him, while they cast looks at Denham 'expressive of mingled pity and contempt'.

Distressed by the attitude of his Muslim companions, Denham was also 'nearly exhausted by the intolerable heat' which his thermometer registered at 113°F. in the best shade he could find. But at Delow, the first town in Mandara, there were springs of beautiful fresh water, fig trees in the valleys and a lovely, sweet-smelling tree with flowers like those of a syringa. The people of Mandara, too, were well favoured. The men, who seemed intelligent and lively, had 'large sparkling eyes, wiry curled hair, noses inclining to the aquiline, and features altogether less flattened than the Bornouese'. The women, Denham continued, 'are proverbial for their good looks, I cannot say beauty. I must allow them, however, all their acknowledged celebrity of form ... A man who took me to be a Moorish merchant led me to his house, in order to show me the best looking slaves in Mandara':

He had three, all under sixteen, yet quite women; for these are precocious climes; and certainly, for negresses, they were the most pleasing and perfectly formed I had ever seen. They had simply a piece of blue striped linen round their loins, yet they knew not their nakedness. Many of these beauties are to be seen at Kouka and Angornou: they are never, however, exposed in the *fsug* but sold in the houses of the merchants. So much depends on the magnitude of those attractions for which their southern sisters are so celebrated, that I have known a man about to make a purchase, regardless of the charms of feature, turn their faces from him, and looking at them behind, just above the hips, as we dress a line of soldiers, make choice of her whose person most projected beyond that of her companions.

At Delow, Barca Gana's forces, now increased to about 3,000 by the accession of several Shuwa chiefs and their followers, were met by the ruler of Mandara and thirty of his sons, all dressed in striped silk gowns of the brightest colours and mounted on 'really beautiful and powerful' horses. After a brief parley Boo-Khaloom felt confident that the ruler, in exchange for some handsome presents, would permit the plundering of a Kerdy town full of unbelievers. That evening Denham accompanied Boo-Khaloom and Barca Gana to the palace to continue the discussions.

They galloped up to the entrance gates at full speed, a perilous form of salutation never to be omitted, though it usually resulted in some accident. On this occasion a man and a horse standing in the way were ridden over in an instant, the horse's leg being broken and the man killed. Ignoring these casualties, the chief's trumpeters greeted their master's guests with loud blasts on their instruments as they were conducted into the presence of the chief who, his beard dyed sky-blue, sat in a dark-blue tent on a mud bench covered with a carpet and silk pillows. He was surrounded by about two hundred men, counsellors and eunuchs, all with their backs turned towards him. Barca Gana approached him, his eyes fixed on the ground and clapping his hands together as he called out, 'May you live for ever! God send you a happy old age! Blessing! Blessing!' These words were repeated by the chief, and then sung out by all the court. Presents were then produced and carried away unopened by eunuchs.

The chief then asked who the white man was. A native of a very distant and powerful nation who had come to see his country, he was told. 'Is he Muslim?' the chief then asked and, on being informed that he was not, Denham was dismissed and never again invited to the palace.

He was, however, allowed to partake of the meal of *gussub* flour paste with hot fat, pepper and onions, 'the very acme of Mandara cooking', which was borne out to the strangers' encampment by forty slaves and a eunuch. Denham judged this meal 'not very unpleasant'; but the myriads of ants and insects which bit him so persistently that his swollen hands and eyes made it scarcely possible for him to hold a pen or see to use it, and the appalling heat, from the effects of which he could escape only by wrapping himself up in blankets and getting his Negro to pour cold water on his head, rendered his time in the encampment exceedingly tiresome. And he anxiously awaited the chief's decision as to how the marauders should proceed.

So did the Kerdy people whose fires could be seen at night in the granite hills which rose high above the plain. By day, with the help of his telescope, Denham could see these frightened people moving higher up into the mountains, 'while others came down bearing leopard skins, honey and slaves, plundered from a neighbouring town, as peace offerings; also asses and goats with which their mountains abound'. They threw themselves on the ground, pouring sand on their heads, and uttering the most piteous cries. They wore goat and leopard skins to which the heads and the skin of the legs and tails of the animals were still attached, fur caps upon their bristly heads and round their necks strings of human teeth extracted, so Denham supposed, from enemies slain in battle. Teeth and bits of bone were also attached to their hair, 'and with the red patches with which their body was marked in different places, and of which colour also their own teeth were stained, they really had a most strikingly wild and truly savage appearance'. These people, so Denham was assured, were Christians, a notion he took leave to doubt, arguing, when they begged permission to regale themselves with the remains of a horse which had died in the camp in the night, that no Christian would eat such food. 'That is nothing,' his Muslim informant riposted. 'I certainly never heard of Christians eating dead horse-flesh but I know they eat the flesh of swine, and God knows that is worse!'

So long as offerings from the Kerdy people poured into the palace, the chief was naturally reluctant for the would-be plunderers from the north to attack them. He was also reluctant to give permission to Denham to go up into the mountains to see these strange people in their own surroundings. His head eunuch, who kept Denham waiting for an hour sitting on the ground in the palace – walking about was prohibited there – said that the chief could not imagine what the white man wanted in the hills. Did he want to catch the Kerdies? It would be much more convenient to buy some. The chief would sell him as many as he wanted. The eunuch then made some remark which was not interpreted and which raised a loud laugh amongst the bystanders. Nettled by this incomprehensible joke which had obviously been made at his expense, Denham replied that he would certainly not go up into the hills if the chief objected. As for catching Kerdies, he would not take them if they were given to him as a present. That 'put all to rights'; and it was now arranged that six men, armed with huge clubs and short daggers, should accompany him into the hills. But these men proved so suspicious of his every action and watched him so closely as he picked up stones and inspected plants that he did not 'venture to sketch the shape of a single hill'. The only Kerdies he saw before his companions insisted on returning were a few naked figures, mostly women and girls, scrambling up the side of the mountain with monkey-like agility.

Soon afterwards the marauding army struck camp and moved south towards Dirkalla in the country of the Fulani against whom the chief had decided that the expedition should be directed. The Fulani, though Muslims, were his natural enemies and a 'troublesome, warlike people'. He himself, with thirty sons and six favourite eunuchs, accompanied the expedition with a strong force of his own soldiers.

The raiding party arrived at the banks of the Makkeray, a few miles north of Dirkalla, on the evening of 27 April. Here the Bornu warriors put on their armour and, as darkness fell, Denham could hear their clumsy, ill-shaped hammers striking against the iron links. Soon after midnight the order to advance was given, the moon affording a clear and beautiful light. The Arabs under Boo-Khaloom led the way, and at sight of the Fulani town of Dirkalla they emitted the piercing Arab war-cry, at the sound of which Denham thought he could perceive 'a smile pass between Barca Gana and his chiefs'. He was inclined to believe that both they and the ruler of Mandara entertained the hope that the Fulani would teach the Arabs a little more respect for the bows and arrows of the black men of which they spoke with such derision.

Dirkalla and a small nearby town were quickly laid waste and set on fire; the few inhabitants found in them, mostly children and old people unable to escape, were 'put to death without mercy or thrown into the flames'. The raiders then passed on to Museifa, a town built on rising ground and protected by a wadi which extended across its front. Beyond the wadi was a swamp. This strong position was further defended by a 'very strong fence of palisades, well pointed and fastened together with thongs of raw hide, six feet in height'. Bowmen were placed behind these palisades, with horsemen beyond them, higher up under cover of the hills.

The Arabs charged with supreme confidence, spurning support from the Bornu and Mandara troops. They were met by a hail of arrows, some of them poisoned; but within half an hour they had broken through the fence and, brandishing their spears or firing their antiquated French muskets, they galloped on, driving the Fulani up the sides of the hills. The Fulani women, who had been bravely assisting their menfolk at the palisades by passing them fresh arrows, now rolled down huge masses of rock, previously undermined for the purpose, upon the heads of their Arab pursuers, killing several and badly wounding others. Barca Gana and his Bornu warriors now entered the battle by riding up to drive their spears through the wounded Fulani by the shattered fence, then advancing into the town. Barca Gana himself hurled eight spears, all of which hit their mark, some of them at a distance of thirty or thirty-five yards. But no other troops moved forward in support; and the Fulani, taking advantage of their caution, made a determined counter-attack.

'The arrows fell so thick that there was no standing against them,' wrote Denham who had ridden by Barca Gana's side, 'and the Arabs gave way', most of them badly wounded. Barca Gana had three horses hit under him. Boo-Khaloom's horse was also hit by a poisoned arrow and he himself was wounded. Denham's horse was badly cut in the neck; his burnous was pierced by two arrows and a third struck his face. Watching the Arabs' defeat from a safe distance, the Mandara troops turned and fled in the utmost confusion, followed by the surviving Arabs and Barca Gana's men pursued by the Fulani horsemen. Denham's wounded horse stumbled and fell and the Fulani were immediately upon him. He shot one of them and managed to remount but the horse soon fell once more, hurling him against a tree. He was again surrounded by Fulani who thrust at him with their spears, wounding him in both hands, and would have killed him had they not been so anxious to leave undamaged the clothes which they stripped from his body, leaving him completely naked. As they began to quarrel over their valuable booty, he crept under the belly of a horse, then dashed away towards the thickest part of the wood, pursued by his assailants, his flesh torn by the prickly undergrowth. He raced towards a mountain stream and, his strength almost spent, was letting himself into the water from the branch of an overhanging tree, when a large *liffa*, 'the worst kind of serpent this country produces', suddenly rose from its coil as if about to strike and so horrified him that he lost his grip on the branch and tumbled headlong into the water. Revived by the shock, he swam to the opposite bank and clambered up, feeling for the first time safe from his pursuers.

Yet scarcely had he congratulated himself on his escape than he thought of the leopards which he knew abounded in these woods. And then, having decided to spend the night at the top of a tamarind tree in order to escape them, he remembered the *liffas*, almost as numerous and equally to be dreaded. Just then he saw horsemen through the trees. He rushed towards them and, with infinite relief, recognized Barca Gana and Boo-Khaloom with some Arabs fighting off a party of Fulani. But the screams of the wounded, the cheers of the Arabs rallying and the reports of their guns and pistols drowned his cries. Maramy saw him, though, and riding towards him, pulled him up behind him and, while the arrows whistled over their heads, galloped off with him to safety.

After they had covered a mile or two Boo-Khaloom caught up with them and asked one of the Arabs to give Denham a burnous to protect his head and blistered neck from the burning sun. They were almost the last words Boo-Khaloom spoke, for soon afterwards the effects of the poison in his wounded foot took effect, and he fell dead into the arms of his favourite follower.

The horses, wounded by the Fulani's arrows, now also began to die, dropping to the earth with blood gushing from their nostrils, mouths and ears. Maramy's horse, however, was unscathed; so, having drunk copious draughts of the muddy waters of a stream, he and Denham were able to ride away towards Mandara.

Having covered more than forty-five miles on the bare back of this lean horse, while Denham's wounds gave him the acutest pain and the burnous, crawling as it was with vermin, insufferable irritation, they reached Mandara after midnight. Denham slid from the horse and lay down, scarcely able to move. Maramy gave him a drink made from parched corn, bruised and steeped in water, and thus refreshed he went to sleep under a tree.

Forty-five of the Arabs had been killed in the disastrous raid and nearly all of the rest wounded. Their camels and everything else they possessed had been lost. Many of the wounded died within the next few days from the effects of the poisoned arrows, their bodies becoming swollen and black and, immediately after death, blood issuing from their noses and mouths. The survivors, who had lost all their former arrogance, were driven to begging Barca Gana for a little corn to save them from starvation. Denham himself was soon to receive a severe reprimand from London for having been on a slave hunt and, by his presence, having seemed to countenance such 'disgraceful proceedings'.

On his return to Kouka, Denham learned that another expedition was planned, this one led by the ruler in person and directed against the unbelievers of Manga, a rebellious people under his nominal rule to the west of the river Gambaron. Despite his previous experiences, as soon as he was sufficiently recovered Denham sought permission to join this expedition, and it was agreed that he should do so at Kabshary, on the Gambaru, travelling by way of the old city of Bornu and the town of Gambaru with one of the ruler's slaves, Omar Gana, acting as guide.

Accompanied by Oudney, he accordingly left Kouka on 22 May with five camels and four servants; and two days later, having covered seventy miles, they reached the Gambaru at a place called Lada. Here, several women and children, believing them to be Tuaregs, threw down their water jugs and fled through the high grass and prickly undergrowth in the greatest alarm. Fear of the Tuaregs had induced the people to dig deep holes at the bottom of which they stuck sharp stakes, hardened by fire, and, over the top, laid grass so skilfully that it was impossible to detect the mantraps' presence. Some of these *blaqua*, as Denham learned they were called, were not a yard distant from the path he had followed, and he 'trembled at the recollection of the various escapes' he had had.

Beyond Lada, where scores of monkeys chattered above them in the wild fruit trees, the country became more and more desolate, 'one continued wood', as Denham described it, 'with narrow winding paths to avoid the overhanging branches of the prickly tulloh'. Footprints of lions, jackals and hyenas were often to be seen. But birds, too, were plentiful and, although the atmosphere was 'dreadfully sultry and oppressive', there was no shortage of good food at night.

On 26 May they reached the old city of Bornu which was said to have once contained a population of about 200,000 behind hard red brick walls that were in many places still standing to a height of eighteen feet. Gambaru, which they reached the next day, had also once been a large town; and it was clear from the ruins of brick houses and mosques that it must in its heyday have had 'an appearance superior to any town' that Denham had seen in Africa.

From Gambaru, Denham and Oudney followed the course of the river, breaking through high grass, dense undergrowth and thickly scattered bamboo. Now and then, by following the tracks of elephants whose ponderous bodies beat down everything in their path, they caught a glimpse of the river, there known as the Yeou. Crossing at a ford, they at length came upon the outskirts of the chief of Kouka's encampment and, passing through numerous groups of his Kanembu spearmen, they arrived at his tent and were regaled with an excellent supper of guinea fowl.

The next day they followed the army to a lake known as Muggaby where the naked warriors entered the water to spear fish as large as good-sized salmon which were then strung on lines made of grass and 'most expeditiously' roasted. Beyond the fishermen, hippopotami could be seen 'constantly throwing up their black muzzles, spouting with water'.

From the lake the army marched on, preceded by five flags, two green, two striped and one red, with extracts from the Koran written on them in gold. Behind the chief rode a Bornu page carrying his armour and weapons and another Negro, fantastically dressed in a straw hat and ostrich feathers, bearing a drum which it was the greatest misfortune and disgrace to lose in action. These were followed in turn by the ruler of Bornu, who usually accompanied these expeditions though he never fought. His attendants and harem included men bearing wooden trumpets ten and twelve feet long, standard bearers and bodyguards with immense spears hung round with charms. The Kanembu soldiers trailing behind, nine thousand strong, were naked apart from goatskin belts and narrow strips of cloth, the money of the country, which they wound round their heads, passing the cloth under the nose. They carried light wooden shields bound with bullock's hide, spears and daggers. They were trained to advance by tribes of about eight hundred each, uttering a shriek 'exceeding anything in shrillness' Denham had ever heard, and striking their spears against their shields. But although the town of Kabshary had been destroyed by the rebels of Munga, the Kanembu warriors were not called upon to wreak vengeance upon this occasion. For the insurgents came into the camp in their hundreds, bowing to the ground in submission and throwing sand over their heads. Their chiefs brought peace offerings; and the *fighi*, a strange-looking man with a thick beard on one side of his face and not a hair to be seen on the other, who had encouraged them to revolt, presented himself bare-headed and in the meanest clothes. Since the rebels could bring 'twelve thousand bowmen into the field' with arrows much longer and even more efficaciously poisoned than those of the Fulani, it was resolved to conciliate rather than to punish them. So they were forgiven and the troops returned to Kouka; and Denham and Oudney went with them to wait there until the rainy season was over.

For much of this time in Kouka, both Oudney and Clapperton were seriously ill and occasionally delirious, tormented by flies, mosquitoes and scorpions, by black ants that raised red marks all over their bodies, and by white ants that made their way into every trunk, consuming blankets, clothes and carpets with equal avidity. While they lay tossing and sweating on their mats, the rain poured down upon the leaking roofs of their huts; and hyenas, howling through the night, seized every opportunity to enter the town by way of insecure gates in the walls and to carry off all defenceless animals they might find in the streets.

Denham retained health enough to go out duck-shooting and otherwise to spend his time profitably by working at the Arabic and other languages, by gaining information about the shores of Lake Chad which he intended to explore as soon as he could, by collecting specimens of birds and other animals, and by adding to his menagerie which included two monkeys, five parrots, three rare Abyssinian hornbills, a civet-cat, a young ichneumon and a baby hyena. He made a study of local medicines, of the uses made of the castor tree and the tamarind, noting that the natives were acquainted with inoculation, which they performed 'by inserting into the flesh the sharp point of a dagger charged with the disease', and that, as Bruce had found in Ethiopia, they had the utmost faith in the curative properties of water drunk from bowls in which had been written sentences from the Koran. He went to dances at which the women turned their backs upon one another and, to the accompaniment of drums, bumped bottom against bottom with such force that they knocked each other over, often breaking the belts that they all wore round their bodies just above the hips and scattering beads in every direction. He attended wrestling matches between slaves whose excited owners, drawing pistols, threatened to shoot them if they were defeated, while promising them handsome rewards for victory. 'Dislocated limbs or death were often the consequence of these encounters' during which weaker men were held high in the air by the hips before being hurled to the ground where they lay covered with blood and unable to resume the contest, or had their spines snapped by sudden hugs and twists and the weight of a gigantic body concentrated in a bended knee. Denham also watched female slaves from Musgow at work in the fields as they tended the *gussub* crops, feeling pity for their patience under their sufferings, knowing that a year seldom passed without several of them being snatched away by the lions which crouched in wait under cover of the ripening corn. Denham described their features which, naturally large and ugly, were artificially rendered even more so by their having their front teeth punched out to make way for the heavy silver plates which they wore in their grotesquely extended lower lips. He also observed with pity the young men from Bagirmi – whose own ruler was said to have nearly a thousand wives and three thousand Bornu and Kanembu eunuchs – paraded in the chief's garden after being castrated in order to qualify them for service in his harem. The old hardened head of the seraglio, who seemed happy that so many of his fellow-creatures were reduced to the same standard as himself, exclaimed, 'Why, Christian, what signifies all this? They are only Begharmis! Dogs! Kaffirs! Enemies! They ought to have been cut in four quarters alive, and now they will drink coffee, eat sugar, and live in a palace all their lives.'

Denham was appalled by the severity of the punishments inflicted on recalcitrant eunuchs and all others found guilty of even minor offences who frequently had their brains knocked out with iron-headed clubs. Regarded with particular seriousness were crimes committed during Ramadan, which was so strictly observed that any man caught drinking water or visiting his wives between sunrise and sunset was sentenced to four hundred strokes with a whip of hippopotamus hide, and the only relief allowed to workers almost fainting with thirst was to have buckets of water thrown over them. One unfortunate man caught asleep in his hut with another man's wife by his side was without hesitation presumed guilty of having broken the Ramadan. The woman was stripped, her head was shaved and she was suspended by means of a cloth, 'in a manner not to be described', and given two hundred lashes which rendered her senseless. The man was flogged to death. A slave who was caught with the wife of a freeman was hanged by the woman's side.

Towards the end of 1823 Clapperton and Oudney were given permission to leave Kouka for Kano; and on 23 January 1824 Denham set out in a south-easterly direction towards Loggun. He was accompanied by Dellal, the chief's representative, 'one of the handsomest negroes' he had ever seen, by six of Dellal's slaves, and Ensign Toole, a cheerful, enterprising and energetic young man in the 80th Regiment. Toole had volunteered to join Denham at Kouka and 'had made the long, dangerous, and difficult journey from Tripoli to Bornu in the short space of three months and fourteen days'.

Denham and Toole went by way of Angornu to Angala where they were received with 'great kindness and hospitality' by the old chief and by his daughter, a 'very handsome, beautifully formed negress', who greeted them surrounded by her favourite slaves, all dressed in fine white shirts reaching to their feet and thickly ornamented about the neck, ears and nose with coral. Four eunuchs stood at her door and a dwarf less than three feet tall, the keeper of her keys, sat before her with the insignia of his office on his shoulder, grinning and slobbering as his mistress laughingly spoke of his inability to procreate children despite his having been given eight of her handsomest and youngest slaves.

From Angala the explorers went on to Showy on the banks of the Shary, a beautiful river, at that point 650 yards wide, with banks 'thickly scattered with trees rich in foliage, and all hung over with creeping plants, bearing various coloured and aromatic blossoms'. Several crocodiles, from eight to fifteen feet in length, disturbed in their slumbers on the banks rolled into the stream and disappeared in an instant. The natives appeared to have little fear of them in shallow water, diving in after the ducks and iguana which the white men shot.

In the centre of the stream was a lovely island with a sandy shore over-hung by steep banks and abounding in game. Denham and Toole had a supper here of venison, buffalo meat, wild duck and fish, all roasted on wooden spits.

They returned to Showy by water, finding it very heavy work rowing against the stream. They endured two days of burning heat and nights tormented by insects, eating sparse meals of Indian corn boiled in the leaking canoes which were ankle deep in water and to which hippopotami came so close that they were struck by the paddles. From Showy they continued the journey inland, through the walled town of Willighi and on to Affadai, beating their way through woods of locust trees covered in jasmine, aromatic plants and flowers growing in wild profusion on every side, the overhanging branches of thorny shrubs tearing their shirts and dragging the loads from the camels' backs. At Kussery they decided to rest for a time, as Toole was feeling dreadfully ill and was constantly vomiting. But Kussery, as they discovered, was the last place they should have chosen for rest, since the swarms of insects were so insistently troublesome that the natives lived in huts composed of one cell within another, five or six in number, in order to escape them. Denham was only able to keep them away from Toole, of whom he had already grown extremely fond, by lighting a fire and constantly supplying it with weeds and wet straw. Finding it impossible to endure the torments of Kussery, Toole suggested that they move on to Loggun, thirty miles to the south, though by now he could scarcely stand and had to be lifted on and off his horse. In Loggun, Denham gave the customary presents of clothes, knives and scissors to the chief who sat on a carpet behind a cane latticework screen. A bundle of silk and shawls, with nothing but his eyes visible, the chief welcomed his visitor in a soft whisper, it being 'extremely ill-bred in a Loggun gentleman to speak out', and asked him if he would like to buy some handsome female slaves: he had hundreds of them and was prepared to sell them as cheaply as anyone.

Some of these slaves visited Denham later, accompanied by their mistresses. They were good-looking and intelligent but 'most immoral' women who examined all his possessions, even going through his pockets and attempting to steal what they could not persuade him to give them. 'Why, how sharp he is!' they said to each other when discovered in the act. 'Only think! Why, he caught us!' Denham was further annoyed the next day to be told that there were two chiefs in Loggun, father and son. He had seen the son, and it was absolutely necessary to give the father at least as much as his offspring had received, otherwise all would be taken from him. He felt obliged to give way, and was then pestered by each for poison with which to dispatch the other, the son sending three female slaves under fifteen years of age as an inducement.

While waiting in Loggun for permission to proceed, Denham, in his usual conscientious way, noted the various crops which were cultivated there and the manner in which the industrious people wove, dyed and glazed their cloth. Toole stayed in bed and grew gradually a little stronger. He might well, indeed, have recovered had not they both been ordered peremptorily to leave because, so they were told, Bagirmi raiders were on their way and no protection could be offered them. They left, therefore, on 19 February, with no provisions other than a sack of parched corn, and a few days later were back in Angala where Toole died. His grieving friend buried him in a deep grave over which was raised a pile of thorns and branches of the prickly tulloh as a protection against hyenas.

The next week, back at Kouka, Denham learned that Oudney also had died the month before at a place called Murmur, near Katagum. Denham, overcome by 'fatigue, heat, and anxiety of mind', now also fell ill again and was confined for ten days to his hut.

While he lay there feverish, the chief's soldiers returned from a campaign against the Bagirmi with an immense amount of plunder including nearly five hundred horses and two hundred female slaves, several of whom were offered for sale in the market. One of them, a girl of fourteen, was pressed upon Denham in exchange for a red cap and an old muslin turban. Delighted by this triumph, the chief was more thrilled than ever when more presents from the English arrived for him by caravan on 22 May. He was particularly taken with a dagger, two gold watches and a parcel of rockets. 'There are no friends like these!' he exclaimed. 'And I see by the Book that if the Prophet had lived only a short time longer, they would have been all Moslem.'

The next month Denham's stock at the palace rose to new heights when he removed a fish-bone from the throat of one of the chief's young sons by persuading him to swallow some large pills of wax candle dipped in honey. 'Everything was now prepared,' Denham wrote, 'for the expedition to the eastern side of Lake Chad.'

He left under the protection of a punitive expedition led by Barca Gana, and reached Maffatai on 20 June. From there he moved on to Showy and, 'crossing the Gurdya by a slanting ford, came more to the eastward than before and by a nearer route'. On the 24th they crossed the Shary where they counted twelve crocodiles basking on the banks, and came upon the camps of the Dugganah Shuwa, a nomadic people living in rush huts and tents of dressed hides, and existing largely on the milk of their camels, cows and sheep. 'They have the greatest contempt for, and hatred of, the negro nations,' Denham discovered, 'and yet are always tributary to either one black sultan or another: there is no example of their ever having peopled a town or established themselves in a permanent home.' He found something 'singularly interesting and expressive' in this people's manners and language.

A girl sits down by your tent with a bowl of milk [he wrote], a dark blue cotton wrapper tied round her waist, and a mantila of the same thrown over her head, with which she hides her face, yet leaves all her bust naked. She says, 'A happy day to you! Your friend has brought you milk. You gave her something so handsome yesterday, she has not forgotten it. Oh! how her eyes ache to see all you have got in that wooden house!' pointing to a trunk. 'We have no fears now; we know you are good ... But ... how it pains us that you are so white.'

Denham was now close to Tangalia at the eastern extremity of the lake and this was as far as he was destined to reach, for Barca Gana was defeated by the rebels and obliged to retire. 'The excursion you wish to make was always dangerous,' he said to Denham, 'it is now impracticable.' Denham, whose provisions were almost exhausted, took the advice and returned to Kouka, catching a glimpse on his way of five giraffe, the first he had ever seen.

No sooner had Denham returned to Kouka than he determined to make another effort to reach Kanem on the far side of Lake Chad, this time by way of Woodie. So, accompanied once again by the chief's representative, Dellal, he set out on 16 August, arriving at Woodie on the 25th. Here they met Barca Gana whose forces were 'in a sad plight, with scarcely thirty horses left, having literally fought their way back' from Kanem where the 'people were all in a state of mutiny'. Dellal wanted to turn back, but Barca Gana said, 'It is dangerous, but I think you may go on if you wish it.' So Denham decided to pursue his journey through the 'continued marsh and swamp' east of Lari and across the northernmost part of the lake. On the way, he was tormented by flies and mosquitoes; his horse sank nearly up to its body in water, while reeds and high grass swayed above his head, for most of the time hiding the lake from sight. On the night of 30 August, after spending almost thirteen hours in the saddle, he reached Mabah 'completely fatigued'. He would have gone on to Kuskoua, but Dellal could not be persuaded to venture any further; and Denham, who had had so many proofs of the man's bravery, 'could not but doubt his fears were just'. So Denham turned back. And by the middle of September he and Hillman were crossing the desert once more on their way back to Murzuk.

'To do them justice,' Denham conceded, 'the Fezzan people seemed as glad we were come back as we were ourselves. "To go and come back from the black country! Oh, wonderful! You English have large hearts! ... Now you are going home. Well, good fortune attend you!" ... All welcomed our return: we had bowls of *bazeen* and *kouskosou* night and morning, and visitors from daylight until long after sunset, notwithstanding we had no tea, coffee or sugar to regale them with.'

Despite their welcoming smiles, however, Denham thought that the women of Murzuk, 'though many degrees nearer our own fair and blue-eyed beauties in complexion', lose much by comparison with the black ones of Bornu. 'That the latter were "black, devilish black" there is no denying; but their beautiful forms, expressive eyes, pearly teeth and excessive cleanliness, rendered them far more pleasing than the dirty half-castes we were now amongst.' These were 'wrapped in a woollen blanket, with an under one of the same texture'; and they seldom took these clothes off and even less often washed, except when they were to be married; their hair was besmeared 'with sand, brown powder of cloves, and other drugs, in order to give them the popular smell; their silver ear-rings and coral ornaments, all blackened by the perspiration flowing from their anointed locks [were] really such a bundle of filth, that it [was] not without alarm that you [saw] them approach towards you'.

From Murzuk, Denham and Hillman moved on to Sebba and Omhul Abeed; and on Christmas Day, their fourth in Africa, they arrived in Temesheen. The next day they came to Sockna where they lodged in the house of a merchant which was cared for in the family's absence by a Bagirmi slave who had been twenty-four years in bondage. When he learned that Denham had visited his homeland and heard repeated the names of towns he had known as a boy, he clapped his hands with pleasure. But, on being asked whether he would like to return, he said, 'No, no. I am better where I am. I have no home now but this; and what will my master's children do without me? ... And who will take care of the garden for his wives and daughters?' No, his country was a long way off and full of enemies. Here he had a home and plenty to eat, thank God. And two months ago they had given him a wife 'and kept his wedding for eight days'.

A month later Denham and his companions reached Tripoli where, so he said, 'Our long absence from civilized society appeared to have an effect on our manner of speaking, of which, though we were unconscious ourselves, occasioned the remarks of our friends: even in common conversation, our tone was so loud as almost to alarm those we addressed.'

He now had 'no other duties to perform,' as he wrote in the last pages of his account of his adventures, 'except the providing for our embarkation with all our live animals, birds, and other specimens of natural history, and settling with our faithful native attendants, some of whom had left Tripoli with us, and returned in our service. And if either here or in any foregoing part of this journal it may be thought that I have spoken too favourably of the natives we were thrown amongst, I can only answer, that I have described them as I found them, hospitable, kind-hearted, honest, and liberal: to the latest hour of my life I shall remember them with affectionate regard.'

Denham sailed from Tripoli in a brig bound for Leghorn whence the baggage and animals were sent home by sea in the care of William Hillman. Denham went to Florence, crossed the Alps and on 1 June 1825 reported his return to England to Lord Bathurst. Then, after the publication of his *Narrative*, he disappeared from public notice. He returned to Africa in December 1826 to take up an appointment as superintendent of liberated Africans on the west coast, and died of fever at Sierra Leone on 8 May 1828.

4

HAUSALAND AND SLAVE COAST

CLAPPERTON AND OUDNEY LEAVE FOR KANO, 1823 ·
OUDNEY DIES ON THE WAY · CLAPPERTON ENTERS KANO
ALONE · HE GOES ON TO SOKOTO · WELCOMED BY THE CHIEF
OF SOKOTO · RETURNS TO ENGLAND · HIS NEW
INSTRUCTIONS TO 'ASCERTAIN THE SOURCE, PROGRESS AND
TERMINATION OF THE MYSTERIOUS NIGER' · HIS
COMPANIONS INCLUDE RICHARD LANDER · THEY SAIL INTO
THE BIGHT OF BENIN, NOVEMBER 1825 · THEIR JOURNEY
TO KATUNGA AND RESIDENCE THERE · THE WIDOW OF
WAWA · ARRIVAL AT BUSSA AND DESCRIPTION OF THE
NIGER THERE · CLAPPERTON ONCE MORE IN KANO AND
SOKOTO · HIS DEATH · LANDER RETURNS ALONE TO
BADAGRY · THE HORRORS OF HIS ENFORCED SOJOURN · THE
FETISH TREE AND THE ORDEAL OF POISON · HIS RETURN TO
CORNWALL

Shortly before Denham had left Kouka for Lake Chad, Hugh Clapperton and Walter Oudney had set out for Kano, accompanied by twenty-seven Arab merchants and various Bornuese bearers, guards and servants. The rivers which formed in the wet season and flowed into the Yeou were still full of water, so rafts had to be constructed by lashing bundles of long reeds across poles. Several of the Arabs viewed these rafts with the greatest apprehension and some of them who could not swim jumped off them into the water 'three or four times before they could muster courage to cross. The camels occasioned a great deal of trouble, one man having to swim before with the halter in his teeth, while another kept beating the animal behind with a stick.'

On 21 December 1823 they arrived at Bera on the banks of a beautiful lake formed by the overflowing of the Yeou. Immediately there was 'quite a fair' in the camp, the women of the town coming with Guinea corn, bean straw, cashew nuts and milk to sell in exchange for glass beads and cloth. Beads seemed welcome everywhere but at these impromptu

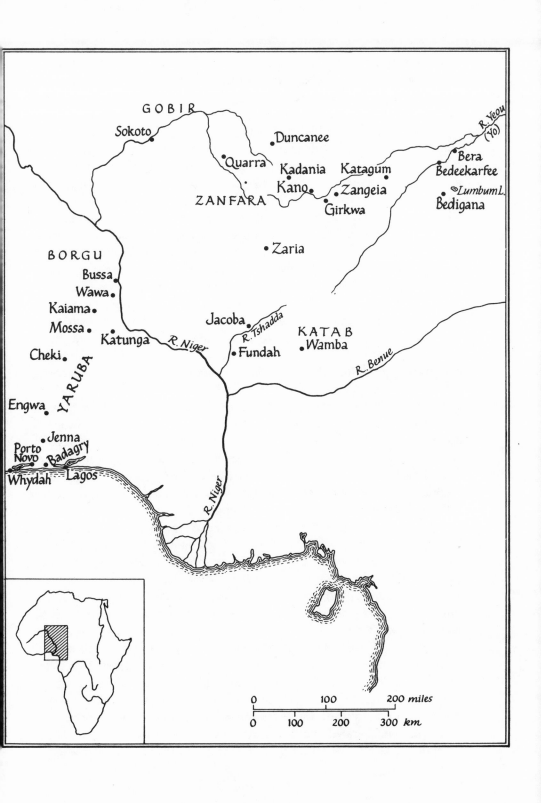

GOBIR

Sokoto

Duncanee

Quarra

Kadania   Katagum

Kano   Zangeia   Bera
                           Bedeekarfee
ZANFARA   Girkwa   Lumbum L.
                                 Bedigana

Zaria

BORGU

Bussa

Wawa

Kaiama   Jacoba   R. Tshadda   KATAB
                                        Wamba
Mossa   Katunga   R. Niger   Fundah

Cheki   YARUBA   R. Benue

Engwa

Jenna
Porto
Novo   Badagry
Whydah Lagos

R. Niger

R. Yeou
(Yo)

0   100   200 miles
0   100   200   300 km

markets further west the natives asked for coral rather than cloth and for gun-powder which was highly valued as a medicine. Christmas Day was spent at Bedeekarfee where they were cordially greeted by the head man whose dwelling, 'large and extremely clean, consisted of a spacious quadrangular enclosure, surrounded with mats fixed to high poles, within which were several small round huts, also of matting with thatched conical roofs, each surmounted by an ostrich egg ... a distinctive mark of the occupant being a man of rank'. The people here were mostly Shuwa Arabs, the women being, in Clapperton's opinion, extremely beautiful, wearing their hair in a strange style resembling a helmet, the side tresses being 'neatly plaited and frizzled out at the ends'.

At Bedeekarfee the caravan was joined by at least five hundred people wait-ing for Arabs armed with guns to escort them through the neighbouring Bedde country which was inhabited by a heathen race regarded as outlaws and said to be unnaturally fond of eating dogs fattened for the purpose. The Fulani, however, seemed to have been more of a menace than the Bedde and on his way to Bedigana, Clapperton passed the ruins of several towns which, he was told, had been very populous before the Fulani invasions. He had little to say of these towns but he described in detail the *goorgee* trees whose dark-red flowers resembled tulips, and the immense *kuka* trees measuring twenty-five feet in circumference and having large white flowers like lilies, and fruit hanging from long stalks 'like silken purses'. In his diary Clapperton also often remarked upon the extraordinary coldness of the mornings when the horses and camels stood shivering outside the tents and, on one occasion at least, when the water in the shallow vessels was crusted with thin flakes of ice and the waterskins were frozen as hard as a board.

Outside Bedigana by a lake called Lumbum where, it was said, an encounter with the Bedee was likely, Clapperton, riding a little way in front of the caravan, met two men, 'one of whom was a Shouaa Arab, the other a Negro' and both of whom carried a bundle of spears. They saluted him civilly and passed on, to be questioned by the Bornuese behind who, receiving unsatisfactory answers, seized, stripped and bound them. Considering it a matter in which he had 'no authority to interfere', Clapperton merely requested that their clothes might be returned to them. 'Oh, damn their fathers!' one of their captors said. 'They are thieves. What would they be doing here if they were honest men?' But when a Bornuese hit the Negro so hard that Oudney thought the blow might have killed him, Clapperton, with a characteristically sudden display of violence, beat the aggressor, forced him to bind up the wound with a strip torn from his robe, and threatened to shoot him if he harmed the man again. At Bedigana the two captives, happening to be well-known in the town, were liberated 'but their clothes were not restored'.

Oudney was by now seriously ill. He struggled through Sansan where, as he noted, the women dyed their arms and legs, hands and feet as well as their hair and eyebrows with indigo, and their fingers, toes and the palms of their hands with henna. He rode into Katagum where he found cowrie shells in circulation as money and a governor who expressed his astonishment that the travellers did not want slaves but merely to see the world. Yet he had not strength enough to mount his horse on leaving Katagum, and he had to be lifted on to a bed fixed to a frame on a camel's back. At daybreak on 12 January 1824 at Murmur, Clapperton saw 'the ghastliness of death in his countenance'. Later that day he buried his friend under an old mimosa tree outside the southern gate of the town.

Clapperton went on unhappily alone into the province of Kano, through a country which had hitherto, as he put it, 'never been trod by European foot'. Women sat spinning cotton by the roadside, offering roast meat and sweet potatoes for sale as well as water and cashew nuts, and from time to time surveying themselves 'with whimsical complacency' in little pocket mirrors. The caravan passed through Zangeia where – between rows of date trees – cotton, tobacco and indigo grew profusely in the shadow of high blue mountains. It was a beautiful country, Clapperton thought, with 'numerous plantations as neatly fenced as in England' and soil of a rich red clay, frequently broken by large blocks of granite appearing above the surface. At Girkwa where he had an attack of ague, a pretty Fulani girl, going to market with milk and butter, as 'neat and spruce in her attire as a Cheshire dairy-maid', spoke to him with 'infinite archness and grace'. After 'much amusing small talk' he jokingly invited her to accompany him on his journey; she 'with roguish glee' referred him to her father and mother. He did not know how it happened but her presence seemed to dispel the effects of the ague and his grief at Oudney's death. He knew that he would not readily forget her.

For his entry into Kano, a large town of some 30,000 to 40,000 inhabitants, half of them slaves, he thought it as well to array himself in naval uniform and make himself 'as smart as circumstances would permit'. But he need not have bothered for not a single inhabitant turned to look at him, so intent were they upon their own business. The place was in other respects, too, a bitter disappointment to him. The square, clay houses, roofed with the trunks of palm trees, were scattered in untidy groups between large stagnant pools of water. An extensive swamp, covered by reeds and frequented by wild ducks, cranes and 'a filthy kind of vulture', cut the town almost in half. Having crossed this swamp by the marketplace, to deliver a letter of introduction from the ruler of Bornu to one of Kano's principal inhabitants, he had to recross it again to the other side of the town where a house had been allocated to him, a gloomy hovel of two floors into whose rooms little holes admitted a glimmer of light.

The governor, however, a fat Fulani of a 'dark copper colour', was friendly and 'seemed highly pleased' with his presents which included some brass badges for children's caps, a tea-tray, a spyglass and a broken thermometer. He bade Clapperton 'a thousand welcomes to the country'. And while Kano itself was a dispiriting place, its market, which Clapperton thought the best-regulated he had seen in Africa, afforded him endless entertainment. The prices were fixed by the official in charge, and if the purchaser subsequently found the goods he had bought of inferior quality the price he had paid was returned to him. The range of goods offered for sale on the neat rows of bamboo stalls was remarkable. Bands of musicians parading up and down attracted the attention of passers-by to booths in which were displayed all kinds of food, silks and ornaments, armlets and bracelets of glass, coral and amber, silver trinkets, pewter rings, scissors and knives of native workmanship, indigo for dyeing hair, eyebrows and legs, and the flowers of the *goorgee* tree for colouring both lips and teeth a deep blood red, sword blades from Malta, coarse writing paper from France, English green cotton umbrellas, and, of course, slaves who were examined with the utmost care by their intending purchasers, required to show their teeth and tongues and made to cough, yet who appeared to Clapperton 'much happier than their masters'. Most of those who were afterwards granted their freedom preferred, indeed, to remain in the country of their captivity rather than return home, still acknowledging their former masters as their superiors and present-ing them yearly with a part of their earnings.

When not in the market, Clapperton occupied his time in Kano watching the women spinning cotton, dyeing cloth and tanning skins. He noted how excessively polite and ceremonious their fathers and husbands were as they idly passed by the working women, saluting one another by laying a hand on the breast, making a bow and inquiring, 'How do you do? I hope you are well. How have you passed the heat of the day?' He was entertained by snake-charmers who made their serpents, some of them over six feet long, perform a kind of dance to the beating of a drum, coiled them round their necks, pointed their fingers at them, exasperated them, raised them into positions as though they were about to strike, then made them retreat by spitting in their faces, and sometimes picked them up and hurled them amongst the spectators. Once Clapperton organized a boxing match, having 'heard a great deal about the boxers of Haussa'; but since the death of one or other of the combatants was usually 'almost certain before a battle' was over, he expressly prohibited all fighting in earnest. Even so, though no eyes were gouged out and no death blows delivered with the heels under the ribs or to the side of the neck, the combatants seized each other's heads under their arms, beat them with their free hand, at the same time sharply raising their knees to deliver agonizing strokes against their opponent's testicles. The contestants had frequently to be separated on Clapperton's orders because they were beginning to lose their tempers.

On 22 February Clapperton left Kano for the Fulani town of Sokoto, observing a custom established by Oudney of slaughtering two bullocks before his departure as an offering to the poor of the town.

Suffering from fever for much of the way, he nevertheless conscientiously kept up his diary, recording the countryside at first as being 'very woody ... crossed sometimes by dikes or ridges of white quartz, sometimes by ravines and the dry channels of rivers, besides which were small plots of onions and tobacco, melons, indigo and wheat'; then, after a week of circuitous travelling, as being 'through little valleys, delightfully green, lying between high ridges of granite ... with many clear springs issuing out of the rocks where young women were employed drawing water'. Clapperton asked for a gourd of water as an excuse to get into conversation with these women. They bent gracefully on one knee, 'and displaying at the same time teeth of pearly whiteness and eyes of the blackest lustre', they presented their gourds to him and 'appeared highly delighted' when he thanked them, saying to one another, 'Did you hear the white man thank me?'

This was outside the village of Kagaria. His guide had taken him through Kadania, Duncanee, Ratah and was soon to lead him into Quarra; and everywhere he stopped for the night he had found the people 'kind and attentive' in procuring for him a house and provisions. In Quarra he waited as he had been advised to do until a guard was sent from Sokoto to conduct him through the states of Gobir and Zamfara which were in a state of insurrection. Here he was besieged by people who took him for a *fighi* and pestered him 'at all hours of the day' to write out prayers and charms for them. Other visitors were the wives of the governor of the place who examined his skin with the most scrupulous attention and informed him that it was a pity he was not black for, if he had been, he would have been 'tolerably good-looking'. He asked one of them, a buxom young girl of fifteen, if she would marry him provided that she could obtain the governor's permission. She immediately began to whimper and, on being asked the reason, said she did not know how she would be able to get used to his white legs. The next day more women came to him and 'evinced much discernment' in their 'curious manipulation' of his person.

Tired of waiting for the promised escort from Sokoto, Clapperton left Quarra without them on 13 March, much to the consternation of his companions who were profoundly relieved to meet the escort on the way. There were about 150 horsemen with drummers and trumpeters. They advanced towards him at full gallop, bidding him welcome to the country in the name of their master, and thereafter riding so close to him and in such dense masses around him that he was almost suffocated with dust. Conscious that this extraordinary respect was paid to him as the servant of the king of the white men, as he was described in the ruler of Bornu's letter, he thought it behoved him to impress them further by looking the part. So he donned his lieutenant's gold-laced coat, white trousers, silk stockings and, to complete the finery, Turkish slippers and a turban. And thus he continued the journey, in clouds of dust, assuming, so he put it himself, 'the utmost serenity of countenance, in order to meet with befitting dignity the honours' the escort lavished upon him.

The chief of Sokoto whom he met on the morning of 17 March bade this important representative of the English king 'many hearty welcomes'. A 'noble-looking man', forty-four years old with a short curling black beard, a surprisingly Grecian nose and large black eyes, he was sitting on a carpet in a room with walls painted blue and white in the Moorish taste. He seemed much interested in England, particularly in the religions practised there. The provisions which were thereafter sent to Clapperton's house regularly arrived in pewter dishes with the London stamp and once in a white wash-hand basin of English manufacture.

During one of his several conversations with Clapperton, the chief asked if the English king would provide him with guns and rockets. Yes, replied Clapperton, if he in return would put down the slave trade on the coast. 'I further pointed out to him,' Clapperton wrote, 'that [Sokoto] was the best situate town in all Northern Africa for commerce, without which a nation was nothing; that rich merchants make rich kings; and that it was in the power of the king of England to make him one of the greatest princes in Africa, when all the trade from the east and west of that continent would centre in his dominions: at the same time advising him strongly to have a port on the sea coast, where he might have ships, and where his people would be taught by the English the art of ship-building . . .'

The chief seemed interested and, although he was warned about the perfidy of the English by the Arabs – who were anxious to ensure that their own trade should not suffer from competition – he agreed to write a letter to King George IV consenting to the proposals which Clapperton had made to him, to the reception of merchant ships at the town of Raba and the establishment of an English consul there. While waiting for this letter to be written, Clapperton suffered from a recurrence of fever during which he found it more irksome than ever to be compelled to receive at his house endless streams of curious visitors including the executioner of Sokoto. This 'ill-looking wretch', so Clapperton was told, had succeeded his brother as executioner at Yacoba, a position he had obtained by going to the governor of that place and boasting of his superior adroitness in the family vocation. The governor had responded to his request by saying, 'We will try. Go and fetch your brother's head.' The man had instantly gone to look for his brother, whom he had found at the door of his house, and without noise or warning had struck off his head at one blow. He then took the bleeding evidence of his skill to the governor who appointed him to the now vacant post. The chief, being afterwards in want of an expert headsman, had sent for him to come to Sokoto where, soon after his arrival, he had officiated at the execution of 2,000 Tuareg prisoners.

On 2 May Clapperton was told that the chief's letter to the king of England would be ready the next day; so, on the evening of the 3rd, he went to fetch it from him. He found him at the mosque and, after waiting for two hours for him to come out, he followed him to his house where an old female slave took him by the hand, led him through a number of dark, low passages and up and down flights of uneven steps until he caught sight of a faint light flickering in a distant room. Here sat the chief who handed him the letter 'with assurances of his friendly sentiments towards the English nation' and his 'anxiety to enter into permanent relations of trade'.

Carrying the letter with him, as well as a map of Central Africa on which the chief had drawn the supposed course of the Kwara river ('which reaches Egypt and which is [there] called the Nile'), Clapperton left Sokoto for Kano by one of the twelve gates in the almost thirty-foot-high walls on 4 May, accompanied by a military escort, four merchants and their slaves. He remained at Kano for ten days, then set out for Kouka by way of Murmur where he found that the clay wall around Oudney's grave had been destroyed and a fire burned over the grave itself. Although assured that an Arab caravan had been responsible for the desecration, not the people of the town, Clapperton was so enraged that he horsewhipped the chief, who with 'slavish submission promised faithfully to rebuild the wall'. A month later he was back in Kouka and on 1 June 1825 once more home in England.

Long before he set foot in England, Clapperton had been planning to return to Africa. He had collected much useful information but had not yet so much as seen the Niger or the Benue, and could offer no certain evidence as to their course. He found Lord Bathurst eager to sponsor a second expedition; and so, within a short time of his return home, he was at sea again. Among his companions was a Cornish servant, Richard Lander.

Lander was then twenty years old and had always, as he put it himself, displayed 'rambling inclinations', delighting in wandering about from place to place, listening attentively to 'tales about the manners and ceremonies of the natives of distant regions of the earth', and harbouring an ambition to travel to those regions himself and to arouse the 'wonder and admiration' of his contemporaries by his descriptions of them. The son of an innkeeper at Truro, he had been briefly educated there before going out with a merchant to the West Indies where he remained three years. Upon his return to England, he had been employed as a servant by 'various noblemen and gentlemen' with one of whom he travelled on the Continent; and, in 1823, he went to South Africa as servant to a Commissioner of Inquiry into the State of the British Colonies. Having travelled widely in South Africa with his master, he sailed home to England the next year and obtained employment with a kinsman of the Duke of Northumberland in whose service his time passed 'pleasantly and thoughtlessly enough'. Stories of the adventures of Denham and Clapperton, however, once more aroused his wanderlust and he determined to 'embrace the first favourable chance' of going abroad again. 'There was always a charm in the very sound of Africa, that always made my heart flutter on hearing it mentioned,' he later wrote; 'whilst its boundless deserts of sand, the awful obscurity in which many of the interior regions were enveloped; the strange and wild aspect of countries that had never been trodden by the foot of a European, and even the very failure of all former undertakings to explore its hidden wonders, united to strengthen the determination I had come to.' As soon as he heard of the British government's decision to send out another expedition to explore Central Africa and to 'ascertain the source, progress and the termination of the mysterious Niger', he offered his services to Clapperton who immediately accepted him as his confidential servant.

Lander was brave, good-natured and humorous, the ideal travelling companion. Very short and fair, with an open, pleasing face, he was as kind, ingenuous and honest as he looked. He was also intelligent and, although susceptible to tropical diseases, his resilient, optimistic spirit was to help him always to recover from them.

Clapperton's party also included a fellow naval officer, Captain Pearce, a charming man and excellent draughtsman and linguist; two surgeons, Dr Dickson and Dr Morrison; a West Indian mulatto named Columbus; and a Hausa from Gobir called Pasko, a roguish cunning little man, no more than five feet in height with hands and arms 'disproportionately long', 'who might have been sixty years of age but looked much older'. His vast mouth, with its lubberly lips and enormous white teeth, was set in a perpetual, demoniacal grin, his nose was 'excessively broad and fat', his cheeks deeply marked by eight broad tribal scars, his dark eyes restless and cunning. 'It is somewhat odd,' Lander wrote of him, 'that Pasko, plain as his appearance most undoubtedly was, should have entertained the strange notion that almost every female who saw him, of whatever hue, nation, or religion she might be, could not help falling in love with him at first sight.' And, indeed, so supreme was his confidence, so self-assured his approaches and so beguiling his eloquence that women were not in the least averse to his advances. He had numerous wives and was to acquire several more on his journeys. He was not a stranger to exploration and adventure. He claimed to be the brother of the chief of Gobir, to have been captured in war, sold as a slave and rescued when the Portuguese ship taking him to Bahia had been overtaken by a British sloop. He had served in the British Navy for a time; had agreed to travel to Timbuktu with the Italian explorer, G. B. Belzoni, upon whose death he had resumed his life as an ordinary seaman; and had then accepted Clapperton's request that he should join his mission as interpreter.

On 23 November 1825, Clapperton and his companions sailed into Whydah in the Bight of Benin. Here Dr Dickson was to leave the rest of the party and to make his way inland to meet the others at Jenné in Yaruba. He was much distressed at parting for he had a presentiment he would not see them again. 'Study the character of the natives well,' Clapperton advised him, 'respect their institutions, and be kind to them on all occasions ... Set a guard over your temper, my dear Dickson,' he added, offering advice which he did not always follow himself, 'and never let it lead you into error.'

'We meet at Jenné, then,' said Dickson with what Lander described as an 'anxious, half-doubting look'. 'We meet at Jenné,' answered Clapperton. 'Once more *adieu*, my dear Dickson, and may God bless and protect you!' The doctor, in Lander's words, 'tore himself from the deck and we saw him no more'.

The ship then sailed on to Badagry where it dropped anchor three days later.

The gentlemen of the mission and the officers of the ship assembled on the quarter-deck to take a final farewell of each other [Richard Lander wrote] and some of the latter were deeply affected, as with a faltering voice and agitated manner they breathed their hopes that success might attend the perilous undertaking to which their enterprising friends had so willingly devoted themselves ... I myself could with difficulty stifle my emotion; and to dispel the gloom which hung upon my mind, I bade the officers a hasty and respectful adieu, and shaking hands with many of the honest seamen on deck, I sprang into a canoe that lay alongside the Brazen; and as two of the natives were rowing it towards the shore, I took the opportunity of playing '*Over the hills and far away*' on a small bugle horn which I had brought with me. This elicited the admiration of the sailors, and I landed amidst the hearty cheers and acclamations of them all.

'After a great deal of palavering and drinking' with their 'African friends', Clapperton and his party – which now included an English merchant named Houtson and George Dawson, an able seaman employed as a servant – left Badagry on 7 December. The men in their canoes were armed with 'small guns in the bow'; but the precautions seemed quite unnecessary as everywhere the natives appeared to be perfectly friendly. At Puka, immense crowds of people crowded round the strangers, the smaller ones scrambling up on to the shoulders of others and a war chief, grotesquely dressed in a ragged red coat with yellow facings and a Portuguese military cap with feathers, prancing towards them on a horse. Clapperton presented him with an umbrella as a sign of peace, whereupon drums beat, hands were clapped and 'fingers cracked at a great rate'. The chief approached the white men, 'capering and dancing the whole way', shook them by the hand, then made a speech about his clothes which came from the white men's country, as did all good things. Therefore his people must be glad when white men came to visit him. The *caboceer*, or chief man of the town, was equally complimentary as he offered them *goora* nuts and water and afterwards sent sheep, yams and firewood to their hut, through the holes in which his wives and young women came to peep at them, running away whenever noticed.

As at Puka so at most other places on their route to Katunga, the chiefs and their people were equally inquisitive, children being lifted up on to the shoulders of parents who pointed out the 'red' men, crying, 'There they are!' as though the strangers had been 'wild beasts', Lander said, 'or monsters of some sort. All, however, behaved with the strictest propriety and kindness.'

At Isako they came came out with lamps to guide the strangers on their way. At Dagmoo one of a party of women carrying plantains to market almost wept when asked for water of which she had none to give, and offered her plantains instead. At Humba the inhabitants sang and danced all night round the white men's house. At Laboo the chief's wives and concubines, about two hundred strong, clapped their hands joyfully as he complimented his guests and 'laughed immoderately' when told a white man had only one wife; and when the strangers left the town they sang in chorus and held up both hands as they passed, while groups of other women knelt down to wish them a safe journey. At Jenna, where the people were getting ready to go on a slaving expedition, the *caboceer* was particularly attentive and particularly gorgeous in his attire. He received his visitors in a yellow silk shirt and red velvet cap, carrying a silver horsewhip in one hand and in the other a child's silver rattle of English manufacture which he shook when he spoke. He offered his guests water in a handsome European chamber pot, then led Clapperton and Houtson by the hand in an African dance, turning up his old withered face to his partners, whisking round on one foot, then marching slowly with solemn gait, evidently very proud to be dancing with white men and delighting the surrounding multitude. When he sneezed all his attendant, clapped their hands and snapped their fingers. Clapperton also noted that he was accompanied everywhere by dogs, animals which were treated in this region with much respect and were provided with coloured collars decorated with cowries. In no other country in Africa that Clapperton had visited were dogs treated with even common humanity.

For much of the time since leaving Badagry, Clapperton had been feeling ill and had had to be carried in a hammock. But, apart from Houtson, his companions were much iller than he. Richard Lander was on occasions delirious, springing out of bed and attacking his master. Dr Morrison, who now looked like a 'walking spectre', was unable to proceed beyond Bachy, and, returning towards the sea with Houtson, died on 31 December. Houtson himself later expired on the coast after an illness of only a few days. George Dawson died at Ega; Captain Pearce, talking distractedly to his mother and answering himself, at Engwa. Dr Dickson's presentiments were soon to be fulfilled. He was to lose his life on his way to Jenna in a quarrel with some natives during which he seems to have lost his hasty temper. By then the mulatto, Columbus, was also dead. Clapperton, having read the funeral service 'in a tremulous voice and agitated manner', left Engwa on 3 January 1826 with the survivors, none of them fully recovered but hoping that a change of air would have a restorative effect.

Beyond Engwa the countryside was beautiful. In the early days of their journey their path had led through the 'thickest woods' Clapperton had ever seen, 'wholly impenetrable by man or beast' except on the track they followed. On approaching Laboo, however, the path had risen over hill and down dale through more open country planted with corn and yams and with finé avenues of trees. By moonlight it appeared 'quite enchanting, being through an avenue of tall majestic trees with fetish houses placed here and there, and solitary lights burning by each'. The scenery continued lovely beyond Assoudo, a walled town of some 10,000 inhabitants which they passed on 5 January. Small villages were perched on the top of hills beneath which in rocky valleys, 'well watered with many fine streams', were fields of cotton and corn and orchards of banana trees. The people were still friendly and generous. At Chiadoo the travellers were escorted out of the town by 'an immense train of men, women and children', the women singing in chorus to the discordant accompaniment of drums, horns and gongs. At Erawa they were provided with fowls and sheep, a goat and a pig. At Cheki they were greeted with 'every demonstration of joy'; and the chief pressed them strongly to stay a day or two longer and asked innumerable questions about England, inquiring in particular, as almost everyone did, how many wives an Englishman had, and laughing uproariously with all his attendants when told but one. At Katunga, where they arrived on 22 January, the crowds of women behind the chief stood up and cheered when their master, wearing a pasteboard and blue-cotton imitation of a European crown, shook their hands and welcomed them to the capital of Yaruba. Throughout their stay at Katunga, so Lander said, the people 'every-where made way for [them] to pass ... and, retreating to a short distance, made a profound obeisance and in some cases even went so far as to prostrate themselves in the dust ... The more respectable parts of the inhabitants used to run up to shake hands with as much cordiality as if they had been acquainted with the visitors since childhood and would very kindly inquire after their health, 'not merely for the sake of having something to say, as is the case in England, but prompted by an interest and concern they could not disguise'.

They remained at Katunga for seven weeks, astonishing the inhabitants with a display of rockets, and receiving regular visits from the chief who always arrived attended by numerous of his women, one of whom carried a chamber pot containing a supply of *goora* nuts, another a carved gourd with a hole into which her master spat when he felt so inclined. On being promised thirty muskets during one of these visits, the chief 'went away dancing, tripped and fell but was soon picked up by his ladies'. They also received regular visits from the chief's principal eunuch, an extremely fat and roguish man through whom all lesser persons had to address their petitions and compliments to the chief while lying prostrate on the ground. The eunuch was frequently drunk, a condition in which Clapperton was never surprised to find him since the man would cheerfully drink two quarts of raw rum before noon and was once seen to swallow upwards of a pint without drawing his breath. He also often cheated the white men of the ample provisions which the chief sent them; and when Clapperton complained about this to the chief the eunuch vehemently denied the charge and the chief took no action against him.

Nor was the chief helpful when Clapperton asked him to set a day for the white men's departure. He made all manner of excuses: the roads were not safe; there were important men coming to Katunga especially to see the white men; there were entertaining performances about to be staged; there were interesting customs to study. Would not Clapperton like a wife? the chief asked him. He was not sure how many wives he had himself, though he was convinced that if they were arranged in a line holding hands they would reach as far as Jenné. He could not offer the white men any of these, as it was death for anyone other than himself to touch them. But his daughters were allowed to take anyone they might choose, either as a husband or a lover.

The days passed and the chief continued to be evasive whenever he was asked when the white men could leave or questioned about the course of the Quarra of which he was, or pretended to be, entirely ignorant. After waiting more than three weeks, Clapperton reminded him that the rains would soon set in: it was essential for the journey to continue. 'Fix a day,' Clapperton begged him. At length the chief said, 'Nine days.'

When this time had elapsed Clapperton reminded the chief of his promise. The chief hesitated and once more gave an evasive answer, this time mentioning the need to provide the white man with a large horse. A small one would do, protested Clapperton. But he could not be provided with a small one either: the chief had only one. Well, could horses be hired? 'What will they say of me,' protested the chief, 'if I allow you to go away in this manner after your king has sent me such good presents?' Exasperated, Clapperton felt that he was no nearer getting away from Katunga than he had been on the day of his arrival. But five days later, on 6 March, the chief came to see him again and at last gave him the permission for which he had waited so long.

Clapperton wasted no time. On the 8th he was at Algi. By the 13th he had crossed the river Moussa, by whose shores the people placed crocodiles' eggs on their huts as a supposed protection against attack, and had reached Kaiama, the principal town in Borgu. Here the chief, having sent him milk, eggs, cheese, curds and bananas, came to visit him accompanied by 'six young female slaves naked as they were born except a strip of narrow white cloth tied round their heads and a string of beads round their waists; each carried a light spear in the right hand'. They danced round their master's horse, singing his praises in loud voices, as he excitedly accepted the presents that were offered him, waving strings of imitation coral beads at his naked girls as much as to say, 'Which of you will get these?' and brandishing a sword above his head as he called out, 'Oh, my white lord! Oh, my white lord!'

This chief, too, attempted to prevent Clapperton's departure, making difficulties over bearers and messengers, protesting that his head men must receive presents as well as himself, then asking if he would take his daughter as a wife. 'I said, "Yes",' Clapperton recorded. 'And I went to the house of the daughter, which consisted of several *coozies* separate from those of the father, and I was shown into a very clean one: a mat was spread: I sat down; and the lady coming in and kneeling down I asked her if she would live in my house or I should come and live with her: she said, whatever way I wished: very well, I said, I would come and live with her, as she had the best house. She kept her kneeling posture all the time I was in the house. I took leave of her, and went home.'

Three days after this, Clapperton was provided with bearers and two horses and allowed to join a Hausa caravan on its way to Wawa. 'Bullocks, asses, horses, women and men to the amount of a thousand, all in a line,' formed a 'very curious sight', Clapperton thought. 'They were a most motley group, from the nearly naked girls ... to the ridiculously and gaudily dressed Gonja traders, riding on horseback.'

'The women with them, as in every other instance that came within the compass of our own observation,' Lander added, 'bore the heaviest burdens and seemed actually sinking to the earth with heat and fatigue without exciting the compassion or obtaining the assistance of the [male] companions of their journey, although several of the latter had little else to do besides keeping pace with the horses.'

117

The long caravan passed slowly across a level plain covered with trees to Wawa where Clapperton had the opportunity of taking another wife, a monstrously fat Arab widow between thirty and forty years old, 'said to be the richest person in Wawa, having the best house in the town and a thousand slaves'. She had set her heart on a white husband and had at first shown a preference for Richard Lander.

She took it into her head to fall desperately in love with me, whose complexion, she affirmed, rivalled her own in whiteness! [Lander recalled] ... And Captain Clapperton who relished a joke with all his heart did his utmost to inflame the lady's passions by passing a thousand compliments on the regularity of my features and the handsomeness of my person. 'See what beautiful eyes he has,' observed the Captain; 'if you were to search from Badagry to Wa Wa you would not find such eyes!' ... For an hour together the widow would gaze intently upon me, while the most amorous glances shot from her large, full, and certainly beautiful eyes, which confused and disconcerted me not a little ... for ... I was [inexperienced with women] and consequently was excessively bashful [in their presence] ... As for my master, he was delighted with these interviews, and with his arms folded on his breast, while thick volumes of tobacco smoke rolled from his pipe, he with the most impenetrable gravity enjoyed the scene and looked as happy and as much at home as if he had been seated by his friends in Scotland. After the widow's departure, it was his usual custom, tapping me on the shoulder, to ask how I felt my heart, and observe what a boast I could make, on our return to England, of so magnificent a conquest.

For several days Lander bore the joke in good part, but then decided that it was no longer a joke but was beginning to wear 'a more serious aspect' than he had anticipated. So he made up his mind to bring it to an end and told the widow bluntly that he would never choose a black wife. But she was a white woman, she protested. Well, then, he could never live in Africa. That was nothing: she would leave it and live with him wherever he wanted. At length he left the room, declaring that he could never love her. Little abashed, she turned her attention to Clapperton, whose curiosity was by now sufficiently aroused for him to visit her house. He found it as large and as full of slaves as he had been told it would be. Its owner was sitting on a carpet on the veranda, chewing nuts and tobacco. On one side of her was a calabash of water with which to rinse out her mouth, on the other a whip. Before her, on the ground, squatted a humpbacked female dwarf, naked except for strings of beads and coral round her neck and waist. Her mistress was also bedecked with coral and with gold and rubies. Her eyebrows and eyelashes were blacked; her hair dyed with indigo, and her hands and feet with henna. 'Around her body she had a fine striped silk and cotton country cloth which came as high as her tremendous breasts.' She invited Clapperton to sit down near her and began to fan him with a piece of stained glass. She sent the humpback to fetch the rest of her jewels which she showed him, assuring him how rich she was. She then took her guest on a tour of her various apartments which were 'cool, clean and ornamented with pewter dishes and bright brass pans'. Her husband had been dead ten years, she said. She loved white men, and would go away with Clapperton. Sending for a looking-glass, she studied her reflection, then handed the glass to Clapperton, remarking that she was a little older than he was but not much, and of what consequence were a few years, anyway. 'This was too much,' Clapperton concluded, 'and I made my retreat as soon as I could, determined never to come to such close quarters with her again.'

This woman, he later learned, augmented her riches by hiring out the more attractive of her female slaves as concubines, a practice which was not considered in the least reprehensible in Wawa where the virtue of chastity, he believed, did not exist. Neither was sobriety held a virtue. He had never, indeed, been in a place in his life where drunkenness was so general. Even the head man's daughter, who used to come to him three or four times a day, 'painted and bedizened in the highest style of Wawa fashion', always arrived half tipsy and departed in tears when Clapperton assured her he had no time to spare for her as he 'prayed and looked at the stars all night'. This seemed most strange to her as the people of Wawa were 'of an easy faith', never praying except when they were sick or wanted something, and cursing their gods indiscriminately at other times. Their Muslim slaves, however, were allowed to worship in their own way. Indeed, the inhabitants of Wawa, 'notwithstanding their want of chastity and drunkenness', were a tolerant, merry, good-natured people. They kept Clapperton awake at night with their inebriated singing outside his hut, with their fiddles, guitars and castanets which they kept on playing until near morning. But they did so with the best intentions and were extremely bountiful with their supplies of food.

On 30 March Clapperton left Wawa and that same day arrived at Bussa where Mungo Park had perished. He found the chief there reluctant to talk of this event, stammering in his replies to Clapperton's questions, and refusing permission for him to visit the spot where Park had died. He knew nothing of Park's papers, he insisted; they 'had gone into the hands of the learned men'; he had been but a little boy when these things had happened. Clapperton asked him if he might inquire of the old people in the town the particulars of the affair, as some of them must have seen it. But the chief 'appeared very uneasy' and did not reply; so Clapperton did not press him further, satisfied at least that the man was otherwise perfectly agreeable. Clapperton was pleased to be asked to stay for breakfast, though when this appeared he wished he had not accepted the invitation, for the meal consisted of dried fish stewed in palm oil, fried alligators' eggs and a large grilled water rat with the skin on.

119

Looking down from the high banks to the waters of the river rushing and foaming past the islands and the jutting rocks, it occurred to Clapperton that 'even if Park and Martin had passed Bussa in safety, they would have been in imminent danger of perishing here, most likely unheard of and unseen'. But, after all the kindness that he himself had received in these parts, it also occurred to him that if Park had not been so ready to fire on natives he had taken to be hostile, he might even so have survived. For the Kambari people who inhabited the riverside villages around Bussa and Wawa seemed, unless provoked, incapable of harming anyone. 'They are apparently a mild ... lazy people,' Clapperton wrote of them; 'in general tall; more stupid-looking than wild ... They go with very little clothing, seldom anything more than a skin round the waist, the young people of both sexes [being] entirely naked until they have cohabited ... The men employ their time in hunting, fishing and sleeping, the most laborious work falling on the women ... They plant a little corn and yams, and keep a few sheep and goats ... They are pagans; and on their temples [are] piled the heads of the hippopotamus and the alligator ... and figures of human beings as well as depictions of alligators, boas and tortoises.'

The rains had come by now and for much of the time Clapperton felt ill; but by eating little and spending the nights in straw huts which, by shutting up as closely as possible, he made as hot as a steam bath, he managed to lower his fever. On his arrival at the walled market town of Koolfu on 2 May, however, both he and Lander grew worse and were obliged to remain there for over a fortnight. They lodged with an old widow who kept a kind of inn where the customers were provided with *booza*, an intoxicating distillation of corn, honey, chillies and the root of a coarse grass on which the cattle fed. Pagan and Muslim alike drank this beverage and agreed 'very well together in their cups', singing extempore songs to the accompaniment of drums, harps and Arabian guitars.

From his bed of sickness, Clapperton watched the activities of the household, the men washing themselves from head to foot on getting up, the women cleaning the house first, then washing themselves as thoroughly as the men in water in which had been boiled the leaf of a bush called *bambarnia*. At breakfast the women and children ate separately from the men, for although 'the greatest man or woman in the country [was] not ashamed at times to let their slaves eat out of the same dish, a woman [was] never allowed to eat with a man'. After breakfast the women and children rubbed themselves with a paste made from the red wood of Benin pounded to a powder and mixed with grease. This lightened the darkness of their black skins. They then put a thick paste on their faces, blackened their eyes with kohl, stained their teeth and the inside of their lips yellow, the outer lip and the eyebrows blue.

The younger women, thus embellished, went off to market, while their mothers stayed at home to spin cotton or to cook; and the children went to fetch water or to go round the town, selling rice balls and fried beans. The men strolled about gossiping, or sat in the shade at the doors of their houses, while the slaves went off to work in the fields or to cut wood.

About noon they return home [Clapperton recorded] when all have a mess of the pudding called *waki*, or boiled beans, and about two or three in the afternoon they return to their different employments, on which they remain until near sunset, when they count their gains to their master or mistress. They then have a meal of pudding and a little fat or stew. The mistress of the house, when she goes to rest, has her feet put into a cold poultice of pounded henna leaves. The young then go to dance and play, if it is moonlight, and the old to lounge and converse in the open square of the house, or in the outer *coozie*, where they remain until the cool of the night.

Clapperton found the people of the town 'of a naturally good disposition', though they seemed incapable of telling the truth, and when detected in a lie, merely laughed, considering it not the smallest disgrace. The men were mostly heavy drinkers, the women 'generally of easy virtue'. They were also 'great cheats'. But although they had an idea that he was possessed of inexhaustible riches, he never had a single article stolen. On the contrary, he was treated with the most perfect respect and civility.

When he left the town all the principal inhabitants accompanied him to the next village where he was introduced to the head man who provided him with a good house, presented him with a sheep and some cooked meat, and spared him the heavy duties – as high as five hundred cowries for a loaded bullock – which were imposed upon the merchants whose caravans he had joined. Being a white man and no commercial traveller, he was allowed to pass through free, having given presents such as scissors and silks in exchange for meat, rice and honey.

On 28 June he reached Wamba, having for the past five days travelled through 'a rich and beautiful valley and over woody hills'. Whenever the caravan had stopped, the encampment had soon been filled with women selling raw goat's flesh, boiled beans, millet and pudding, every two or three of them accompanied by an armed man to see fair play. They were 'a fine, active, clean-looking people: most of the men had a bastard kind of greyhound following them, whose necks were ornamented with colours and strings of cowries'.

Most days were dull and cloudy and often wet; and Lander fell seriously ill again. He lagged behind the others; and, dismounting from his horse, rolled upon the earth in the hope of relieving the agonizing pain in his limbs. When his absence was noted, Clapperton had large fires lit and by the smoke of these Lander was led to the rest of the party. On reaching his tent he threw himself down groaning upon his mat. Whenever the travellers reached a stream which was too deep for him to ford and across which he was too weak to swim, Clapperton, much taller than he, lifted him on to his shoulders and carried him 'often at the imminent risk of his own life'.

The countryside continued beautiful and, within four or five miles of Zania, became altogether clear of wood. The pastureland was now richly planted with rice and millet; and herds of splendid cattle fed in the valleys. Zania itself, recognized 'by its tall trees, like a long avenue of gigantic poplars, running across the horizon, from north to south', was a town of some 50,000 people, mostly Fulani. The head man here told Clapperton that he would have to wait for three days for the return of a messenger who had been sent to Kano to warn the chief of his imminent arrival. Clapperton accepted this decision patiently, for the head man was 'a very good fellow', though in great distress over some private misfortune which he hinted at but was reluctant to discuss. On the third day the poor man's secret came out: he was unable to make love adequately to his many wives. Clapperton thought it 'too serious a matter, and lay too near the man's heart', for him to say he had no medicine for such a complaint. So he 'gave him a box of Seidlitz powders, the effervescence of which surprised him very much. He was made perfectly happy, and fully believed in their virtue.'

Clapperton himself was now feeling extremely unwell again, and during a storm on 27 July on his way from Kano to Sokoto he scarcely had the strength to remain on his horse until his weakness was slightly relieved by vomiting. Soaked to the skin yet with a burning thirst, he looked about for a place to lie down, but all he could see was swamp with not a vestige of dry land anywhere. So he was forced to struggle on to Jaza in the province of Katsina where he had to be helped off his horse. Never possessed at the best of times with 'a sweet and passive temper', as he readily admitted, he was always worse when ill; and he lost his temper with the head man of Jaza who 'made a great many difficulties' and he shouted at him 'in all the Haussa language' he possessed. But it was all to no purpose. 'These Kashna bears are rude,' he decided, delivering himself of a harsher verdict than he had felt himself called upon to give elsewhere on his journey, 'though they pride themselves on being the most polite and the best in Haussa, calling all the rest infidels ... I suffered severely during the night with ague and cramp.'

His temper was not improved when he was told the next day that the roads ahead were impassable and that he would have to return to Kano and wait until after the rains before proceeding to Sokoto. August and September had accordingly to be spent in Kano but, as he lost his journal for these months, nothing is known of his sojourn there.

The diary continues on 11 October when Clapperton and Lander began their travels again, taking with them a great quantity of presents with which they had equipped themselves, including, as well as the usual umbrellas, silks, cloves, fowling-pieces, pistols, swords, knives and rockets, a silver-mounted message cane, a ream of English foolscap paper and two bundles of black lead pencils, coloured prints of the Royal Family, a dozen pairs of white cotton gloves, two watches, a pen, a dressing-case, a magnifying glass, two trunks, numerous medicines, the New Testament, the Koran and Euclid's *Elements* in Arabic, a history of the Tartars and the Psalms of David. At Sokoto, Clapperton had several conversations with the chief who, on one occasion, having discussed the white man's taste for pork and the eating of dogs by the people of Fezzan, said it was strange what food people would eat. In the district of Umburm, for instance, they ate human flesh. When Clapperton expressed his doubt that any people existed on the face of the earth who ate their own kind as food, the chief replied that he had himself seen men from Jacoba eat parts of a Tuareg who had been hanged for theft. 'Whenever a person complained of sickness amongst these men,' the chief added, 'even though only a slight head-ache, they are killed instantly, for fear they should be lost by death, as they will not eat a person that has died of sickness ... When they went to war, the dead and wounded were always eaten, the hearts being claimed by the head man. When asked why they eat human flesh, they said it was better than any other; that the heart and breasts of a woman were the best part.'

The ruler of Jacoba later told Lander that all this was quite true: after a battle his people returned to the field 'and bearing off a great number of dead bodies, roasted them before large fires, kindled for the purpose, and devoured them without yams, corn or, indeed, any other provisions!'

Lander, who had been left behind at Kano because he had been too ill with dysentery to travel, joined Clapperton at Sokoto on 21 December, bringing Pasko with him. Twice Pasko had run off, taking various valuables with him, and on each occasion he had been forgiven. A third robbery could not, how-ever, be condoned and he was dismissed from Clapperton's service. But the wily old fellow soon set himself up as a snuff merchant, then added to the ever-growing number of his wives an extremely ugly, bearded woman who was acknowledged to be one of the best cooks in Sokoto. His former masters acknowledged they were better off without him; but they missed his company, for he was endlessly amusing and a wonderful source of improbable anecdote. They found each other's company pleasant enough, however; and in the evenings, when Clapperton returned from his shooting expeditions, they would talk for hours over their cigars, the only luxury which they had left, telling each other about their homes and families, laughing at 'jests which had been laughed at a thousand times before'. Sometimes they would read aloud to each other or sing songs, or Lander would play tunes on his bugle-horn, 'Sweet,

Sweet Home' being a favourite. 'Anything that reminded my master of his native Scotland was always heard with interest and emotion,' Lander wrote. 'The little poem, "My Native Highland home", I have sung scores of times to him, as he sat with his arms folded on his breast opposite to me in our dwelling.' But on 12 March, 'all thought of further enjoyment ceased' with the sudden illness of Lander's 'dear, kind master' who was attacked with dysentery on that day.

Lander, though ill himself, nursed him tenderly, fanning him for hours on end in the appalling heat, reading to him from the Bible, feeding him fowl soup and milk and water, the only sustenance he could swallow. For a time Lander borrowed a female slave to help him, but she ran away and, having no one else to turn to, he sent for Pasko who fell upon his knees by his master's side, begging for forgiveness. Clapperton slept but little and, when he did, he had frightful dreams in which he called out in Arabic. In his waking hours he spoke constantly of his home and his friends, and, when he felt himself to be dying, he struggled to give Lander instructions as to how to get home and to deal with his papers, fainting several times while speaking. 'He said, "My dear boy I will tell you what to do," ' Lander reported in a letter. ' "Take great care of my journals and when you arrive in London go to my agents and tell them to send directly for my uncul and tell him it was my wish that he would go with me to the colonoal office and delever the journals ... My little money, my close and evrything i have belongs to you ... Writ down the names of the towns you go throw and all purticulars ... Bear yourself up under all your troubles like a man and an english man, do not be affraid and no one will hurt you." ' In the fifth week of his illness he rallied for a while. He ate some guinea fowl and asked Lander to shave off the long, full beard which had 'excited the envy and admiration of the Arabs'. Two days later, however, Lander was greatly alarmed to hear a peculiar rattling noise issuing from his master's throat and a low, hurried cry of 'Richard!' He rushed to the bed in which Clapperton was sitting bolt upright, staring wildly about him. He took him in his arms and felt the violent beating of his heart. Clapperton tried to speak and died.

Lander held his master in his arms for some time, overwhelmed with grief. Later he washed the body and sent a messenger to ask the chief where the burial could take place and if it might be conducted in accordance with the manner of the dead man's country. The chief granted his permission and sent four slaves to dig a grave five miles south-east of the city. Lander took the body there on a camel's back, covered with the British flag. In tears he read the funeral service from his prayer book, the slaves quarrelling with each other the whole time.

Lander now faced with gloomy apprehension the long journey home by himself. He would have preferred to go south to the coast at Badagry rather than north across the desert with the Arabs whom he detested. But Clapperton had advised him to go to Fezzan and the chief said it would be quite impossible for him to travel by the southerly route. So, on 4 May, he and Pasko joined an immense caravan of about four thousand people, merchants, slaves and pilgrims bound for Mecca, and set out across that wild uncultivated tract of ground known as the Gobir Bush. The heat and dust were insufferable; Lander's horse was soon exhausted; and he felt obliged to dismount and rest under a tree, sending Pasko ahead after the camels to fetch water to quench his parching thirst. As the Fulani and Tuaregs rode past him he begged them for water, but they passed him by, saying to each other, 'He is a Kaffir! Let him die!' At length a young Fulani took pity on him and offered him a calabash. He gratefully drank some of the water, sprinkled some drops into his horse's mouth and, much refreshed, rode on. But soon he was in as bad a condition as before: his legs and feet swelled so much that his boots split and fell off, and he 'experienced the most acute pain in every part of his body'. After an hour or so he came upon Pasko sitting contentedly with a camel driver under a tree, drinking from a calabash, Lander's provision bucket lying open before him. Losing his temper, Lander pulled a pistol from his belt and was on the point of shooting the dreadful man when he pulled himself together, replaced the pistol and demanded an explanation of the man's conduct. 'The old fellow answered with his usual demoniacal grin, and as composedly as if nothing was the matter, said, "I was tired."'

At Kano an Arab who owed Lander for some of Clapperton's possessions which had been sold to him, refused to part with the money, giving him instead a female slave and various goods to sell on his journey. Lander was not altogether displeased by this arrangement, for his lack of money made it impossible for him to travel north with the disagreeable members of the caravan. His camels were weakened and diseased, and he could afford neither to buy more nor to purchase presents for the chiefs of the towns on the road to Fezzan. So he decided to turn south towards Fundah on the banks of the Niger and, if possible, trace the course of the river to Benin.

By the end of the first week of June he had reached Fullindishie where the people, perfectly naked, laughed immoderately at the sight of him, while he in turn laughed at them. Their 'locks were bedecked with huge lumps of red clay and grass – their bodies shone with clammy unction, anything but agreeable to the eye or pleasant to the smell – a messy piece of blue glass hung from a hole in the upper lip – and from the lobe of the ear dangled a misshapen fragment of red wood'. 'Their features', Lander continued, 'do not resemble, in the slightest degree, those of the Negro, but are fine, regular and handsome, bearing a striking similitude to the European ... Yet, with all their pretensions to superiority over their neighbours in personal appearance, they yield to them in cleanliness and decency; for ... the Bowchee people are filthy in their habits, and disgusting in their manners ... A most intolerable odour is exhaled from all their dwellings. They ... appear to have no affection for their offspring ... and they sell their children as slaves to the greatest strangers in the world, with no greater remorse of conscience than if they had been common articles of merchandise.'

At Katab, too, he found 'a considerable traffic' in slaves who were exposed for sale in a daily market next to bullocks and sheep. Lander was given a sheep by the local chief, as well as parts of two bullocks and stewed rice 'sufficient to satisfy the appetites of at least fifty men', in exchange for some damask, prints of King George IV and of his brother, the Duke of York. The chief's wives expressed the 'most rapturous delight' at the look of the gilt buttons on the white man's jacket; so he obligingly cut them off and presented them to the women who accepted them with shouts of laughter, stuck them in their ears and danced away.

At Dunrora, however, the chief, who considered himself a much more important ruler than his neighbour at Cuttup, returned Lander's presents of scissors and needles with a contemptuous message to the effect that they might come in handy for a less exalted man but were certainly of no interest to himself. Here at Dunrora, Lander's journey was brought abruptly to a halt by four armed men who galloped up to him, their horses covered with foam, and ordered him peremptorily to return immediately with them to Zaria where the chief was deeply offended that he had passed through his capital without paying his respects to him. After seventeen days' perilous travelling from Kano, with 'a fair prospect', as he put it, 'of reaching the celebrated Fundah in twelve or thirteen more', Lander felt inclined to resist the horsemen's demands, but they were backed by the chief of Cuttup, whom he had offended by his meagre presents, and by a thousand of his men armed with bows and arrows. So, with bitter disappointment, Lander felt obliged to submit and to go back with his escort to Zaria.

He arrived there on 22 July when further presents with the chief were exchanged. Those given to Lander included 'a really pleasing female slave named Aboudah for a wife'. 'I was almost frightened to death at the very sound of wife,' Lander confessed, 'yet I accepted her with the best grace I could assume, not only to avoid offending [the chief] ... but also that I might at least have the satisfaction of giving the poor creature her freedom if I ever reached the sea-coast.' Having been deserted by one of his servants, and 'convinced that no dependance whatever could be placed on the fidelity of hired domestics', he added another woman to his party by buying a slave named Jowdie for seven dollars in the market. With these two women to attend upon him, he left Zaria on 24 July, making not for Fundah, as he had nothing good enough left now to give its ruler, but for Badagry by the more familiar route through Koolfu, Wawa, Kaiama and Katunga. For much of the time the rain fell in torrents but the people were friendly, provisions plentiful and Aboudah delightful. When Lander was tired she used to bathe his temples with the juice of limes, wash his feet and either sing or fan him to sleep.

There threatened to be trouble at Kaiama where the masterful ruler – who required all his women to walk about naked while men wore clothing as a token of their superiority – asked him how he dared to enter his territory without previous notice of his approach and demanded that he instantly return an hour and a half's journey before sending on a messenger. Lander was in the act of complying with this request when the chief bawled after him, 'I forgive you this time, Christian, but never be so remiss again.' There was trouble, too, at Mossa where the immensely fat chief refused to supply Lander's party with food on the grounds that there was none to be had and he himself was starving to death; and it was not until Pasko was grudgingly granted permission to cut grass in the chief's garden for the horses, and discovered an enormous pile of yams concealed there, that their hunger was satisfied.

At most places, though, they were greeted with pleasure, treated with kindness and bidden farewell with noisy regret, in some places the people's cries being so loud that Lander's horse trembled with fear. At Katunga, where he remained a month, 'experiencing every species of friendship and good nature from its inhabitants' who prostrated themselves before him as a sign of their respect, the head man asked him to remain as chief minister and, as an inducement, offered him four of his daughters as wives. As Lander felt it impolite to resist the chief's pressing solicitations, he pointed out four of the prettiest princesses, who stood before him giggling, and declared that as they were the 'most lovely of their sex', they were certainly worthy to share the bed and fortune of a prime minister. As soon as he could, therefore, he would return to marry them and to take up his appointment.

They were by now nearly at the end of their journey. On 11 November they reached Jenna where they found Dr Morrison's grave in perfect condition; and soon afterwards they heard of the death of Mungo Park's son, Thomas, who had come out to discover the place where his father had died and the manner of his death and who, eating unreservedly the food of the natives, adopting their customs, even to the anointment of his head and body with clay and oil, and exposing himself, with scarcely any clothing, to the heat of the sun, had soon contracted a fatal fever.

At Badagry, Lander found the slave trade rather less active owing to the vigilance of British men-of-war off the coast. But this was scarcely a comfort to the many thousands of slaves kept prisoner in the five large factories there.

For when no buyers could be found in the overstocked markets, the expense of maintaining them was reduced by the simple expedient of pinioning together the weaker and less healthy amongst them and throwing them into the river. As an Englishman, Lander was heartily disliked by the Portuguese who now mainly conducted the slave trade; and, by their machinations, he found it impossible to persuade anyone to take a message by canoe to his fellow countrymen at Cape Coast Castle, informing them of his arrival at Badagry.

Lander's enforced two-months' sojourn at Badagry was beset with unpleasant incidents. During the early days, two of the chief's wives had their throats cut outside his house for 'having spoken their mind with too much frankness'. The next morning Lander found their bodies hanging from the branches of a fetish tree. Later, while walking through the forest along the coast in an attempt to secure a passage in a ship which was reported to be anchored off Adjeedore and which turned out to be manned by Portuguese and Brazilian pirates, he came across a much larger and infinitely more horrifying fetish tree. For some time before reaching the clearing where it stood he had been sickened by a poisonous smell which, becoming ever more overpowering, obliged him to cover his mouth and nose with a thick handkerchief. As he came within sight of it thousands of screaming vultures rose, flapping their wings as the branches, released of their weight, rose and waved sluggishly. On these branches were hung putrefying fragments of human bodies, arms, legs, trunks, heads, upon which the vultures, scared away by the intruders, now swooped down again to continue their interrupted meal. Around the base of the tree, the largest Lander had ever seen, were irregular heaps of skulls, the accumulation of many years of human sacrifice. Overcome with horror, Lander fainted and was carried away from the frightful scene by Pasko and his slave.

Lander related how these human sacrifices to the Badagryan gods were performed. Criminals, prisoners of war and unpurchased slaves were beheaded from time to time in the fetish hut and their blood collected in calabashes. Their hearts were cut out and offered to the chief and his women who made incisions in them with their teeth while the chiefs and officials within the hut chanted in chorus. The bodies, heads and calabashes of blood were then paraded through the town among the chanting people to whom were also displayed the hearts upon the points of long spears. Some of the people bit the hearts and drank the blood. Finally the hearts were thrown to the dogs and the other parts of the body, further mutilated, were attached to the fetish tree.

Lander himself came near to death in the fetish house. It had long been the custom at Badagry for those suspected of crimes to be taken there and, surrounded by rows of skulls and bones, to be required to drink from a vessel of poisoned water. If they died their guilt was proved; their innocence was established by the improbable event of their survival. Lander, accused by the Portuguese of plotting against the chief, was commanded one morning to attend at the fetish house to answer the charges.

'You are accused, white man,' one of the priests cried out in a loud voice, 'of designs against our chief and his government, and are therefore desired to drink the contents of this vessel, which, if the reports are true, will surely destroy you; whereas, if they be without foundation, you need not fear, Christian; the fetish will do you no injury, for our gods will do that which is right.'

Lander, so he says, took the bowl in trembling hands, offered a prayer to his Christian God while the priests and elders watched him silently, then put the clear liquid to his lips and drank it all. It tasted disagreeably bitter and made him feel slightly dizzy, but to the evident surprise of the spectators and the delight of his slaves, he managed to walk back to his hut where he took a strong emetic, and thus vomited the poison from his stomach. 'The dreadful charm, having been thus providentially broken,' he wrote, 'all the cold reserve and stiffness of [the chief and his counsellors] suddenly disappeared; and they visited me voluntarily a few days afterwards with presents of provisions, observing frequently that the Portuguese were wicked men, but that I was a good man.'

He had not long to wait now for his deliverance. One morning a man came running breathlessly towards him with a letter and a bottle of gin addressed to 'The Englishman at Badagry'. They came from the master of a British vessel then lying off the town. Within a few hours, beside himself with joy, he was being welcomed aboard Captain Laing's brig, the *Maria*, with 'three tremendous cheers from the throats of British seamen'.

At Cape Coast, he gave his faithful slaves, including the loving Aboudah and Jowdie, their freedom, a state which they were most unwilling to accept, crying and covering their heads with sand and dust as they begged him to take them with him, and recovering their composure only when the governor, Colonel Lumley, generously gave them all some money and a plot of ground, and Lander assured them that he would one day soon return. Pasko travelled with him to Portsmouth aboard the sloop, the *Esk*, and then returned to his wife at Cape Coast Castle but not until, 'after much entreaty', he had been given permission 'to pay his addresses also to Aboudah'. Lander reported to the Colonial Office and, having remained in London for three or four weeks and prepared a copy of his journal, he returned to his friends in Truro after an absence of almost thirteen years.

5

THE MOUTH OF
THE GREAT WATER

Home in Truro, Richard Lander accepted an appointment in the Excise Department, and, upon the salary he received and a modest annuity of £80 which had been intended for the dead mulatto, Columbus, he married and soon afterwards his wife gave birth to a daughter. But the tedious work entailed his spending much time in the cold open air, and since this aggravated his already poor health he applied for a different post. He was given one as a weighing-porter; but this, too, was 'much exposed to the weather' and brought him no more than £50 a year. His dissatisfaction with his life was brought to an end in 1829, however, when John Barrow, the first chairman of the Geographical Society with which the African Association was merged, recommended him to the Colonial Office as 'the fittest person' to send to Africa to settle once and for all the problem of the Niger. Barrow had been asked to advise on the plans of two other young men who had proposed them-

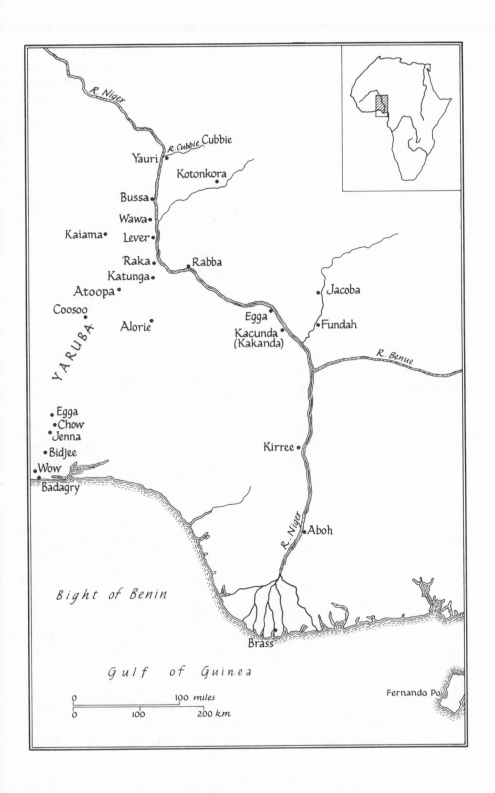

R. Niger

R. Cubbie Cubbie

Yauri•

Kotonkora•

Bussa•

Wawa•

Kaiama• Lever•

Raka• Rabba•

Katunga•

Atoopa•

Coosoo• Jacoba•

Alorie• Egga•

Kacunda• Fundah•
(Kakanda)

R. Benue

Y A R U B A

•Egga
•Chow
•Jenna

•Bidjee

•Wow

Badagry

Kirree•

R. Niger

•Aboh

Bight of Benin

Brass

Gulf of Guinea

Fernando Po

0   100 miles
0   100   200 km

selves as explorers to the Colonial Office. He had not liked these plans – which were nevertheless carried out independently by the two inexperienced adventurers, both of whom died at the outset of their journeys – and had recommended Lander instead. 'No one in my opinion would make their way so well and, with a bundle of beads and bafts and other trinkets, we could land him somewhere about Bonny and let him find his way.'

The idea of employing Lander recommended itself to the Colonial Office not only because of his previous experience but also because he did not ask for much money. He required no more than £100 for his wife while he was away and an annuity of £100 for himself upon his return. His only other request was that his brother John should go with him.

John Lander was then twenty-two, three years younger than Richard. He had stayed at school longer and had been apprenticed as a compositor in the offices of the *Royal Cornwall Gazette*. He was of a more studious and reflective turn of mind than Richard, less adventurous and less humorous.

But, as was to be seen, he had the same courage, perseverance and resilience. He also had a gift for writing and, no doubt, saw in the proposed expedition an opportunity to exercise his talents. Since he required no remuneration, the Colonial Office raised no objection to his accompanying his brother and provided them with personal stores to the value of £96 and presents worth about £260. The stores included a tent, mattresses, sheets, blankets, cooking equipment, a limited amount of foodstuffs, mostly tinned soup, and various medicines, including opium, carbonate of soda, calomel, Epsom salts, Seidlitz powders, tartar emetic, citric acid and eight ounces of blue laxative pills. Among the presents were fifty yards of cloth, fifty razors, a hundred combs, a hundred Dutch pipes, 110 mirrors, 50,000 needles and two silver medals.

The Landers left Portsmouth on 9 January 1830 and their ship, the *Clinker*, dropped anchor in the roadstead opposite Badagry on 19 March 1830. Three days later they climbed down into a canoe which was waiting at the edge of the breakers and were paddled over a tremendous surf to be 'flung with violence on the burning sands'. Beyond the beach were the neat bamboo huts of the little town outside whose doorways were earthen pots which, baited with palm nut, were used in fishing; and beyond the leaf-thatched roofs of the huts could be seen fields of yam and Indian corn, orange and lime trees, coconuts, plantains and bananas. Bullocks, sheep, goats and poultry all seemed plentiful. The people by the shore were perfectly friendly. At the approach of the white men they could not restrain their laughter at their strange clothes, their immense straw hats, long scarlet Muslim gowns and baggy Turkish trousers; but in the town the groups of men selling provisions and cloth beneath the spreading branches of the trees rose to their feet and bowed or sank to their knees respectfully. The brothers found the chief, Adele, sitting in his hut surrounded by a great quantity of muskets and swords hanging on the bamboo walls together with 'a few paltry umbrellas and a couple of horse tails' which were used as fly whisks. Compared with his people, Adele appeared very reserved. He was evidently in deep thought, his head in his hand. He glanced up but said nothing, languidly accepted the offered handshake with a pressure of the fingers so soft as to be scarcely perceptible. An ancient adviser squatted at his feet, smoking a pipe of extraordinary length. His eldest son and heir apparent knelt at his side. In response to a polite inquiry as to the state of his health he smiled with weary resignation, then relapsed into his former thoughtfulness. Nor did the presents, which were displayed upon the floor, arouse the least flicker of interest. They were briefly and un-enthusiastically inspected before being carried off by servants as silent as their master. Soon afterwards Adele, without apology or explanation, abruptly left the room.

When he returned he was puffing at a pipe which emitted such dense clouds of smoke that his melancholy countenance was almost concealed from view. He seemed as discontented as ever but he was at least prepared to explain his gloomy mood. He was, he said in a very low tone of voice, recovering from a severe illness and from a variety of misfortunes. He had lost his most able generals who had either been killed in battle or had perished by some other violent means. One of them had been captured; his right hand had been nailed to his head while his left had been lopped off at the wrist. In this state he had been paraded about among his captors who, their curiosity being satisfied, had watched as the head was severed from his shoulders then placed in the sun to dry before being dispatched back to Badagry. To add to his calamities, Adele's house which contained an immense quantity of gun-powder had caught fire and been blown up together with all his possessions including the valuable presents he had received from Captain Clapperton and from other Europeans, traders and dealers in slaves. The inhabitants of the town had flocked towards the sound of the explosion and many of them had been shot in the legs and other parts of the body by the loaded muskets which had discharged their shot in all directions. The fire had spread and des-troyed a large part of the town.

For the next week the Landers' life at Badagry was as dreary as Adele's account of his misfortunes. Their quarters were constantly besieged by visitors who styled themselves the 'principal men' of the kingdom and who came for no other purpose than the consumption of large quantities of rum. Among these frequent visitors were two mulattos, one named Hooper who acted as Adele's interpreter and confidant, the other a slave who could write English tolerably well. Both of them were confirmed drunkards, Hooper 'always getting intoxicated before breakfast, and remaining in a soaking state all day long'. They pestered the travellers for liquor and presents, advising them at the same time to be equally generous to Badagry's 'noblemen and gentlemen'. One of these, 'a great bully', dissatisfied with what he had received, begged everything he saw and, when gratified to the Landers' best ability, became very abusive and noisy, his huge, round face inflamed with anger and rum as he accused them of lying when they explained the purpose of their mission. It was not long before John Lander conceived a deep aversion not only to these self-styled principal men but to all the black figures that surrounded him, the 'old fat-headed and pot-bellied men, and skinny, flap-eared women' whose importunity was 'really disgusting'.

Adele was quite as importunate as his subjects. He declared that one of the presents with which he had at first appeared highly satisfied – a naval surgeon's coat, admittedly old-fashioned but in good condition and made showy with the addition of a pair of gold epaulettes – was wholly unacceptable: it was intended for a boy not a man; its offer was an insult. He came in person to examine the white men's boxes, to ensure that they did not contain finer presents reserved for other chiefs. Dressed in an English linen shirt, a Spanish cloak and a turban, he was borne in a hammock to the Landers' hut attended by three little boys, one carrying a long sword, another a pistol, the third a bag of tobacco. He accepted several glasses of brandy which the boys were required to taste before passing it on to him, then smoked his pipe with infinite complacency as the contents of the boxes were shown to him, handling everything that caught his fancy and giving those items he intended to keep to his little minions who secured them between their knees. He went away with numerous items including a roll of fine scarlet cloth and two children's farthing whistles with which, he said, he could amuse himself in his retirement. Yet he was still not satisfied. A few days later the Landers were summoned to his presence, informed with a gracious smile that the road inland was still unsafe, an excuse they knew to be unfounded, then asked to write down a list of a few things Adele would require to be sent over from England in return for his protection. Among other articles enumerated were 'four regimental coats, such as are worn by the King of England, for himself, and forty less spendid than these, for the use of his captains; two long brass guns to run on swivels; fifty muskets; twenty barrels of gunpowder; four handsome swords and forty cutlasses ... two puncheons of rum, a carpenter's chest of tools, with oils, paints and brushes' – Adele interjected here that he was himself a carpenter and painter as well as a blacksmith, and indeed had the skills of every trade except those of a tailor – 'a half-dozen rockets and a rocket gun with a soldier capable of undertaking the management of it'. The Landers asked sardonically if that would be all. The chief pondered the question for a few moments while strings of bells tied to the tails of cats tinkled in the quiet air, then, having discussed the matter with his attendants, replied that he had forgotten to mention the want of a large umbrella, four casks of grape-shot and a barrel of flints. He later remembered his need of a gunboat with a hundred men from England and a few tobacco pipes. Declining to part with any more tobacco pipes for fear lest they would have nothing left to give other chiefs during their journey, the Landers agreed to issue a futile order for the remaining items on Adele's list. In exchange for this they were given leave to proceed from 'the abominable place of Badagry' where, so they had been informed, a sacrifice of no less than three hundred human beings, of both sexes and all ages, was shortly to take place.

They were accompanied by a messenger from Jenné; by the little old Hausa, Pasko; by one of Pasko's numerous wives; by Jowdie, the former slave who had been employed on the last mission; two Bornu men, Ibrahim and Mina, who were 'well acquainted with English manners' and could act as interpreters; 'a young man of colour named Antonio, son to the chief of Bonny, who eagerly embraced the opportunity of proceeding to the interior'; and twenty of Adele's men to carry the baggage.

They left on a clear, moonlit night and were punted upstream in Adele's war canoe which the chief had been prevailed upon to lend them. From the banks came the hoarse croaking of frogs and the voices of invisible priests who replied to the greetings of the canoe-men in the same sepulchral tones in which they were addressed. As the darkness lifted the Landers saw that marine plants almost covered the surface of the narrowing river from whose banks evil-smelling marsh miasmas rose like thick clouds. Then the river widened again into a clear stream full of crocodiles, hippopotami and wild ducks and shaded by a canopy of trees in which parrots and monkeys chattered ceaselessly.

The travellers landed at Wow where most of the people, never having seen a white man before, rushed down from the market to meet them and to conduct them to the chief whose attendants appeared to the sound of a horn, bearing large silk umbrellas. They were welcomed with kindness as well as curiosity and liberally regaled with water from a calabash. But since the 'regulations of the fetish' permitted neither a white man nor a horse to sleep in the town, the party had to move on again, through heavy rain and 'a most melancholy-looking forest', to a village where the Landers were shown into a hut, one end of which was occupied by goats and the whole decorated with strings of rattling human bones, written charms, sheepskins and bows and arrows. After a night plagued by mosquitoes and ants they moved on to Bidjee where, so John Lander recorded, 'the natives testified the wild delight they felt at our visit by clapping of hands and loud bursts of laughter. The chief shook hands with us in great good humour.' He was surrounded by women the skin of whose foreheads was raised up in little lumps like marbles, whose cheeks were scarred and similarly deformed and the lobes of whose ears were pierced with big holes plugged with ivory and wooden ornaments. At Jenna as at Bidjee the travellers were immediately upon their arrival surrounded by immense crowds of pushing, inquisitive, smelly, noisy, friendly people, 'an amphitheatre of black woolly heads and teeth set in jetty faces'. The chief was in the 'prevailing finery' of crimson velvet gown and cap, both edged with gold lace. 'At his right hand sat his wives and women. The women sang the praises of their master in a loud unpleasant voice, in which they were assisted by the music of drums, fifes, clarionets and horns.'

As their journey continued the Landers were treated with increasing interest, respect and kindness. At Chow the head man, who was violently agitated when Richard Lander entertained him with a tune on his bugle-horn which he took for some sort of snake, seemed to regard them as demi-gods rather than men and presented them with lavish provisions including highly prized *goora* nuts. At Coosoo the chief plied them with milk, bananas, a basket of *caffas*, a 'vast quantity of yams' and a fat goat. At Acboro they were sent a sucking-pig with a message from the chief: 'White men do nothing but good, and I will pray that God may bless you, and send more of your countrymen to Yaruba.' There were certain unfriendly places. At one they were sent nothing but stale eggs; at another, where John Lander fell seriously ill with fever, the people 'made a hideous noise by singing and drumming in celebration of their fetish' and could not be persuaded to desist. Yet for most of the way the brothers had little to complain of apart from the utter lack of peace or quiet, the perpetual bleating of sheep and goats, the constant fluttering of pigeons, the barking of numerous half-starved dogs, 'the incessant chatter of women's tongues, to say nothing of the exertions of horrid bands of native musicians'.

From Coosoo the path led through a delightful country and past many small towns composed of clay huts with thatched roofs and floors of mud and cow-dung. These towns were very dirty, yet the sheep, as indulged as ladies' lap-dogs in England, were washed thoroughly every morning and followed their owners about with the utmost faithfulness in all their peregrinations. There was no lack of food. Crops grew plentifully; and the rivers abounded in fish and in hippopotami whose flesh when young was eaten with relish. There were distressing sights: naked boys were encountered on the march towards the slave markets at Badagry; yet these young slaves seemed as unconcerned by their fate as the women who walked beside them bearing on their heads burdens that looked as though they would have exhausted a mule, and little wooden figures of children who had died.

136

Six weeks after leaving Badagry the Landers came within sight of Katunga. It was 13 May, a cooler day than the Landers had known since landing from the *Clinker*, with the thermometer standing at 71°, a temperature which made the natives clutch their blue and white cotton dresses over their shivering limbs. The white men's own clothes were much travel-stained by this time; and King Majotu of Katunga, his wives and eunuchs and subjects of all sorts laughed so long and so heartily at them, 'with such good will, and such power of lungs', that their guests felt constrained to join in the general merriment. Majotu himself was extremely expensively if rather eccentrically dressed in a patchwork gown of green and crimson silk and velvet, English cotton stockings and a hat like a bishop's mitre ornamented with strings of coral and tied under the chin to prevent it being blown off. Having recovered from their mirth the eunuchs prostrated themselves before the king, rubbing their faces in the ground which they kissed 'fervently and repeatedly', and then sat down before him, their lips and faces stained with the damp, red soil.

After some conversation his guests were given a kid, a calabash of *caffas* and two thousand cowries, then conducted to a hut which had been repaired and cleaned for them. Majotu himself soon visited the hut and, looking about, expressed great admiration for the bugle-horn which was accordingly presented to him to his obvious delight.

Warned by an enormously fat and influential eunuch named Ebo, whom he had met on his previous visits to Katunga, not to mention to the king the real purpose of his mission for fear lest suspicions were aroused, Richard Lander let it be known that he had come to Katunga on his way to Yauri where the head man was believed to be in possession of certain papers belonging to a 'fellow-countryman' who had perished at Bussa twenty years ago. He said that the King of England had instructed him to procure the restoration of these papers and to take them back to London. This explanation appeared to satisfy Majotu who readily agreed to send a messenger to Yauri to acquaint the ruler there, as well as the rulers of other provinces on the route, of the white men's intention to pay them a visit. When the messenger returned the Landers would be free to depart. In the meantime, Majotu added, his guests could remain at Katunga undisturbed: any impertinent individual who proved troublesome would promptly be beheaded by Ebo, public executioner as well as chief eunuch.

The Landers settled down to wait at Katunga for the messenger's return, dispirited by the gloomy atmosphere of the place and the apathetic unconcern of the people at the encroachments of the Fulani who threatened to overrun the district as, indeed, they were to do in 1837. Resigning themselves to a long delay, they sowed cress and onion seeds. It was, therefore, to their 'infinite surprise and pleasure' that, on the night of 19 May, Ebo hurried into their yard with an encouraging message from the king whose total avoidance of them since their arrival had led them to fear that he regretted his initial friendliness and that he intended to detain them in Katunga during the continuance of the rains. It now appeared that they were to be permitted to depart almost immediately and that they might well be in Yauri within a fortnight, even though, the direct route being considered unsafe, they were to be sent back to Atoopa and thence proceed on a safer path through Kaiama.

On the morning of 21 May they said good-bye to the king who on this occasion was wearing a cap 'very much resembling in shape those which were worn by elderly ladies in the time of Queen Elizabeth'; and on the evening of the 28th they were welcomed by King Yaru of Kaiama, a kindly, elderly man, almost toothless, with a beard as white as wool. His hut was adorned with scraps of paper containing sentences from the Koran and excellent prints, given to him by Hugh Clapperton, of George IV, the Duke of York, Wellington, Nelson and an unidentified officer in the Light Dragoons accompanied by 'a smartly dressed and happy-looking English lady'. The Landers' own presents consisted of 'six yards of red cloth, a quantity of printed cottons, a pair of silver bracelets, a looking-glass, two pairs of scissors, a knife, two combs and a tobacco pipe', all of which were received with 'much apparent satisfaction'.

After a delay of five days in Kaiama occasioned by the Muslim festival of Babbar Salla, during which they attended the exciting horseraces commonly held there at this time of year, the Landers left on 5 June, arriving at Bussa on the 17th. John had fallen ill with fever on the way, so ill, in fact, that his brother had expected every moment would be his last. But now that the Niger was reached he had completely recovered; and, while disappointed by the sight of the river, so narrow here and filled with black, rugged rocks rising from the centre of the stream, he thought the surrounding countryside delightful. Rice, corn and yams grew abundantly in the fertile soil; fish were plentiful; guinea-fowl, pheasant, partridge, deer and antelope were all to be found in the greatest abundance.

The king was kind and welcoming, 'affable, obliging and good-natured': he claimed that he and his wife had been weeping for the death of Captain Clapperton, 'whose untimely end they would never cease to lament', at the very moment when their guests arrived. And, although the Landers could discern no evidence of this sorrow, they were touched by its confession. Encouraged by his friendliness, they broached the unhappy subject of the fate of Mr Park. At first the king denied all knowledge of it: he had been a little boy at the time; all traces of the white man had been lost. The next day, however, the king came to see them accompanied by an attendant with a book under his arm. Treated with the utmost reverence, it was enveloped in a large cotton cloth. It had been salvaged from the Niger, the Landers were informed, after their countryman had been drowned. Their hearts 'beat high with expectation' as the book was slowly unwrapped, for they felt sure it must be Park's lost journal. They were chagrined, however, to discover that it was a book of logarithms. It had evidently belonged to Park, though, for between the leaves was an invitation to dinner addressed to him by some people in the Strand. The proud possessor of the book took it back, wrapped it up as reverentially as he had unfolded it, and bore it away as a household god, quite unperturbed by the white men's disappointment.

Presented by the generous King of Bussa with a bullock, sheep and turkeys as well as a horse, the travellers now moved on to Kagogie, a pleasant little walled town inhabited solely by the king's slaves. Here a canoe was provided to take them upstream to Yauri.

About midday the workmen having finished [repairing] our canoe [John Lander recorded in his journal] we embarked with our people, and were launched out into the river. We found it flowing from north to south, through a rich and charming country, which seemed to improve in appearance the further we advanced. Beautiful, spreading trees adorned the country on each side of the river, like a park; corn, nearly ripe, waved over the water's edge; large, open villages appeared every half-hour; and herds of spotted cattle were observed grazing and enjoying the cool of the shade ... The river was as smooth as a lake; canoes, laden with sheep and goats, were paddled by women down its almost imperceptible current; swallows, and a variety of aquatic birds, were sporting over its glassy surface, which was ornamented by a number of pretty little islands.

Yauri was reached on 27 June; and the following day the Landers were conducted to the ruler, Muhammad Ebsher, whom they found sitting alone in the centre of a square 'on a plain piece of carpeting, with a pillow on each side of him, and a neat brass pan in front. His appearance was not only mean, but absolutely squalid and dirty.' He accepted his presents coldly; and, when Richard Lander hinted, briefly and indirectly, at the reason for his visit to Yauri, the ruler answered brusquely, 'with an affected laugh', 'How do you think I could have the books of a person that was lost at Bussa?'

He continued to deny all knowledge of Park's effects throughout the Landers' stay in Yauri, which proved to be a most unpleasant one. They both felt ill; their quarters were invaded by swarms of mosquitoes, myriads of gnats, cockroaches and black ants as well as by bats which fluttered in front of their eyes; the air was 'humid and unwholesome, being impregnated with all manner of noxious effluvia from the large pools of impure water which existed more or less in every quarter of the town'. The inhabitants seemed poor and were certainly ill clad and perpetually complaining of their bad condition. Women who could afford the time to do so made themselves look most unappetizing by the application of henna to their teeth, blue indigo to their plaited hair

139

and yellow and blue stain to their lips. To add to their discontent, the Landers found it difficult to buy provisions and impossible to procure a canoe for their journey down to the sea, since their supply of acceptable currency and presents was running low. The ruler was eventually persuaded to offer twenty-five thousand cowries for a piece of red cloth, two pairs of scissors and a canister of powder, and two hundred cowries for every little button that could be produced. But when the time came for payment, complaining sadly of poverty, he asked the Landers to be satisfied with a female slave instead of the cowries. They considered it useless to demur and so accepted the girl whom Pasko took over as yet another wife. Realizing that they could expect nothing further from Muhammad Ebsher, the brothers sent a messenger back to the more accommodating King of Bussa, asking him to provide them with a canoe to take them down to the salt-water at the mouth of the Niger. To their 'unspeakable joy' the king agreed to procure them a canoe. But Muhammad Ebsher 'put off their departure from day to day', under a variety of 'nonsensical excuses' which convinced them that his intention was to detain them until he had extorted from them all their remaining possessions. One of these excuses was that he wished to increase the number of ostrich feathers which he had already had plucked for them to give to the King of England. The ostrich, however, could not be expected to undergo a further plucking at so cold a time of year, so they must wait until the bird had regained its plumage. Two thousand cowries' worth of butter (for which the recipients of the feathers would naturally be required to pay) would be diligently rubbed into the bald patch to encourage regrowth.

At length a messenger arrived from the King of Bussa requesting the white men's immediate release. So on 1 August they thankfully went to take their farewell of Muhammad Ebsher. They discovered him smoking a pipe of huge dimensions in a room continually crossed and recrossed by young naked servants, male and female, carrying dirty calabashes; everything was spattered with the droppings of swallows' nests, full of twittering young, which were attached at different points to the ceiling. They returned with relief to their quarters where the ruler's daughters came to beg for medicine and buttons, and remained there noisily bartering and wrangling until sunset.

The Landers' route back to Bussa took them through the country of the Kambari, an extremely dirty people who wore earrings of coloured wood as well as long pieces of glass passed through holes in the septum of their noses and crocodiles' teeth inserted through both lips. They lived in round clay huts, thatched with palm leaves and raised above the ground on wooden posts 'so as to secure the inmates from the annoyance of ants, snakes, and the wet ground, and even for protection from the alligators which prowl about at night in search of prey'. In their cooking these people used wood ash instead of salt which they could not afford; a meal thus prepared was naturally to European taste 'a most unsavoury repast'. The Landers were accordingly delighted to be back in Bussa on 7 August and to be greeted by the king who came towards them with 'joy beaming in his countenance'. He had decided that they must continue their journey by way of Wawa whose ruler could offer them more protection than himself and whose canoes were much superior to those made in his own territories.

The aged King of Wawa, who was married to the King of Bussa's sister, seemed to be quite as helpful as his brother-in-law, though 'the grave, eccentric old man' shook hands with his visitors without removing his arm from his gown or even condescending to look them in the face. He accepted the few and meagre presents offered him with expressions of perfect satisfaction, supplied them with yams, milk and eggs every morning, and undertook to sell his guests a canoe 'with the greatest pleasure'.

His promise of an excellent canoe was not, however, fulfilled. Returning to Bussa in expectation of its being sent on to them there, the Landers were bitterly disappointed to receive a small boat wholly inadequate for their purpose. They were also disturbed by the changing attitude towards them of the King and Queen of Bussa. 'Their benevolent feelings are growing colder every day,' John Lander wrote in his journal on 6 September. 'Our resources at the same time are diminishing rapidly and when they are gone, we know not what we shall do. We now receive only a calabash of *caffas* from the King once in three days, so that we are compelled to eat them at times, either in a state of putridity or go without; and our men are half-famished ... Our powder is reduced to a very small quantity, and in all probability we have not half so much as we shall require on the Niger.'

Occasionally stewed elephant's flesh arrived instead of the *caffas* or hippopotamus meat, but elephant except when very young is tough and rancid, and hippopotamus 'rank and fat'. The Landers sent one of their men to a nearby town to sell an ass and as many needles as he could; but he returned with 'very little money indeed', having disposed of the ass for less than half of its worth and finding hardly anyone interested in needles.

The days and nights passed with dreadful slowness. Once they were diverted by 'a long and gay procession, formed by the female followers of the ancient religion of the country ... walking and dancing alternately, with large spreading branches of trees in their hands'. 'The priestess had just swallowed fetish-water and was carried on the shoulders of one of the devotees,' John Lander recorded. 'Her body was convulsed all over, and her features shockingly distorted ... [She] was believed to be possessed with a demon; indeed to us they all appeared to be so, so indescribably fantastic and so unseemly did they disport themselves ... Their motions were regulated by the sound of drums and fifes, and to this music they joined their wild shrill voices. They presented one of the most extraordinary and grotesque spectacles the human mind can conceive.'

Another day 'an old Mahommedan priest, whose countenance seemed to radiate with meekness, simplicity, loving-kindness and good-nature', called at the hut and entreated the white men to give him a quantity of deadly poison. This request, he added, 'arose from the desire he felt to administer the poisonous drug to a neighbour whom he longed to put out of the world'.

In the second week of September the brothers decided that they could bear to wait at Bussa no longer. They had both been ill again and felt that if they did not get away immediately they would remain there for ever. Making up their minds to go down the river to the island of Patashie and to wait there until another canoe promised by the King of Wawa arrived, they began to collect as many provisions as their severely limited resources would allow. By Sunday, 19 September, everything was ready, and on that day to their 'unspeakable joy' messengers arrived from the King of Nupe who had received valuable presents from Clapperton and was 'delighted with the intelligence that white men were to honour his dominions with their presence'. One of these messengers was the King of Nupe's own son, the other a guide who would conduct the strangers 'even as far as Funda, which is beyond the limits of the empire'.

The next day the Landers said good-bye to the King and Queen of Bussa who, as though to compensate for their past inhospitality, had presented them with a considerable quantity of rice, honey, corn and onions and two large pots of butter. The royal couple were in tears at their guests' parting, though whether or not these were symptoms of genuine grief it was impossible to say. The tears of the ordinary people – four-fifths of whom at Bussa, as elsewhere in these territories, were slaves – seemed more sincerely induced. 'Neighbours, friends and acquaintances all fell down on their knees to bid us good-bye,' John Lander recorded. 'The eyes of many were streaming with tears, and all were more or less affected. As we passed by these poor creatures, we spoke to them all, and thanked them again and again for their good wishes.'

The island of Patashie they found to be 'unspeakably beautiful' and well cultivated by the people who, while active, honest and prosperous, were as timid as hares. If the visitors happened to look fixedly at their faces for a moment, most of them, and particularly the women and children, would 'start back with terror as if they had seen a serpent in the grass'. And at the approach of the strangers they would run away screaming as though in danger of falling into the jaws of a crocodile, so horrified were they at the mere sight of a white man and so frightful did their imaginations picture him to be. But the local chief, 'a venerable-looking old man, of advantageous stature and exceedingly corpulent', expressed the 'utmost delight and satisfaction on seeing white men before he died', a pleasure his father and mother had never enjoyed and 'a gratification which his ancestors had never hoped for'. He looked upon a book of natural history which his visitors showed him 'with silent astonishment' and 'became at first uneasy, and afterwards perfectly wild with amazement' when a watch and mariner's compass were produced for his inspection and their uses explained to him. 'No one in the world could express more naturally or forcibly the emotion of wonder, or the passion of fear, which the countenance of this old man displayed as he looked at the watch; nor could he be persuaded for a long time but that it was in possession of life and being.'

Unwelcome news awaited the travellers at Patashie: the King of Wawa had, indeed, procured them a canoe which was waiting for them at Lever; but 'it would not be paying him that respect which his rank and situation demanded,' his messenger announced, 'were the white men to leave his dominions and country altogether without first coming to pay him their respects.' Yet when Richard Lander, in obedience to this summons, arrived at Wawa the king, 'with the greatest indifference', said, 'I have not yet been able to procure you the canoe ... But I have no doubt that the ruler of Patashie will have it in his power to supply you with one to your satisfaction.'

Having returned to Patashie and thence gone on to Lever, Richard Lander, after consultation with his brother, decided that they must appropriate two canoes belonging to the chief of Patashie. 'It grieves and saddens us beyond expression to do this thing,' he wrote in his journal defensively; 'for this island ruler is a simple, kind-hearted, and good, very good old man. But what can we do? We have not the means of purchasing his canoes, for the King of Wawa has deprived us of them. Our resources are nearly exhausted, and how should we be able to prosecute our journey?'

So, it was in these stolen canoes that the Landers were paddled downstream into the kingdom of Nupe. Passing a fishing town on the small island of Madjie on 5 October, they came on the 6th within sight of the smoke of the 'far-famed' town of Rabba. But this was as much as they were to see of it, for a message arrived from its Fulani chief, Mallam Dendo, to the effect that while he shared the King of Nupe's favourable opinions of the white men, he did not recommend a visit to Rabba: the travellers would be more comfortable on an island named Zagozhi on the opposite side of the river whither the King of the Dark Water would escort them on the morrow.

The arrival of this majestically titled official was heralded the next morning by the sound of men singing and keeping time to the motion of many paddles. Presently two canoes appeared; the bigger of the two was rowed by 'twenty very fine young men' and was of extraordinary length. In the bow were three or four little boys all of the same size and neatly dressed; in the stern were a number of musicians, several drummers and a trumpeter. Under a colourfully decorated mat awning in the centre of the boat sat the King of the Dark Water himself, a tall, elderly, fine-looking man, 'his skin as black as a coal', dressed in an Arab cloak, Hausa trousers and sandals of coloured leather. He was attended by two pretty little boys who flicked the flies from his person with an ornamented cow's tail and by six of his wives, 'fine handsome jet-black girls, dressed in neat country caps edged with red silk'. On shore he behaved with great dignity and benevolence, presenting the visitors with a pot of excellent honey, two thousand cowries and a large quantity of *goora* nuts which were 'held in so great esteem, that the opulent and powerful alone' had the means of procuring them.

Before moving on again the Landers thought that their own canoe should be given a smarter appearance for its arrival at Zagozhi so that it should not be completely overshadowed by the splendid craft of the King of the Dark Water. They therefore hastily constructed an awning from their sheets, and above it erected a staff to which they fastened a Union Jack. Richard Lander put on an old naval uniform coat which he had with him for 'state occasions'; his brother dressed himself in 'as grotesque and gaudy a manner' as their means allowed; and their attendants arrayed themselves in white Mahommedan gowns. Thus clothed, the party was paddled on to the island of Zagozhi where the people's huts stood on poles above the marshy water. And here, soon after their arrival, messengers arrived from the ruler to say that they would introduce themselves early the next morning for the presents the white men intended to give their master who would not put them to the trouble of going to see him as the town was 'full of Arabs whose begging propensities would be very inconvenient'.

Although their stock of presents was running low and had to be supplemented by a pocket compass and a camera obscura, the articles were all gratefully received and the visitors were given in return ample stores of provisions, including a fine sheep and a large pot of honey, as well as enough strong beer for a whole regiment of soldiers. They were also able to replenish their stock of cowries for, unlike other places, Rabba – where young slaves, mostly captured in war, were offered for sale in large numbers – was such a good market for needles that Jowdie and Ibrahim were able to dispose of them for eight thousand cowries. The Landers' contentment was further increased when they were told that the King of the Dark Water would supply them with a commodious canoe, to take the place of the two smaller ones stolen at Patashie, and a guide and interpreter to accompany them as far as the sea. Their satisfaction was, however, roughly shattered when Pasko was summoned to Mallam Dendo and informed that, far from pleased with the presents, as they had previously been led to suppose, he considered them all perfectly worthless, with the exception of a looking-glass and that was fit only for a child. If they could not send him something more useful and of greater value he would seize their guns, pistols and powder before permitting them to leave Zagozhi. Dismayed at the thought of losing their weapons, which would have been 'a death blow' to all their hopes, they sent Ibrahim to Mallam Dendo with a magnificent gold-embroidered crimson damask gown given to them by the King of Bussa who had supposed it to have been the property of Mr Park. This splendid *tobe* was accepted 'with rapturous admiration'. 'Ask the white men,' Mallam Dendo said to Ibrahim, 'what they would desire, and if Rabba can supply them with it, they shall have it.'

All they needed was a canoe; yet this was still curiously difficult to obtain. And when at length one was said to be available they were informed that it was worth much more than their own two poor little craft: if an exchange was required an additional payment of ten thousand cowries would be required. Enabled by the sale of their needles to afford this sum, the Landers agreed to the bargain; and the canoe was produced. Not nearly as big as they had hoped, it also proved to be extremely leaky and 'patched up in a thousand places'. But rather than enter into what they knew would be an interminable dispute, they transferred their baggage into it and set off downstream, their men using paddles which – having failed to induce anyone to sell these essential pieces of equipment – they had been forced to steal at night.

Then 'a fresh evil arose', as an 'incredible number' of hippopotami came 'plashing, snorting and plunging' all around the canoe. Shots, instead of frightening them off, summoned many more and this so alarmed the paddlers that they 'trembled with fear and apprehension, and absolutely wept aloud', their terror increased by dreadful peals of thunder and the powerful glare of forked lightning. At midnight the wind grew so furious that the waters of the river were swept over the side of the canoe and the storm seemed certain to achieve what the hippopotami had so far failed to do. Driven about by the gale, the canoe was quite unmanageable until it was swept against the branches of a tree to which it was eventually secured. Utterly exhausted, its occupants huddled together in their wet clothes and tried to sleep, dangling their legs over the sides of the boat for lack of room to lie down in any other posture. After a few hours' rest the journey was continued in the pouring rain as the men struggled to bail out the water before the craft sank. At dawn they landed at a small fishing village, having covered some hundred miles in the previous twenty-four hours.

The next day, a Sunday, was less tempestuous; but on Monday, the rain fell more torrentially than ever, the wild wind rose again and the canoe, half-filled with water, was tossed about like a coconut shell. The men exerted their muscles to pull the canoe among the rushes by the bank where 'a frightful crocodile of prodigious size', disturbed in his sleep, plunged underneath it with extraordinary violence 'to the amazement and terror' of them all. Surviving this hazard, the canoe passed on downstream, past the island of Fofo, and, beneath hills which rose high on either side, into a creek which led to the landing place of the town of Egga. The white men were immediately conducted to the old white-bearded Muslim chief who, smoking a pipe about three yards long, inspected them from head to foot, then delivered himself of the opinion that they were 'strange-looking people, well worth seeing'. He called in his wives to satisfy their own curiosity before giving instructions for his guests to be accommodated 'in a hut fit for a king' where they were subjected to even closer examination by the entire population who gazed at them in 'amazement and terror', rushing backwards in the greatest trepidation whenever the strange figures approached too near the doorway.

At sunset the chief himself arrived and, anxious to show how active he was despite his great age – the Landers thought he looked at least a hundred – he performed a most lively dance, capering about and shaking his hoary locks so energetically that his people displayed their admiration by their customary loud laughter. He would, it seemed, have continued all night had his strength permitted it, and would certainly have detained his audience of white men in Egga had they not been determined to proceed. He warned them of the dangers of their enterprise, declaring that the banks of the river downstream were 'inhabited by a people who were little better than savages and plundered everyone who came near them'. Having already heard such stories from his people, most of the Landers' men now mutinied, refusing to go any further. They would have run away there and then had they not been owed their wages and feared that to be left behind at Egga would mean their instantaneous enslavement. It was accordingly with much ill grace that they climbed back into the leaky canoe and, having listened moodily to the Christian prayers which their masters read to them every day, pushed off from the landing-place at Egga early on the morning of 23 October.

Later on that morning their gloomy spirits were lightened by the sight of a sea-gull flying overhead and a dozen large white pelicans swimming gracefully on the water. But at sunset they had further cause for fear and complaint when the inhabitants of a waterside village rushed down to the water's edge shouting war cries and brandishing weapons, evidently supposing them to be hostile Fulani. The Landers cried out in Hausa that they were peaceful Christians on their way to the sea; but the villagers understood not a word until there appeared on the bank an old woman who spoke a little Hausa and who was able to set their minds at rest. Even so they refused the white men permission to land, and advised them to go on to Kacunda. Here, despite the tribal scars which lent their faces a savage appearance, the inhabitants were a harmless, hospitable people who offered the travellers shelter. But the chief repeated the warnings they had been given at Egga about the dreadful tribes downstream: 'If you go down the river you surely fall into their hands and be murdered.' And when his people said good-bye to their visitors, who departed at half past four on the afternoon of 24 October, they appeared to think they were proceeding to their death.

The rest of that day, however, passed without incident. At midnight the lights of a village were seen, and the noise of people dancing, singing and laughing outside their huts was heard across the water; but the canoe moved quickly to the other bank and glided silently past. The next day the direction of the river changed to the south-south-west, running between immensely high hills; and at five o'clock in the morning the Landers caught sight of 'a very considerable river, entering the Niger from the eastward'. It was the Benue, the great tributary of the Niger. They were the first Europeans to have seen it.

As the travellers progressed downstream the gloomy prognostications of their recent hosts seemed less and less likely to be fulfilled. While resting on the bank on the morning of the 25th they were alarmed to see a party of tribesmen with muskets, bows and arrows, knives and cutlasses rushing towards them. The Landers, unarmed, went bravely forward to face them, holding out their hands in greeting. The chief, who had an arrow poised in his bow, hesitated, then dropped his weapon, accepted the offered hands, burst into tears, apologized, and asked for the white men's forgiveness. The next day the travellers were similarly threatened, but when they offered no show of resistance the natives merely inquired what the strangers wanted. And on the 27th, after failing to respond to the shout of 'Halloa, you Englishmen! You come here!' from a little squinting black man in an English soldier's jacket, they were chased by a dozen canoes much larger than their own; but, having been overtaken, were only requested to go back to the village of Damugoo where they had omitted to pay respects to the king. The king turned out to be perfectly friendly and invited the white men to remain in his village until an agent from the King of Bonny, who had come to Damugoo to buy slaves, returned to his own country. The agent was the little squinting man in the red jacket. He had picked up his English, and, perhaps, his coat, from the sailors of the Liverpool ships that frequented the Bonny river, taking on cargoes of palm oil. His presence at Damugoo gave the travellers cause to hope that their long journey was nearly over.

The Landers were well treated at Damugoo, provided with palm wine, eggs and bananas as well as yams, and invited to shoot a wild bullock which they were asked to roast under the temple of a little god so that he could enjoy the savoury smell of the cooking meat. But they were exasperated here as elsewhere by the hosts of inquisitive people who clustered round their hut staring in at them. They complained to the chief who advised them 'seriously to *"cut off their heads"'*.

To ascertain whether or not the time was propitious for his visitors to continue the journey, the chief consulted his gods and the entrails of fowls. He then pronounced the omens to be inauspicious. Even so, the Landers insisted on leaving on 4 November; and, finding their determination fixed, the chief presented them with another canoe so that the rest of their journey would at least be more comfortable. At a riverside farewell party, during which palm wine circulated freely, a fatted goat and a decanter of rum were offered as leaving presents while other goats, several elephants' tusks and six complaisant slaves were packed into the canoe as gifts for the King of Bonny. The party was followed by 'a fetish ceremony', so that it was dark before the Landers were able to set off in the chief's canoe, Pasko having already left with the baggage, presents, animals, slaves and servants two hours before. Once out in the stream, however, the canoe sped quickly through the dark water, the Damugoo boatmen keeping their paddles in time to the rhythm of their song, and Pasko's heavily laden canoe was soon overtaken. Indeed, as the old canoe was in danger of being left far behind, Richard Lander got into it, took up a paddle himself, and wielding it vigorously, encouraged the others by singing 'Rule Britannia'. This had the desired effect, he wrote, 'and we continued on very pleasantly. But at seven a.m. we saw ... a great number of canoes were lying near the bank. They appeared to be very large and had flags flying on long bamboo canes ... As we approached I observed the British Union flag on several, while others, which were white, had figures of a man's leg, chairs, tables, decanters, glasses and all kinds of such devices. The people in them, who were very numerous, were dressed in European clothing, with the exception of trousers. I felt quite overjoyed by the sight of these people ... and congratulated myself that they were from the sea coast.'

Lander's joy was premature, for these were the people against whom he had been warned at Damugoo and Egga. They attacked his canoe and, overwhelming the crew, plundered it of all its contents. They then advanced upon the other canoe, rammed it with such force that two or three of the Damugoo boatmen were knocked into the water, then capsized and sank it.

Both brothers and their men were rescued from the robbers by the people of the nearby town of Kirree; and a few of their possessions were recovered, either from the robbers' canoes or from the river into which they had been cast. But the travellers were told that they must consider themselves as prisoners, that they would be conducted next day to the King of the Ibos who would examine them and whose 'will and pleasure' concerning them 'would then be explained'.

The Landers' captors were a savage-looking race, strong, athletic and well-proportioned, wearing nothing but a tiger's or leopard's skin fastened round their waists. Their hair was plaited and plastered with red clay, their faces deeply cut and dyed with indigo. On the way to their king at Aboh they stopped from time to time to buy yams at riverside villages. The silent bargaining was conducted by old women who directed all the vendors to place their yams in rows and distinctly separate bundles. The purchasers would place articles, such as cloth or flints, amounting to what was considered their value beside each bundle. The woman would then either take up the articles if she deemed the offer fair and hand them to the vendor, leaving the purchaser to remove the yams, or if the offer were not fair, she would allow a moment or two for it to be increased, then if it were not, she would direct the owner of the yams to remove them, indicating to the would-be purchaser that his bid had failed. The Ibo people boiled the yams, then skinned them before energetically mashing them into a paste with the addition of a little water. They offered some of the resulting concoction to the white men who, having seen the dirty hands of the cooks and the streams of sweat which fell into it, felt for it 'an invincible disgust'. They preferred to go hungry, and hungry they had to remain.

Unlike his subjects who had brought the strangers into his presence, the King of the Ibos was a pleasant-looking young man with alert, intelligent eyes. He shook hands cordially with his visitors, complimenting them frequently with the word 'Yes' to which his knowledge of their language was confined. He wore a close-fitting Spanish coat of red cloth, ornamented with gold epaulettes and gold lace, and so covered with coral decorations as to be scarcely discernible beneath them. His cap, shaped like a sugar loaf, was also covered with coral as well as with bits of looking-glass. Necklaces of coral encircled his throat; thirteen or fourteen bracelets surrounded each wrist, and a string of little brass bells each ankle. Thus splendidly clothed, smiling at his own magnificence, 'vain of the admiration which was paid him by his attendants, and flattered without doubt by the presence of white men, who he imagined were struck with amazement at the splendour of his appearance, he shook his feet for the bells to tinkle, sat down with the utmost complacency, and looked around him'.

On hearing their story he declared that by the laws of his country he was not only entitled to the white men's persons but also to those of their attendants. He would, however, take no further advantage of his good fortune than exchange them for as much in English goods as would amount in value to twenty slaves.

The Landers listened to these words with horror, doubting that the masters of the English vessels at the mouth of the river would have the ability or the inclination to ransom them. And for several days they waited at Aboh, close to starvation, occasionally receiving a yam or a fowl which, while an adequate meal perhaps for the two of them, was parsimonious fare indeed for a party of ten. They, therefore, considered it 'heavenly news' when a man known to them as King Boy, one of the rulers of Brass, the country by the sea, offered to pay the amount demanded for their ransom on the understanding that he would be repaid by the master of the brig *Thomas* which was then lying at anchor off his shores and that he would receive in addition the value of fifteen slaves and a cask of rum for the trouble and dangers he would incur in conducting them to the shore.

The offer was immediately accepted and on the morning of 12 November 1830 the Landers and their men set off for the town of Brass at the mouth of the river, accompanied by the favourite daughter of the King of the Ibos who had expressed a desire to see white men's ships. The huge canoe, with forty boatmen dashing their paddles into the water in perfect unison, swept along at first with the speed of a dolphin, then slowed as it entered a small branch of the river in which it became entangled for a time in shoots of mangrove and evil-smelling brambles dripping with ooze. Occasionally the canoe stopped for the crew to purchase yams, bananas and coconuts, parts of which King Boy always threw into the water, before eating the rest, as offerings to the 'spirits of the water'. These spirits were further propitiated by him after breakfast on 15 November when 'fetish priests' marked his naked body with chalk circles, lines and a variety of fantastic figures, and placed on his head a little cap made of grass and decorated with buzzard feathers. His boatmen were decorated in the same way, while the Landers' men were merely chalked on the forehead.

The next day the town of Brass was reached. It was 'a wretched, filthy place' surrounded by rank, impenetrable vegetation. Half-starved animals and human beings, looking equally famished and dirty and covered with odious boils, wandered about between the decayed huts most of which seemed on the point of sinking into the marshy ground. King Boy's father, the ruler of this depressing place, was found sitting half drunk with a number of his wives and dogs in a small and dirty hut. He demanded money from the white men before granting them permission to leave the town; and when he was given a bill on the captain of the English vessel aboard which the Landers hoped to sail, he said to Richard Lander, 'Tomorrow you may go to the ship. Take one servant with you. But your mate [brother] must remain here until my son, King Boy, shall bring the goods for himself and me.'

Obliged to accede to this demand, Richard Lander went on with King Boy to the *Thomas* where he found half the crew of eight had just died of fever and the other half, prostrate in their hammocks, looking as though they would soon follow them. The captain, Lake, who had himself recovered from a serious attack, turned out to be as brutish a fellow as most other masters who traded in these waters, one of whom had recently had the black members of his crew whitewashed with lime, an operation which had rendered one of them blind in one eye. On Lander's asking him to guarantee the ransom demanded for the release of himself, his brother and men, Lake 'flatly refused to give a single thing, and, ill and weak as he was', did so with the most offensive and shameful oaths Lander had ever heard. 'If you think,' he said, 'that you have a —— fool to deal with, you are mistaken. I'll not give a bloody flint for your bill. I would not give a —— for it.'

'Petrified with amazement, and horror-struck at such conduct, I shrunk from him with terror,' Lander recorded. 'I could scarcely believe what I had heard, till my ears were assailed with a repetition of the same.' He reported Lake's reaction to King Boy whom he asked to take him on to Bonny where there were plenty of other ships. But Boy proved as unaccommodating as Lake. 'No, no,' he said. 'If this captain no pay, Bonny captain no pay. I won't take you any further.' So Lander returned to Lake who repeated his refusal, giving way to the extent only of undertaking to take Lander's people aboard his ship if he could get them there. But, he insisted, he would sail without them if they were not on board within three days. And, no doubt, he would have done had not a strong sea breeze risen on the morning of 23 November and raised too high a bar. The next day both Landers were aboard the *Thomas* and before the end of the month the brig managed to pass over the bar at the edge of the breakers and set sail for the island of Fernando Po. Here the Landers disembarked and secured a passage aboard the *Caernarvon*, an English vessel bound for Rio de Janeiro where they found the *William Harris*, a government transport, to take them to England. They arrived at Portsmouth on 9 June 1831 and the next day Richard Lander was in London reporting to Lord Goderich, the Colonial Secretary, his discovery of the termination of the Niger, a likely means of carrying on 'a water-communication with so extensive a part of the interior of Africa that a considerable trade will be opened'.

The rewards and acclaim enjoyed by the Landers on their return to England were far from extravagant. Richard received the first annual premium of fifty guineas from the Geographical Society. But he had to be content with the bare £100 bounty which the Government had agreed to pay him and which they did not increase. John received nothing. John Murray, the publisher, offered them a thousand guineas for their journal and King William IV granted them an audience; but the newspapers took little notice of their achievements.

Richard Lander went to work in the Customs House at Liverpool; and in this commercial city the economic advantages of his discoveries were recognized. An African Inland Commercial Company was established and an ambitious trading expedition was proposed: two steamships, the *Quorra* of 145 tons burden and the *Alburkah* of 55 tons, were to sail up the Niger with almost fifty men and to establish a trading post at the confluence of the Niger and the Benue. The leader of the expedition was to be Richard Lander. A naval officer was to be sent with him to make a survey of the Niger, but otherwise the Government did not choose to involve themselves with an expedition which was recognized as simply commercial, although its instigators expressed the hope that it would at the same time help to strike a blow at the slave trade and to impart the 'traits of Christianity' to peoples abandoned to paganism.

The two steamships were in the Niger by October 1832 and at first all went well. King Boy, whose debts had already been paid, was further placated by a Scottish Highland uniform amongst other pleasing presents; and at Aboh, the coral-encrusted ruler also extended a friendly welcome to Lander who entered the town in a general's uniform complete with a plumed cocked hat. But thereafter disaster followed upon disaster: there were quarrels between the ships' officers and Lander whose leadership they questioned; the ruler of the Igala people who inhabited the left bank of the Niger below the confluence with the Benue proved hostile and arranged for the poisoning of Pasko who had joined Lander once more; the amount of ivory offered for barter was far less than had been hoped; the navigation of the river was difficult; fever attacked all the white men, many of whom died. The *Quorra* which had grounded near the confluence and was stuck there for several weeks was sent home to Liverpool.

In the *Alburkah*, the first sea-going ship ever constructed of iron, Lander decided to sail up the Benue in an attempt to confirm reports that this unexplored river was an outlet of Lake Chad. After a hundred miles he had to turn back, however, as provisions were sparse and opportunities for trade discouraging. Steaming up the Niger instead he was again obliged to turn back after calling at Rabba, this time because the engine failed. The ship's stores were also very low; so, when the engine had been repaired, the *Alburkah* steamed back to Fernando Po where, no cowries being available, Lander went on to Cape Coast Castle to buy some, leaving the ship's surgeon, R. A. K. Oldfield, to take her back up the Niger. Returning up the Niger on his way to the *Alburkah* himself, Lander and his party were threatened by a relative of King Boy who said to them, as 'his eyes sparkled with malignity', 'White men will never reach Ibo this time.' The threat was soon carried out in a narrow part of the river by natives on both banks. Three of his men were killed in the attack and Lander was wounded. 'After receiving the wound I was very faint,' Lander reported to the Superintendent of Fernando Po. 'Had we remained ten minutes longer, not a soul would have been alive. We were now followed by a great number of war canoes, and with them we kept up a running fight for five hours ... I have lost all my papers ... I fear if these savages are not chastised immediately it will never be safe to go up in a boat or canoe. I am afraid some white men have a hand in this, as they were placed in so formidable a position and their numbers I suppose about 8,000 or 10,000 all armed with muskets and swords, Bonny, Benin and Brass people.'

Lander survived his wound to reach Fernando Po; but a few days later, on 2 February 1834, he died in the Superintendent's house and was buried on the island. His wife was granted a pension of £70 a year, their daughter a gratuity of £80. His brother, John, who had been found employment as a tide waiter in the Custom House, soon afterwards died in London at the age of thirty-two of a malady originally contracted in Africa. When questioned by the Superintendent of Fernando Po, King Boy disclaimed all responsibility for the attack which had resulted in Richard Lander's death, maintaining that the assailants were outlaws who were enemies of the peoples both of Brass and of Aboh who had declared that the river was theirs, and that no white man should ever go up it. King Boy undertook to destroy the town from which they came, to kill all its male inhabitants and to make slaves of all their women. The Superintendent indicated that some rather less drastic revenge would be considered adequate; and in the end nothing was done.

6

THE MYSTERY OF TIMBUKTU

HANMER WARRINGTON, THE ECCENTRIC BRITISH CONSUL-
GENERAL IN TRIPOLI · HIS CONCEITED SON-IN-LAW,
ALEXANDER GORDON
LAING · LAING'S PREVIOUS ADVENTURES IN WEST AFRICA
AND EXPLORATION OF THE ROKELLE RIVER · LAING
TRAVELS BY WAY OF GHADAMES ACROSS THE DESERT TO
TIMBUKTU · ATTACKED AND LEFT FOR DEAD BY TUAREGS ·
LATER MURDERED BY TUAREGS IN SEPTEMBER 1826 · RENÉ
CAILLIÉ, THE SON OF A DRUNKEN BAKER, SETS OUT FOR
TIMBUKTU · HIS EXTRAORDINARY ADVENTURES AND
RESOURCEFUL PERSISTENCE — HIS LIFE WITH THE BRAKNA
MOORS · IN THE GUISE OF AN EGYPTIAN MUSLIM HE REACHES
JENNÉ · HIS SLOW AND MISERABLE JOURNEY BY CANOE TO
KABARA · HE ENTERS TIMBUKTU, APRIL 1828 · AN
AGONIZING CROSSING OF THE WESTERN SAHARA TO
TANGIER · HIS RETURN TO FRANCE ·

At the time of the Landers' journeys in Africa, the British Consul-General in Tripoli was Hanmer Warrington. He was a rich, eccentric, irascible man who drank heavily and, in his cups, related improbable stories of his days of exciting service in the Dragoon Guards and of his nights spent gambling with his old friend, the Prince Regent. He was also an expert judge of horseflesh and an acknowledged authority on north African affairs. Few travellers who called upon him at his large house just outside Tripoli did not, for one reason or another, soon find themselves indebted to him. One such traveller in 1825 was Alexander Gordon Laing.

Laing, then aged thirty-two and recently promoted major in the Royal Africa Corps, came from Edinburgh where his father had opened the first classical academy in the city. He had attended this academy until he was thirteen and had afterwards taught in it, having in the meantime attended Edinburgh University. Soon tiring of a schoolmaster's life, he had joined the army and,

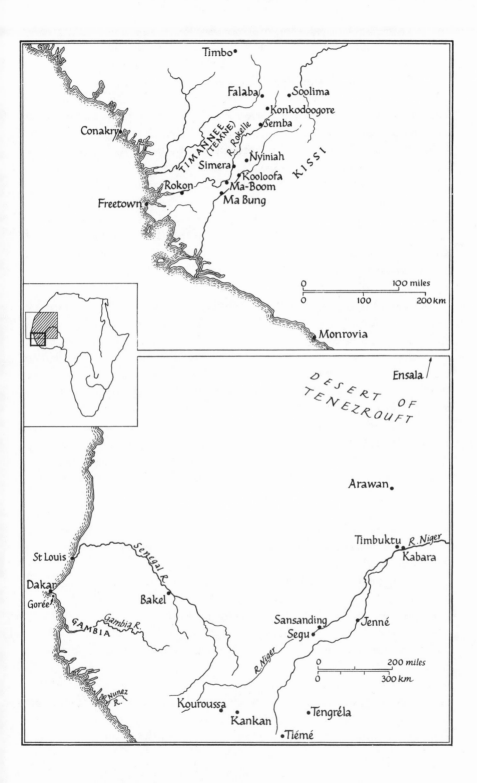

Timbo

Falaba • Soolima
• Konkodoogore
Semba
Conakry

TIMANNEE (TEMNE)

R. Rokelle

Nyiniah

Simera
Kooloofa
Rokon Ma-Boom
Ma Bung

Freetown

KISSI

0   100 miles
0   100   200 km

Monrovia

Ensala

DESERT OF TENEZROUFT

Arawan •

Timbuktu R. Niger
Kabara

St Louis
Senegal R.

Dakar
Bakel
Gorée

GAMBIA   Gambia R.

R. Niger

Sansanding
Segu
Jenné

Nunez R.

0   200 miles
0   300 km

Kouroussa
• Tengréla
Kankan
• Tiémé

after service with the 2nd West India Regiment, he had found himself at the beginning of 1822 in Sierra Leone where his obvious cleverness, conceit and habit of expressing his opinions didactically in a pronounced Scottish accent did not endear him to his fellow officers. At his own suggestion, he had been authorized by the Governor to leave the regiment and to make an excursion into the Kambrian and Mandingo countries to find out how the natives there felt disposed towards trading with the Europeans on the coast. Although he did not say so to the Governor, Laing hoped that he might be able to extend the scope of the mission and go on to Timbuktu and discover the source of the Niger.

Accompanied by a guide, two soldiers, eleven carriers and a fifteen-year-old servant boy, Laing had left Sierra Leone by boat up the Rokelle River on 16 April. And two days later, at three o'clock in the afternoon, he had reached Rokon, the principal Timannee town of the district. The next morning he was summoned to an audience of the king; and, learning that 'his majesty was fond of a little pomp', he ordered ten of his party to go with him, carrying their firelocks and three rounds of blank cartridges each, so that the king could be saluted in accordance with the supposed custom of the country. They found the king to be about ninety years old, with a mottled, shrivelled skin the colour of an alligator, greenish eyes sunk deep in his head and a bleached, twisted beard hanging down about two feet from his chin. His legs were swollen 'like those of an elephant'. He wore a necklace of coral and leopards' teeth and carried a staff of office to which were attached several bells. Unfortunately the salute which his visitors accorded him produced a very different effect from that intended. 'For the old man started back a few paces, muttered some angry expressions, bit his lips, gave [Laing] a hasty and savage look, then turning round, hurried away in a violent fit of passion.' Persuaded to return by one of his chief people, he did so with a most suspicious look upon his face and sat down on his chair of state 'with an air of consequence and authority truly ludicrous'. Why had he been fired at? he asked at length. Assured that the firing had been purely to do him honour, he said, 'Why did you point your guns to the ground?'

'That you might see our intention was to show you respect.'

'But the pebbles flew in my face. Why did you not point in the air?'

'Because we feared to burn the thatch of your houses.'

'Well, then, give me some rum.'

Having been indulged in this respect, he became much more good-humoured. But Laing found it even more difficult to obtain permission to move on than he had feared: the discussions, supervised by a garrulous orator, seemed endless; the presents were deemed insultingly paltry; and, when at last permission to leave was obtained, the king 'made his appearance in a frightful rage', complaining that one of the white man's party had had the effrontery to wear a red shirt finer than his own and declaring that it was the law of the country – a law that he had himself just invented – that any man dressed better than the king, especially in red, had to forfeit his clothes. The man was ordered to change his shirt which was given to the king who was also presented with tobacco and rum. But Laing had not long left Rokon when a man fantastically attired and masked as if in the guise of some outlandish bird overtook the party and, representing himself as the king's 'greegree man', attempted to seize some other clothes which had taken their fancy.

Travelling by way of Ma Bung, a town of about 2,500 inhabitants, the travellers arrived at Ma Yerma on 3 May. Here one of the bearers found a gun missing from his load. Laing's guide insisted upon seeing 'the greegree man of the town' who presented himself to the visitors, 'less disguised but more hideous to look at' than the king of Rokon's. His head supported 'an enormous canopy of skulls, thigh bones and feathers, and his plaited hair and beard, twisting like snakes, appeared from beneath it'. There were bells around his knees and a fringe of grass round his waist. He made several circuits of the assembly, demanded the cause of his summons, then, waving his rod in the air, he retired into the bush whence, after a quarter of an hour's meditation, he returned to name the culprit who, he said, was now halfway to Ma Bung with his prize. Laing did not believe a word of this but he gave the man some tobacco and was later glad that he had done so, for the named culprit was discovered and the gun returned after Laing's party had reached Mayasa.

The people of Mayasa were much more friendly than those in the places they had passed through earlier, presenting the strangers with yams, plantains and rice, 'the only remuneration desired or wished for being a sight of the white man ... The palaver for permission to pass was easily settled.' Elsewhere, however, Laing had 'little to offer in defence of the Timannee people'. They seemed to him to be 'depraved, licentious, indolent, avaricious ... and superstitious'. Before eating or drinking they invariably threw a small portion of their food on the ground as an offering to the dead, and regularly passed provisions and palm wine through the small apertures which were made for this purpose in the walls of the charnel-houses where the remains of their headmen were placed. The men, Laing observed, were most scantily clothed, usually contenting themselves with 'a small square piece of coarse cloth or woven bark attached to a string, and tied round the middle', the women sometimes wearing nothing at all, even 'over-grown women' who were 'quite unconscious of the disgust which their appearance excited'.

Although equally avaricious, and inclined to treat his presents with ridicule, the people of Ma-Boom and Kooloofa were, in Laing's opinion, much more industrious and agreeable. Most of them were Mandingos, neatly dressed and welcoming. At Kooloofa, the chief expressed himself as being 'extremely happy' to receive the travellers, while the people of the town, out of compliment to the first white man who had ever set foot there, 'commenced such a din of drums, flutes and various other instruments, accompanied with dancing and singing that sleep was impossible'. At Simera the satisfactory 'palaver was closed with a fine fat cow'. At Nyiniah, Laing was presented with an equally fine young bull, although he did not manage to enjoy much of it himself, since as he wrote:

> On occasions of this kind, certain parts are claimed by different people, so that when the whole are provided, the breast is all that is left to the person to whom the present is made. The maraboo who slays the animal is entitled to the head, neck, and feet; the guarange expects the hide, liver and other parts of the inside; the head-man of the town receives the right hind-leg for his portion; and the blacksmith [and others] all come in for a share, which is theirs by right of ancient usage and custom.

By the beginning of June, Laing was in the country of the Koorankos, 'by no means so handsome or so intelligent a race of people' as the Mandingos. Unlike their Muslim neighbours, most of them were pagans and shared with the Timannee 'an unlimited faith in greegrees'. They were, nevertheless, quite friendly, presenting the strangers with eggs, milk and fowls at Semba, and at Konkodoogore welcoming them with the greatest excitement. The chief, who was 'almost beside himself with joy', solemnly took off his cap, 'lifted his aged eyes to heaven and fervently thanked his Creator for having blessed him with the sight of a white man before he died'.

Further inland, at Falaba, the capital of the Soolima people, a town which he had always been 'most eager to see', Laing's reception was even more encouraging. Two thousand armed men were assembled to greet him with 'a heavy and irregular discharge of musketry' which so alarmed his horse that he was almost thrown from the saddle. Thirty horsemen followed by two thousand more soldiers then dashed forward firing in all directions and performing various movements and evolutions for about half an hour. Arrows were shot, more muskets were fired, drums were beaten, fifes, flutes and harps were played, and songs were sung by bawling women, all with such determination to produce the most deafening noise that Laing thought the din 'sufficient almost to crack the tympanum of ordinary ears'. After this display was over, the King of Falaba pointed to a horse, 'nicely caparisoned in the Moorish style', and told all the chiefs to witness that he gave it to his guest. Finely dressed men 'exclaimed "Kaase, Kaase! 'Tis true, 'tis true," and sung loud and long to the praise of the King's liberality. They made him out to be the greatest potentate upon the earth, except the King of the white men, who, they admitted, had more money, but not so many horses, nor so fine a country.'

Riding his new horse out into the country, Laing saw a crowd of about three thousand people, marshalled under flags of various devices, awaiting the arrival of the king and entertaining themselves with music and dancing. On the appearance of the king they fell into silence. The king's *herald* then 'exhorted them all to work hard, and to water the ground with the sweat of their brows, as their king was so good to them. He pointed to three fat bulls, which were tied under the shade of a cotton-tree. "These," he said, "are to be killed by the king for his people; therefore, those who would eat beef let them work." ' At the conclusion of this speech the people were drawn up in two lines which then advanced with astonishing speed and regularity, the first line scattering the seed, the second covering it with hoes.

While these matters were going forward, I sat with the king and a large party of his head-men under the shade of a tree [Laing recorded]. They appeared highly delighted at the interest I took in the scene, and every now and then congratulated the king on his great name, which had induced a white man to travel from the waterside to see him. At this the king would smile and turn his head to one side. A *Jelle* man observing this commenced a song, the purport of which was the power of the Soolima nation, and of its great chief.

The king was delighted with the presents, including weapons, coral beads, red handkerchiefs, cowries, flints, a cocked hat with a gold band, a laced coat, a silver chain and a medal of George IV, which Laing produced for him. But his evident pleasure did not make it any the easier for Laing to obtain permission to proceed to the source of the Niger, which, so a caravan of merchants from Kowia informed him, 'might easily be reached in three days'.

'White man, it is impossible,' the king said, shaking his head. 'I am at war with the people of Kissi, the country from which the river comes, and if they were to know you came from me, they would that moment kill you.' By 30 July, however, Laing had induced the king to let him go in that direction, and he spent a sleepless night 'highly delighted at the prospect before [him] of penetrating further into the interior of this vast continent'. But no sooner had he set off early the next morning than the king summoned him back.

'What are you taking with you on the road to pay your expenses?' the king asked him.

After Laing had enumerated various articles, the king said, 'What! Have you no tobacco?'

'No.'

'No salt?'

'No.'

'*Alla Akbar*! To think of travelling through Kooranko without tobacco and salt! They would turn you back and give me a bad name. They would say, I sent a white man to make fools of them. No, my white stranger, you cannot walk that country without tobacco and salt.'

But when Laing had obtained these commodities, the king was still reluctant to allow him to go: the people of those regions were savage and suspicious; they entertained all kinds of superstitions about the river which was looked upon as the greatest in the universe. They would think that the white man had come to 'make some greegree to let the salt-water in upon the river's head'. In any case, how would the white man cross the rivers? Laing replied that he would swim across upon gourds.

'*Alla Akbar*! There are deep swamps on the way in which you will sink to the neck. How will you pass over them?'

'I must do as the people of the country do; and, if that will not answer, I must fell trees, and, laying them across, scramble over their branches. But I tell you, once for all, that even a river of fire shall not deter me, if you are kind enough to give me your passport.'

'*Alla howla! Taha*! God is powerful. Go!' And so saying, the king got up and left.

The next morning at dawn, Laing set out again. But, once more, a messenger from the king caught up with him on the road. 'The king has had a very bad dream about you,' the messenger said, 'and he has sent me to bring you back.' So Laing returned with the utmost reluctance and 'at a sluggish pace' to the town where the king, after talking at length about his dream, eventually admitted under pressure the reason – Laing believed it to be the real reason – why he was so reluctant to allow the white man to proceed. He said with great emphasis, 'When the Kissi meet my people they cut their throats; and when my men meet the Kissi people, they cut their throats in return. Nobody is safe going into that country from me; that is the truth. I am ashamed to have been so long in telling it to you.'

Chagrined as he was to be told this, Laing was, as he admitted, considerably relieved when his disappointment had subsided. The frustrations of the past few weeks had begun to affect his health; he had already exceeded by two months the period allowed him for the performance of his journey; and, moreover, he could not 'reasonably have expected men who had been hired at a small expense to carry loads from Sierra Leone to the Soolima country, to have exposed themselves to danger for what they would deem little better than idle curiosity'. After all, the mission on which he was employed was not intended to be one of discovery but had been arranged, at his own suggestion, for the purpose of 'enlarging the commerce of Sierra Leone with countries supposed to be rich but hitherto known only by report'.

So Laing told the king that he would return to Sierra Leone within three weeks. He used that time to explore the source of the Rokelle which he traced, at no great distance from Falaba, to the foot of a hill where, springing from under a large rock and shaded by the thick foliage of date palms, 'it bubbles up and scatters itself over a wide surface of red clay, in appearance like a stream

20. Major Alexander Gordon Laing, who, with his 'obvious cleverness, conceit and habit of expressing his opinions didactically in a pronounced Scottish accent did not endear himself to his fellow-officers'.

21. René Caillié makes notes while pretending to study the Koran.

22. René Caillié's sketch of Timbuktu, from his *Travels*. 'The character of the single dwellings was well represented by that traveller,' Barth commented, 'the only error being that in his representation the whole town seems to consist of scattered and quite isolated houses, while, in reality, the streets are entirely shut in, as the dwellings form continuous and uninterrupted rows.'

23. The serious, self-righteous James Richardson travelling in disguise in north Africa, as depicted in his *Travels in the Great Desert of Sahara*.

24. Heinrich Barth. 'recognized as an authority without equal on north and central Africa'.

25. A sandstorm in the Sahara, from Richardson's *Travels*.

26. An encampment of Tuaregs. 'Some of the leathern tents were open, presenting a view of the interior of these simple movable dwellings,' Barth wrote. 'Beyond was a swampy creek enlivened by a numerous herd of cattle half immersed in the water.' From Barth's *Travels and Discoveries.*

27. Ederi, between Tripoli and Murzuk, from Heinrich Barth's *Travels and Discoveries*: 'We ascended the narrow streets of the old town and from the highest part, which is 190 feet above the bottom of the valley, obtained a very interesting view of . . . black sandstone . . . green fields of wheat and barley . . . date trees scattered in long narrow strips.'

28. Mbutudi, a village in Bornu, 'situated', wrote Barth, 'round a granite mount of about 600 yards circumference and rising to a height of about 300 feet. It had been a considerable place before the rise of the [Fulani] . . . but it has been greatly reduced, scarcely more than 100 huts now remaining.'

29. Musgo, a village south of Lake Chad. 'We entered upon stubble-fields with numerous groups of huts and wide-spreading trees whose branches were all used for storing up the ranks of nutritious grass of these swampy grounds for a supply in the dry season . . . Several artificial ponds enlivened the hamlet . . . the tops of the granaries were provided with a sort of "fennel" covered in by a roof of straw.'

30. Richard Burton. He 'prided himself on looking like Satan, as indeed he did'.

31. People of the Wazaramo tribe whom Sir Richard Burton encountered soon after leaving Zanzibar with J.H. Speke: 'The Wazaramo are no exception to the rule of barbarian maritime races . . . Their distinctive mark is the peculiarity of dressing their hair. The thick wool is plastered over with a cap-like coating of ochreish clay, brought from the hills and mixed to the consistency of honey . . . [The women's] hair is allowed to grow in a single or double dense thatch.'

32. Ladies smoking near Unyamyembe as depicted by Sir Richard Burton: 'All the feminine part of the population assemble together and . . . apply themselves to their long black-bowl'd pipes. They smoke with an intense enjoyment, slowly and deeply inhaling the glorious weed and exhaling clouds from their nostrils; at times they stop to cool the mouth with slices of raw manioc or cobs of green maize.'

33. John Hanning Speke, Burton's rival, who had 'an immense and abnormal fund of self-esteem, and who ever held not only that he had done his best on all occasions but also that no living man could do better'.

34. Speke's escape from the Somali attack at his camp near Berbera, from his *Journal*.

35. Speke and Grant at a levee held by Mutesa, Kabaka of Buganda, from Speke's *Journal*. 'When he spoke to them his courtiers were required to throw themselves to the ground in humble submission.'

36. Kamrasi, King of Nyoro, receives his first Bible lesson, from Speke's *Journal of the Discovery of the Source of the Nile*.

37. Grant dancing with Ukulima, the Bugandan Queen Mother, as portrayed in Speke's *Journal*.

38. J. A. Grant, too ill to walk, is carried by his bearers, from Speke's *Journal*.

formed by the bursting of a water-pipe in the streets'. Then, with the satisfaction of having examined the source of a river 'so important to the colony of Sierra Leone' to compensate him for not having been able to visit the source of the Niger, Laing prepared for his journey back to the sea in the second week of September, having received a bundle of presents sent up to him from Sierra Leone. These included two pairs of shoes of which he was sorely in need, some fireworks 'for the gratification of the King and his people', and a lancet together with two glass plates of preserved vaccine virus. He was permitted to inoculate several children, beginning with those of the king himself, and observing that it was 'an interesting fact that a nation so far in the interior of Africa should have so readily admitted, at the instigation of a white man, who was almost a stranger to them, to an operation against which so much prejudice existed for so many years in the most enlightened and civilized countries in Europe!'

On 16 September, at a cost of 7s. 6d., Laing gave 'a grand entertainment and ball for the ladies, who appeared in the gayest attire' and who danced until an early hour next morning. On the 17th he said good-bye to the king who squeezed his hand affectionately and, turning away and covering his face with his hands, said, 'Go, and return to see us.' Laing felt, he said, as though he had parted from a father. Six weeks later he was back in Sierra Leone.

Having returned to England to write an account of his adventures which was published as *Travels in the Timannee, Kooranko and Soolima Countries in Western Africa*, Laing was invited by Lord Bathurst, the Colonial Secretary, to undertake an expedition from Tripoli to try to reach Timbuktu and the source of the Niger from the north. He readily agreed and left almost immediately for Tripoli and thus made the acquaintance of Hanmer Warrington.

Warrington at first found him 'most agreeable', a man of 'extreme Gentlemanly manners, Honorable Conduct, sound moral principle . . . of Enthusiastic Spirit and Indefatigable exertion'. At the time of writing these encomia, however, Warrington had not considered Laing in the character of a son-in-law; and when he learned that this poor Scotsman of humble birth wished to marry his daughter, Emma, he made his displeasure plain. But his 'wishes, exertions, Entreaties' were alike 'quite futile and of no avail; [so] under all circumstances, both for the Public good, as well as their mutual happiness', Warrington felt obliged to perform the wedding ceremony in his office as Consul, while making the stipulation that the bride and bridegroom must not live together until the marriage had been confirmed by an Anglican clergyman.

Two days after the wedding, Laing set out upon his journey in company with a sheikh named Babani. He travelled by way of Fezzan, Ghadames, Ensala, and through the desert of Tenezrounft, sending back worried reports which revealed his anxiety about Emma, about the possibility that someone might reach Timbuktu and solve the question of the Niger before him, and about other officers being promoted before him. Babani died on the way; and Laing himself was almost killed by a party of Ahaggar Tuaregs who, suspecting him to be a Christian, shot him while he slept and then, as he leapt to his feet, wounded him so savagely with their swords that he was left for dead with gashes all over his body, his right hand almost severed, his jaw broken, part of an ear cut off and his scalp slashed in five places. He was lifted up and tied to a camel by the Moors whose caravan he had joined, and was carried by them into Timbuktu on 18 August 1826. What happened to him thereafter is not known for certain. It seems that, having slowly recovered his strength in a house belonging to a Moor, he went about the town quite openly in European dress, was occasionally stopped and asked to repeat that there was but one God and Mahomet was his prophet, an injunction which he obeyed by repeating the first part of the declaration only. But otherwise he was not ill treated, although he was sometimes suspected of being a spy and much disliked because he came from the same country as Mungo Park whose reputation as a ruthless murderer of defenceless men had spread throughout West Africa. On leaving Timbuktu on 26 September 1826 for the north with a Moorish caravan, however, Laing was stopped by a nomadic sheikh of the Berabich Tuaregs in the Zawât desert near Arawan. The sheikh, it seems, ordered one of his people to kill the infidel. The man refused, whereupon two black slaves were summoned who tied a turban round Laing's neck and strangled him. His papers were torn up and burned so as to destroy their magical properties, and all that he had discovered about Timbuktu was thereby lost.

When news of Laing's death reached Tripoli, another young explorer came forward: he had long since set his heart upon reaching Timbuktu and winning not only fame in doing so, but also the 10,000 francs offered as a prize by the Société de Géographie in Paris.

René Caillié was a frail-looking, thin young man with a prominent nose, large dark hooded eyes and abundant brown hair. He looked more like a thoughtful clerk in a Bordeaux counting-house than the intrepid explorer he was to prove himself to be. He had been born at Mauzé near the Biscayan coast at La Rochelle in 1799, the son of a drunkard who had been sentenced to twelve years' imprisonment for a robbery of which he might not have been guilty. His mother was the daughter of a master baker for whom his father had worked. She died when René was eleven, her husband having died, still in prison, two years before. The boy had been brought up with his elder brother and two sisters by his grandmother. He left the village charity school early and was apprenticed to a shoemaker. It was not a trade that appealed to him. Indeed, no trade appealed to him, so he said, 'owing to the reading of voyages and travels' which occupied all his leisure moments.

The History of Robinson Crusoe, in particular, inflamed my youthful imagination [he recorded in a passage which might well have been written by Richard Lander]. I was impatient to encounter adventures like him; nay, I already felt an ambition to make myself famous by some important discovery ... Geographical books and maps were lent to me: the map of Africa, in which I saw scarcely any but countries marked as desert or unknown, excited my attention more than any other. In short, this pre-dilection grew into a passion for which I renounced everything. I no longer joined in the sports and amusements of my comrades. I shut myself up on Sundays to read all the books of travels that I was able to procure. I talked to my uncle, who was my guardian, of my desire to travel. He disapproved of it, forcibly representing the dangers which I should incur at sea, and the regret I should feel far away from my country and my family.

But René persisted: nothing would ever satisfy him if he could not get to Africa where he might make a name for himself, and where no one need know that his father had been a convict in a chain-gang at Rochefort. So, at last, his uncle, an innkeeper, gave way. And on 27 April 1816, the sixteen-year-old boy, who had never before travelled even as far as Paris, set out for Senegal as an officer's servant with sixty francs in his pocket. Just over ten weeks later the brig *La Loire* dropped anchor at St Louis, at the mouth of the Senegal River, a crowded port smelling of dried fish and reverberating with the throb of drums. But there had been some misunderstanding. The English there, who were to have given the place back to the French under the terms of the Treaty of Paris, had as yet received no orders to do so; and until such orders arrived the French colonists who had sailed with Caillié were not permitted to land. They were taken instead to the village of Dakar, and there Caillié stepped ashore in the Africa that had bewitched him, and experienced for the first time those torrential African rains that beat down trees to the ground and washed away the flimsy native huts. Here his master died; and here most of his companions lost all the desire they had ever had to settle in Africa. But Caillié was not disheartened. And as soon as he heard that an English expedition, under a Major Peddie, was about to set off for the interior he longed to go there, too. The English mission was a tragic failure: Peddie died of fever on New Year's Day 1817 having got no further than Kadonky. Captain Campbell, who succeeded him, was turned back by a native ruler and also died on his arrival at the coast. The British then prepared to mount a third expedition under Major Gray who was to attempt a different route by making his way up the Gambia. Caillié determined to join him. He had no money, so he could not take passage in a ship, nor would he be welcome in a caravan. He would have to walk. He found two Negroes who were returning south and he persuaded them to allow him to go with them on the three-hundred-mile journey.

By the time he reached Goree, Caillié, who had had to run for much of the way to keep up with his companions, was utterly exhausted. Yet he might well have tried to struggle on to the Gambia, had not the French commandant at Goree persuaded him that Major Gray could scarcely be expected to welcome a companion in such a weakened condition and that he would do much better to satisfy his craving for travel by sailing to Guadeloupe for which a free passage could be procured for him. So Caillié sailed to Guadeloupe where he obtained 'a petty appointment' and where his longing to return to Africa was inflamed by reading Mungo Park's account of his adventures on the Niger. By the end of 1818 he was back at St Louis 'with scanty resources' but more determined than ever to make a name for himself as Mungo Park had done. He found that, although six months had elapsed, Major Gray was still 'standing in need of hands'; and he immediately offered his services to Gray's agent, a mulatto named Adrien Partarrieu, who had been sent to St Louis to replenish Gray's stock of presents which had been much diminished by the avarice of Gambian rulers and, in particular, by the *Almamy* of Bondou. Partarrieu listened to the young man's pleas without enthusiasm, accepting his employment only on condition that he received no pay.

From St Louis to Gray's camp at Bondou entailed a circuitous journey to the east lasting over three months; and these long weeks that Caillié spent with Partarrieu's caravan of sixty or seventy men and thirty-two camels were an experience far more fearful than his previous walk south to Goree. Following the caravan on foot, tired out and constantly thirsty, Caillié was, as he confessed, 'reduced to extremity'. 'I have since been told that my eyes were hollow,' he wrote, 'that I panted for breath, and that my tongue hung out of my mouth. For my own part I recollect that at every halt, I fell to the ground from weakness, and had not even the strength to eat ... I was not, however, the worst off, for I saw several drink their urine.'

Partarrieu at length took pity on him, offered him water from his calabash and introduced him to the *neoe*, a fruit with a white pulp of an agreeable flavour which for a time quenched his burning thirst. Peppermint drops which had been packed in the camels' baggage were also a relief; but Caillié was almost constantly thirsty, and when he came to a village where water was for sale he ignored the swarms of parched bees that settled upon the calabashes and stung the faces and lips of all who drank from them.

Bondou was reached at last; but there was little comfort to be found there. The *Almamy* affected to be disgusted with the presents which Major Gray was now able to offer him and refused him permission to proceed in the direction he had hoped to follow. Denied access to the wells, he was forced into the territory of the Fulani of Futa-Toro who demanded outrageous prices for water and plundered the caravan. Gray left his men to seek help from the French fort at Bakel; but on his return to the caravan with a party of hired Moors and volunteer seamen he was attacked by Fulani who attempted to tear the clothes off his men's backs and led him away into captivity. Caillié and Partarrieu then also made for Bakel to fetch help. But the help was not needed, for soon after their arrival Gray was released and joined them there.

Caillié now fell ill with fever and had to be carried out of Bakel in the torrential rain. He was taken back to St Louis where, following weeks in the makeshift hospital, he was faced with the prospect of having to earn his living again. He worked for a time as a cook in St Louis; then, returning to France, was employed by a firm of wine merchants. He saved money as the months passed; but it was not until his employer lent him enough to buy 'a little *pacotille*' – a small stock of cheap goods for use as presents – that he was able to realize his ambition of returning to Africa. He arrived back in Senegal soon after his twenty-fourth birthday in 1824 with new plans for himself as an explorer. He had learned, from his experiences with the English, at what disadvantage the traveller in Africa placed himself by moving about with so obviously large and tempting a supply of goods as Major Gray had done. He would travel with very little; and he would travel alone. He would wear the clothes of a Moor and behave as a Moor; he would learn a language that Moors would understand. He would present himself as a young man intent upon learning how to be a good Mohammedan. And then he might be able to reach Timbuktu.

He confided his plan to the French governor of Senegal who endeavoured to dissuade him from the enterprise but, finding him resolute, added to the *pacotille* with which his former employer had provided him. And, on 3 August 1824 at four in the afternoon, he left St Louis on foot for the country of the Brakna Moors. It was to be another dreadful journey. With his bundle of goods on his head, he walked through the marshy land beside the Senegal River and across country where sharp flints cut his feet and the thorns of prickly plants lacerated his legs. There were sandstorms and storms of drenching rain. He drank water so muddy he was obliged to suck it through his teeth. But after weeks of travelling he reached the Brakna country and sought out the ruler's marabout to tell him his story. He was, he said, the son of a well-to-do Frenchman who had recently died and left him his fortune, part of which was now stored at St Louis. In France he had 'met with a French translation of the Koran' in which he had found 'important truths' with which he was 'deeply impressed'; and, having 'heard the wisdom of the Braknas highly extolled', he had 'determined to come and live among them' and train himself to become a worthy Mussulman. The marabout, obviously interested in the young man's account of his wealth, appeared to accept this story and undertook to conduct him to the ruler who, when the stranger had been twice thoroughly washed as a purification, agreed to see him and appeared also to believe his account of himself.

So Caillié settled down to share the life of the Braknas, to eat their unappetizing food of mushy couscous and sour milk, to learn their ways, to tolerate the inquisitiveness of the women who peered at him from between the legs of the men and, at every movement he made, 'drew back their heads with loud screams', to suffer the torments of children who pulled off his covering while he tried to sleep, pricked him with thorns and threw stones at him crying, 'Come and see the Christian!' He accompanied them on their nomadic journeys from one grazing ground to the next, watching as the new camp grew as filthy as its predecessor and the grazing was exhausted, affecting to feel no distaste when women rubbed rancid butter and pounded cloves into their hair or endeavoured to make their daughters fatter, and therefore more desirable and valuable, by forcing stodgy food into their mouths until they were sick, and to improve their appearance in the eyes of Brakna men by forcing their front teeth out over the lower lip. At Ramadan he fasted rigorously under the eyes of spectators eager to condemn the slightest lapse.

On the sixth day I thought I could no longer endure these privations [he wrote]. The east wind blew violently; the heat increased; my throat was parched; my tongue, dry and chapped, was like a rasp in my mouth, and I thought I should sink under my sufferings ... Besides being compelled to observe a most rigorous fast, I had to bear the insolence of a number of travelling hassanes, with whom my sufferings were a subject of ridicule. If they found me lying upon my mat, they pulled me by my clothes, and pinched me and tormented me in a thousand ways to force me to answer their questions, which were all intended to insult me. They commonly concluded by asking me if I would not drink a little brandy and eat pork, and whether I did not intend to be circumcised. At each of these questions, to which I refused to reply, they laughed violently, and answered for me, affecting the most cutting contempt.

Having endured the torments of life with the Braknas and having assimilated enough of their manner to render his further journeys less hazardous, Caillié returned to St Louis – accompanied by a member of the tribe to ensure that he came back to them with his supposed riches – in the hope of persuading the governor to advance him 6,000 francs for the furtherance of his mission. To his bitter disappointment he was offered only 1,200 francs, which he declined; and was once again compelled to seek employment in the hope of saving up enough money himself. This time he managed to obtain an extremely well-paid appointment from the British authorities at Freetown in Sierra Leone. He was to be paid no less than the equivalent of 3,600 francs a year as manager of an indigo works. It was only later that it occurred to him he had been offered this tempting sum by the British to keep him contentedly occupied in Sierra Leone, leaving Major Laing – who had left Tripoli about eight months before – without a rival in his attempt to reach Timbuktu.

Caillié never lost hope of getting there himself. He saved as much money as he could; he continued with his studies of the Koran and the languages of the desert; he consulted the Mandingo merchants and workers in Freetown; he walked for miles, training himself to estimate accurately the distance he covered and the direction in which he was advancing without the use of those instruments to which other explorers had recourse but which he would not dare to show he possessed; he studied the conditions which the Société de Géographie had attached to their prize, the detailed information about Timbuktu and its surroundings which the winner would be expected to supply; and he perfected the story which he would tell on his next journey: the story of his being born in Egypt of Arab parents, of his being taken to France when young; of his being later taken to Freetown by his French masters who had released him from their employment there; and of his anxiety to return home to his family in Egypt and to 'go on in the Mussulman religion'.

When he had saved 2,000 francs, Caillié decided the time had come for him to set out on his travels again. With most of his money he bought presents; the rest, in silver and gold, he placed in the pockets of a belt. And, so, in Arab dress once more, taking with him, as well as his presents and money, medicines given him by some Scotsmen who had befriended him in Freetown, two pocket compasses and several loose sheets of the Koran, he took ship in March 1827 for the mouth of the Rio Nunez in what was to become French Guinea.

He was befriended at Kakandé not only by a French trader who put him up, and by two English merchants who took him on a cautionary excursion to the tombs of Peddie and Campbell, but also by the local Muslims whom he joined in prayer. And, while waiting for a caravan which he could join on its way to the interior, he studied the ways of the surrounding tribes – the men of the Landoumas, some of whom had two hundred wives, and the boys and girls of the Bagas who were betrothed when they were seven or eight years old and married when it was perceived that 'the young virgin had ceased to be so', which was 'ordinarily at the age of eleven or twelve years'.

Caillié had to wait for scarcely more than a fortnight for a small caravan to assemble at Kakandé; and on 19 April he set off in company with five Mandingos, three slaves, a Fulani porter, a guide and the guide's wife. It was a journey as exhausting and unpleasant as he had learned to expect. The air was oppressively hot; the narrow path led through thick grass that waved above his head, up mountain paths, through fast-moving streams and soggy morasses, across the slippery trunks of trees insecurely spanning rivers. The route was tortuous, dictated by the needs of the caravan; and for days Caillié found himself stumbling along in a direction far from that in which he had intended to go, changing direction as many as fifteen times in a day. Secretly he made notes when he could, using the loose pages of the Koran so that if he were discovered he might pretend to be engaged in some religious study, committing to memory the names of places until it was safe to write them down. In villages he remained quiet, retiring, self-effacing, always tactful, most scrupulous in his payment for hospitality. Only once did he forget himself and laughed out loud when an old man, attempting to display his scholarship, took the Koran from his hand and declaimed a passage to the crowd, holding the page close to his eyes upside down. Angered by the mockery, the old man shouted that Caillié was a white man and an infidel. Most of the time, however, Caillié was treated with respect as the Egyptian student he pretended to be. He was offered fruit and kola nuts and given a pair of sandals for the comfort of his lacerated feet.

On 10 May, having covered well over two hundred miles in three weeks, he reached Cambaya; and a month later he crossed the Niger near Kouroussa, uncomplainingly waiting for several hours for a place on the ferry. Beyond Kouroussa he came to Kankan, a large neat town of relatively sophisticated people whose leading men, having questioned him closely, declared at a meeting in the women's mosque – commonly used for such purposes as it was not so much in demand for religious practices as the men's – that the stranger was, indeed, a young man of truth and merit. In the country of the Ouassoulous, too, he was treated with much respect, though not as a follower of the Prophet, for the people here were pagans, but as a handsome visitor, courteous and pleasant, and possessed of an extraordinary instrument which he called 'un parapluie' and which he furled and unfurled for their curious inspection. They stared wonderingly also at his white skin, at night-time lighting wisps of straw to examine it more closely. 'They liked the looks of me,' so Caillié said. 'Many gave me milk, and a pretty good supper of boiled yams with gombo sauce and seasoned with a little salt to which pistachio nuts were added.'

From Ségala, the principal town of the Ouassoulous, Caillié passed on to Samatiguila and thence to the Mandingo village of Tiémé. And at Tiémé, where he arrived on 3 August 1827, he fell dangerously ill. He was suffering from a severe attack of fever; also, for some time now, his foot had been badly infected by some parasite which had caused an agonizingly painful blister. He was forced to shelter in a mud hut where he was looked after by an old woman of the village who spread a bullock's hide on the ground for him to lie on and gave him 'some soup, consisting of herbs stewed in milk' and seasoned with a few grains of her precious salt. When he was a little better her son, who was named Baba, found him a larger hut where he lay on a mat which was spread on the damp ground and was 'the only furniture of the place'. For weeks he lay there, the sore on his foot growing worse instead of healing, while the rain poured down, filtering through the thin walls.

I could not kindle a fire [he recorded], on account of the intolerable smoke. Throughout all the interior of Africa, the negroes never make chimneys. They kindle their fires in the middle of their huts, and leave the smoke to find its way through the roofs, which are in consequence thickly lined with soot ... I intended to set out about the end of August; but at that time another sore much larger than the first broke out on the same foot. I suffered considerable pain, and my foot was so swelled that I could not walk ... About the end of October the rains ceased and the days became exceedingly hot ... My host Baba, who had paid me great attention at first, no doubt because of the pretty presents I had given him, began to neglect me ... On the other hand I was tormented by the women of the village who came in crowds to ask me for glass beads. I was at once an object of curiosity and aversion to them. They ridiculed my gestures and my words, and went about the village mimicking me and repeating what I had said ... My sore foot was the object of their ridicule, and the difficulty I experienced in walking excited their immoderate laughter ... By 10 November the sore in my foot was almost healed, and I hoped to profit by the first opportunity for setting out for Jenné. But at that very time violent pains in my jaw informed me that I was attacked with scurvy, and I experienced all the horrors of that dreadful disease: the roof of my mouth became quite bare, part of the bones exfoliated and fell away, and my teeth seemed ready to drop out of their sockets. I feared that my brain would be affected by the agonizing pains I felt in my head, and I was more than a fortnight without sleep. The sore in my foot broke out afresh, and all hope of departure vanished ... Baba's good old mother brought me a little rice-water twice a day which she forced me to drink ... and at length after six weeks of indescribable suffering I began to feel better.

By New Year's Day 1828 he had sufficiently recovered his strength to move on again. A caravan arrived at Tiémé that day bringing in a supply of kola nuts; and Caillié determined to join it on the northward journey to Jenné which was to be resumed after the hungry men had satisfied their voracious appetites: in a week of almost continuous eating they consumed five or six meals a day and sometimes got up in the middle of the night to enjoy another. On the 9th the caravan moved off, the men wearing bells which jingled as they walked; the women naked apart from belts decorated with cowrie shells and cotton thread. They were a large and happy group, their number swelling to over five hundred before their destination was reached. On their heads, with apparent effortlessness, they carried bundles of kolas so heavy that Caillié could scarcely lift them. They walked fast, increasing their pace as the night's resting place drew near, a messenger running ahead to warn of their approach, while the women hurried after him to heat water and prepare meals for the men. Refreshed by food and washing, the young men and women danced round bonfires, leaping up and down as though celebrating their release from their heavy burdens, kicking their bottoms with their heels and shaking tambourines.

Caillié chose not to join them in their meals for the effects of scurvy had made it difficult to eat without painful slobbering and the fear that a piece of loose bone from his palate would fall out – as once a piece did – into his mouth. Nor did he join them in the huts because of the insufferable smoke, preferring to sleep outside despite the cold of the nights, shivering in his thin worn clothes, frequently catching cold and once spitting blood. At Tengréla, though, he shared with some others a hut of surprising commodiousness, containing not only two doors but even a window. Here, while the others drank quantities of honey-beer, on which they became so drunk as to be incapable of speech, he, careful as always to maintain his reputation as a devotee of Allah, declined to touch the calabash when his turn came round.

When the caravan reached Jenné, Caillié's assumption of the character of an Egyptian intent upon returning to the Mohammedanism of his forebears was once again most closely questioned. On his arrival in the town he was lodged at first in an exceedingly wretched and dirty room reached by means of a narrow stairway of earth leading out of the ground-floor store-room; and from these evil-smelling quarters he was conducted by their Mandingo owner to the house of the sherif, the leader of the Moorish community in the town.

The sherif and his fellow-Moors made him repeat his story more than once, cross-examined him interminably, and required him to appear before the aged Negro chief of Jenné to whom he had to repeat his story yet again. But at length the story was accepted; and the old Negro decreed that, 'until an opportunity should occur' of the young man's going to Timbuktu, he 'should remain with the sherif who, as a rich man and a descendant of the Prophet, would take care that I should be well treated'.

Although the sherif appeared 'not very well pleased' at being burdened for an indeterminate time with a stranger as his guest, Caillié was, indeed, well treated. He was given a first-floor room considerably more salubrious than the one he had at first occupied; he was offered the services of a barber who removed his turban and shaved his head most skilfully with a blade of European manufacture; he was provided with food infinitely more enjoyable than the almost inedible mush he had been obliged to eat virtually every day since leaving Freetown. A female slave brought to his room large dishes of good rice seasoned with meat and small onions; and, on a subsequent visit to the sherif's house, he was given not only excellent stewed mutton and onions but also fine fresh bread and tea served in small porcelain cups.

'We each took four of these cups of tea with white sugar,' Caillié remembered. 'And, after dinner, at which the sherif did the honours admirably well, we took a walk on the banks of the river. We sat down for a few minutes to see the canoes pass by, and, afterwards, we all said the evening prayer together, it being too late to go to the mosque. We then returned to our homes. I found a great difference between the Moors of Jenné and the Brakna Moors.'

Caillié was much impressed by Jenné and its inhabitants. The houses were unfurnished apart from the bullocks' hides or mats on which the people slept, and the leather bags which contained their belongings and were sometimes hung on lines to divide apartments into two; but they were well constructed and some even contained water-closets. There were schools and a fine mosque begun in the eleventh century. The people, Mandingos, Fulani and Moors alike, seemed lively and intelligent. Everyone was well dressed, the men in white *coussabes*, white trousers and red caps around which a large piece of muslin was rolled like a turban. The women were also in white with plaited hair, gold ear-rings and nose-rings, necklaces of glass, amber and coral, and rings of plated iron round their ankles. All of them, and their children, wore gaily coloured leather shoes, 'very neatly made'.

After spending eleven days in this pleasant town, Caillié prepared for his journey by canoe to Timbuktu. He sold the few remaining articles of his *pacotille* for 30,000 cowries and with these purchased goods that would be useful to him on his northward journey. He gave his umbrella to the sherif who had made no secret of his desire to possess so extaordinary and useful an apparatus, and who was so pleased to have it that he not only arranged a passage for Caillié on board a canoe but also gave him presents of dates and fine water-melons every day until his departure, as well as food and candles for use on the river journey.

This journey, at first on the river Bani which flows parallel with the Niger and then on the Niger itself, began on 23 March 1828. Two days later, at Couna, some fifty miles below Jenné, Caillié and the other passengers were transferred to a larger canoe, a vessel almost a hundred feet long constructed of planks lashed together with hempen ropes and the leaves of palm trees, and caulked with pounded straw and clay. It appeared to Caillié extremely fragile and was obviously not watertight, members of the crew being constantly employed in bailing. But all the other canoes were in a similar state and apparently did not sink. They were covered with mats and laden with rice, millet, cotton, honey and butter. Most of them also carried slaves. Their rate of progress was extremely slow, perhaps not more, so Caillié thought, than two miles an hour. Where the banks permitted it, they were dragged along by ropes; where ropes could not be used, they were pushed along by poles and in deeper water paddled. Occasionally the slaves had to be set on shore to lighten the craft; and once the fifty or so in Caillié's canoe, temporarily released from their chains, began to leap and dance as though in celebration of their freedom. This so offended a party of Fulani who happened to see them that they came aboard the vessel armed with bows and pikes to complain of such behaviour during Ramadan and to demand payment of a fine of 5,000 cowries. 'The master, to whose charge the slaves had been committed, earnestly defended the cause of his employer. A spirited altercation arose but ... at length the dispute ended at the expense of the poor slaves who, as a punishment for dancing during this sacred season, were each condemned to receive five lashes on the back. The sentence, however, was not executed with much severity, and did not restrain the slaves from resuming their dance as soon as the fanatical [Fulani] departed.'

Tediously slow and constantly interrupted, the journey north was a dreadful ordeal for Caillié.

I had the misery of being the only white man among the negroes, and with their language I was unacquainted [he wrote]. This circumstance, joined to my being a stranger, and almost destitute, emboldened them to insult me in the grossest manner ... During the day the heat was excessive ... and this brought upon me an attack of fever ... During my illness I was permitted to go into the cabin; but the place assigned me there was very cramped. I was with a Mandingo and his female slave; and they allowed me so little room I could not lie straight; my head touched my knees. I had been particularly recommended to this negro by the sherif; but he paid no regard to the instructions he received and showed as little pity for me as the rest of the crew ... And the slaves, following this example, behaved with the grossest insolence towards me.

The sight of the 'immense monstrous plains' that stretched far and desolate beyond the banks of the river added to Caillié's misery. Sometimes he saw a group of slaves working on the land or a party of their black and woolly-haired masters, armed with pikes and bows and arrows, watching the canoe from the shade of the mimosa trees at the river's edge. Occasionally the lowing of distant oxen was to be heard, or the grunting of hippopotami and the shrill cries of the trumpet-birds upon the sand banks. From time to time young naked girls appeared running along the banks, offering for sale dried fish and sour milk. Once, feeling less ill, Caillié went ashore to a Fulani village and entered one of their huts, a circular structure 'made of a very pretty kind of matting' and 'surrounded by quickset hedges of *celane*, a euphorbious plant which grows spontaneously on the sandy shores'. 'The only dress of the women was an apron tied round their waists,' he recorded. 'They were all exceedingly clean ... They came in crowds to see me, being very curious, and apparently, very devout, for when I was going away they took up some sand in their hands and earnestly requested me to pray over it. I complied with their wishes, gravely muttering some verses of the Koran. They then carefully rolled up the sand in their aprons.'

But such diversions in the long and tedious days were no longer possible once the canoe drew close to Timbuktu, for here, beyond Saféré, the river banks were controlled by pillaging Tuaregs who extorted tribute from the passing boats. Caillié was told that his pale skin would attract the notice of the marauders and that he must therefore conceal himself in the covered part of the canoe under matting. In the stifling heat of this hiding-place he thereafter passed his days until the canoe arrived at Kabara, the port of Timbuktu where, on 20 April, a party of slaves belonging to Sidi-Abdallahi Chebir, a friend of the sherif of Jenné, came out to meet him and to conduct him across the desert to Timbuktu. He arrived there just as the sun was touching the horizon and, on entering the 'mysterious city', experienced 'an indescribable feeling of satisfaction'.

Yet, when he looked around him, his disappointment was bitter; for Timbuktu was very far from being the magical place of legend. It 'presented, at first view, nothing but a mass of ill-looking houses, built of earth. Nothing was to be seen in any direction but immense plains of quicksand of a yellowish white colour. The sky was a pale red as far as the horizon: all nature wore a dreary aspect, and the most profound silence prevailed; not even the warbling of a bird was to be heard.'

He had supper of couscous and mutton that evening with Sidi-Abdallahi Chebir, a small, fat, pock-marked, middle-aged merchant who greeted him in a friendly way and accepted without question the story of his provenance and desire to reach his Muslim family in Egypt. And, after a sleepless and oppressively hot night in the lodging which Sidi-Abdallahi Chebir's servants had prepared for him, he went out the next morning in the hope of finding Timbuktu less desolate than it had seemed the evening before. But he was again disappointed. The place, which he estimated contained some ten or twelve thousand inhabitants, was neither so large nor so populous as he had expected; and its commerce was 'not so considerable as fame' had reported. The streets were not crowded as they had been at Jenné. Occasionally a trail of laden camels was to be seen, or water-sellers and nut-vendors crying their wares, or a group of women, their 'deep black' faces unveiled, their eyes lined with antimony, their hair braided or bunched into tight balls, decorated with coral, their bodies swathed in long, loose white robes and scented with musk and cloves, their feet encased in brightly coloured sandals. But the overriding impression was one of inactivity and indolence. Most of the Negroes sat on mats, engaged in desultory conversation; the Moors slept in the shade before their doors. Sometimes an open door revealed a store-house filled with goods from beyond the desert. Timbuktu produced nothing of its own, the soil being totally unfit for cultivation. Food was, therefore, expensive. So was the water which, warm and sandy, was sold by women in the marketplace at a cowrie for half a pint. Firewood was scarce and used only by the wealthier merchants; the poor had to make do with camel dung. Everyone was terrorized by the Tuaregs who not only plundered caravans on their way into the town, but entered the town itself, forcing their way into houses, helping themselves to food and drink, stealing what took their fancy and even demanding payment before leaving. There was a Negro king in Timbuktu, a man of 'a very dark black' whom Caillié was taken to see by Sidi-Abdallahi; but he was of little consequence when the Tuaregs were about. It was the Tuaregs, Caillié now learned, who had so brutally assaulted Major Laing and left him for dead.

Caillié could not help being afraid that such a fate might await him in the Saharan desert which he would one day soon have to cross. He considered going home by a less hazardous route, through Segu and Sansanding to the

Senegal coast; but he reflected that 'jealous people' might then doubt that he had reached Timbuktu at all, 'whilst by returning via the Barbary States, the very point of [his] arrival, would impose conviction on the envious'. So, at the beginning of May he said goodbye to Sidi-Abdallahi who loaded him with presents, protesting that all the care he had taken of his guest was 'for the love of God and the Prophet', and accompanied him some distance from his house. The caravan had already left and Caillié had to run so fast to catch up with it that he fainted on reaching it and had to be picked up and placed on a loaded camel where he sat among the packages.

The journey to the Mediterranean across the Sahara, a journey which no European was known to have attempted, was the most agonizing of all Caillié's ordeals. As the caravan, which soon comprised 1,400 camels and 400 merchants, travellers and slaves, trudged across the seemingly endless sands and the desolate rocky wastes at a rate of less than two miles an hour, there was at first the danger from Tuareg marauders, two of whom rode up, veiled and spectacularly armed, to batten on the travellers until they chose to ride off again. There was the ever-present threat of sandstorms. There was the relentless glare of the sun and the choking heat of the sand-filled air which blistered the lips and burned the throat, despite the strips of cloth which desert travellers wore over their mouths as well as over their eyes. There were the long silent night marches and the fear that the camel with his awkward gait would throw off a sleepy rider who might be stunned by the fall and left to die alone. There was the dreadful monotony of the paste of flour and honey which was served out as food and of which, though he had paid for it, Caillié received less than his share from the Moorish villain, Sidi-Ali, into whose care he had been entrusted by Sidi-Abdullahi and whose delight in petty cruelties was intolerable. An ugly, spiteful little man with a pretence of piety, he teased and bullied Caillié mercilessly, threatening to sell him into slavery, encouraging his companions to call him 'Gageba', the name of his camel which, with his long nose, he contended Caillié resembled, handing the slaves branches of thorns to thrust into his face and pieces of wood to drive through his nose so that he might be led like a camel.

Worst torture of all was the perpetual, parching thirst. The wells were far apart and some were dry. The stores in the *gerbas* did not permit of more than a small ration which was issued once a day in the afternoon; and when Caillié asked if he might have a smaller ration more often he was angrily told that he must abide by the customs of the caravan or get no water at all. On one long agonizing march between well and well it seemed that the caravan's supply of water must run out. The slaves bit their fingers to suck their blood; some drank their urine. A party of men was sent out to search for a water-hole off the main route, but they got lost and were reduced to killing a camel to drink the greenish liquid stored in its stomach. They would have drunk the blood, too, had not the Koran forbidden it. As the east wind blew hotter than ever, Caillié thought of nothing but water. 'Rivers, streams, rivulets were the only ideas that presented themselves' to his mind. At the camping-places he went from tent to tent, with his prayer-beads in his hand, begging shamelessly for 'a little water for the love of Allah'. This 'useless fatigue' augmented his torments and when he got back to his own tent he fainted. And at this 'horrible time' a huge pillar of sand crossed the camp, overturned all the tents and whirled their occupants about like straws.

Through the shouts and prayers and the roaring of the wind I could distinguish at intervals the low plaintive moan of the camels who were as much alarmed as their masters, and more to be pitied as they had not tasted food for four days [Caillié recorded]. About half past four in the afternoon we left the place where we had experienced this terrible hurricane and proceeded on our way towards the north. The camels walked slowly and with effort for they were almost exhausted ... The sight of this numerous caravan, destitute of water, scattered over the arid land, was truly dismal ... The plain was interspersed with hills of coarse red sand mixed with gravel. The soil was very hard, covered with rocks and red and black granite, in flaky strata like slate ... The heat was stifling ... The allowance of water was every time more and more scanty. We suffered beyond all expression.

At last the well was reached. It was filled with sand 'which the Moors immediately fell to work to clear out'. The camels sensing that water was near became unmanageable and had to be beaten off with whips. They ran off a little way, then came crowding round the well again, laying their heads on the damp sand which had been thrown out of it. The water drawn up was black and muddy, but the camels fought for it with fury and Caillié went in amongst them to drink.

This was at the wells of Telig near the salt mines of Toudenni where blacks worked in conditions of appalling squalor and where the water in the wells was so foul that within a few years it poisoned all those who had to drink it regularly. The caravan had already passed through Arouane, a trading post of some 3,000 people with deep wells containing unwholesome brackish water and surrounded by sand dunes as far as the eye could reach, the 'most unpleasant place' that Caillié had ever seen. From Telig it moved on to the wells of Cramès; then, on 1 June, to the wells of Mayara where the water was 'detestable'; then to Amoul-Gragrin where the well was filled with sand, and huge fat snakes, almost six feet long, crawled out of holes in the middle of the night. In the camps set up between the wells the Moors made sure that their camels' loads were secure. But, in spite of this examination which was repeated at every halting-place, the camels were often galled by their loads and developed sores and wounds which their owners scarified and filled with salt to prevent mortification. After doctoring his own camels in this way, Sidi-Ali mixed the food with filthy hands, thrusting his arms into the paste up to the elbows. When occasionally he washed his hands, he gave the water he had used for his slave to drink. If the camels' feet were cut their owners stitched them together with patches of hide, using the same needle when necessary to sew together the cracks in the soles of their own feet.

Caillié's camel bolted just before the caravan reached El-Harib and he was thrown to the ground with such force that he almost broke his back and thought that he had fractured his skull. He was in pain for weeks. Sidi-Ali's family lived at El-Harib where Caillié was lodged in the camelhair tent of Ali's sister, a malicious, verminous woman who provided him with a mess of food like porridge which was full of hairs because the woman used the same butter for cooking as she did for rubbing into her scalp. He tried to make do with dates but these were so hard as to be virtually inedible, since his attack of scurvy had made it impossible for him to chew without severe pain. He was driven to going from tent to tent begging for camel's milk as he had begged for water further south. The people he saw in these tents were repulsively dirty, their children covered with sores. When he returned to his own tent to forget his hunger in sleep, women jabbed him with pieces of wood, pulled him by the legs, took away his coverings and threw water into his face. Young men, Ali's sons, presented themselves to him naked, making the 'most obscene gestures'.

To his infinite relief the caravan left El-Harib on 12 July and soon the desert became less harsh. Wells were plentiful; there were glimpses of green foliage; amiable Berber women with tattooed faces and red and white cloths round their heads smiled at him invitingly; once he saw a plough. On 23 July the caravan reached the oasis of Tafilalet where date palms grew in abundance beside melons and apple trees. The desert journey was over; and he now had but to cross Morocco to the sea. This, though, was not easy. He had a few pieces of gold and English silver left in his money-belt; but there were difficulties and risks in changing them and he had to sell some of his clothes before he could buy enough food and hire an ass to carry him across the Atlas Mountains to Fez.

From Fez he went to Meknès where, thrown out of the mosque in which he had hoped to spend the night, he felt compelled to risk the dangers of changing some of his silver so that he could reach Rabat. He did reach Rabat in safety but his hopes of obtaining there the protection of his own countrymen were dashed when the door of the French consulate was opened by a Moroccan Jew. Another Jew was acting as consul. The French Consul was away in Tangier.

On 7 September, Caillié reached Tangier two hundred miles away and, utterly exhausted and in rags, made his way to the Consul's house. The Consul, he was told, was dead; but the Vice-Consul, M. Delaporte, to whom he announced simply, 'I am a Frenchman. I have been to Timbuktu', took him in his arms and, overcome with emotion, kissed him. But he dared not keep him in his house which he had been seen entering. He sent him away, and the next day when Caillié returned, Delaporte shouted to the guard, 'Turn out this dog of a beggar!' And it was not until he secretly returned on the third day that Delaporte agreed to harbour him if he could slip into the house that night unseen. This Caillié managed to do; and for over a fortnight he remained there, lying in blissful comfort between Delaporte's sheets, eating thankfully the food and drink that Delaporte brought him, until he was able to leave in the uniform of a sailor and return to France aboard the *Légère*.

In his own country he was greeted as a hero. He received the prize offered by the Paris Geographical Society; he was awarded a pension of 3,000 francs and soon afterwards he married and bought a farm near Mauzé. He had children; he prospered and was elected mayor. But there were those who were strongly critical of his having denied Christ in his pretended character of a Mohammedan; and there were others, particularly in England, who doubted the truth of his story, as James Bruce's stories had been doubted. It was even alleged that he had somehow come into possession of the papers of Major Laing and had used them to concoct his own account. 'I must confess,' Caillie wrote at the end of his *Travels*, 'that these unjust attacks have affected me more deeply than all the hardships, fatigues and privations which I have encountered in the interior of Africa.' When he died from consumption at the age of thirty-eight, his story was still not wholly credited and it was not until another explorer entered Timbuktu that its truth was fully established. This explorer was Heinrich Barth.

7

10,000 MILES THROUGH NEGROLAND

HEINRICH BARTH AND JAMES RICHARDSON LEAVE
TRIPOLI, MARCH 1850 · THEIR JOURNEY ACROSS
THE DESERT TO TINTELLUST · BARTH IS THE
FIRST CHRISTIAN TO ENTER AGADES · HIS DESCRIPTIONS
OF TASAWA AND KANO · RICHARDSON'S DEATH
NEAR KUKAWA · BARTH GOES SOUTH TO YOLA ON THE
BENUE · HE JOINS ARAB ROBBERS AND GOES TO
MANDARA · A MARAUDING EXPEDITION IN
MANDARA · SOUTH TO MASENA AND EAST TO
TIMBUKTU · HIS RETURN JOURNEY ACROSS THE SAHARA
TO TRIPOLI WHERE HE ARRIVES IN AUGUST 1855

When he set out upon the long journey that was to take him across the Sahara to Timbuktu, Heinrich Barth was already an experienced traveller. Born in Hamburg in 1821, he had read classics at the University of Berlin and had afterwards studied Arabic in London, becoming as fluent in that language as he also was in Italian, English and Spanish. At the age of twenty-four he had made his way throughout the length of North Africa, travelled widely in Egypt, ascended the Nile to Wadi Halfa and crossed the desert to Berenice. His account of his *Wanderungen* was published in 1849. In that year he was recommended by Professor Karl Ritter of the University of Berlin who had been asked by the German ambassador in London to suggest a suitable fellow-countryman to join a British expedition then being planned under the direction of James Richardson.

Richardson, fifteen years older than Barth, had also travelled widely in North Africa and had published a book about his experiences. A serious, rather self-righteous man, he had been educated for the evangelical ministry and had become a leading opponent of the slave trade. It was with the intention of discovering how the trade was carried on that Richardson had

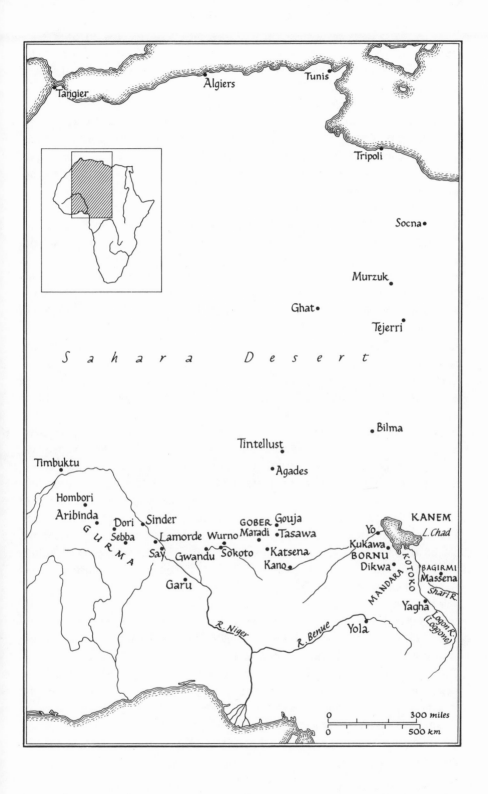

Tangier

Algiers

Tunis

Tripoli

Socna•

Murzuk•

Ghat•

Tejerri•

S a h a r a   D e s e r t

Bilma•

Tintellust•

•Agades

Timbuktu•

Hombori•
Aribinda•

Dori•
Sebba•

Sinder•

G U R M A

Lamorde•

Say•

Gwandu•

Garu•

Wurno•

GOBER• Gouja•
Maradi• •Tasawa

Sokoto•

•Katsena

Kano•

Yo•

Kukawa•
BORNU
Dikwa•

KANEM

L. Chad

M A N D A R A

K O T O K O

BAGIRMI
Massena•

Shari R.

Yagha•

Logon R.
(Loggone)

R. Niger

R. Benue

Yola•

300 miles
0

0
500 km

journeyed across the desert to Murzuk, Ghadames and Ghat; and one of the principal objects of the expedition which Barth was now to join was to discover ways in which it might be abolished and to promote other forms of trade in its place. Barth himself, however, thought that the main object of the mission should be the scientific exploration of Central Africa and hoped that, having reached Lake Chad, the explorers would be authorized to continue their journey either east to the Nile or Zanzibar, or west to Timbuktu. These hopes were shared by Adolf Overweg, the Prussian astronomer and geologist, who was also to be of the party.

'Seated in solemn state' upon their camels, the three explorers left Tripoli on the first stage of their journey on 24 March 1850. By way of Murzuk, the oasis of Ghat and the small town of Barakat, they made their way south slowly and uneventfully through the desert until, near the village of Selufiet towards the end of August, 'a large mob of lawless people' came about their camp in the middle of the night 'howling like hungry jackals'. Barth thought that they might well have been tempted by the ten large iron cases which were amongst their baggage and which, though they contained nothing but dry biscuits, were supposed by the tribesmen to be filled with 'enormous wealth'. The travellers escaped, however, with the loss of but a few camels and reached Tintellust in safety before the end of September. They were welcomed here by an old chief who observed that although, as Christians, they had come to his country stained with guilt, the difficulties of their journey sufficed to wash them clean and they now had nothing to fear but climate and thieves. As if in obedience to his prediction, the Europeans' camp was soon afterwards invaded by marauders; but, little disconcerted by this or by the jackals that roamed about the tents all night, Barth found Tintellust a delightful place after the rigours of the desert. It rained heavily, yet this was a pleasure after the sandstorms; the camp was surrounded by masses of granite blocks, wide-spreading bushes and luxuriant trees from which fresh leaves sprouted every day; monkeys played around the tents, and ring doves and hoopoes fluttered constantly in the overhanging foliage. Parting company with his companions, Barth left for Agades in good spirits on Friday, 4 October.

With a stained skin and wearing a black tobe and white burnous, Barth entered Agades a few days later, the first Christian, as he believed, ever to set foot there; but despite his disguise, he was recognized as a Christian immediately. Yet, although women and children occasionally broke out into 'little explosions of fanaticism', he was treated well enough and no objections were raised to his walking as a tourist through the town with his pencil and sketchbook. He was admitted into the clay houses, the principal items of furniture in which were enormous four-poster bedsteads covered with canopies and mats; he was allowed to watch the labours of the leather workers and blacksmiths and to visit the markets upon which greedy vultures peered down from the pinnacles of the ruined walls; he entered the mosque and inspected the adjoining tower, a clay structure almost a hundred feet tall, its four walls united by thirteen layers of beams crossing its entire breadth and width. And he was given 'a fair sample of the state of morals' in the town when five or six girls came to his house with a proposal that he should 'make merry with them'. 'Their demeanour was very free,' Barth commented, 'and I too clearly understood the caution requisite in a European who would pass through these countries unharmed and respected by the natives to allow myself to be tempted by these wantons.' Having spent three weeks in Agades, Barth returned to Tintellust and then made south again for Tagetel where, without enthusiasm, he again met Richardson for whom he had conceived an antipathy which was mutual.

The explorers now decided to part company once more; and when Barth said good-bye to Richardson, he had the feeling that he might not see the Englishman again. Richardson had certainly found the going far more difficult than his German companions. 'The fatigue,' he had written in his diary some time before, 'is killing. I read nothing nowadays but a few verses of the Greek testament and write only these miserable leaves of journal. I must save my strength. I am very weak.' 'He was quite incapable of bearing the heat of the sun,' Barth wrote in one of those frequent passages expressive of disapproval of his fellow-explorers, 'for which reason he always carried an [old broken white] umbrella, instead of accustoming himself to the sun's heat by degrees. There was some sinister foreboding in the circumstance that I did not feel sufficient confidence to entrust to his care a parcel for Europe. I had sealed it expressly that he might take it with him to Kukawa [where they had arranged to meet] and to send it off from that place with his own dispatches immediately after his arrival; but at the moment of parting I preferred taking it myself to Kano.'

So, leaving Richardson to make for Kukawa, and Overweg to make an excursion to Gobir and Maradi, Barth went on alone in January 1851 to Tasawa, 'the first place of Negroland proper' which he had seen. It made 'the most cheerful impression' upon him, 'manifesting everywhere the unmistakable marks' of the comfortable, pleasant sort of life led by the natives. The clay and red-thatched houses were shaded by spreading trees and enlivened by groups of children, goats, fowls, pigeons and, where a little wealth had been accumulated, a horse or pack-ox. The people, of whom he estimated there were about 15,000, seemed perfectly happy, 'rather given to women, dance and song, but without any disgusting excess', and drunken people were rarely seen. The men – most of whom had two wives, one of their own age, the other a young girl – were clothed in wide shirts and trousers dyed with indigo; the women wore cotton dresses fastened under or above the breast, with strings of glass beads around their necks. In the markets there were piles of bread made from the fruit of the magaria tree, morsels of roast meat on sticks, bales of red cloth and calabashes filled with roasted locusts.

Kano, which was reached at the beginning of February, Barth found just as 'animated and exciting'. Here, having presented gifts to the Fulani governor, who received him in a dark but stately hall, clothed in all the 'mixed finery of Hausa and Barbary', he rode freely about the town, looking into the rows of shops which were 'filled with articles of native and foreign produce' and into the sheds where the half-naked and half-starved slaves anxiously awaited purchasers. He admired the scrupulously clean rows of earthenware pots and wooden bowls, and the neatly dressed women whose children played in the sand; he admired the fine trees and watched the slaves who were kept busy pounding corn. He saw caravans arriving from Gonja with cargoes of kola nuts, natron and the luxuries of the north; marvelling at the variety of races from olive-coloured Arabs to black, broad-faced Mandingos.

Leaving Kano on 9 March 1851 on his unsightly black nag, with three well-loaded camels swaying after him, a fortnight later he entered Bornu where he learned that Richardson had died on 4 March before reaching Kukawa. Expecting this news, he was not disconcerted by it, and went forward on his way without pretence of deep regret. His path, at times well marked, at others scarcely distinguishable, led through the walled town of Gobalgorum and Kashimma, across lofty sandy ridges and thickly overgrown hollows, beneath trees full of locusts and a sky darkened by dense flocks of hawks. Occasionally an antelope was seen, once a gazelle, and the ground was covered with the deep footprints of elephants. At Ngurutuwa, once a celebrated place, now decayed, he came upon Richardson's grave which, protected by thorn bushes, had been dug beneath a large fig tree. And at Kukawa he found Richardson's servants, clamouring for their wages, and Richardson's baggage, under the protection of the local ruler, 'a very simple, benevolent, and even cheerful man' with a remarkably black and glossy skin. But agreeable as the ruler was, he declined to hand over the whole of the impounded possessions some of which had already, in fact, been sold. And it was not until Overweg arrived in Kukawa on 7 May that Richardson's boxes were released and then without Richardson's watch to which the ruler had taken a particular fancy, and only on the understanding that various other articles would be given as presents both to the ruler and to his chief minister. Despite his depredations, the ruler was a likeable rogue with a harem of some four hundred female slaves in which he took an ethnological as well as sexual interest, displaying great pride in certain rare specimens such as a beautiful Circassian. Occasionally lamenting that his collection lacked a girl from some particular tribe, he would instruct his servants to catch him one, as a rich lepidopterist might order a valuable butterfly.

Despite the intrigues of the Arab traders, who were as always afraid that the

English would rob them of their business, Barth succeeded in borrowing money to pay Richardson's servants and in arranging for himself to go south to Yola, while Overweg remained behind to explore the shores of Lake Chad. So, accompanied by one of the ruler's officers named Billama, a tall, handsome man from Bornu mounted on a splendid grey horse, and by various other companions, Barth left Kukawa on 29 May.

Immediately south of the town the country was densely inhabited, and the people who had never seen a European before were astonished by the sight of Barth; but they knelt by the roadside to pay their respects to the Bornu officer who had once been governor of the district. The land, well cultivated for some distance, soon gave way to forest and dense forests of reed grasses so high that they reached above the riders' heads. The inhabitants, though Muslim, wore little clothing or went about naked; some were quite black but others, whom Barth presumed to be characteristic of the original tribe before their inter-mixture with surrounding nations, were of 'a pale or yellowish-red complexion, like rhubarb'. They were pleased by Barth's evident admiration of their beautiful bodies but grew frightened when he set about sketching them.

As he progressed south through the occasionally heavy rain, Barth saw 'jet black slave girls, well fed, and all neatly dressed in long aprons with their necks adorned with strings of glass beads being marched out to their daily labours'. The camels of the travellers caused these girls the greatest astonishment, and two of them, 'slender as antelopes and wearing nothing but a light apron of striped cotton round their loins', jumped about laughing at them; others crawled under their bellies, protesting that they must surely be sacred beasts. These strange animals seemed, indeed, to arouse more curiosity than Barth himself, though he was, more than once, taken for some kind of god and required to give the people his blessing.

At length, in the middle of June, Barth reached the Benue. The river's banks rose to a height of thirty feet, and as he looked down upon the broad and majestic stream which flowed through 'an entirely open country from which only here and there detached mountains started forth', Barth felt that this was 'one of the happiest moments' of his life. The sight of the frail canoes, however, which were used to cross the wide expanse of water rather alarmed him, though in fact the crossing was made without mishap. The horses swam calmly by the sides of the canoe, while the drivers of the camels thrashed them as the only way in which they could be induced to enter the water at all. Beyond the river there were straggling hamlets and rich cornfields in the shadow of rugged mountains, meadows beautifully adorned with white, violet-striped lilies, and then Yola, a large town of conical huts surrounded by spacious courtyards. The governors of this place were not welcoming. Although the chief himself was prepared to accept the word of the ruler of Kukawa that Barth was a learned and pious man 'who wandered about to admire the works of the mighty creator', some phrases in the letters presented to him by Billama, which laid claim to various disputed territories, caused such offence that the travellers were advised to return without delay to the country from which they had come.

Having returned to Kukawa, Barth decided that before travelling westward, he would make a journey round the north side of Lake Chad to Kanem. So, leaving Kukawa on 11 September, he arrived a few days later at Yo, a town of closely packed streets smelling strongly of dried fish. There he met Overweg once more. Having salvaged just in time his leather bags and mats which were in the process of being destroyed by hordes of white ants, he and Overweg crossed the river which flows through the town into the waters of Lake Chad and made their way north beside the shores of the lake. On their way they encountered 'one of the most interesting scenes which these regions can possibly afford', a herd of ninety-six elephants marching as though in military formation down to the river, the males in front, the young ones behind, the females in a third line followed by five males of immense size.

The fine pasture-grounds where the elephants lived gave way after a while to a morass in which Barth's horse stumbled and fell, throwing the rider into the bog and then collapsing on top of him. Extricating himself with difficulty, Barth emerged covered in mud and rode on to find a snake over eighteen feet long hanging in a threatening attitude from the branches of a tree. Pierced by several balls, the snake fell to the ground where its head was cut off, and some natives who had attached themselves to the explorers' party cut the body open and removed the fat which they declared to be excellent.

On 1 October Barth and Overweg came upon a band of Arab robbers with whom they now continued their journey for three weeks. During this time the marauders captured three hundred head of cattle, fifteen hundred sheep and goats and fifteen camels. On 20 October the Arab camp was attacked by an army of natives who lost thirty-four men in the assault, while killing only four Arabs and getting away with little more than a few cooking utensils and a prayer-book which had belonged to Richardson.

The next month Barth and Overweg joined another marauding expedition, this time led by the ruler of Kukawa who announced his intention of enforcing obedience from the vassal state of Mandara but who was really intent upon replenishing his coffers and capturing slaves. Barth naturally regretted associating himself with such an expedition but, excusing himself on the grounds that he might not otherwise have been able to get so far south, and that by accompanying the expedition he might 'prevent a deal of mischief and might likewise have a fair opportunity' of seeing for himself whether or not the reported cruelty of these forays was exaggerated, he joined the army, riding in the rear-guard with the camels and other baggage animals. The army passed through Dikwa at the beginning of December and a few days afterwards entered another walled town, Zogoma, where the chief's cruel minister, thinking to entertain the European, brought into his presence two criminals whose necks were both secured in *begos*, large heavy pieces of wood which caused the greatest pain at every movement. These two men were forced to flog each other with whips of hippopotamus hide; and it was 'with great difficulty' that Barth succeeded in persuading the minister that the 'horrible sight' was 'far from agreeable' to him.

As the army approached Mandara the chief of that place, Adishen, gave notice of his intention to resist the army's advance; and, on learning this, the Bornu soldiers ceased their war songs and fell into a dejected silence. But then came news that the chief, who was said to 'indulge in amorous intercourse with his female slaves before the eyes of his people', had changed his mind: ten of the more beautiful of these slaves were led into the camp as a token of his submission. Far from content with such meagre spoils, the army marched on deeper into the territories of Mandara, through extensive stubble fields of millet intermixed with beans, vast expanses of wild rice and cotton fields; then through forest where the ground was covered with brushwood and where giraffes and elephants could occasionally be glimpsed beyond the mimosa and kalgo trees, across regions 'never before trodden by European foot'. Aroused at dawn by three heavy strokes on a drum, the army moved in an extended line of battle, the heavy cavalry in coats of mail or thick wadded clothing, their tin helmets glittering in the sun; the light cavalry in thin shirts and mounted on 'weak unseemly nags'; the spearmen almost naked but for their torn aprons and barbarous headdresses, carrying wooden shields and bundles of spears and shouting war cries in a 'wild native manner'. In the hope of appeasing them the chief, Adishen, followed up his present of slave girls with gifts of horses and oxen; but, encouraged by these signs of weakness, the army proceeded to pillage deserted villages, gorging themselves on roast hare and elephant's flesh and on the fish which were caught in huge quantities in the small lakes beside the line of march. Adishen then appeared in person, a short, stout man about fifty years old, dressed in a black robe. He knelt before his acknowledged masters, sprinkling sand upon his head as a sign of submission. He was accordingly clothed in a rich silk robe and an Egyptian shawl and ceremoniously installed as an official of Bornu, while the leaders of the army looked down upon him, treating him with scorn in their 'proud consciousness of a higher state of civilization'.

Adishen's submission did not prevent further ravaging of the surrounding country. Hundreds of slaves were rounded up and scores of other natives, tall, bearded, ill-featured men with dusty black skins and coarse black hair, were slaughtered, most of them being left to bleed to death, having had their legs cut off. The local horsemen, who used no saddles but kept their seat by making a broad open wound on the backs of their animals and scratching their own legs so that the blood glued them to the horses' flanks, were no match for the cavalry of Bornu. Nor were the men of Demmo against whom the Bornu army now marched. Villages in this area were ravaged as mercilessly as those further north. 'Slaughtered men, with their limbs severed from their bodies, were lying about in all directions, and made the passer-by shudder with horror. Such is the course of human affairs in these regions.' Believing that healthy young slaves were to be found south of Demmo, along the banks of the Loggun river, the army pursued its course in that direction; but the people had fled from their houses and, while Barth and Overweg were 'greatly satisfied with [their] day's work' which had afforded them a sight of 'this fine stream', the army were bitterly disappointed to capture only a few slaves, some animals, a little corn and a stock of groundnuts. And when, on 7 January 1852, the army began its return march to Bornu, they took with them scarcely more than 3,000 of the 10,000 slaves they had hoped to capture, many of these being old women, and children under eight years of age.

Barth had been back in Kukawa for little more than a month when, on 4 March 1852, he set out again on a journey which was to take him round the southern shores of Lake Chad to Massena. It took him over the Loggun river and across the Shari, a river 'certainly not less than 600 yards across' at Mele. From Mele he went to Burgoman, then to Bagirmi, then, obstructed by local chiefs who were suspicious of his intentions, he was compelled to return to Mele where he was arrested and put in irons. His arms and baggage, his compass, watch and journal were all taken away from him. They were returned to him, and his fetters removed, only after an influential Arab whom he had met on a previous journey interceded on his behalf.

Immediately upon his release he resumed his easterly march and arrived at Massena on 27 April. Although the capital of Bagirmi, it was a depressing place in a ruined condition, devastated by civil war, its frail, leaky, clay houses scattered in dilapidated groups behind a decaying wall. The gloomy atmosphere of the town affected Barth's spirits until, on 6 July, there arrived from Kukawa letters which made him regard this day as 'one of the most lucky' of his whole life: he found himself authorized by the British government to continue the explorations which Richardson's death had interrupted and provided with sufficient means to carry them out satisfactorily. On 10 August, therefore, he left Masena for Kukawa with the intention of setting out as soon as possible for Timbuktu. At Kukawa, however, he found Overweg, who had returned from a trip into the south-western districts of Bornu, in a weaker and more exhausted condition than he had ever seen him. Soon afterwards Overweg was 'seized with a terrible fit of delirium, and muttering unintelligible words, in which all the events of his life seemed to be confused, he jumped up repeatedly in a raging fit of madness, and rushed against the trees and into the fire'. He died the next day at the age of twenty-nine.

The sole survivor of the expedition now, Barth left Kukawa for Timbuktu on 25 November 1852. He was accompanied by five servants, four of them Arabs, the fifth a Shuwa from Kotoko, and two liberated Negro slaves. They travelled by way of Katsina, where the governor politely accepted various presents but asked in addition for a pistol which he thereafter carried about with him everywhere, taking delight in 'frightening everybody by firing off the caps in their faces'. And passing through Sokoto, they approached the Niger at Say in the second week of June 1853.

We were now close to the Niger [Barth recorded]. And after a march of little less than two hours [on the morning of 20 June] through a rocky wilderness covered with dense bushes, I observed the first sight of the river ... gliding along in a noble unbroken stream ... hemmed in on this side by a rocky bank. On the flatter shore opposite, a large town spread out, the low rampart and huts of which were picturesquely overtopped by numbers of slender *dum* palms ... My camels, horses, people, and luggage having crossed over without an accident, I myself followed, about one o'clock in the afternoon, filled with delight when floating on the waters of this celebrated stream the exploration of which had cost the sacrifice of so many lives.

From Say, Barth struck out west for the hilly country of Gurma, reaching Champagore on 25 June and pausing there to sketch its extraordinary corn magazines, quadrangular buildings about fifteen feet in height, raised on stilts in order to protect them from the ants, their walls gradually sloping inwards towards the top where there was a single aperture through which the corn was poured in and taken out. At Sebba, the capital of the province of Yagha, Barth took out his sketchbook again to make a drawing of the interior of the hut which had been placed at his disposal by the governor whom he had discovered sitting in front of his house near the mosque in the midst of a large congregation of people to whom he was reading and interpreting various passages from the Koran. The walls of the hut, which measured about twenty feet in diameter, were made of matting coated with clay, the roof supported by a pole rising from the middle of the floor. There were fixed clay seats on either side of the entrance as well as movable wooden seats; two shallow holes in the floor in which dishes were placed at meal times so that they were not upset; a semi-circular area behind a low wall for the storage of luggage; and a cooking area protected from gusts of wind by another low wall and by huge polished clay urns, as high as a man, used for the storage of corn. There were smaller vessels for other kinds of food and water; and, hanging from the roof, small baskets for various implements such as weaving-tools.

Barth remained at Sebba two days to allow his camels a rest; and on 9 July

moved on to Dori, the capital of the province of Liptako. On 25 July he came
to the Bugyoma river. But his party was unable to cross and, in the hope of
finding a ford higher up, they struck out into the forest where they were
suddenly surrounded by some two hundred half-naked men, beating their
shields and brandishing spears over their heads. Barth reached for his gun but
one of his companions urged him to ride on quietly and shouted out to the
natives that his master was a sherif carrying a number of books from the east.
Immediately the men dropped their spears and crowded round him, begging
him to give them his blessing. They then guided him to a place where they
assured him the river was fordable. The boggy nature of the ground, however,
inspired Barth with little confidence and, as on his journey to Kanem, his horse
fell in the middle of the swamp and he under it. His clothes and possessions
were all soaked and his horse only extricated with the greatest difficulty; but on
the far side of the river the going became easier and they reached Lamorde,
the capital of the province of Aribinda, before nightfall.

In heavy rain the journey continued through Kubo, Isaye, past the Hombori
mountains, on to Bambara and Sarayamo where he succeeded in hiring a boat
which was to take him north all the way to Kabara, the harbour of Timbuktu.
He arrived at Kabara on 7 September 1853; and, hiring eleven donkeys for the
transport of his luggage, he left behind him the fertile banks of the river and
entered the path, lined with thorny bushes and stunted trees, which led across
the desolate desert. The trees and bushes had been cleared away in places to
make it more difficult for the Tuareg tribesmen to lie in ambush. A few days
previously two travellers had been killed near a place halfway between Kabara
and Timbuktu known as Urimmandes ('he does not hear') because from here
the screams of the Tuaregs' victims carried to neither place. But, travelling in
the guise of an important Muslim visitor, Barth was not harmed on his journey;
and, once he had entered the town, though denounced as a Christian and
threatened with assassination, he bought himself protection from a Muslim
resident with the lavish gifts he had brought with him. He remained at first in
Timbuktu itself, then for over seven months in his protector's encampment outside it before he was given permission to leave. Meantime he took stock of the
town, which had changed little since the time of Caillié's visit.

Finally, he set out on his return journey on 19 April 1854, following the
course of the Niger, passing unmolested through Tuareg camps where he gave
looking-glasses to the prettiest women and needles to the rest, until he arrived
before Gogo, the ancient capital of Songhai on June 20. He had, so he said,
a 'more ardent desire' to visit this place than he had had to see Timbuktu, for,
'according to the unanimous statement of former writers [it was] the most
splendid city of Negroland'. Once again, however, he was disappointed. The
place had degenerated from its former glory into the 'desolate abode of a small

and miserable population' of only a few hundred poor people. All that remained of the great mosque was a massive ruined tower. On going down to see the river he found nothing but a small creek and a swampy lowland extending to the Niger far in the distance; on attempting to converse with any of the inhabitants he found them sullen and uncommunicative; on trying to buy Indian corn he was sulkily told they had none. Thankful to leave, he travelled on through Garu and Sinder, through Say, Gwandu, Sokoto, Wurno and Kano. Just beyond Bundi, on 27 November, he saw approaching a horseman 'of strange aspect – a young man of a very fair complexion with a white turban wound thickly round his head'. This was a fellow-German, Eduard Vogel, who had been sent to reinforce the expedition and had long since given Barth up for dead. Barth's pleasure at seeing a European face once more was marred, however, when he discovered to his aggrieved surprise that Vogel did not possess a single bottle of wine. 'For having now been for more than three years without a drop of stimulant except coffee, and having suffered severely from frequent attacks of fever and dysentery,' Barth explained, 'I had an insuperable longing for the juice of the grape.'

A further disappointment awaited him in Kukawa where he found that the boxes which he had left there had been plundered, and he was unable to pay his long-standing debts. It was not until after a caravan had arrived from Fezzan with money for the mission – addressed to Vogel in the presumption that Barth was dead – that he was able to settle his obligations and leave Kukawa for Fezzan on whose frontiers, at Tejerri, he arrived on 6 July.

The whole population of the village came out to congratulate the travellers on their safe arrival after their journey through the desert with so few companions. Barth had hoped to be able to rest his animals in Tejerri but, the only supplies he could obtain there being a single fowl and a few dates, he was obliged to take the road to Murzuk on which, at the village of Yess on 13 July, he met Hanmer Warrington. Together they spent a happy evening, Barth 'deeply affected, after so long an absence, to be within reach of European comforts'. A few weeks later he spent an equally cheerful evening with the British Vice-Consul in Tripoli. And, having spent four days in the town, he embarked in a Turkish steamer for Malta. Sailing from Malta to Marseilles he arrived on 6 September 1855 in London where he was most kindly received by Lord Palmerston as well as by Lord Clarendon, who took 'the greatest interest in the remarkable success which had accompanied [his] proceedings'.

During the five years he had spent travelling 10,000 miles in Africa, Barth had formed a deep affection for Africans with whom he had lived for most of the time on terms of mutual respect, eating their food, speaking their languages, wearing a black Sudan *riga* over a white tobe and a white burnous, observing when necessary the outward forms of Islam. The commercial treaties which he induced chiefs in Bornu, Sokoto and Gwandu to sign eventually came to nothing; but his explorations of the Benue, and of the places described in his scholarly and monumental *Travels and Discoveries*, enabled him justly to claim that he had 'opened up to the view of the scientific public of Europe a most extensive tract of the African world, and not only made it tolerably known, but rendered the opening of a regular intercourse between Europeans and those regions possible'. When he died in Berlin in 1865, two years after being appointed Professor of Geography, he had been recognized as an authority without equal on north and central Africa.

8

THE MOUNTAINS OF THE MOON
AND THE INLAND SEAS

LUDWIG KRAPF AND JOHANNES REBMANN · THEIR MISSION
AT RABBAI MPIA AND THE INTRACTABLE NATIVES · WANIKA
SUPERSTITIONS · REBMANN'S SEARCH FOR MORE
RESPONSIVE PEOPLE IN THE INTERIOR · HIS JOURNEYS TO
KADIARO AND JAGGA · HIS DISCOVERY OF KILIMANJARO ·
KING MASAKI AND KING MAMKINGA · KRAPF MEANWHILE
EXPLORES THE COUNTRY TO THE SOUTH · HIS JOURNEYS
TO USAMBARA AND UKAMBANI · HIS DISCOVERY OF MOUNT
KENYA · HE ACCOMPANIES KING KIVOI TO THE RIVER
DANA · AN ATTACK BY ROBBERS · KRAPF'S ESCAPE ·
PRIVATIONS DURING HIS FLIGHT TO THE COAST · BURTON
AND SPEKE · THEIR ADVENTURES · ATTACKED BY SOMALI ·
THEIR ARRIVAL IN ZANZIBAR, DECEMBER 1856 · THEIR
JOURNEY TO THE INTERIOR AND DISCOVERY OF LAKE
TANGANYIKA · SPEKE GOES ALONE TO VICTORIA NYANZA ·
HIS QUARREL WITH BURTON AND THEIR RETURN TO
LONDON · SPEKE'S NEW EXPEDITION · HIS COMPANION, J. A.
GRANT · THEIR JOURNEY NORTH THROUGH BUGANDA · THE
KABAKA, MUTESA · SPEKE REACHES THE WHITE NILE AT
URONDOGANI, JULY 1862 · HE AND GRANT MEET SAMUEL
BAKER AT GONDOKORO · BAKER AND HIS TRANSYLVANIAN
CHÈRE AMIE DISCOVER LAKE ALBERT · BURTON'S ESCAPADES
IN DAHOMEY · HIS RETURN TO ENGLAND TO CONFRONT
SPEKE WHO IS KILLED IN A SHOOTING ACCIDENT,
SEPTEMBER 1864

While Richardson and Barth were travelling in north Africa, far to the south
near Mombasa two obscure German missionaries were building themselves a
house in a village of the Wanika and trying, with ever-decreasing hope of
success, to convert the unresponsive inhabitants to Christianity. The elder of

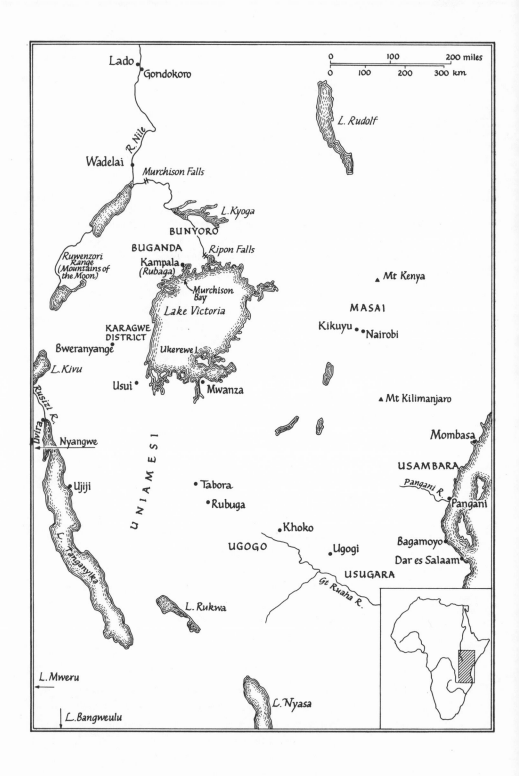

the two was Ludwig Krapf, the son of a farmer from Derendingen near Tübingen, who had been in Africa since 1842 and had been searching ever since for tribes prepared to listen to the word of God.

Born in 1810, Krapf had been so savagely beaten by a neighbour at the age of eleven that he had been seriously ill for six months; and, while lying in bed, the reading of the Bible, particularly the Old Testament, had become his main source of pleasure. During his convalescence he repeated the stories he had read to the labourers in the surrounding fields who told his father they felt sure the bright young boy was destined to become a parson. His father thought so too, and, with the intention of training him either for the church or for the law, he sent his son to the local grammar school where, after a time, in the perverse way of children, Ludwig conceived 'an ardent desire to become the captain of a ship and to visit foreign lands'. When objections were raised to this ambition he turned his mind to the idea of becoming a missionary, and in 1827 entered the Missionary College at Basel. After his studies there he was ordained; and in 1837, under the auspices of the English Church Missionary Society, left for Abyssinia. Having spent some time as a missionary at Adowa and at Ankober, the capital of the hilly region of Shoa, he returned to the coast. Imprisoned and robbed on the way by the soldiers of a local chieftain, he reached Massawa in May 1842, sailed to Aden and thence to Egypt where he married a German girl who was soon to die in Africa having given birth to two daughters neither of whom survived.

Krapf landed in Africa at Zanzibar, and from there travelled north to Mombasa, where he diligently studied the Swahili and Kinika languages and prepared himself for the conversion of the peoples of the hinterland, the Wanika and Wakamba, neither of whom proved much disposed to listen to his preaching. The Wanika, whose lands had been invaded by the Wakamba during a prolonged famine, were potentially unpromising converts, characterized by 'drunkenness and sensuality, dullness and indifference'. One of their chiefs openly declared that there was no God since he could not be seen and that the Mohammedans – whom the Wanika did not distinguish from Christians – were outright fools to fast and pray so much. The chief did not prevent his people attending Christian services. But Krapf's congregations listened to his sermons without interest and gradually slipped away one by one for more entertaining pursuits. When Krapf asked his way to the next village, the path was pointed out to him but he was warned to beware of the young men celebrating their *ugnaro*, a sporting festival during which they smeared their naked bodies with white and grey earth and departed for the forest where they remained until they had killed a man and returned home to feasting and carousal.

After the arrival of his fellow-countryman, Johannes Rebmann, a young missionary from Württemberg, Krapf nevertheless decided to establish a mission at Rabbai Mpia, a small village of some twenty-five huts about a thousand feet above the sea from which fine views of Mombasa and the ships in its harbour could be obtained between the trunks of the coconut trees. So he and Rebmann, both suffering severely from fever, struggled up to Rabbai Mpia in August 1846 and there they themselves finished building the mission house which the Wanika, although well paid for their meagre and slapdash efforts, had left in a quite uninhabitable condition. In dirty and tattered clothes, bleeding from wounds caused by the thorns and sharp stones, still weak from fever and suffering from the heat of the sun, the missionaries dug foundations which the Wanika had omitted to provide, flung mud on the walls in the native fashion and plastered them with the palms of their hands, laid a roof of the plaited leaves of the coconut tree, and then, at length, stood back to admire a house twenty-four feet long by eighteen broad, complete with kitchen, stable, store-house, oven and a hut for public worship.

On Sundays Krapf would fire a gun and ring a bell as a signal that a service was to be held, but the congregations that assembled were never large, and the missionaries were warned that they would never increase unless the people were given some inducement to attend. One man asked how much his children were to be paid for attending the white man's lessons. Another wanted to know what food was to be provided. 'If the Wanika received rice and a cow,' he explained, 'they would always come; but if not, they would stay away.' Most of them continued to stay away, distressing Krapf by their complete in-difference 'to the means of salvation through the Saviour', by their belief that the adoption of Christianity would anger the spirits of the dead and bring drought and pestilence, and by the tenacity with which they clung to their old superstitious practices, in particular to their reverence for the *muansa*, a hollowed-out piece of wood which was 'made to give out a frightful sound by rubbing'. Only the elders were allowed to see this instrument, the very sight of which would bring sudden death upon all women and children. At night, when it was made to emit its loud, unearthly sound in the forest, it took upon itself the form of a wild beast, and the elders, as though in response to its bellowing, began to shriek and dance and sing, fortifying themselves from time to time with 'large draughts of palm-wine, which rekindled their flagging powers and rendered them more uproarious'.

Faithful as they remained to the *muansa*, despite the missionaries' objections and explanations, the Wanika reposed equally unimpaired faith in rain-makers, in the magical ceremonies of clapping, dancing, wailing and singing which were performed around the prostrate forms of the sick, in the omnipotence of those spirits that flitted from the grave to the clouds in a thunderstorm, and in the efficacy of determining the guilt of suspected criminals by such means as the passing of a red-hot needle through their lips and watching for the blood which always flowed from the wounds of evildoers but never from those of the innocent. They continued, too, to hand over misshapen babies to their chiefs so that they could be strangled and buried beneath the trees; and, when Krapf earnestly preached against this heartless infanticide, one female member of his congregation expressed what seemed to be the opinion of the rest by letting out a great shout of laughter.

In the course of time, so Krapf confessed, perhaps despairing of the conversion of these intractable people, he and Rebmann came to the conclusion that it was their duty not to limit their missionary labours to the coastal tribes but 'to keep in mind as well the spiritual darkness of the tribes and nations of Inner Africa'. Thus began that series of explorations which were to bring them both fame and derision and which were to lead their successors towards the fabled Mountains of the Moon described by Ptolemy.

Rebmann was the first to leave. On 14 October 1847, having prayed with Krapf for God's blessing upon the enterprise, he set out for Kadiaro. It was a journey beset with dangers, for the wilderness through which he had to pass was infested with wild beasts and with robbers who lay in wait in the bush for caravans bearing ivory to the coast. As a protection against these dangers the Wanika who accompanied him wanted to take with them two magic staves which had been burned black and wreathed round at the top with bark, protesting that these staves were to them what his Bible was to Rebmann; but the missionary would have nothing to do with such heathen protection against the powers of darkness and hurled the staves into the bush. After long and sulky protests the Wanika followed him apprehensively towards the mountains of Teita; and to their relief and evident surprise in the protective qualities of the Bible they reached without mishap that part of Teita called Kadiaro on 19 October. It was 'a solitary mountain mass, stretching about one league and a half from south to north, and near its centre reaching its highest summit which consists of an enormous mass of rock and is, for the most part, completely perpendicular'.

At the village of Maguasini, the huts of which were built among immense rocks protruding from the mountain, Rebmann conversed for the first time with Teita people. They were scantily dressed in pieces of cloth and leather aprons with their arms encircled and their ears hung with brass wire, the females adorned also with loads of beads around their necks and ankles. They were quiet and reserved but not unfriendly, and they listened politely when Rebmann assured them that he had not come to build a fortress in the fastness of their rocky land, as they supposed, but to preach the gospel of Christ, the Saviour. Rebmann decided that a mission to this people would be 'very feasible and very desirable'.

Encouraged by his reception, Rebmann determined after his return to Rabbai Mpia to penetrate even further inland, beyond Kadiaro to Jagga. So, in April 1848 he set out once again, making his way westwards through the lands of the Teita, across a pathless wilderness, over plains and beneath towering mountain masses, seeing many herds of giraffe and zebra, rhinoceros, buffalo and elephant. And at about ten o'clock on 11 May, when the mountains of Jagga could be distinctly discerned, he fancied he saw the summit of one of them 'covered with a dazzingly white cloud'. He pointed this out to the guide who merely said, *'Beredi'*, meaning cold. 'It was perfectly clear to me, however,' Rebmann recorded in his journal, 'that it could be nothing else but snow.' He was confirmed in his belief when the guide told him that long ago the king's father had sent an expedition to climb this mountain to investigate the whiteness of the summit which he had believed might be made of silver. Only one man had survived; the guide had seen him; his hands and feet were bent inwards by the cold. Rebmann realized that the man must have been suffering from frost-bite and that he himself had, indeed, seen the snow-capped summit of Kilimanjaro.

What impressed Rebmann quite as much as Kilimanjaro, however, was the 'lovely country, bursting with plenteousness' which lay at the mountain's foot. A beautiful, sparkling river flowed through a valley, covered with 'the richest vegetation of a perfect perpetual summer'. Between the magnificent trees grew lush grass as high as a man's waist. The guide tore out some blades of this grass and pressed them into Rebmann's hand, telling him that when he was presented to the king he must hold out the grass towards him, for this was the usage of the country.

Soon afterwards he met the king, Masaki, a lively, intelligent young man, who presented him as a token of friendship with a small piece of skin from the forehead of a slaughtered sheep which was fastened to Rebmann's little finger. Rebmann was then taken to a hut, 'in the midst of a whole forest of bananas', where he offered the king in return gifts of calico and beads, scissors, needles and thread, and a knife and fork. The king placed the fork in his hair as an ornament. Rebmann explained its proper use. 'He laughed but did not seem to understand.'

Nor did Masaki understand how Rebmann had been able to make so long a journey without spear or shield or the use of any magical enchantments, carrying with him nothing but an umbrella and a Bible. And, as though searching for an explanation of the mystery, he, his relations and advisers closely examined every part of the missionary's clothes, even his trouser buttons. Rebmann then took up his Bible and showed it to the king as his only talisman. To visit his country was of little importance to him, Rebmann declared, but to teach him and his people the contents of this book was what

196

he desired above all. The king took the Bible into his own hands and 'amused himself by turning over the leaves'. Neither he nor his advisers seemed wholly convinced by Rebmann's claims, but he agreed that his visitor should be allowed to return to his country as a teacher when the necessary preparations had been made. So Rebmann returned to the coast, content in the knowledge that, despite the shocking state of the route which led to it, a missionary in Jagga would 'find there facilities denied him among the Wanika'.

Anxious to see more of this promising land, Rebmann returned to Jagga in November 1848, and on 7 December was once more in the presence of King Masaki who greeted him with friendly courtesy. But when Rebmann explained that he wanted to journey even further westward, Masaki raised objections, being unwilling, so Rebmann thought, to see the presents of calico and beads pass out of his kingdom into that of his neighbour. There happened, however, to be some soldiers with Masaki from the neighbouring kingdom; and when Rebmann told them of his desire to visit their master, King Mamkinga, these soldiers immediately declared that they would take him to him, as he had but recently announced his intention of sending to the coast for a European to remain in his suite as one of his sorcerers. So, unwilling to offend his powerful rival, Masaki gave permission for Rebmann to leave his domains and go to Mamkinga.

Accordingly on 4 January 1849, accompanied by Mamkinga's brother who had come to escort him, Rebmann left Masaki's territory and, passing by night beneath the heights of Kilimanjaro whose majestic snow-clad summit he could distinctly see by the light of the moon, he began his journey to the west. It was as cold as in Germany in winter; and, as the path rose up into the mountains through a bleak and uninhabited country, it grew colder still. But then the path led down again, across a river and into a valley where the ground was covered with banana trees whose rotting fruit filled the air with the smell of putrefaction. Further rivers were crossed; the valley gave way to jungle, then to fine open country; and at the beginning of the second week of January Rebmann entered Majame and was conducted to a hut where he was asked to wait for a few days while the king's sorcerers made arrangements for his reception by their master. These arrangements took a considerable time, for they entailed the preparation of a mixture of the blood of a slaughtered goat and medicine made from the juice of a certain plant which had to be fetched from a distance. And it was not until 12 January that the king's chief medicine-man entered the hut and, without a word of warning or explanation, produced a cow's tail and splashed Rebmann's face and body with a generous dose of the noisome mixture with which all visitors to King Mamkinga had to be spattered. Annoyed though he was by this procedure, Rebmann was delighted with his reception by the king who assured him frequently of his great affection for him and indicated that he would look favourably upon him as a teacher should he wish to return to Majame in that capacity. But when Rebmann did return two months later he found Mamkinga far more anxious to plunder him of his possessions than to listen to the word of God. Rebmann had hoped to pass through Majame on his way to Uniamesi as he considered it his 'duty to name the name of Christ where it had never been named before and to make Christians at home acquainted with the unknown countries of the African interior so that they might be stimulated to promote the Gospel more energetically'. But Mamkinga proved so avaricious that the missionary's entire stock of goods with which he had hoped to promote his journey to Uniamesi were gradually taken from him. Exhausted by fever and dysentery, Rebmann one day burst into tears in the presence of the king who told him not to worry: he would be well compensated with ivory to take back with him to the coast. When Rebmann was strong enough to depart, however, he was informed that messengers of the word of God should not covet ivory; and he had to content himself with a single old tusk of just sufficient value to purchase food on the way. His Wanika bearers, who had been robbed quite as mercilessly as himself, were even required to deliver up their last remaining beads as payment for the honour of being ritually spat upon with the saliva of peace which was customarily bestowed upon all departing guests by the people of Majame whose territories Rebmann was only too thankful to leave.

While Rebmann was exploring the country west of Mombasa in his disappointing search for sites for possible mission stations, Krapf was engaged in similar activities to the south. In July 1848 he left for Usambara with a guide and seven bearers, first across the edges of the wilderness which 'stretches as an immeasurable plain into the interior of the African continent', then through a country 'covered with high grass, acacias and other trees and shrubs'. They passed through dense woods and by pools frequented by elephants, and penetrated thickets of euphorbia, spurge and wild aloe so thick that Krapf was unable to ride his ass; by night they slept beside fires of ebony which were kept burning as a protection against wild beasts, 'traces of whom, especially of the rhinoceros, were to be observed in the jungle'. At the foot of the mountain known as Pambire there were rice plantations and hillocks covered with sugar cane and banana trees; and as he crossed the Engambo River and began to climb Mount Makueri the air became cool and pleasant; water trickled from the granite rocks; and small groups of huts could be seen surrounded by patches of Indian corn. As he approached Salla he began to fear that the king, Kmeri, might kill him as a spy; but, in fact, he was welcomed graciously both by him, by his several hundred wives, and by his people who had not dared approach him until Kmeri, the 'only true lion', had given his approval.

Satisfied that a mission might be established in Usambara, Krapf turned north towards Ukambani, the country of the Wakamba who, when he reached Kikumbuliu on 17 November, gazed at him as though he were 'a being from another world'. 'Hair, hat, shoes and umbrella, excited their liveliest attention and they hopped about like children.' They asked him if he could make the badly needed rain fall; and when it did rain three days later they ascribed it to his supernatural powers. As he advanced towards Ukambani his fame went before him. The Wakamba came out of their villages to offer him the meat of giraffes (which he enjoyed very much) and elephants (which he found far too tough), as well as fowls; and at the village of the king, Kivoi, they rushed in crowds towards him. The king himself was amiable and told him of a white-capped mountain, even greater than Kilimanjaro, which could be seen from a hill a little way from his village. Krapf accordingly made an expedition to see this great mountain, but was disappointed to find the view obscured by clouds. A few days later, however, he did catch sight of it, and was thus the first European to see Mount Kenya. Kivoi invited Krapf to accompany him on an expedition to fetch ivory from Kikuyu upon which he was to embark the following month. But Krapf was anxious to return immediately to Rabbai Mpia and to make his report to the Church Missionary Society. When this was eventually done, Krapf was authorized to found a missionary station in Ukambani, the first, it was hoped, of a chain of missions that would be established across the entire continent.

With this end in view Krapf returned to Ukambani the next year accompanied by about thirty Wanika as bearers and escort, and some hundred Wakamba returning to their homes. He had been on the march for ten days when, in the midst of a dense thicket, he heard terrified cries of '*Aendi! Aendi! Aendi!* Robbers! Robbers! Robbers!' from the Wakamba who were bringing up the rear. Immediately his own Wanika threw down their loads and vainly endeavoured to escape into the impenetrable bush, crying, 'Shoot! Fire the guns!' although the man who was carrying Krapf's double-barrelled gun had run off with it. The Wakamba, in contrast, did not give way to panic. A few of them dropped their burdens and fled, but most stood their ground, shot their poisoned arrows at the robbers and managed to kill at least three of them before driving the others off.

Three days later, after what Krapf described as 'a very toilsome march', the travellers reached Kikumbuliu in safety; and on 26 July 1850, having crossed the Adi, they began to ascend the high land of Yata where Krapf hoped to establish his mission. But as soon as they arrived at Yata his Wanika bearers, who had undertaken to build him a mission house there, hastily threw up 'a miserable hencoop scarcely six feet high' and then, without staying to roof it with grass, ran off to join a caravan which was returning to the coast. Thus abandoned by his bearers, and by his servant who took the opportunity of going home with them, Krapf decided to seek the protection of Kivoi who had seemed friendly enough the previous year. Kivoi was still friendly; when Krapf told him of his desire to create a mission station at Yata the king replied that he would do all he could to help him but first he must accompany him on a journey to the River Dana.

So, carrying with them a quantity of the wood which was used in the manufacture of the paste that poisoned their arrows and which could be exchanged for tobacco and ivory with the people on the other side of the Dana, Krapf and King Kivoi set out on their expedition on 24 August. It was to prove a fearful journey. In its early stages Krapf, hungry and thirsty, was exasperated by Kivoi who imposed lengthy delays upon the expedition, first by commanding a halt when he noticed that the umbrella which he had appropriated had lost its handle and insisting on returning to make a thorough search for it, then by stopping again to look for ostrich feathers a few of which one of his wives had seen scattered in the grass. Soon after the expedition had been put in motion again it was for a third time brought to a halt, this time when Kivoi's slaves pointed to a party of men armed with swords and bows and arrows emerging from the forest into the plain. Immediately the cry of 'Robbers!' went up; shots were fired; and, at Kivoi's orders, the grass was set alight so that the wind might blow the flames into the robbers' faces. On approaching Kivoi the men assured him they were not robbers, however, and invited his men to proceed: they would not interfere with them; indeed, they would lead them to the river. The travellers moved on apprehensively, Kivoi appearing to Krapf to be 'much troubled', as, in fact, he had good cause to be, for soon the men who had offered themselves as guides suddenly wheeled round and discharged their arrows at Kivoi's people, while others attacked them from the rear. All was now confusion as poisoned arrows whistled through the air; Kivoi was killed; bearers screamed and hurled down their burdens before leaping away into the undergrowth; and Krapf, unable to distinguish friend from enemy in the turmoil, ran off, too, impeded by his heavy gun and the ammunition in his pockets. In trying to jump across a dried-up stream-bed, he lost his footing and fell, broke the butt of his gun and nearly broke his leg. Scrambling up the bank, he ran along beside the course of the stream until he suddenly came upon the robbers carrying off their spoil. He retreated immediately across the bed of the stream and was then obliged to change direction again when he came face to face with two rhinoceroses. Escaping also from them, he resumed his flight for ten minutes until, utterly exhausted, he threw himself down at the foot of a tree. He was now parched with thirst; and, at the risk of being seen by the robbers, determined to make his way to the River Dana which he now supposed to be close at hand beyond a line of lofty trees. He made his way stealthily towards the trees and to his profound relief soon caught sight of the gleaming water. He drank deeply, filled the leather case of his telescope and the barrels of his now useless gun, the mouths of which he stopped with grass and bits of cloth torn from his trousers. Although driven to the river-bank by extreme thirst rather than geographical curiosity, he took the opportunity to make some exploration of the Dana, to take notes of its width and course, and to describe a high mountain which he saw on the other side and which he named Mount Albert in honour of the Prince Consort who had concerned himself with missionary activities. Then, concealing himself in the bushes, he waited until nightfall when he intended to try to find his way back to Kivoi's village. As darkness fell he rose to his feet and, since the wind had been at his back on the outward journey, he judged that if he now walked with it blowing in his face he would be going in the right direction. And so it proved. He came to the plain where Kivoi had set fire to the grass; he passed beneath a mountain which he had noticed before and which he called Mount William in honour of King Frederick William IV of Prussia; and he began to hope that, if he did not starve or die of thirst, he might reach safety. On he went, drinking the remains of the gunpowder-flavoured water from his gun barrels, chewing leaves and roots, eating elephants' excrement and ants until, on 28 August, he heard the chattering of monkeys beside a dry and sandy river bed and realized he must be near water. He followed the course of the bed and came to a pit dug by monkeys in the sand and here at last he did find water. Having quenched his thirst, he once again filled his gun barrels and telescope case and made use also of his powder horn, tying up the emptied powder in his handkerchief. To assuage his hunger he ate some of the powder together with the young shoots of a tree which grew nearby, a strange fare which gave him severe stomach pains. But he was near to human habitation now; and the next day, his mouth so dry that his tongue clove to its roof and he could not speak, he came to a village where lived a relation of Kivoi. Here he drank water and ate bananas before falling into a heavy sleep. The people were unfriendly, though, for they blamed him for the death of Kivoi and of those of his people who had perished in the fight with the robbers. Some said he should be punished by death. Krapf believed that this might well be his fate; and, having been tormented the next day by villagers who came to stare at him and to examine his Bible, paper, pencil and telescope, all of which were universally deemed the equipment of a sorcerer, he made up his mind to escape as soon as it was dark. Creeping out of his hut while the other occupants were asleep, he therefore resumed his flight, jumping over the thorn hedge which surrounded the village, pushing his way with difficulty through the tall grass, falling into pits and over stones, his clothes and fingers rent by thorns, snatching beans for food and cutting sugar canes, listening for the croak of frogs which would indicate the presence of water, until he came to Kivoi's village where he intended to throw himself upon the mercy of the dead king's wives and brothers. He did well to do so: instead of being angry with him they took pity upon him; and, when he promised them a share of the possessions he had left behind at Yata provided they would accompany him there, they readily agreed to go with him.

He arrived at Yata on 13 September 1851 and, further stay there being impossible because of his weak state of health, left four days later, having with difficulty persuaded Kivoi's kinsmen to be content with a portion instead of the whole of his possessions; indeed, on arrival he found that the man he had employed as caretaker was in the very act of opening them, believing him to be already dead.

The return journey to the coast was beset with vexatious incidents. The Wanika bearers were even more exasperatingly timid than in the past, throwing down their loads and running away at the sight of elephants or clambering up trees when they caught a glimpse of a buffalo. A shortage of water was followed by heavy rains which made the lighting of fires a performance of extreme difficulty. And one day Krapf trod on a sharp piece of wood which pierced the sole of his shoe, wounding his foot and making walking thereafter most painful. He reached Rabbai Mpia on 28 September 'weary and worn' and filled with regret that he had 'not been privileged to make a longer missionary experiment in Ukambani' where he believed it might have borne fruit.

Krapf comforted himself, however, with the thought that by making another journey to Usambara he might procure a confirmation of the permission he had been given by the king in 1848 to found a missionary settlement there. So, a few months after his return from Ukambani, on 10 February 1852 he set out again for Usambara, this time travelling by way of the River Pangani. On his arrival the king expressed his perfect willingness for the establishment of a mission, though Krapf was only too well aware that the Christian message meant nothing to him personally and that he was far more interested in the presents that the white man brought with him. Nevertheless, on his return Krapf was able to report, 'It is certain that the King of Usambara is now, as previously, disposed to admit missionaries to his country ... and that Usambara is a country with many and large villages where a missionary can address masses of people when he is master of the language.'

By the time these words were written Rebmann and a fellow-missionary, Jacob Erhardt, had bought a plot of land at Kisulidini where they constructed another mission house. Here one day at the beginning of 1857 they were visited by two Englishmen, Richard Burton and John Hanning Speke, who were to extend the explorations in East Africa which the German missionaries had begun.

*

202

Burton was a tall, broad-shouldered man with a scarred face, an abrupt manner and what Frank Harris, who later met him in London, described as 'imperious, aggressive eyes, by no means friendly'. 'The heavy jaws and prominent hard chin gave him a desperate air,' Harris added. 'He wore a heavy moustache ... and looked like a prize-fighter ... His intellectual curiosity was astonishingly broad and deep ... He would tell stories of Indian philosophy or perverse negro habits of lust and cannibalism, or would listen to descriptions of Chinese cruelty or Russian self-mutilation till the stars paled out ... It was the abnormalities and not the divinities of men that fascinated him.' He 'prided himself on looking like Satan', another observer thought, 'as, indeed, he did'. Arthur Symons wrote of his 'tremendous animalism, an air of repressed ferocity, a devilish fascination'.

Burton's father was a retired army officer of Irish descent and uncertain temper who, when Richard was a child, had taken his family to the Continent where they had wandered about in France and Italy, settling in some places for a few months, in others for years. Neither Richard nor his brother had any regular education, attending for a short time only a preparatory school in England before returning to France to the care of a tutor who beat them with a horsewhip even more severely than their father did. Unruly and, on occasions, uncontrollable, they nevertheless acquired a wide variety of knowledge and when, in 1840, Richard entered Trinity College, Oxford, to which his father sent him with the improbable intention of training him for the church, the wild, disdainful, nineteen-year-old undergraduate – who protested that England was the only country in which he never felt at home and that his staid fellow-undergraduates were an assortment of grocers – was recognized as a potential scholar with remarkable linguistic talents. He himself, however, had other ambitions than the fellowship which his father had planned for him; and, contriving to get himself rusticated, he obtained a cadetship in the Indian army and set sail for Bombay. He remained in India for seven years doggedly learning several of the twenty-nine languages he was eventually to master, and becoming one of the army's most skilful intelligence officers. Living like a 'white nigger', as his disapproving and resentful fellow-officers put it, he adopted the dress and customs of the natives in order to gather information, smoked opium and took bhang, discovered the arts of Hindu love making, and found in his work a satisfying fulfilment of his passion for the exotic and the forbidden. Required by Sir Charles Napier to investigate the homosexual brothels of Karachi, he undertook the work with such fascinated verve and compiled a private report of such detached thoroughness that when his findings reached the secretariat at Bombay suspicions there that Burton's attitudes and interests were incompatible with those of a British officer and gentleman seemed all too fully confirmed.

When Burton returned home in 1849 he brought with him an extensive collection of oriental manuscripts and curios, notes for several linguistic articles, materials for four books about India and a further volume on the use of the bayonet – which the War Office later reprinted, granting him one shilling reward – as well as a desire that became an unquenchable ambition to make the pilgrimage to Mecca. Without enthusiasm, the East India Company agreed to grant him an additional year's leave for this enterprise on the grounds that he might thereby 'pursue his Arabic studies where the language is best learned'. Within the prescribed term, Burton, in various disguises, fulfilled his purpose and in so doing provided himself with material for yet another book.

But other Europeans, most recently the Swiss ethnologist, Johann Ludwig Burckhardt, had been to Mecca before him; and Burton, who was to write after climbing one of the highest peaks in the Cameroon mountains, 'to be first in such matters is everything, to be second nothing', now resolved to go where no European had preceded him and to win the renown to which he felt himself entitled. His opportunity came in 1854 when the authorities in Bombay granted him permission to explore Somaliland and to fulfil a new ambition of penetrating through the mountains to the upper waters of the Nile. In this adventure he was to have three British companions; but first he determined to travel by himself, in the guise of an Arab merchant, to Harar. So, setting out alone, he sailed by steamer to Zayla where he spent a month making preparations for his journey and studying Somali customs, particularly their sexual customs, with that passionate curiosity which he brought to all his anthropological investigations. Somali women, he noted for instance, preferred making love with strangers, 'following the well-known Arab proverb, "The new comer filleth the eye"'; their sexuality was little diminished by the practice, common in many parts of Africa, of excising the clitoris. He recorded the signs they used to indicate their willingness to commit adultery and the special positions they adopted to enjoy sexual intercourse, as well as the custom of slicing off part of the labia and of stitching up the vagina of young girls with horsehair or leather thongs to preserve their virginity until marriage. It was then expected of the husband that he would attempt to force a way through the blockage with his penis; he usually failed to do so and had to make use of a knife. The aperture was then usually sewn up again by a jealous husband; but if she were so minded, Burton wrote, the wife would break the suture herself and 'sew it up again when her [desires] were satisfied'.

Having completed his researches and his preparations for the journey, Burton moved towards Harar, regretting on the way that he had not provided himself with walnut juice to darken his skin, for he was suspected of being a Turk and that, as he was warned more than once, would be sufficient to cost him his life when he reached his goal. Entering the town openly as an Englishman, he was greeted respectfully by the young amir who was anxious not to cause offence to a nation which had the power to interfere with the slave trade. Yet while the amir was accommodating, his small town, a pile of stones overshadowed 'by two gray minarets of rude shape', was a sad disappointment. Its narrow streets were littered with immense rubbish heaps between which wandered Muslim *wadads* who lived by selling charms and cures to those persuaded to believe in their efficacy by the vendors' ability to recite a few passages from the Koran. Only the young women of the place, who glanced at Burton through kohl-bordered eyes shaded beneath pale blue headscarves, relieved the gloom of a town which, though no white man had succeeded in entering before, he left lamenting 'how melancholy a thing is success'.

By the time of his return to Aden, however, he had recovered his high spirits and was eagerly looking forward to the new, extended expedition on which he was to be accompanied by three other officers. These were Lieutenant S. E. Herne, a friend he made in India; Lieutenant William Stroyan; and another young lieutenant, John Hanning Speke of the Bengal Native Infantry.

Speke, then aged twenty-seven, was six years younger than Burton whom at this time he seems to have admired, if not revered. He came from a well-to-do Somerset family on whose estate he had developed that passion for shooting wild life which was never to abate. His father had served in the 14th Dragoons and he himself, after unhappy schooldays, had gone out to join the army in India when he was seventeen, sending back to Somerset numerous specimens of the heads and skins of animals he had shot. He had fought in the Punjab campaign and was present at several battles in the Sikh War, including Chilian-wala. But he never considered himself a soldier so much as a 'sportsman and traveller'. Whenever the time for leave came round he left for the Himalayas or Tibet to shoot, to collect botanical and animal specimens, to explore un-known tracts of land, and to practise mapping. He had what Burton was to call 'an uncommonly acute "eye for country" '. Long before he left India he had decided to widen his horizons, and perhaps win fame in another continent. The day after that upon which his ten years' service was complete, he sailed from Calcutta for Aden. Refused permission by the British Resident to go out shooting alone, he was advised to attach himself to Burton's expedition and, in preparation for the main journey, was instructed to lead an expedition him-self to the Wadi Nogul before joining the others at Berbera. This preliminary expedition was a complete failure. Unlike Burton, he was no linguist – he had not even mastered Hindustani in all the years he had spent in India – and largely owing to his inability to communicate properly with his guide who, in his own words, was 'a vile-conditioned man from whom he could never get one true word', he had not succeeded in the main purpose of his mission. He had, never-theless, returned from it with a characteristically eclectic collection of skulls, skins, bones and feathers.

Despite his apparent incompetence in dealing with fraudulent servants, his naivety, touchiness and occasional disturbing excitability, Speke was warmly welcomed by the other officers at Berbera. Tall and strong with abundant fair hair, his looks were as pleasing as his apparently rather diffident and simple manner. He was known also to be determined, strenuous and brave, and these were qualities soon needed. For, as they were waiting in camp outside Berbera for various instruments to arrive from England, the officers were suddenly attacked one night by a party of Somali whose chiefs believed them to be spies working for the British Government against the slave trade. As the natives began to beat down the tent, Speke leapt outside only to be driven back by a volley of stones. 'Don't step back,' Burton told him roughly, 'or they'll think we are retiring.' Provoked by this remark, which he took as a slight on his 'management of fighting', Speke 'stepped boldly to the front', as he put it, 'and fired at close quarters into the first man before' him. But then, struck by a war club, he fell to the ground with 'a dozen Somali' on top of him. The man he had tried to shoot snatched his pistol with one hand and with the other made a grab towards his genitals, which 'sent a creeping shudder all over' him and made him feel as though his hair were standing on end. For he feared that these men belonged to a tribe notorious for the mutilations they inflicted upon their enemies. 'Indescribable was my relief,' Speke continued, 'when I found that my most dreadful fears were without foundation. The men were in reality feeling whether, after an Arab fashion, I was carrying a dagger between my legs, to rip up a foe after the victim was supposed to be powerless.' Yet, even if spared castration, Speke expected to die, for he was bound and kept captive all night, obliged to witness a victory dance round the crumpled tents, derided for being a Christian and savagely tormented by a Somali who kept thrusting a spear at him, eventually driving it through his thigh. At this Speke leapt to his feet, lunged at his assailant with his bound fists, unbalanced him and then fled away, almost naked. He was pursued by hurtling spears, several of which struck him, but he managed to release his bonds with his teeth and, covered in blood, to reach the sea. Herne also escaped to the sea, astonishingly unhurt except for a few bruises inflicted by the Somalis' clubs. But Stroyan had been killed; and Burton, hit by a javelin which had passed right through his jaw, knocking out four of his teeth and splintering the roof of his mouth, had been forced to fly for his life with the weapon still embedded in his face, its point emerging from his right cheek. The wound was so serious that when he arrived back in Aden the British doctor there, noting as a complicating factor that Burton had 'recently suffered from secondary syphilis', recommended that he 'immediately proceed to Europe'. The same recommendation was made in respect of Speke.

Having recovered from their wounds, both Burton and Speke volunteered for service in the Crimea and when the war there was over they were back together in Africa, having secured leave from the Indian Army and won the support of the Royal Geographical Society, as well as a Foreign Office grant of £1,000, for an important journey of exploration. It was hoped that they would discover the source of the Nile in the region of the inland seas of which the German missionaries in East Africa had given indeterminate reports. They arrived in Zanzibar on 20 December 1856 and it was soon after this that they went to seek the advice of Rebmann at Kisulidini.

Rebmann warned them not to attempt a journey west from Mombasa: plundering bands of Masai had made the route impassable, he said. The Englishmen would do better to go south to the mouth of the Pangani and make their way inland from there. They followed this advice but on reaching the Pangani they both contracted yellow fever and were obliged to go back to Zanzibar where, when he was feeling better, Burton learned Kiswahili and collected materials for his two-volume *Zanzibar: City, Island and Coast*, a work which graphically describes the horrors and squalor of the noisome port, the capital of the East African Arab empire. Its 'disorderly lanes and alleys' were heaped with offal and rubbish; its wells covered in slime; its air reeked of decay, of putrefying molluscs in the cowrie shells piled upon the shore, and of coconut flesh drying in the sun; its people suffered from all manner of diseases, from malaria, dysentery, hepatitis, yellow fever, syphilis, gonorrhoea, sarocele, hydrocele, elephantiasis of the arms and legs, and of the scrotum which was often so swollen it reached the knees; its slave dealers, who, despite all efforts to prevent their traffic, disposed of thousands of Negroes each year with as callous an indifference to their sufferings as that of one Spanish merchant who, finding some of his stock suffering from dysentery, sewed them up so that they did not spoil his chances of a sale.

After spending six months in this dreadful place, Burton and Speke set out for the interior in the middle of June 1857. Their caravan was a large one, eventually comprising over 130 men and 30 animals. All were heavily loaded. They carried beds, chairs, tents, blankets, mosquito nets, a folding table, numerous instruments, fishing tackle, presents of cloth, brass wire and beads, food, carpenters' tools, books, umbrellas, ammunition, firearms, hatchets, knives, daggers, shields, bullet moulds and a dozen bottles of brandy. Their route to the mysterious inland seas – which were uncertainly indicated on the map which Erhardt had drawn for the Royal Geographical Society as a single elongated splodge – lay through Usugara and Tabora, first through dank forest and slimy bogs, then through open country dotted with mimosa and gum trees through whose foliage could be seen the shapes of antelope and the stripes of zebra. But long before they had crossed the Usugara Mountains much of their heavy and extensive baggage had been lost. Alternately cajoled and whipped by Burton, bearers had deserted in considerable numbers; presents had been stolen, and the half-caste Arab who had been appointed to direct the caravan turned out himself to be a thief and had to be replaced with an African, a former slave, known as Sidi Mubarak Bombay. Later to be recognized as an invaluable servant, Bombay was at this time considered vain and shifty, a man whose almost constant ill-temper frequently erupted into violence and whose gruesome aspect was rendered even more malevolent by incisor teeth filed down to resemble the sharp points of a saw. Ill with fever and exhausted by long and arduous marches, neither Burton nor Speke could summon the strength to control their bearers or to withstand the exorbitant demands made upon their resources by the chiefs through whose territories they had to pass. Burton's mouth became full of ulcers, and his feet were so swollen that he could not walk. By day he found it as much as he could do to maintain his balance on a donkey; by night he lay sleepless on his bed, overcome by depression and fear that the expedition was destined to fail, and finally lapsed into a delirium in which he saw weird beasts, fearful hags and monstrous men with heads growing out of their chests. Speke was in little better shape. They were tortured by mosquitoes and flies, earwigs, beetles and scorpions, by white ants that ate through their bedding and by huge pismire ants whose mandibles, strong enough to pinch a rat to death, bit agonizingly into their legs.

Finding the country intolerable, both Speke and Burton considered that most of its inhabitants were quite as unpleasant. Speke, little interested in them anyway, viewed them initially with disdain, as idle, obstinate and untrustworthy, 'hideously black and ugly'; and found it difficult to overcome his embarrassment at the women's nakedness. Burton had no such inhibitions. He delighted in the sight of the healthy, young nude bodies of the black girls and in their unselfconsciousness; and he hinted in his books that he had enjoyed the pleasure of these bodies himself. He wrote of the 'splendid development of limb' of such women as those of the Wasagara tribe, and of the imposing size of so many African men's penises. He was perfectly open in this admiration: he measured the penis of one man and found that 'when quiescent, it numbered nearly six inches'. 'This is a characteristic of the negro race,' he decided. 'Moreover, these imposing parts do not increase proportionally during erection; consequently the "deed of kind" takes a much longer time and adds greatly to the women's enjoyment.' In other passages a hint of envy creeps into such descriptions; and his evident belief that the black man was sexually more accomplished than the white may well have coloured his often strongly disapprobatory view of African society generally. It was his not untypical opinion, for instance, that the Wanika people were 'a futile race of barbarians, drunken and immoral; cowardly and destructive; boisterous and loquacious; indolent, greedy and thriftless'. And it did not much surprise him when one of his own bearers, having bought a slave girl who could not keep up with the pace of the caravan, cut her head off, not merely as a punishment but so that no one else should have his property for nothing. Burton, in fact, agreed with Speke that the Negro was inferior to the white man but, unlike Speke, he looked for a scientific rather than a biblical explanation.

The relationship between Burton and Speke, which was to become so violently antagonistic, was already becoming strained. Burton was discovering that beneath Speke's quiet, amenably tactful demeanour was a character far less docile, a man of relentless ambition who harboured slights until they hardened into ineradicable grievances, who had, as Burton was later to write when their differences had broken out into public quarrels, 'an immense and abnormal fund of self-esteem, who ever held, not only that he had done his best on all occasions, but also that no living man could do better'.

For his part, Speke maintained that it was Burton who had this overweening sense of his own importance, who was one of those men 'who never *can* be wrong, and will not acknowledge an error'. He remembered with rancour how Burton had told him to hold his ground in the collapsing tent at Berbera, as though he were a coward who would not or could not fight. He was bitterly affronted by the way in which Burton had made use of his diary in his *First Footsteps in Africa*, relegating it to an appendix, making light of Speke's difficulties with his guide during his ill-fated journey to the Wadi Nogul, and paraphrasing Speke's words in the third person as though he could not write. More recently he had felt a lingering resentment at Burton's refusal to halt the caravan to allow Speke time to shoot more game. A teetotaler himself and, at this time, sexually prim, he could not but feel disturbed by Burton's indulgence in alcohol and drugs, by his unbridled curiosity about the genital organs and sexual life of Africans, and by his obvious eagerness to participate in that life himself. Burton was 'a blackguard', Speke was to conclude: he had 'gone to the Devil' in Africa.

For the moment, however, their mutual antipathy was kept in check. They arrived at Tabora, at the beginning of November, and there learned what they had for some time suspected, that the huge 'Sea of Ujiji' drawn on Erhardt's map was not one lake but several, and that two of these lakes were much larger than the others. One lay to the west of Tabora, the other to the north. Believing that there might be a river joining them, that this river might be the upper Nile, and that the more southerly of the two large lakes was, therefore, probably the source of the Nile, Burton decided to go west in search of it. Both he and Speke were now desperately ill again, Burton with malaria which paralysed his legs and obliged him to be carried in a hammock; Speke with an infection of the retina which made him almost blind. But on they went through Usagozi, along the course of the Unyamwezi, across the Ruguvu and Unguwwe rivers until on 13 February 1858, on the summit of a hill which had proved so steep and hard to climb that Speke's ass had collapsed and died during the ascent, Burton caught sight of the waters of the lake, at first but dimly through the veil of trees and then the whole expanse of it. The sight of the shining waters beneath the surrounding hills filled him with 'admiration, wonder and delight'.

Exhilarated as he was by this discovery of Lake Tanganyika and refreshed by the cool milk, eggs, tomatoes and artichokes they found in Ujiji, the principal town on the lake's shore, Burton's health deteriorated still further now that he had reached the end of his journey. He lay on the ground for days on end in Ujiji, feeling too ill to talk. When he had recovered slightly he sent Speke, whose eyes had improved, to hire the only sailing craft on the lake, a dhow in which he hoped they might explore its shores and reach a river that was reported to flow out of it to the north. But when Speke returned after nearly four weeks' absence – and with an agonizing inflammation in his ear from which he had unsuccessfully tried to prise a burrowing beetle with a pen-knife – he reported that the Arab merchant to whom the dhow belonged refused to part with it for less than 500 dollars and then not for three months. Endeavouring to conceal his anger with Speke, who had 'done literally nothing', Burton himself obtained at an exorbitant price two leaky dug-outs; and in the larger of these he determined to find the river, the Rusizi, which, so some Arab slave dealers had assured Speke, did indeed flow northwards out of the lake. Still unable to walk, Burton was carried down to the shores of the lake in his hammock and, with the Union Jack flying above the heads of the native paddlers, he and Speke were taken northwards across the waters of the lake, past the settlements of the Wamembe who were, according to Burton, cannibals to a man and cannibals with a decided preference for raw flesh. Returning Burton's gaze, they balefully looked upon him, so he thought, 'in the light of butcher's meat'.

At Uvira near the northern end of the lake, Burton was dismayed to hear that the waters of the River Rusizi did not flow out of the lake but into it. Anxious to settle the matter himself – since, if the reports were true, his whole theory about the Nile would be upset – Burton ordered the canoemen to take the dug-outs on to the Rusizi. But they had gone far enough. The tribe that inhabited that part of the lake, the Wavera, were supposed to have an even stronger relish for human flesh than the Wamembe: the canoemen would not endanger their lives by entering Wavera waters. Burton endeavoured by persuasion, money and threats to make them change their minds; but in the end he had to give way, for his tongue and mouth, covered in ulcers, were so swollen that he could no longer speak. Dispirited and miserable, he and Speke returned to Ujiji in the pouring rain, crouching in the dug-out, surrounded throughout the month-long voyage by sacks of sodden flour and disgusted by the stench of excrement and putrefying offal which could not be thrown overboard for fear lest they attract the attention of the crocodiles.

Prevented by lack of supplies from following his original plan of exploring the south of Lake Tanganyika and then going down to Lake Nyasa, Burton decided that he and Speke must now return to Zanzibar. So, on 26 May they left for Tabora. Here Burton announced that they would rest for a while until his legs grew stronger. This was no hardship for him as it provided him with an opportunity to pursue various anthropological and linguistic studies. But for Speke it was a time of utter boredom. 'This is a shocking country for sport,' he wrote to a friend. 'There appears to be literally nothing but Elephants, and they from constant hunting are driven clean away from the highways; all I have succeeded in shooting have been a few antelopes and guinea fowls beside hippopotamus near the coast ... There is literally nothing to write about in this uninteresting country. Nothing could surpass these tracts, jungles, plains for same dullness, the people are the same everywhere in fact the country is one vast senseless map of sameness ... Burton has always been ill.'

Burton himself reported that Speke, now almost completely recovered from his illness, was a most irksome companion, restless, sulky, irritatingly high-handed with the Arab merchants, whom he 'treated as niggers', and apparently resentful of Burton's easy fluency in conversations from which he, with scant knowledge of the languages employed, was always excluded. So, when Speke suggested an exploration north from Tabora to the northern lake, the Ukerewe, which was reported to be not far off, Burton was only too pleased to be rid of him for a while, expecting, no doubt, that he would be no more successful in this venture than he had been on previous occasions when Burton had sent him out on his own.

But in this expectation Burton was quite wrong. After little more than a fortnight's easy march, Speke, accompanied by his interpreter, Bombay, came within sight of a massive expanse of water that looked even more extensive than Lake Tanganyika. Bombay asked one of the natives how far it was to the northern shore. The native did not know: his people had never ventured so far; the water perhaps stretched out to the very edge of the world. After these words had been reported to Speke it came upon him with the force of a divine revelation that he had 'solved a problem which it had been ... the ambition of the first monarchs of the world to unravel'. He had discovered, he was convinced, the true source of the White Nile. Spending only three days by the shores of the lake, which he named the Victoria Nyanza after his 'gracious sovereign', he hurried back to Tabora with the exciting news.

Burton, listening to him, seemed unimpressed. Speke might have stumbled upon 'one of the feeders' of the White Nile, but to say that the so-called Victoria Nyanza was its source was to claim far too much. There might perhaps be reasons to suppose it so, yet they were reasons which no reputable geographer could possibly accept. Speke urged Burton to come back with him to the lake and see it for himself. Burton, however, declined. He was older than Speke, he reminded him, and he was still unwell. They must return together to Zanzibar, recover their health, obtain more funds and then, having reported on what they had done, return to complete their whole journey. In the meantime, it was tacitly understood between them that the subject of the Nile was one that was better left undiscussed.

For much of the return journey, indeed, Speke was in no condition to discuss it. He was seized with agonizing pains, tormented by terrifying visions and convulsed by fits in one of which he barked like a mad dog. In his delirium he raved about his grievances, not just about Burton's disinclination to recognize his claims about the Nile but about earlier slights and insults, real and imagined. Burton, nursing him, could be in no doubt as to the depth of Speke's resentment and that Speke was now a rival rather than a friend.

For the moment, however, the appearances of friendship were maintained; and when they arrived in Aden all seemed outwardly well between them. Burton was advised to remain in Aden to convalesce, and when Speke sailed home alone aboard the *Furious* his words of farewell, so Burton said, were, 'Good-bye, old fellow. You may be quite sure I shall not go up to the Royal Geographical Society until you come to the fore and we appear together. Make your mind quite easy about that.'

On board the *Furious*, however, was the rich, homosexual travel writer, Laurence Oliphant, who was returning to London with Lord Elgin after a futile diplomatic mission to the Imperial Chinese court. Evidently attracted by Speke, he spent much of his time on board ship in his company and persuaded him not to wait for Burton, into whose shadow he would inevitably be cast, but to go directly to the Royal Geographical Society and put forward his own claims. Speke followed this advice, found Sir Roderick Murchison far more ready to listen to him than Burton had ever been, and was persuaded to speak at a meeting of the Society before Burton returned. And by the time Burton did return to England towards the end of May 1859 a new expedition had been organized; funds of £2,500 had been promised; and Speke had been given the command. The quarrel between the two explorers, exacerbated by squabbles over money, now erupted in public. Speke accused Burton of all manner of sins and mistakes, describing in print his own achievements while making it appear that Burton's were of secondary importance, making claims about Lake

212

Victoria which the evidence did not warrant, and suggesting in private that, had Speke not been with him, Burton could never have undertaken the journey at all. At first Burton left it to his friends to support him and to refute Speke's allegations. But when the time came for him to write the preface to his *Lake Regions of Central Africa*, Burton made it quite clear how he himself felt about Speke who had arrogated so much importance to himself, yet who, being neither a linguist nor a man of science nor even 'an accurate astronomical observer', was, in fact, 'unfit for any other but a subordinate capacity'. 'Can I then feel otherwise than indignant,' Burton asked, 'when I find that, after preceding me from Aden to England, with the spontaneous offer, on his part, of not appearing before the Society that originated the Expedition until my return, he had lost no time in taking measures to secure for himself the right of working the field I had opened.'

When these words appeared in print Speke had already embarked on the expedition to which Burton referred. And having repeatedly rejected any suggestion that he would ever be subordinate to anyone again, Speke had found an ideal companion in James Augustus Grant, a quiet, retiring officer from his own regiment, a man as agreeable, amenable and even submissive as Burton was abrasive and overbearing.

At thirty-two Grant was the same age as Speke, well over six foot in height, powerfully built and extremely good looking. The son of a Scottish minister, he had been granted a commission in the 8th Native Bengal Infantry when he was nineteen and had been wounded while fighting gallantly after the mutiny of the regiment. He was as keen and good a shot as Speke, a talented artist and an expert botanist. Humourless and dull, his was not a striking personality, but his unassuming nature – which masked a strong streak of jealousy – had won him many friends in his regiment including Speke whose invitation to accompany him on his next exploration in Africa was immediately accepted. It was Speke's intention, so he told Grant, to move inland again from Zanzibar to Tabora, march north to Lake Victoria, and then to make his way up the side of the lake to the northern shore where he would find the outlet which was the beginning of the White Nile. His expedition would be passing through the uncharted areas of central Africa and would settle, once and for all, not only the problems of the Nile and the inland lakes but also of the Mountains of the Moon.

It was a most exciting vision, but Grant had not been long in Africa before the high price that would have to be paid for its realization was brought home to him. All the evils which could beset a mission of exploration had fallen upon theirs: disease, robbers, deserting bearers, chiefs demanding extortionate *hongo*, and tribal wars. And it was not until the end of 1861 that he and Speke managed to advance north from Tabora and to enter Karagwe, the most southerly of the three kingdoms which had been established centuries before in Uganda by people from the highlands of Ethiopia who had in many respects reached a higher state of civilization than the aboriginal inhabitants of the northern and western shores of Lake Victoria.

The people of Karagwe, and of the two other kingdoms of Buganda and Bunyoro, had no written language and had not discovered the wheel or even the plough. But, as Speke discovered to his surprised admiration, they lived in large, well-constructed conical huts of cane and reed, some of which were as high as fifty feet; they washed their hands before sitting down to appetizing meals of chickens, beef stews, fish, sweet potatoes, sugar cane and bananas; their bodies were neither scarred nor tattooed and their gowns and capes were sewn with expert skill. Their slaves were treated compassionately, and they behaved with civility towards strangers.

Rumanika, the King of Karagwe, seemed particularly pleased to see the first white men he had ever come across when they arrived at his capital, Bweranyange. He greeted them hospitably, offered them his most commodious huts, and sent them presents of food and *pombe*. He encouraged them to go out shooting the plentiful game – lions and elephants, giraffe and rhinoceros, buffalo, zebra, antelope and hyena – and was delighted to admit them to his harem which was filled with women of so unbelievable a fatness that they could not stand up. In order to attain this formidable size young girls were fed on quantities of rich milk, and were threatened with a beating if they did not consume enough. Speke, with unaccustomed bravado, asked one of these women if he could measure her. He discovered her naked chest to measure 52 inches, her thighs 31.

Leaving Grant, who had a painfully infected leg, in the care of King Rumanika's physician at Bweranyange, Speke marched northwards in January 1862 to Buganda where he found the young *kabaka*, Mutesa, a far more formidable figure than the easy-going Rumanika and a man whom it was impossible to treat with his customary condescension. Strong, intelligent, self-confident and cunning, Mutesa had, in the manner of his ancestors, established a tyranny which seemed to European eyes one of monstrous cruelty, having thirty of his brothers burned alive upon his accession in order to pre-empt a family rebellion, and having since executed hundreds of his subjects who were decapitated to the roll of drums for such negligible offences as talking too loudly in his presence. When he himself spoke, his courtiers were required to listen in rapt silence, then to throw themselves to the ground in humble submission to his commands or grateful acknowledgment of his wisdom, repeating a strange repetitive cry, '*N'yanzig, n'yanzig, n'yanzig!*' The *kabaka* walked about amongst them in his toga, strings of beads around his arms and legs, stepping stiff-leggedly upon his toes in a manner intended to represent the movements of a lion.

214

Dressing his men in red blankets, Speke set out with his presents to be received by this formidable ruler on 20 February; but, required to wait in the blazing sun outside the palace while another delegation was admitted, Speke lost his temper and marched back to his hut. Unnerved by this astonishing breach of etiquette, and no doubt frightened that it might provoke wholesale executions, a party of courtiers rushed after him, apologized for the mistake, begged him to return and said that he would be allowed the unprecedented privilege of bringing a chair into the *kabaka*'s presence. Soon afterwards, accompanied by the royal band of harps and trumpets, Speke was led through outer courts to the *kabaka*'s throne room where for an hour he sat in this chair beneath an umbrella while Mutesa inspected him, making occasional remarks to his courtiers and accepting beer from his pages. After the hour had elapsed the *kabaka* left the room with his leonine gait to have his dinner; and it was only after this meal was over and night had fallen that Speke was allowed to offer his presents and to receive in return various comestibles including fish, fowls, porcupines and rats. These gifts were followed by several virgins from the *kabaka*'s harem, naked girls smeared with grease who had been presented by their fathers to the *kabaka* in propitiation for some offence. Girls, her daughters, also came from the *kabaka*'s mother, a fat woman who was usually drunk and who was once seen by Speke surrounded by attendants on all fours drinking beer from a trough like pigs. These girls, so Speke recorded, were distributed as wives amongst the bearers. But not all, in fact, were handed over. One, named Meri, was taken into his own hut and it appears from extracts in his journal, which did not find their way into print, that he fell in love with her. Before he left Buganda he had fathered a child.

Among the presents Speke gave the *kabaka* was a carbine and at a subsequent reception, after Speke had been required to demonstrate the power of his own pistols by shooting four cows, Mutesa handed this gun to a page and ordered him to go out and shoot somebody in the courtyard. The boy went out, fulfilled his commission and returned to the *kabaka* who asked him, 'And did you do it well?' The boy replied that he had done it very well indeed. 'I never heard,' Speke commented, 'and there appeared no curiosity to know, what individual human being the urchin had deprived of life.'

Considering, perhaps, that human bodies were too easy a target, Mutesa thereafter strutted about the town, followed by his wives, pages, courtiers, the girls of his harem and the musicians of his band, firing into the trees and occasionally hitting a vulture, a demonstration of his powers which would be greeted by his attendants falling in admiration to the ground and giving vent to their strange cry, '*N'yanzig! n'yanzig! n'yanzig!*'

Both Mutesa and his mother were reluctant to let Speke depart, for his presence was a diversion and more presents might be extracted from him, particularly guns which Mutesa coveted as a means of maintaining his power. Also Mutesa, whom Speke treated with a carefully limited respect, was anxious, as he admitted, to 'learn new things' from the white man whose wearing of trousers and a hat and whose habit of sitting in a chair he later adopted. But on 7 July 1862, after Grant had joined him, Speke was given permission to leave; and the two men set off eagerly towards a river which, so they had both been told, flowed out of the nearby lake to the north. Speke and Grant both felt sure that they must be approaching the climax of their journey.

Yet two days after leaving Mutesa's capital, it was decided that Speke and Grant should part company again, that Grant should make for Chagsi, the capital of King Kamrasi of Bunyoro whose territories they would next have to traverse, while Speke should make his way alone to determine the spot where the White Nile emerged from Lake Victoria. Both men were afterwards to maintain that this was a decision to which they had mutually agreed; that Grant's leg, not yet fully recovered, made it impossible for him to cover the twenty miles a day which Speke required on the dash to the Nile, and that it was necessary 'to communicate quickly' with John Petherick, an ivory trader and British Consul in Khartoum, who had been paid to bring supplies for the expedition to Gondokoro and who was believed to be in the vicinity. But it was afterwards said, of course, that Speke, in his determination not to share his triumph with anyone, took advantage of Grant's loyal and modest nature to promote his own glory. And glory there was to be. For, on 21 July 1862, Speke reached the White Nile at Urondogani, forty miles downstream from Lake Victoria, 'a magnificent stream, 600 to 700 yards wide, dotted with islets and rocks', as he described it, with crocodiles and hippopotami to be seen beneath the high banks, and herds of hartebeest beyond them. Speke excitedly told his men that they ought to shave their heads and bathe in 'the holy river, the cradle of Moses'. But Bombay prosaically reminded him that being Mohammedans they could not look upon these things so fancifully; they were 'contented with the commonplaces of life'.

Speke himself was even more excited when, having marched upstream for a few days, he came upon the roaring flood of a waterfall. For he was convinced that it was here, where the waters of Lake Victoria plunged down in cascades of foam, where passenger-fish leapt 'at the falls with all their might', where native fishermen 'stood on all the rocks with rod and hook', and hippopotami and crocodiles lay sleepily in the stiller water downstream, that the Nile began its long course to the sea. Naming the cataract Ripon Falls, in honour of Lord Ripon, the future Viceroy of India who had had much to do with the planning of the expedition, Speke made his way north again to join Grant in Bunyoro, impatient now to get home and to announce his great discovery to the world.

216

King Kamrasi, however, was quite as reluctant to let him leave as King Mutesa had been; and it was not until he had acquired Speke's gold chronometer that permission was forthcoming.

Had his possessions and stores not by now been so reduced, and had he had more time to spare, Speke would have gone west rather than north; for he had heard reports of another lake in that direction known as the Luta N'zigé, the 'dead locust', which might well prove to be another source of the Nile. But he decided he must be content with what he had already achieved; to risk more might be to lose all; the journey home would be long and arduous enough as it was. And so it proved to be. When he and Grant reached the Nile again they tried to make use of it by continuing their journey in canoes; but cataracts and hostile tribesmen drove them back on to land; and it was not until the beginning of December that they reached Faloro, the most southerly Egyptian trading-post on the upper Nile, and not until the middle of February 1863, almost two and a half years after their exploration had begun, that they approached Gondokoro. To Speke's anger there was no sign there of Petherick; but the figure of a European could be seen running to welcome them. This was Samuel Baker.

Baker, like Speke, was an enthusiastic, not to say insatiable sportsman. The more animals he killed, the more deeply he was satisfied. He delighted, he confessed, in 'whole hecatombs of slaughter'; and had been known in Scotland to dispatch a stag by plunging a twelve-inch-long, double-bladed knife through the creature's shoulders into its heart, 'ten times better sport', in his opinion, 'than shooting a deer at bay'. He had had plenty of opportunities to indulge in his tastes. His father was rich and his grandfather had left him a great deal of money. Educated at home by tutors, he had been spared the rigours of a public-school education and had been left much to his own devices. Married when young, he had gone to live abroad, first in Mauritius, then in Ceylon where he had shot more elephants than any man before him. Soon after his return home his wife died, leaving him with four daughters; and 'with no plans for the future', as he put it himself, he decided to wander about for a while and trust to fate – 'anything for a constant change'. But while boar-shooting expeditions in the Turkish mountains were a pleasant enough diversion, he was discontented with his aimless life and began to consider ways of spending it more profitably. He had much to offer: he was the proud possessor of enormous strength which he delighted in displaying; he was a gifted linguist and a fluent writer, the author of two books on Ceylon; he could sketch with facility and had a remarkable talent for getting the likeness of a face on paper; he had a splendid bass voice, capable of making windows rattle and much in demand when his friends were in the mood for a stirring, patriotic song; he could tell an excellent story; he was also, in the words of a friend, 'a very well-informed man, having some knowledge of geology, botany and medicine, as well as an eager longing after everything that concerns natural history'. Not conventionally handsome, as Speke and Grant were, his features were striking without the least hint of that satanic cast that could make Burton's alarming. Good humour, as another friend put it, seemed to radiate from his sparkling blue eyes. Yet he was not a man given to intimate friendships. 'Made up of queer materials', in his own estimation, he was unable 'to fit in . . . ever unhappy when unemployed, and too proud to serve'. He was also dogmatic, overbearing, aggressively self-confident and unalterably convinced of the superiority of the British over all other peoples and of the inferiority of the Negro whose intellectual capacity, he was to conclude, it was 'preposterous to compare' with that of the white man.

Aware of most of these failings and of his reputation as a rich and rather eccentric sportsman, the people to whom Baker applied, when he had made up his mind that Africa was the best solution for his restlessness and might fulfil his desire for a more enviable reputation than the one he possessed, were unresponsive. Sir Roderick Murchison, the President of the Royal Geographical Society, for example, declared that Baker's application, which had been passed on to him, was 'out of the question'. So concealing his disappointment as best he could, he set out once more for Turkey and on his way through the Balkan town of Widdin he caught sight of a young woman who was to transform his life. She was a slight, fair girl from Transylvania, about seventeen years old; and she was being offered as a slave in the market. Baker bid for her, bought her and fell in love with her. Accepting the impossibility of taking her back to England with him, he applied for an appointment with the Danube and Black Sea Railway in order to stay with her; and then decided to go with her to Africa. 'You know that Africa has always been in my head,' he wrote home in explanation to his family. 'I am going to Khartoum, and thence, God only knows where, in search of the sources of the Nile.'

By the middle of June 1862 Baker, then aged forty, had reached Khartoum, capital of the Egyptian Sudan, with the girl he called Florence and was later to marry in London. She had long since outgrown her early timidity; and, while submissively devoted to the man who had rescued her in Widdin, had proved herself a woman of strong character, resourceful and adaptable, with a robust sense of humour that complemented his own. When Baker had suggested that they go in search of Speke she had immediately consented to the plan; and by the end of December she could have been seen, in 'trousers and gaiters and a belt and a blouse', sailing up the Nile towards Gondokoro where they landed on 2 February 1863.

A transit camp where slavers and ivory dealers waited for boats to transport them downstream, Gondokoro was a 'perfect hell of a place', Baker thought, suffocatingly hot, disgustingly smelly and intermittently violent. Suspected of being agents for anti-slavery organizations, he and Florence were far from welcome; and when a boy, sitting on one of his boats, was shot through the head, Baker could not but conclude that many people in Gondokoro would have been delighted had the same fate overtaken himself. Yet he felt he could not escape from the place until he had some reliable news of Speke and Grant about whom nothing had been heard for so long. He would have gone out in search of them anyway had his men been more trustworthy; but, since they were on the verge of mutiny, he felt obliged to stay where he was. It was, therefore, with infinite relief that on the morning of 15 February he heard that the white men were on their way. Walking fast up the river bank, he soon caught sight of them and, recognizing Speke whom he had met years before on a steamer bound for Aden from India, he broke into a run, waving his hat in the air and shouting words of welcome. Both Speke and Grant looked utterly exhausted and painfully thin. Speke's shirt was badly torn; Grant's knees could be seen through the holes in his tattered trousers. But the excitement of the meeting seemed to give them new strength. They shook hands vigorously; they could not, Speke said, 'speak fast enough'. Still talking they were led away to Baker's boat where, on seeing Florence, Speke made a tactless remark to Baker to the effect that he thought his wife was dead. Baker introduced Florence as his '*chère amie*'.

Delighted as Speke professed himself to be at seeing once again his 'old friend', Baker, his pleasure was overcast by his angry feelings towards Petherick whom he unjustly accused not merely of ineptitude in failing to come down with the stores which were so badly needed, but even of a wilful disregard of his instructions in the furtherance of his own private trade. And when Petherick did arrive on 20 February, Speke refused to accept anything from him, choosing to believe that he had become involved in the slave trade and making much of a story that the heads of three natives killed in an ambush had, on Petherick's orders, been boiled so that the skin, flesh and brains could be removed before the skulls were sent to London to be sold to the Royal College of Surgeons. Petherick's devoted and capable wife, who had almost died on the journey and who had arrived at Gondokoro in so weak and worn a state that her wasted figure was scarcely recognizable, begged Speke not to refuse her husband's help, to consider what damage his refusal might do to 'Peth's' reputation in England. But Speke was unrelenting: he would not, he said, 'recognize the succour dodge'.

Harsh as he was with the Pethericks, Speke behaved in a perfectly friendly way towards Baker who could not conceal his disappointment that there seemed little now left in Central Africa for him to do. He complained wistfully that Speke and Grant had arrived too soon, adding that he had hoped to discover they were in some fearful plight from which he could rescue them. And later, hearing the full story of Speke's discoveries, he asked, 'Does not one leaf of the laurel remain to me?' Speke assured him that there did, indeed, remain such a leaf – the discovery of the lake known as Luta N'zigé into which, Speke surmised, the Nile flowed from Lake Victoria and out of which it flowed to the north. Speke obligingly wrote some notes for Baker to help him find it, and Grant drew him a hypothetical map.

As soon as he heard of it, Baker determined to go to the Luta N'zigé, though the difficulties of getting there appeared almost insuperable. The rapids above Gondokoro would prevent him going by boat, the tribes beyond the rapids were known to be fiercely hostile to travellers, and the men who had come with him to Gondokoro were unwilling to venture further south with an Englishman who would undoubtedly be attacked by slave dealers. Baker thought of making a dash on horseback to the lake with Florence, accompanied by only two reliable servants on camels and taking nothing with them other than beads with which to buy food. But he was advised that the tribes through whose lands he would have to pass would not accept beads in exchange for food. 'You can do nothing here,' he was told, 'without plenty of men and guns.' And it was not until he heard of a trading party which was shortly to be dispatched to the south by a friendly Circassian slaver that Baker was able to seize an opportunity to leave Gondokoro for the Luta N'zigé. By keeping close to this party Baker thought that his own smaller caravan might get through; and on the afternoon of 26 March, when he knew from the sound of drum beats and gunshots that the traders were about to depart, he had his donkeys and camels loaded and with seventeen of his men who had agreed to go with them, he and Florence mounted their horses and rode off. At first the traders refused to have anything to do with them. But Baker offered them money and gave their Syrian leader a double-barrelled gun, while Florence suggested that, were they to follow the explorers, they might well be taken into lands where ivory was to be found in abundance. The Syrian was clearly impressed by the idea that the intriguing articles in the Englishman's baggage when given to local chiefs might well open up territories that he had not previously been able to enter. So an uneasy bargain was struck: the two parties would go on together.

At first the path was an appallingly difficult one over steep, rough, stony ground on which the camels frequently fell, shedding their loads; and the faces and bodies of the riders were cut by the thorny bushes dangling from the rocks. Held up when the rains came by swollen rivers too deep to ford, both Baker and Florence suffered from intermittent bouts of malaria; and their animals, bitten by the tsetse fly, began to die. In their hut swarms of white ants crawled about in their blankets. Their escort, reduced first to twelve men, then to nine when three others deserted after Baker had knocked one down for threatening mutiny, grew ever more sullen.

After the rains had stopped, however, they were able to move on at the beginning of 1864 and on 22 January, after marching through streams and deep swamps, they reached the White Nile between Lake Victoria and the Luta N'zigé and soon entered the kingdom of Bunyoro.

King Kamrasi was in even more rapacious mood than usual. Having accepted present after present, clothes, shawls, shoes, ornaments, necklaces, a Persian carpet and a double-barrelled rifle, he demanded that his visitors' bags be opened up to satisfy himself that they had nothing left to give him. He then announced that if Baker wanted to go to look for the lake he was welcome to do so provided he left him his little white woman in exchange for a few of his own wives. Baker leapt to his feet in fury, held a revolver to the king's head and threatened to pull the trigger if he ever suggested such a thing again. The king asked for Baker's kilt and his compass instead. And it was not until these were handed over that he granted him permission to proceed, providing him with a noisy, prancing escort of painted warriors who appeared before him in leopard and monkey skins with antelopes' horns on their heads, cows' tails hanging from their buttocks and false beards on their chins.

Under the doubtful protection of what Baker called 'The Devil's Own Regiment', who proved themselves readier to plunder villages than to fulfil their duties as guards, the expedition continued into lands which Baker believed had never before been entered by strangers. The heat was intense; the air humid; there was no quinine left; fever dogged the travellers. Baker once fell off his ox; Florence was so ill that she suffered a seizure then lapsed into a coma. Baker abandoned all hope for her and gave orders to the men to dig a grave. She regained consciousness to the sound of pickaxes striking the hard earth.

They struggled on painfully, and on 14 March 1864 they came upon the lake, 'a grand expanse of water', which he named Lake Albert. Gripping a stout bamboo, Baker led the way towards it. Florence, 'in extreme weakness', tottered down the pass after him, supporting herself on his shoulder and having to rest every twenty paces. 'After a toilsome descent of about two hours, weak with years of fever, but for the moment strengthened by success, we gained the level plain below the cliff,' Baker recorded. 'A walk of about a mile through flat sandy meadows of fine turf interspersed with trees and bush, brought us to the water's edge. The waves were rolling upon a white pebbly beach: I rushed into the lake, and thirsty with heat and fatigue, with a heart full of gratitude, I drank deeply from the Sources of the Nile.'

A few days later he and Florence were sailing up the eastern side of the lake in a dug-out to which he had fitted a mast, a yard and a sail made from a Highland plaid. And after nearly a fortnight's northward voyaging, during which they almost perished in a storm, they reached the point where the Nile entered the lake. Then, continuing up the river to the east beyond a village deserted but for numerous immense crocodiles, they soon came upon the splendid sight of a thundering cataract where the waters of the river fell 130 feet and the Victoria Nile became the Albert Nile. Baker named this cataract the Murchison Falls.

He would have liked to have crowned his achievement in discovering both lake and falls by tracing the course of the river northwards from its exit; but the paddlers of the canoes would not risk their lives by entering the territories of the savage tribes along the river's banks. They had narrowly escaped drowning during the storms and had almost been eaten alive by crocodiles when their canoe had been lifted half out of the water beneath the falls by a huge hippopotamus. They were all anxious to go home. So, too, was Baker; but it was to be many months before he reached England again. Delayed by attacks of fever during which he sometimes lapsed into unconsciousness, haunted by visions of his parents and of his dead wife, he was delayed also by King Kamrasi who wanted him to join in a war against a rival chief and attempted to starve him into submission when Baker refused to fight for him. Week followed weary week. There was little to eat except mildewed grain, sweet potatoes and a sort of wild spinach, little to drink but tea made from wild thyme and alcohol which Baker, ever inventive, distilled from potatoes. Both he and Florence often thought of death, and sometimes felt that they would have welcomed it as a release from suffering. In September, however, an Arab caravan arrived from Gondokoro with stores and mail; and Kamrasi, who had extracted from him almost all his remaining possessions, at last gave Baker permission to travel with the caravan when it went back to Gondokoro. Among the mail was a letter from Speke enclosing a picture of himself and Grant from the *Illustrated London News*.

On his return to England the year before, preceded by a telegram in which he had announced categorically, 'the Nile is settled', Speke had been welcomed as a hero. At Southampton a band had played triumphant airs and the mayor had invited the great explorer to a banquet. In London, at the Royal Geographical Society, where windows had been broken in the rush to hear him lecture, his appearance had been greeted with acclamation. But this enthusiasm had soon abated, for Speke was not a man to accept his triumph modestly or to tolerate any questioning of his achievement. He had already arrogantly informed the Royal Geographical Society from Khartoum that he was intent on returning to Africa as soon as possible and travelling right across it from east to west. 'Unless I do it,' he had declared, 'it will not be done this century.' Now that he was home, in the excitement of his fame, his self-satisfied arrogance had increased and his attacks upon his rivals and those whom he took to be his enemies became more outspoken than ever. Sir Roderick Murchison, who had previously spoken of his feat as being 'far more wonderful' than anything that had been accomplished in his lifetime, was now thoroughly disillusioned with the man and his 'aberrations' and exasperated by his reluctance to write a paper for his Society's journal in case it should interfere with the profits from his forthcoming book. John Petherick was so incensed by Speke's allegations about him that he was eventually driven to instigate an action for libel. James M'Queen, an influential geographer, angered by Speke's treatment of Petherick and disgusted by his philandering at King Mutesa's court – about which Speke himself seems to have spoken indiscreetly, perhaps boastfully, in London – compiled a vituperatively abusive review of Speke's *Journal of the Discovery of the Source of the Nile*. But of all Speke's opponents the most formidable was the one who had once been his friend but who was now to conclude that his erstwhile companion's extremely shaky knowledge of geography had invested the Nile 'with an amount of fable unknown to the days of Ptolemy'.

Burton had returned to London in August 1864 from West Africa where he had been serving as consul at Fernando Po. He had been as active as ever. He had explored the delta of the Niger and the Brass and Bonny Rivers; he had spent three weeks in Abeokuta, north of Porto Novo; he had climbed Mount Victoria, the highest peak in the Cameroon Mountains; he had gone up the Gabon River in search of gorillas and of gorilla's brains which were reputed to be a powerful aphrodisiac and, although he had only seen one of these animals, he was able to describe them in one of his numerous books more accurately than his friend, Paul du Chaillu. This French explorer, who had travelled extensively in the equatorial regions of West Africa from 1855 to 1863, had gained considerable knowledge of the estuary of the Gabon and the delta of the Ogowé, had studied the habits of the Fon who, though a handsome people and expert craftsmen, were 'real, unmistakable cannibals', and had told many incredible tales of the 'Kings of the African forest' whose 'hellish expression of face' had appeared before him 'like some nightmare vision'.

On his second journey up the Gabon, Burton had also studied the Fon who, he claimed, lived in a state of perpetual warfare broken only by feasts upon the bodies of the slain. He had then gone up the Congo as far as the Yalalla rapids. And he had gone twice to Dahomey for the Foreign Office to report upon that 'blood-stained land' where, so it was said, the death of every king was attended by the sacrifice of 2,000 of his subjects, and to endeavour to impress upon the present king the undesirability of these human sacrifices and of the continuance of the slave trade.

His first visit to Dahomey was a disappointment. 'Not a man killed, or a fellow tortured,' he reported jocularly to his friend, Monckton Milnes, an avid collector of erotic and sadistic literature. 'Poor Hankey [a mutual friend of depraved tastes who delighted in watching public executions while playing with prostitutes and who had asked Burton for some skin stripped from a living female body] must wait still for his *peau de femme* ... At Benin ... they crucified a fellow in honour of my coming – here nothing!' On his second, longer visit to Dahomey, Burton had more opportunities to study the annual sacrificial ceremonies and to indulge his passionate interest in cruelty to the full. The victims, about five hundred a year, were made drunk at the time of their dispatch and given messages to take to the dead. The king, so Burton heard, himself executed the first on New Year's Eve by cutting off his head; his ministers executed the rest and mutilated the bodies after death. Female victims were beheaded separately 'by officers of their own sex'. Burton formally protested to the king on behalf of the British Government about this 'revolting slaughter' and apparently succeeded in ameliorating some of its customary horrors. But he joined with evident enthusiasm in the ceremonies of dancing and drinking with which it began, performing a *pas seul* and then, with the king, a *pas de deux*, which elicited wild applause from his subjects and which encouraged the king to drink to his partner from a human skull.

As well as recording the details of these human sacrifices which, despite all protests, were continued until the French conquered Dahomey in the 1890s, Burton wrote at length about the king of Dahomey's celebrated army of Amazons. Hoping to find thousands of delightful virgins, he was disappointed to discover that the army consisted of about 2,500 elderly, hideous women, most of whom had been discovered in adultery and had been handed over to the king as a punishment. Several of them were pregnant. Their uniforms of red and white, brown and blue were certainly impressive and their blunderbusses and huge knives intimidating; but Burton did not think they were nearly so effective a military force as their reputation suggested. Their officers appeared to have been chosen for the size of their bottoms. Following the custom of the country, the women's bodies were scarred, not only on the face and on the back but also on the inside of the thigh, a practice which, so Burton noted with his accustomed relish, was supposed to increase sexual pleasure. Again, in accordance with the country's customs, the clitoris was not excised but elongated, it being held in Dahomey that, unless a female child's genitalia were manipulated by professional old women for this purpose, the mother would be accused of neglecting her daughter's education and denying her future husband the pleasure of 'handling the long projections'.

While Burton was compiling his *Mission to Gelele, King of Dahomey*, the controversy about Speke and his strident claims to have discovered single-handedly the source of the Nile was at its height. Geographers, journalists and the public at large had taken up the positions from which they were to attack their opponents with increasing vehemence and, in several cases, with growing disregard for the established facts. With Speke himself insisting that Lake Victoria was 'without any doubt ... the great source of the holy river' and Burton now maintaining that, on the contrary, Lake Tanganyika was that source, it was eventually decided that there should be a public debate between the two men at the annual conference of the British Association for the Advancement of Science at Bath in September 1864.

Speke cannot have been looking forward with pleasure to this confrontation which he would have avoided had he not been provoked by others into agreeing to it. He had none of Burton's talents as a speaker and, being now rather deaf, he might not catch all that his opponent said. Also he was aware that some of the claims he had made would not stand up to scientific scrutiny. The day before the date fixed for the debate Speke, who had gone out shooting with an uncle who lived nearby, was found shot through the chest with his own gun which, the coroner's verdict decided, had gone off accidentally while he was climbing over a stone wall. 'By God,' Burton is said to have exclaimed when told of Speke's sudden death, 'by God, he's killed himself.' Others thought so, too. Always careful with firearms, Speke was never known to have had an accident with one before. 'It is a mystery,' wrote a correspondent in the *Athenaeum*, 'to compare with the still unsolved mystery of the Nile itself.'

9

BEYOND THE SAHARA

W. G. BROWNE IN DARFUR · J. L. BURCKHARDT ·
GERHARD ROHLFS CROSSES AFRICA FROM THE
MEDITERRANEAN TO THE GULF OF GUINEA · GUSTAV
NACHTIGAL MEETS ROHLFS IN TUNIS AND ALEXANDRINE
TINNÉ IN TRIPOLI · NACHTIGAL ALMOST DIES OF THIRST
IN THE DESERT · HIS ADVENTURES WITH THE TUBU
OF TIBESTI · HIS ENFORCED STAY WITH THEM
AND ESCAPE TO FEZZAN · GEORG SCHWEINFURTH · THE
SHILLUKS AND THE DINKAS, THE BONGO AND THE
NIAM-NIAM · EVIDENCE OF CANNIBALISM · KING MUNZA
OF THE MONBUTTO · PYGMIES · ATTACK BY A-BANGA
WARRIORS · WILHELM JUNKER · HIS JOURNEY TO THE
SOURCE OF THE UELE AND HIS EXPLORATIONS IN
THE NILE–CONGO WATERSHED · THE TRIBES OF
THESE AREAS AND THEIR CUSTOMS · HIS RETURN TO
ZANZIBAR, 1888

While controversy as to the true source of the Nile continued to rage in Europe, German explorers were travelling in unknown regions to the west of it, in Bornu and Bagirmi, in Wadai and Darfur and in the Congo Basin.

Their predecessor in Darfur was an Englishman, William George Browne. A quiet, gravely contemplative, and immensely resourceful young man, Browne had abandoned his legal studies when an inheritance from his father, a well-to-do wine merchant, had enabled him to fulfil his long-held ambition of becoming an explorer in Africa. He had sailed to Alexandria in 1791 with the intention of making his way up the Nile in the footsteps of James Bruce whose adventurous volumes had enchanted him. Having journeyed three hundred miles across the desert to Siwa, he returned to Cairo to learn Arabic, then set out for Ethiopia. Prevented by warfare from reaching Ethiopia by the direct route through Aswan, he decided to join a caravan to get there by way of Darfur. Although cheated and betrayed by the agent whom he had employed

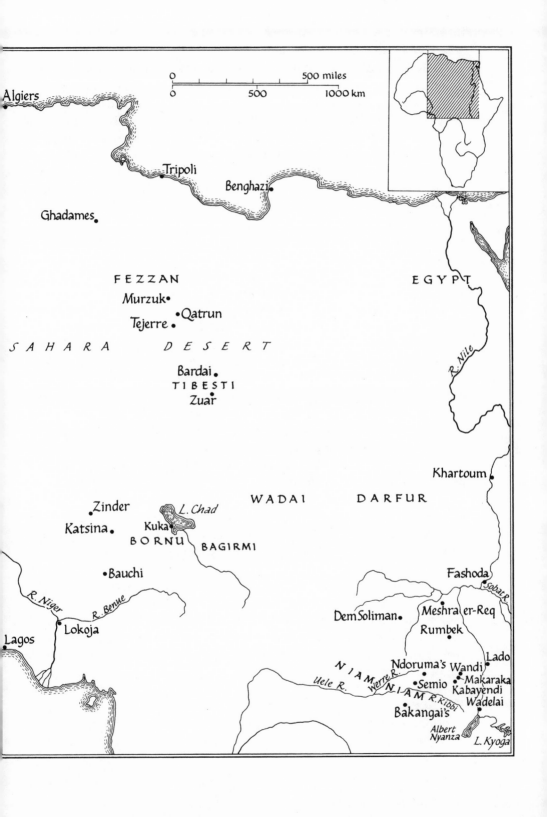

Algiers

Tripoli

Benghazi

Ghadames

FEZZAN
Murzuk
Tejerre •Qatrun

EGYPT

SAHARA   DESERT

R. Nile

Bardai
TIBESTI
Zuar

Khartoum

WADAI   DARFUR

Zinder   L. Chad
Katsina   Kuka
          BORNU   BAGIRMI

Fashoda
Sobat R.

•Bauchi

Dem Soliman   Meshra er-Req

R. Niger   R. Benue

Rumbek

Lagos   Lokoja

Lado

NIAM   Ndoruma's Wandi
Uele R.   Werre R.   •Semio   Makaraka
      NIAM R. Kibbi   Kabayendi
                    Wadelai
Bakangai's

Albert
Nyanza   L. Kyoga

500 miles

500   1000 km

to accompany him, and suspected of being a spy because of the open way in which he took notes and asked questions, he arrived at Cobbe unharmed. After spending some time there he went to El Fasher where he fell ill with malaria, had most of his goods seized by the Sultan's representatives and landed himself in deeper trouble by accidentally pulling off the loin cloth of a slave girl whose master, accusing him of violating her, demanded ten more slaves in compensation. Prevented from leaving Darfur, he was obliged to set himself up there as a doctor until a caravan bound for Cairo was permitted to leave the country and he was allowed to go with it. After an absence of six years he returned to England where, having published an extremely boring account of his adventures, he settled down to study before undertaking further travels in the Middle East. He was murdered by Kurdish bandits in 1813 at the age of forty-five.

While living in London, Browne had had long conversations with Johann Ludwig Burckhardt, a young man from Basle of about his own age, who had come to England with letters of introduction from Professor Blumenbach under whom he had studied at Göttingen University. He had hoped to obtain employment in the diplomatic service but, disappointed in this ambition, he had been encouraged by his talks with Browne and with Professor Blumenbach's friend, Sir Joseph Banks, at whose house in Soho Square he was a frequent visitor, to consider African exploration instead. Anxious 'to be of some use in this world', he offered his services to the African Association, which accepted them.

In preparation for his journeys, he studiously applied himself to lessons in Arabic, practised wearing Arab dress, energetically took long walks in the hottest weather, made himself accustomed to living on little food and assiduously attended lectures on surgery, astronomy and other subjects which he thought might prove of future use to him. At the beginning of 1807, his training in England completed, he sailed for Syria, where he spent a further two and a half years perfecting his Arabic and learning to behave like a Muslim. From Syria he made his way to Egypt where he passed himself off as a Turk in search of a relative who had disappeared on a trading mission to Sennar. He joined a caravan of Egyptian slavers who treated him with contempt and in whose unpleasant company he passed through Berber to Shendi, one of the busiest markets of the eastern Sudan, where spices, horses, gold, sandalwood, slaves and skins, leatherwork and corn, ostrich feathers, ivory, rhinoceros horn, honey, scents, soap and medicine, cambric and muslin were all offered for sale in riotous array. From Shendi, Burckhardt made the dangerous crossing east to Suakin through the territory of hostile tribes. From Suakin he sailed across the Red Sea to Jiddah, then made his celebrated pilgrimage to Mecca before returning to Egypt through Medina where he nearly died of dysentery, an illness which so weakened him that when he suffered a recurrence of the complaint in Cairo in 1817 he did not recover. By then, however, his accounts of his travels were complete.

Inspired by these accounts, a German doctor's son, Gerhard Rohlfs, determined to follow Burckhardt's example. Essentially an adventurer, Rohlfs, who was born near Bremen in 1831, had interrupted his haphazard education by running away to sea and had then joined the army in order to fight the Danes in Schleswig-Holstein. After the war was over he spent some time as an in-attentive medical student before enlisting in the Austrian army from which he deserted in order to serve in the French Foreign Legion in North Africa. Discharged from the Legion, he set out to explore Morocco in the guise of a Muslim. At first he had little success as an explorer: his disguise was penetrated; he contracted malaria; he was more than once robbed. But he did display an uncomplaining resignation in adversity, an adaptability and a determination that were to redeem many faults. Once near Tafilet he was almost killed by marauders who shot him through the thigh and almost severed his left arm and right hand; yet, although these wounds were to trouble him intermittently for the rest of his life, he rarely complained of them and was never disheartened. Stiff in manner and prejudiced in his outlook, he was sensible in his approach to exploration, maintaining, for example, that the common practice of wearing thick woollen underwear in hot climates was absurd, that the explorer should become familiar with native food as soon as possible rather than burden himself with European provisions; that he should avoid 'large and luxuriously conceived expeditions which were a hindrance rather than a help', and that he should not only be prepared to put up with hardship, hunger and thirst but also with 'insult and abuse'. Rohlfs himself lost his temper from time to time and threatened to shoot men who exasperated him, but he never actually fired his revolver at anyone.

He was always prepared to change course in his explorations, to go where circumstances, instinct or fancy drew him, rather than to pursue a fixed object. For him, as with Stevenson, to travel hopefully was better than to arrive.

Raising money where and from whom he could, he travelled widely in Morocco; in 1865–7 he crossed the Sahara by way of Murzuk to Kouka, went on south to Lokoja and reached the coast near Lagos, becoming the first European to traverse Africa from the Mediterranean to the Gulf of Guinea. He made journeys in Ethiopia; then, having attended a conference in Brussels sponsored by King Leopold in 1876, he travelled from Benghazi down to Aujila and then across the desert to Kufra, covering over fifty miles a day for five days.

After his return from Ethiopia, Rohlfs was entrusted with some presents which the King of Prussia wished to be given to the ruler of Bornu in recognition of the protection and support accorded to him and to other German explorers in the area of Lake Chad. Rohlfs took these presents to Tunis and there entrusted them to a German physician working in the town, Gustav Nachtigal.

The son of a Lutheran pastor, Nachtigal was born at Eichstedt in 1834 and, after completing his medical studies, had become a military surgeon. But as the climate of Germany exacerbated a lung complaint from which he suffered, he had been advised by his old professor at the University of Greifswald to go to live in North Africa where, while employed as physician to the Bey of Tunis, his health was completely restored. He was on the point of returning home, with the intention of setting up in practice as an eye specialist, when Rohlfs arrived in Tunis with the presents for the ruler of Bornu. Having long 'ardently wished to see more of the mysterious continent to the north coast of which fate had led' him, Nachtigal grasped at the opportunity to make 'a memorable journey'. He admitted that he 'lacked experience as a traveller' and was 'expert in none of the natural sciences' but, as well as his medical qualifications, he had a good knowledge of colloquial Arabic and of Muslim customs. And, since 'no better person could be found', his offer to take the presents to Bornu himself was accepted. Soon afterwards Nachtigal set out upon his journeys which were to last for over five years and during which he was to cover well over 6,000 miles.

He was glad to have the service of Muhammad el-Qatruni, a patient, silent, ugly, toothless servant who had been Barth's faithful companion on his journey to Timbuktu and who had served Rohlfs with equal steadfastness in Bornu. Nachtigal was also pleased to be able to leave Tripoli for Murzuk in the company of a European companion, Giuseppe Valpreda, a Piedmontese baker whom he had 'got to know as a cook and servant in the house of a friend', a rather timid and unadventurous man whose natural misgivings about the undertaking seem to have been overcome by a groundless hope of becoming rich in the countries to the south. There was at that time another European bent upon reaching Fezzan, a rich and intrepid Dutch woman, Alexandrine-Pieternella-Françoise Tinné, whose ambition of penetrating into the Tuareg country had been in no way diminished by the deaths of her mother and aunt and two European maids with whom she had arrived in Africa and all of whom had succumbed to the climate after ascending the White Nile above Gondokoro and exploring part of the Sobat. Alexandrine Tinné's 'aristocratic, seemingly cold features and her distinguished aloof demeanour' intimidated Nachtigal at first, as he readily confessed, and filled him 'with shy respect'. Known in Tripoli as *bint el-re*, the King's daughter, she was accompanied by a large retinue including 'two Dutch sailors, some Negroes from the Upper Nile who belonged to her, Algerian women, Arabs from Tunis and Algiers, freed Negro slaves who were hoping under her protection to get back to their homes, and Adolf Krause, a young German, who in his enthusiasm for travel in Africa, had left the Gymnasium'. 'Her ample means and numerous motley entourage made the idea of a joint expedition to Murzuk not particularly desirable,' Nachtigal wrote, 'and since she had concluded her preparations I allowed her to travel ahead.' Nachtigal followed in her footsteps on the cool, fresh morning of 18 February 1869.

He arrived in Murzuk just over five weeks later and was welcomed there by 'one of Fräulein Tinné's Dutch servants with friendly greetings from his mistress and a fat sheep, eggs, bread, butter, onions and the like'. Nachtigal began to change his opinion of the formidable woman who, when next he met her, was 'as always, quiet, serious and distinguished but more cordial and warmer than in Tripoli'. She, in turn, considered him, unlike most African travellers, 'discreet, unassuming and honest'. It was agreed that if by the end of the summer no merchant caravan with which they could proceed upon their journey had assembled in Murzuk, they would join forces and go on with the assistance of an armed escort to be hired by her. In the meantime they both planned to make separate expeditions, she to the Tuareg country, he to Tibesti, the country of the Tubu.

Alexandrine Tinné left first and Nachtigal said good-bye to her on 5 June. It was a fond farewell for, while they had been together in Murzuk, he had 'learned to value highly the intellect and the courage of this lady'. It was also a farewell overcast with foreboding. Muhammad el-Qatruni murmured as they watched her ride off through the western gate, 'We shall never see her again, *sidi*.' 'You have said it, Muhammad,' Nachtigal replied. 'There is nothing more to be done but to commend her to the protection of Allah.'

Nachtigal regarded his own journey amongst the unexplored lands of the Tubu with equal foreboding, for they were reported to be 'a faithless, treacherous, greedy, thievish and cruel people'. And as he advanced south from Murzuk, through Qatrun and Tejerri, he was warned time and again of their bad character, their arrogance, perfidy and avarice. The path to the lands of these unpleasant people seemed horribly appropriate. The hilly, sandy country of south Fezzan became more arid and stony, a difficult, rocky, mountainous region in which the camels stumbled and faltered. Few men of any race had ever been this way before. There were no traces of paths, no piles of stones to guide the traveller, no rocks or hills of conspicuous shape. Above all there was no water. From time to time the guide climbed a rock and looked about him for signs of the well of whose position he seemed to be uncertain. The travellers closely watched the expression on his face, and more and more discouraging 'became the plain answer given by his uncertain glance and his frequently repeated "*ma zal*, not yet, not yet" '. They went on without a word, their noses and mouths covered with turban cloth, 'over stony desert plains, through eroded sandy valleys ... across endless stretches of country covered with large slabs of gray, slate-like stone from which [their] footsteps or the blow of a staff or a lance drew a metallic clang, and from the crevices of which some miserable withered stunted vegetation struggled out'. The guide and other desert experts warned Nachtigal that neither man nor beast would reach the elusive well unless they left the baggage behind and mounted the whole party on the animals' backs. So this was done while Giuseppe Valpreda distributed the last drops of water. The Tubu guide was the last to drink. He pushed back his veil, took a mouthful, then spat it out in a long stream through a gap in his teeth, as if it were 'just the usual contents of a Tubu mouth, green tobacco juice'. He handed what was left in the cup to Nachtigal with the remark that he did not need any more but that he well understood 'the People of the Water' could not endure this privation of thirst 'which indeed was only just beginning'. 'It is, in fact,' Nachtigal commented, 'an opinion generally circulated in these regions that Christians live a semi-amphibious life huddled together on marshy islands in the middle of the sea.'

Refreshed by water, the hopes of the party rose when there suddenly opened up before them a wide riverbed at the source of which the well was believed to lie. There were footprints of camels, donkeys and antelope in the sand of the bed; and, to his delight, Nachtigal noticed those of an ostrich, sure signs, so it was considered, that a well was near. He tried to close his mind to the thought that it might be empty.

Now that their course was marked out for them, the travellers drove their exhausted animals forward between the dark, rocky banks of the dried-up stream with ramrods and cudgels. The sun poured down upon them through the breathless air of the narrow valley. Their mouths were parched; their eyes burned painfully; and it seemed to Nachtigal that an iron ring was pressing ever more tightly around his forehead. Repeatedly his camel sought the shade of the withered acacias that were to be seen here and there, and it had to be driven on by redoubled blows and whipping. But at length the animal, displaying all the stubbornness of her species, refused to submit to her master. Ignoring the flogging, she forced her way between the branches of an acacia, whose long thorns tore into Nachtigal, and fell to the ground, immovable. Her companions followed her, and Nachtigal, incapable of further effort, decided that they should remain where they were until evening in the hope that the guide who had gone on ahead would bring water back to them.

The minutes, so Nachtigal recorded, crept sluggishly by while the sun's piercing rays compelled him to move his position constantly as he sought the inadequate shade of the camels' bodies and the leaves of the acacia tree. Valpreda brooded in silence; another of his companions lapsed into a state of semi-consciousness; a third wearily reproached him in the hoarse voice with which they were all now afflicted for having brought them into this dreadful country until Muhammad el-Qatruni, fatalistic and stoical as always, reprimanded him, reminding him that everything was determined by Allah and that all that the white man could do was himself to die if that were so ordained. Thereafter no further sound disturbed the deathlike stillness of the afternoon. Gradually Nachtigal began to lose consciousness as dreams and memories from his past merged with present experiences. Then, towards evening, he opened his eyes at the sound of what he took at first to be an immense goat advancing towards him. Slowly the misty vision cleared and he saw that it was a man on a camel. The man carried two water bags. At the sight of these he began weakly to cry, and Valpreda fainted. But, as little moved by his salvation as he had been by the prospect of death, Muhammad el-Qatruni warned the others not to drink after so long and painful a thirst without at the same time eating. So, rummaging in the provision bag, he produced a dozen biscuits and crumbled them into the water which was already full of mouldering matter. Disregarding its disgusting state, Nachtigal drank gratefully, then fell into what he described as the soundest, deepest, most refreshing sleep he had ever had in his life.

At the well which they reached the next day, a solitary Tubu was watering a laden camel. The guide arranged his clothes so that only his eyes were visible and, grasping his lance and throwing iron, cautiously approached the stranger. He, too, pulled his *litham* up over his nose in obedience to Tubu custom and, squatting down at a distance of about six paces from the guide, began that interminable ritual of greeting, of question and answer, of song and countersong, of allocation and salutation, which accompanied all such Tubu encounters and which was conducted with a studied lack of interest on either part, the two men rarely looking at each other, letting their gaze wander towards the horizon or intently gazing at the ground by their feet.

Ten days later the travellers reached Tao in Tibesti where they came upon another Tubu who, apart from an aunt, another elderly woman and a few slaves, was the sole occupant of the village. Nachtigal was not favourably impressed by the man's appearance or his manner. He had 'a flat pendulous nose, a large mouth with thick lips, a protuberant chin and a wary look which lent his face a most disagreeable expression'. He did not attempt to disguise his suspicion and dislike of the stranger whom he nevertheless plagued with the most shameless begging, while his aunt, a masculine woman in a dirty blue shirt, chewed tobacco 'with a man's virtuosity, spitting green saliva through gaps in her teeth with a force and accuracy that would have done credit to an old sailor'.

These unattractive people, so Nachtigal soon discovered, were only too representative of their race. At Zuar the notables surrounded the place where he had pitched his tent and demanded a large share of his meal; then, having eaten greedily, they further insisted upon being paid the taxes which, so they claimed, it was their right to exact. There ensued an argument which lasted throughout the day and ended, of course, in Nachtigal's defeat. This gave rise to a discussion of his motives in coming to their country. No Christian had been there before; and they were not in the least anxious to see another. Obviously he had come to make money, since Europeans, supposed to be clever, would never be so stupid as to risk their possessions and their lives in a starvation-ridden country merely to see its barren mountains and dried-up river valleys. They were after gold and were intent upon driving out the Tubu in order to possess it.

The fluency of the Tubu's chief spokesman, the skill with which he evaded or treated as irrelevant the arguments put forward in Nachtigal's favour, could not but be admired. If a point supporting the white man's case was raised he would immediately take up another which had nothing to do with it and then turn the whole discussion on to a different plane, exhausting his opponents and eventually taking their exasperated silence for assent. Nachtigal at last felt driven to suggest that the Tubu notables take from his baggage whatever they thought due to them. To this proposal they retorted indignantly that they were not robbers. He thereupon wearily announced that he would have to go back to Fezzan. They raised no objection to this but artfully indicated that were he to carry out this intention they would be released from their obligations of hospitality to strangers, and what would become of him then? After further lengthy discussions and arguments an agreed amount of goods by way of taxes was settled upon, and Nachtigal was free to proceed on his journey to Bardai.

At Bardai he found the Tubu even more grasping and deceitful than they had been at Zuar. 'Good nature seemed not to exist,' he wrote, 'only obstinacy and vindictiveness.' Crowds of people squatted about his tent arguing amongst themselves, estimating the stranger's riches, discussing methods of dealing with him, spitting out jets of saliva and tobacco juice, occasionally falling silent while one or other of them more influential than the rest carefully removed the quid from his mouth and, placing it upon a stone or throwing iron for later use, embarked upon a complicated exegesis of his own opinions. A few defended the stranger. Among these was a man who, alone among his race, chose not to chew tobacco but to smoke it through a hole pierced in a lump of camel dung. But he, like most of those who supported him at first, changed sides when it appeared that the Christian really did not have the treasure with which they hoped to be rewarded by coming to his assistance. Another of his defenders, a powerful chieftain called Arami, who feared that ill treatment of the European might lead to trouble with Fezzan, was not above cadging presents for himself and his family and threatening to withdraw his protection if they were not granted.

The days passed and the debates continued. Nachtigal was kept a virtual prisoner in his intolerably hot tent, existing on a diet of indifferent dates, while streams of importunate Tubu passed in and out, irritating him with the 'brainlessness of their arguments', wheedling, threatening, inspecting what few objects there were to be seen, laughing derisively, and attempting to frighten him with ferocious speeches. Once a visitor from Borku closely examined both Nachtigal and Valpreda, and, entering into negotiations with Arami for their purchase, declared them useless as working slaves but offered to exchange them for a camel. Twice Nachtigal attempted to leave his tent. On the first occasion he was driven back by children who stoned him mercilessly, and on the second by a drunken man who, encouraged by shouts of 'Down with the infidel!', hurled his throwing iron at him.

The ruler of Tibesti, Tafertemi, a man without riches and commanding little respect, was himself quite as avaricious as any of his subjects. Professing himself wholly dissatisfied with the presents which had been offered him, he demanded more so insistently that Nachtigal angrily suggested that he should search the tent for the treasures it was alleged to contain. Tafertemi immediately accepted the offer, flung open the white man's boxes, pushed aside the books and meteorological instruments, examined the mattress and bed cover, and retired disappointed.

'Where are you going, King?' Arami called after him as he strode back to his huts. 'Have you not come here today so that a decision can finally be made about the fate of the stranger? ... Why don't we let him go back to Fezzan? What do we want to do with him? To kill him? So far as I know it is not our practice to drink men's blood, to make water bags out of their skins or to eat their flesh. And yet he has no other possession worth mentioning. Why are we holding him then? Our brothers and cousins are living in Fezzan; our trade calls us there. If we kill this Christian who is more powerful than the whole Government at Murzuk, we will no longer be able to go to our markets there ... Let him go. He does not know the road; his camels are useless; without food and water he will perish on the way. But God will have killed him, not we.'

Unmoved by this plea, Tafertemi walked on. 'I have seen the empty boxes,' he said, 'and I am going home ... The man has brought us empty timber, I have nothing more to do here.'

'Why has he come here with so few possessions?' other voices called out. 'What business has he here? He has come as a spy to discover our treasures. If we don't kill him he will betray us, and foreigners will take over our country. Why all this fuss about a Christian?'

So the debate continued, week after week. August ended and September began. News arrived in Bardai of the murder by Tuaregs of Alexandrine Tinné and there were renewed demands for the execution of Nachtigal. The Tuaregs, it was said, knew how to protect their lands from prying Christians. Why did the Tubu allow themselves to be deterred by fear of the Turks from killing their enemies? The time to act had come.

Nachtigal now accepted that the only hope for him lay in flight from Bardai under cover of darkness. He persuaded Arami to allow him the use of his camels; and, having dug up a few dollars he had buried beneath his tent, he rode away for the mountain pass that led back to Fezzan. He was back in Murzuk by the beginning of October; but since there was no caravan with which he could travel to Bornu he had to spend Christmas in a cold and leaking hut in the town; and it was not until the middle of April that he was able to leave for Kuka and thence to travel east into Wadai and Darfur. After his return to Europe in 1874, his six-year journey completed, his *Sahara und Sudan* gained him recognition as Gerhard Rohlfs's worthy successor, one of Germany's greatest explorers. Appointed President of the Geographical Society of Berlin and later German Consul-General in Tunis, he was, until his death at sea in 1885, a man whom subsequent travellers beyond the Sahara went to for advice and never went in vain.

When Nachtigal had begun his great African journey at Tunis in 1868, his fellow-German, Georg Schweinfurth, was travelling up the Nile to Khartoum. Born in Riga in 1836, Schweinfurth was the son of a merchant. Educated at Heidelberg and Berlin, he was a doctor of philosophy, an expert botanist and a draughtsman of outstanding skill. He had already spent two and a half years in Africa and, when his money had run out, had returned to Germany with a remarkable collection of plants. Anxious to go out to find more, he had submitted to the Royal Academy of Science of Berlin a plan for the botanical exploration of the equatorial districts to the west of the Nile, and had been given a grant by the Humboldt Institution of Natural Philosophy and Travels to carry out his proposals. He was consequently back in Egypt in July 1868 and, having spent some time botanizing in the mountains of south Nubia, he reached Khartoum on 1 November. Here he employed six Nubians who had already travelled in different parts of the upper Nile, two women slaves to grind corn and a cook named Riharn who had once worked in the kitchens of Shepheard's Hotel in Cairo; and with these companions and a huge sheep-dog, which he had brought with him from Europe, he sailed up the Nile in a boat belonging to one Ghattas, a Coptic merchant who had established trading settlements and depots along the Gazelle River (the Bahr-el-Ghazāl) and who undertook to provide Schweinfurth with an armed escort to take him to them.

The journey from Khartoum to Fashoda took nearly three weeks during which Schweinfurth's ears were assailed by the gurgling and snorting of hippopotami which, 'heard far over the waters', grated as harshly as the incessant creaking of the rudder. Occasionally the roar of a lion and the splash of crocodiles' tails could be heard, and antelope could be seen coming down to drink by the banks where troops of maraboux paddled beneath the acacia trees in which monkeys swung from branch to branch. Buffaloes could also be glimpsed in the long grass through which snakes and iguanas slid and rustled. All manner of birds from eagles to waterfowl flew overhead, and Schweinfurth, firing at random at the flocks of geese, retrieved a number as the wounded bodies fell around him. Later he shot at the swarms of crowned cranes which stood in their thousands in the grass. 'One had but to discharge a load of good-sized shot,' he commented with the guiltlessness of his time, 'and the destruction was marvellous.'

From time to time Shilluk tribesmen came down to the water's edge, marvelling at the sheep-dog, which they took to be some kind of tame hyena, and at the white man in his Mexican sombrero. The men were quite naked, their lean, bony bodies plastered with the ashes either of cow dung, which gave their skins a rusty-red tint, or of wood which rendered it as grey as that of a mouldering corpse. They wore their hair in fantastic shapes which were maintained by the repeated application of clay, gum, cow urine and dung. In consequence they smelled abominably; and since they also used cow urine for washing their milk vessels to compensate for a lack of salt, the strangers did not relish drinking with them.

In the country of the Shilluk the boat was attacked by a swarm of bees and Schweinfurth was stung so painfully that in desperation he flung himself into the river; but this defensive action caused him more pain than ever, for, as he dived down in the water the bees continued to sting him about the face and, on clambering up the muddy bank, he lacerated his hands on the sharp edges of the grass. Lifted back on board, he cowered under a linen sheet, crushing the bees that he had enclosed inside it and suffering periodical stings through the linen, while the insects buzzed loudly and uninterruptedly. He felt that he would rather face an encounter 'with half a score of buffaloes or a brace of lions rather than have anything more to do with bees'.

A little way upstream there were further trials when the boat entered a tributary of the Nile and was swallowed up in what Schweinfurth described as 'a world of weeds'. Here thick and tangled masses of grass, pulpy creepers, ambatch and water plants covered the whole surface of the river, and dense thickets of papyrus, fifteen feet high, loomed over the banks. Standing on the floating mass the Nubians hauled and tugged for hours on end in their efforts to force the boat along, shrieking at the tops of their voices, both as an

237

encouragement to each other and in order to frighten the hippopotami whose huge heads surrounded them on every side. For several days they struggled on in this way until they arrived once more in open water, reached the Gazelle river and disembarked at a landing place known as Meshra er-Req where Schweinfurth's journey into the interior was to begin.

He waited here for several days while the caravans of various Khartoum merchants assembled for the joint march into the ivory country. Each caravan had its own coloured banner emblazoned with the star and crescent of Islam with the exception of that of Ghattas who, as a Copt, had a white flag on which was worked, in addition to the crescent, a Christian cross. And when all were ready the merchants' companies moved off in a long single file behind their respective banners towards the land of the Dinkas.

These were a people, so Schweinfurth discovered, whose 'every thought was how to acquire and maintain cattle'. They never slaughtered their cows which, if sick, were segregated from the rest and carefully tended in large huts built for the purpose. Only animals that died naturally or by accident were used as food. Cow dung, burned to ashes, was used for sleeping on; and cow urine, as with the Shilluks, was used for washing and as a substitute for salt. But, while smelly, the huts of the Dinkas were spacious and clean, their roofs supported by the neatly cut trunks and spreading branches of acacia trees. In these roofs snakes lay coiled and undisturbed, treated as domestic animals and known as 'brethren' whose slaughter would be a crime. The men went about entirely naked, regarding clothing as effeminate and referring to Schweinfurth, who always appeared in a complete suit of clothes, as 'the Turkish lady'. Some shaved their heads except for a tuft of hair at the crown which was ornamented with ostrich feathers; others trained their hair up into tall points and, by continually washing it in cow urine, dyed it a foxy red so that it looked like tongues of flame springing from the scalp. Both sexes broke off the lower incisor teeth, an inexplicable mutilation which led amongst the old to their upper teeth projecting hideously from their mouths. Both sexes also pierced their ears in several places for the wearing of iron rings and bars with iron tips, the women, in addition, piercing the upper lip for the admission of iron pins. They also wore as many iron bracelets round their arms and ankles as they could afford. Schweinfurth estimated that some wives of the rich carried about with them 'close upon half a hundredweight of these savage ornaments' which clanked and resounded like the fetters of slaves. In many respects, however, the Dinka were a cultivated people. They were expert cooks, surpassing, in Schweinfurth's opinion, both Egyptians and Arabs; and they were most polite at meals, never dipping their hands into the same dish, but helping themselves singly and passing the dishes from hand to hand. Everything they used was washed and returned to its appointed place.

Having studied the Dinka, Schweinfurth passed on through Ghattas's settlement to the land of the Bongo whose culinary customs were utterly different.
The Bongo ate rats, mice, snakes, vultures, hyenas and termites with equal
avidity. They fell greedily upon slaughtered cattle, competing for the half-
digested contents of the stomach and for amphistomoid worms which they put
into their mouths by the handful. They relished the putrefying remnants of a
lion's meal. After eating they smoked, passing their pipes from hand to hand, or
chewed tobacco, placing their quids behind their ears when they had had
enough. Their women extended their lower lips with plugs of wood until they
were five or six times their normal size. They also pierced both upper lip and
nose and fitted into the holes iron rings, copper plates, nails or pieces of straw.
Yet hideous as this made them appear in Schweinfurth's eyes, and disgusting as
he found their eating habits, the Bongo were far from untrained savages. They
were highly talented as smiths, wood-carvers, basket-makers and potters; and
they were enthusiastic musicians, skilful builders and conscientious farmers.

After spending several months among these people, Schweinfurth crossed the
river Tondy in November and made south for the lands of the Mittoo and the
Niam-niam, passing through the settlements of various Sudanese merchants
where he was invariably treated as an honoured guest. Cool drinks and water
were brought to him upon his arrival, followed by 'flasks, calabashes and
gourd-shells containing butter, milk, honey, spirits, *merissa* – in short, every
delicacy that the country could offer'. On 19 March, having crossed the river
Linduku a fortnight before, the first European to have seen these waters
between the Nile and the Congo, Schweinfurth was making his way through
banana plantations and villages whose houses were made of bark and rattan
cunningly joined together, when he came upon 'the great river', the Uele, the
long northern tributary of the Congo. As he gazed upon the 'unforgettable
sight' of its brownish, turbid waters surging westwards between steep banks,
he 'could picture the sensations of the Scottish traveller, Mungo Park, when
he stood for the first time on the bank of the hitherto semi-mythical Niger'.

The Mittoo, with whom Schweinfurth spent two months, had the same
predilection for iron ornaments as their northern neighbours, and the same
'revolting and unnatural practice' amongst the women of extending and
piercing the lower lip, accompanied by an extension of the upper lip for the sake
of symmetry. This self-imposed deformity obliged them to elevate the upper lip
with their fingers when they wanted to drink and to pour the liquid into their
mouths; it also, however, served a useful purpose. For 'the projections of the
iron-clad lips' were of great service in quarrels during which, by means of them,
women could 'snap like an owl or a stork'.

Interesting as Schweinfurth found the Mittoo, the Niam-niam were far more
so. A hunting people, they were 'girded with skins. High upon their extensively-

dressed hair they wore straw-hats covered with feathers and cowries, and fastened on by means of long bodkins of iron or copper. Their chocolate-coloured skin was painted in stripes, like those of the tiger, with the juice of the *blippo* (*Gardenia melleifera*)'. Outside their huts, whose conical roofs extended to an extraordinary height, they fixed posts on which hung trophies gained in hunting or war, skulls of both wild animals and men. 'These were in some cases quite entire,' Schweinfurth wrote, 'whilst in others they were mere fragments ... Too decisive to be misunderstood were the evidences of the propensity to cannibalism which met our astonished gaze. Close to the huts, amongst the piles of refuse, were human bones which bore the unquestionable tokens of having been subjected to the hatchet or the knife; and all around upon the branches of the neighbouring trees were hanging human feet and hands more than half shrivelled into a skeleton condition, but being as yet only partially dry, and imperfectly sheltered by the leaves, they polluted the atmosphere with a revolting and intolerable stench.'

The Italian traveller, Carlo Piaggia, the discoverer of Lake Kyoga, who had spent a year among the Niam-niam some time before, came across only one instance of cannibalism when a 'slaughtered foe was devoured from actual bloodthirstiness and hatred'; but, although some of the chiefs Schweinfurth spoke to 'vehemently repudiated the idea of eating human flesh', he himself had 'no hesitation in asserting' that the Niam-niam were cannibals. They made, he said, no secret of their savage craving but ostentatiously displayed the teeth of their victims round their necks. Also, human fat was universally sold; and when eaten in sufficient quantities was believed to have an intoxicating effect. 'Indeed, according to the statements of the Niam-niam themselves there were no bodies rejected as unfit for food except those of people who had died from some loathsome cutaneous disease.'

When Schweinfurth asked the people to bring him the human skulls left over from their meals for his osteological collection, the stock of bones that were brought to him was quite astonishing and removed 'any lingering hesitation' he might have had 'in believing the cannibal propensities of the people'. Some of the bones, indeed, 'afforded indubitable proof that they had been boiled in water and scraped with knives', while others, he suspected, 'came straight from the platters of the natives', for they were still moist and had the odour of being only just cooked. Once Schweinfurth came 'unexpectedly upon a number of young women ... engaged in the task of scalding the hair off the lower half of a human body'; upon another occasion in a hut he 'observed a human arm hanging over the fire, obviously with the design of being at once dried and smoked'; and he described as never to be erased from his memory a scene in a farmstead where an old woman sat surrounded by boys and girls, all busily employed in cutting up gourds and preparing them for eating, and a man composedly played a mandolin, while on a mat, exposed to the full glare of the noonday sun, lay a newborn baby, feebly gasping, the child of a slave, 'destined to form a dainty dish'.

Yet for all their ghoulish tastes, the Niam-niam seemed to Schweinfurth a pleasant and artistic people. They admittedly had the appearance of savages. They tattooed their faces; they filed down their incisor teeth to points 'for the purpose of effectually gripping the arm of an adversary'; the men arranged their long hair into all kinds of strange topknots, tufts and plaits; they clothed themselves in skins and bark. But their manner was polite: 'at their meals,' Schweinfurth noticed, 'and when several are drinking together they may be observed to wipe the rim of the drinking vessel before passing it on'. They had 'an instinctive love of art', while music 'rejoiced their very soul'. They took infinite pains in the manufacture of their favourite musical instrument, 'something between a harp and a mandolin', on which they would play for hours on end. Many of their other handicrafts were exquisitely designed and constructed.

Their inquisitiveness was, however, intolerable to Schweinfurth. So many people thronged around him that he felt compelled to encircle his tent with a thorn hedge; but, undeterred by this, they continued to swarm about him, disturbing him at every moment with their intrusions. 'My next resource,' he recorded, 'was to have a lot of water dashed over the encroaching rabble, and finding that fail, I fired some grains of gunpowder, and, in the hope of alarming the natives, I proceeded to set light to a few shells; but even the explosions of these did not take much effect.' When he went out into the country to collect botanical specimens he was pursued by crowds of people who trampled down the rare flowers he had laboriously collected until he was 'almost driven to despair'.

Among the most inquisitive of all the people he encountered south of the River Uele were the wives of the Monbutto king, Munza, an alarming ruler who was said to have a baby roasted for his table every day and who, like lesser chiefs, had been known, for the purpose of exhibiting his power, to feign a fit of passion and, singling out a victim from the crowd, to throw a rope around his neck and cut his throat with a scimitar.

One day Schweinfurth was invited to an audience with King Munza. He put on his plain black suit and heavy Alpine boots and, with three black servants carrying his rifles and revolver and a fourth his cane chair, he set out for the royal reception hall where he was greeted by the beating of drums and the loud blasts of trumpets. The hall had recently been constructed, the natural brown polish of the woodwork looking as though it were gleaming with the lustre of new varnish. The king, however, was not there, the process of his 'anointing, frizzling and bedizening at the hands of his wives' having taken an abnormally long time. When, however, he did appear, striding into the hall, looking neither to right nor left, as ringers swung iron bells and trumpeters flourished away on huge ivory horns, he was a most impressive sight, as Schweinfurth's portrait well indicates. His entire body was smeared with powdered camwood 'which converted the original bright brown tint of his skin into the colour that is so conspicuous in ancient Pompeian halls ... With arms and legs, neck and breast, all ornamented with copper rings, chains and other strange devices, and with a great copper crescent at the top of his head, the potentate gleamed with a shimmer that ... reminded one almost unavoidably of a well-kept kitchen!'

Without a glance at his visitor he sat down in his chair of state and studied his bare feet, meantime helping himself to the delicacies which were placed by his side on two beautifully carved little tables and concealed from view by napkins of fig bark. 'In his eyes gleamed the wild light of animal sensuality, and around his mouth lurked an expression [which combined] avarice, violence and love of cruelty and which could, with the extremest difficulty, relax into a smile.' When Schweinfurth's numerous presents were laid before him, the king regarded them with close attention, but said nothing, though his wives gave frequent half-suppressed utterances of surprise alternating with shouts of delight when a mirror was passed admiringly from hand to hand. At length, however, Munza rose to his feet and made a speech which lasted half an hour, pausing between his sentences to allow his audience to cheer him, to shout '*Eee, ee, tchupy, tchupy, ee, Munza, ee!*' and to give an opportunity for his band to join in the chorus of approval. When the harangue was concluded, Schweinfurth took his leave, thankful to escape from the noise and tumult, particularly as, upon his departure, the king immediately began a new oration.

The Monbutto people over whom Munza ruled were, in Schweinfurth's opinion, a noble race of men who displayed a national pride and 'an intellect and judgment such as few natives of the African wilderness can boast'. Their wood carving was superb, their pottery exquisite. Unlike the tribes to the north, the men were 'scrupulously and fully clothed' while the women went about almost entirely naked, their bodies tattooed and painted in an almost inexhaustible variety of stars, stripes, crosses, squares, bees and flowers. They were well formed and graceful, and it was rare to find among them those monstrously fat bodies so common among the Dinka.

From them Schweinfurth learned of a race of pygmies to the south, the Akka; and one day, to his deep gratification, he came upon a party of Akka who were serving in the army of King Munza's brother, 'a kind of viceroy in the southern section of his dominions'. At first he thought they were impudent little boys and was irritated by their behaviour as they jumped about him making mock warlike gestures. But he was assured they were men and soon realized that this was so. He took one of them, who was about 4 feet 7 inches, into his service as a slave and kept him with him when he returned north.

On his return journey Schweinfurth was nearly killed. He was accompanied by an enterprising Nubian ivory merchant, Muhammad Aboo Sammat, who ordered a halt in the march when, on approaching the territory of a hostile A-Banga chieftain, he saw, suspended from the branches of a tree, an ear of maize, the feather of a fowl and an arrow, a symbolic warning that whoever touched the chief's property would die by the arrow. Having established that there was no immediate danger, Muhammad gave orders for the caravan to advance. They went on cautiously, occasionally catching sight of a gleaming spear in the grass or the waving of a plume in a hat; and the next day, though they had offered no provocation, they were ambushed and attacked. Muhammad was badly wounded by a deep spear cut in his thigh; two of his bearers were speared in the back. The assailants were driven off by gunfire; but, knowing they would return, Muhammad gave orders for the construction of a fortified camp. Immediately his men pulled down the huts of nearby villages to form an abattis. They ransacked the granaries, and ran off in search of women and children to seize as hostages and, failing to find any, captured instead some boys whom they soon released, 'persecuting them with gun-shot and lances as they took to flight'. They also brought back with them some heads of A-Banga warriors who had been killed in the fighting. Schweinfurth appropriated these to add to his collection of skulls, boiling them in a cauldron in his tent to remove the flesh which he offered to his dogs who would not eat it.

The next day the fortification came under attack, the A-Banga 'dancing about and jumping up and down behind the bushes as though they were taking part in a pantomime', leaping out of cover from time to time to display their war-dress and to discharge an arrow before crouching behind cover again. Then, clambering to the top of high white ant-hills, they shouted their version of Muhammad's name, clamouring for food for their cauldron, calling, 'Mbahly! Meat! Meat! Meat! Meat! Give us Mbahly! We want meat!'

Provoked by these taunts the wounded Muhammad ordered his servants to carry him to the top of an ant-hill himself; and from there, prominent in a straw hat decorated with red feathers, he shouted back at the A-Banga, insulting them, challenging them to attack, shouting, 'Here I am! Mbahly is not dead yet!'

At dusk they did attack and their 'wild cries, like the howling of a coming storm, testified to their overwhelming numbers'. But their weapons were no match for the guns of the Nubians which were all loaded with heavy shot; and soon they were in headlong flight, strewing the ground not only with shields and lances but also with their clothes and artificial chignons.

After this the caravan met no further opposition, and Muhammad's men moved on, plundering the natives' huts, cutting down their maize, taking as many of their women as they could capture into slavery, and slaughtering their dogs which they spitted on their lances 'in the most remorseless fashion'.

On 24 June 1870 they crossed the Tondy by its tottering bridge. On 3 July they reached Sabby, and not long afterwards Schweinfurth was back in Ghattas's settlement where, at midday on 1 December, a fire, which he had long feared would break out somewhere in the crowded huts, destroyed most of his manuscripts, journals and records, his entomological collection, his registers of meteorological events, his vocabularies, his measurements of the bodies of natives, and all his examples of native industry. That night Schweinfurth sat in misery amidst the remnants of his possessions, mournfully munching a half-burned lump of pickled meat while his dogs howled with the pain of their blistered feet and his servants resignedly began to repair the damage, walking about in the white ashes, calm and unconcerned, having lost nothing themselves for they had nothing to lose.

Ten days later new huts were ready for Schweinfurth's occupation; but, having lost his clothes, his guns, his ammunition, his instruments and paper, he was forced to abandon the second journey to the Niam-niam which he had planned to make. So he 'came to the resolution of quitting the scene' of his disaster, and on 16 December, followed by a small herd of cows, he turned his back 'upon the *seriba* that had so soon arisen from the ashes of its predecessor'. By the end of September 1871 he was back upon the shores of the Red Sea, and on 2 November he landed in Sicily. 'Thus, after an absence of three years and four months,' so he wrote, 'I was back once again upon the soil of Europe.'

He returned to North Africa from time to time, but most of the rest of his long life was spent at Dahlem near Cologne where his herbarium occupied over a hundred large cases in the museum. He died in 1925 in his ninetieth year and was buried in the botanical garden at Dahlem which he had helped to create.

Four years after his return from Africa, at the Paris Geographical Congress of 1875, Schweinfurth met Wilhelm Junker, a physician born of German parents in Moscow, who had long held ambitions to become an explorer of Africa himself. Schweinfurth drew his attention to the lands south of the Libyan desert, 'a region at that time ... still shrouded in the veil of an awe-inspiring mystery'. Within three months Junker was in Alexandria. From there he went on to Cairo where he met the zoologist, Theodore von Heuglin, who suggested that, before he went up the Nile beyond Khartoum, he should travel from the Red Sea port of Suakin through the still unexplored regions of the Khor Báraka to Kassala. So, taking into his employment a young forester from Württemberg named Kopp who had come out to Egypt with the intention of studying zoology, Junker sailed to Suakin and set out south along the Báraka valley, across 'almost virgin hunting ground' in which abounded elephants, lions, gazelles, jackals and hyenas as well as 'herds of thousands of camels, magnificent beasts with huge humps ... very different from the ordinary pack-animals'. These and numerous other animals Junker found in captivity in Kassala where a German American, George Schmutzer, had established a menagerie from which he exported wild beasts to the circuses and zoos of the United States. 'Here were giraffes, ostriches, all kinds of waterfowl freely moving about,' Junker recorded, 'large and small elephants standing quietly together, while the little three-year-old daughter [of the manager of the establishment] was playing on a couch with a young lion, a leopard, monkeys and young hyenas, tossing balls from one to another.'

After nine days in Kassala, Junker and Kopp started on 7 April 1876 for Sûq-Abû-Sinn, the capital of the province of Qedaref. It was a town inhabited mostly by Bedouins whose beringed and braceleted women went unveiled, the girls 'often wearing nothing but thonged belts, attended by their female slaves in carelessly worn cotton smocks'. Most of these branded slaves were Abyssinians, young girls from seven to fourteen years old, 'kidnapped in the southern vassal states and borderlands of Ethiopia, and brought hither to recruit the Sudanese harems'. They were often 'really beautiful', Junker thought, though they were 'disposed of like so many camels or mules'.

He was distressed by the sight of this callous traffic in young girls and by the 'wild orgies' in the beer-shops around the market where *merissa* brewed from corn was drunk in enormous quantities. Yet Sûq-Abû-Sinn was a pleasant place with a healthy climate, much favoured by Greek merchants who had settled here to trade in gums, cotton, durra and other local produce. The market was the most lively in Qedaref, offering for sale a wonderful variety of commodities, from ostrich feathers and gold dust to water melons, sesame, hides, spices, dates and soap. The people were friendly, the women delightfully decorative and so lavish in their application of unguents and scents, so fond of sitting over charcoal fires to sweat in the vapour of burning sandalwood, cinnamon, cloves, ginger, myrtle and chips of the *talha* acacia, that a group of freshly oiled and anointed young women could be smelled a hundred yards away. Junker confessed his reluctance to leave for Khartoum.

In Khartoum he met the Italian Romolo Gessi, plenipotentiary of the Governor of the Sudan, General Gordon. Gessi, who had circumnavigated Lake Albert, invited Junker to accompany him on an expedition up the Blue Nile and the Sobat in the steamer *Ssafia* to victual outlying military stations founded by General Gordon and to search for fresh sources of ivory. Steaming south towards Fashoda, through treeless steppes inhabited by giraffes and flocks of ostriches, the *Ssafia* entered the territories of the Dinka who lived on the right bank and of the Shilluk whose villages could be seen on the left and whose fishermen, armed with harpoons, knelt amongst the reeds on ambatch rafts, light manoeuvrable craft with upturned prows which gave them, from a distance, the appearance of Venetian gondolas. Beyond the territories of the Shilluk were those of the Nuer who stood gazing at the *Ssafia* from their huts, their long black bodies powdered with grey ashes, 'their woolly heads either plastered over with a peculiar grey coating or else died red'.

All these people had been described by Schweinfurth; but Junker, abandoning his plan to visit the Darfur regions, which he felt had been sufficiently explored, was now to visit places which Schweinfurth had never seen. He went south to Lado and stayed with the Bari, a reserved, pastoral people who stood on one leg with the sole of the other foot planted against the thigh like long-legged waterfowl. He went to Makaraka where dead chiefs were kept for a year before burial on an *angareb* and smoked over a slow fire, with food and beer placed before the body. He travelled to Kabayendi and to the people known as the Mundu whose chiefs were buried with as many as fifteen live slaves, happy to be sacrificed since their master would provide for them for ever. He went to the territories of the Bombeh, who wore the skins of apes and the horns of antelope, to those of the Abaka whose women wore polished quartz cones almost two inches long in their upper lips, and to those of the Moru whose ears, pierced with as many as fifteen holes, held straws and strings of white beads. He went north to Rumbek and west to Semio. Near Wandi he witnessed funeral rites which lasted uninterruptedly for four days and nights during which the bereaved women, naked but for foliage around their waists and in their hair, paraded about, shouting to the noisy accompaniment of huge kettle-drums, wailing, somersaulting and creeping under the projecting straw roofs of their master's huts in elaborate pretence of looking for him. Dispensing with their foliage, they seized his clothes. One donned his long sleeping robe, another a shirt, others vests; still others brandished above their heads his lances and his large Abyssinian sword. 'When it is added that the women showered ashes on their heads,' Junker recorded, 'smeared their bodies with dirt, and wallowed in the mire during a tremendous downpour, some idea may be formed of the picture presented by this wild scene of fantastic orgies, which the longer they lasted the more they acquired the character of revelries.'

On some of these journeys Junker was accompanied by Kopp, but in June 1877 Kopp fell victim to the climate, and Junker's last important expedition was carried out alone. This was to the Kibbi, the source of the Uele, an objective he 'had long steadily pursued'. Yet, so he said, he was unable to take any pleasure in his successful journey into these 'regions hitherto untrodden by any white man', for he had undertaken it in the company of an expedition which had been raised to plunder the tribes of the area as well as to procure ivory, an expedition which aroused such terror that the people took flight at its approach, abandoning homes and cornfields to the mercilessness of the marauders. 'The constantly recurring scenes of savage brutality,' Junker wrote, 'the floggings liberally dispensed every day to the slaves and servants ... my indignation at the robbers, the Nubians being the worst, my pity for the poor plundered negroes ... all made it impossible to feel comfort or satisfaction.'

He returned to Russia soon afterwards without any thoughts of returning to Central Africa. But a few months later he changed his mind; and by the beginning of February 1879 he was on board the *Ismaila* steaming up the Nile once more to Fashoda. He relieved the tedium of the journey in the cramped ship by shooting at the rats which invaded his cabin and by conversations with his assistant, Friedrich Bohndorff, a former goldsmith's apprentice from Mecklenburg who had been a kind of steward or store-keeper in General Gordon's service and had since wandered about in Darfur and the territories of the Niam-niam. From Fashoda the *Ismaila* steamed on to Meshra er-Req where Junker and Bohndorff disembarked to travel south through the lands of the Dinkas, then west to Dem Soliman before proceeding south again to the capital of the powerful Niam-niam chief, Ndorama.

For their reception by Ndorama, Junker had his black servants dressed in fezzes and Russian peasant costumes of bright cotton shirts and trousers of which he had brought several dozen with him as presents. The chief was himself attired in a most eccentric costume which he had evidently put on expressly for the occasion – crimson trousers, once part of a hussar's uniform, which were far too short and narrow for his brawny legs, and an Arab jellaba, also much too tight for him, compressing his arms and shoulders while leaving his great chest and paunch fully exposed. Even so, he was a most impressive man, dignified, alert and intelligent. He displayed great interest in the unusual presents which his visitor had brought with him and in the illustrated books and musical instruments, including a barrel-organ, that Junker 'always found useful in amusing a black audience'. He expressed his astonishment that the white man intended travelling through his country and other strange lands without an escort of any kind, but promised to help him as best he could.

So Junker decided to make his headquarters at Ndorama's, leaving Bohndorff in charge while he made excursions into the surrounding countryside. Huts were soon erected, a stout palisade was built around them as a protection against leopards, and a garden was dug and planted. While this work was in hand, Junker kept the chief and his wives and courtiers entertained with picture-books and music, frequently offering them presents of glass beads, trinkets and cheap European toys which, of no interest to their children, were seized upon by the women who gave 'shouts of delight and then would echo the long-drawn-out *akooh*'. 'Astonishment was also produced by children's penny whistles, while a large accordion caused universal amazement,' Junker recalled. 'The performance, especially of the musical-boxes, usually struck the listeners dumb with amazement, so that a solemn stillness would pervade the audience. Occasionally, when the soft and weird-like notes were suddenly emitted, and when I myself feigned surprise, looking round about the hut to discover the agency at work, my visitors would be overcome by an unmistakable sense of fear and alarm at the uncanny sounds and would stealthily disappear one after the other.'

Having spent two months in his encampment on the banks of the Werre at Ndorama's, Junker set out on the first of his expeditions. This was to a neighbouring chief, Semio, a ruler of the Zandeh, who was to embark upon a march into the territories of a vassal chief to collect tributes of ivory. Semio agreed to take the white man with him. So Junker was able to proceed further south in a long procession headed by a trumpeter, whose five-foot ivory horn occasionally emitted hollow, ominous notes, by men ringing iron bells and by a vanguard of armed warriors. These were followed by Semio, his personal attendants and a corps of musketeers armed with Belgian elephant guns. Behind them came more warriors with shields and spears, then a meandering line of carriers, servants, slaves and, of course, women without whom no African expedition was ever complete. In the rear marched several hostages who were to be exchanged for ivory should there be any difficulty in its collection. Thus accompanied, Junker began his journey to the 'long-sought' Uele-Makua, accepting on the way the gift of a little female slave about five years old who was passed on to him by Semio and who presented herself before him with all her possessions, a few ivory hairpins, a carved stool, two small straw mats and a basket suspended on her shoulders by a headband and containing a box of red powder for dyeing the skin.

On reaching the Uele-Makua, 'a majestic stream some three hundred yards wide', Junker passed into the lands of the Mangbattu whose chief, Mambanga, a young man with an expression of 'unbridled sensuousness', greeted him in a friendly manner. He was a nephew of King Munza, whom Schweinfurth had visited during his journeys in the area, and his people, like Munza's, were, so Junker said, 'beyond dispute' cannibals. Once, when a witch had been killed and her gall-bladder, wherein her magical powers were supposed to reside, had been torn out and burned, her cooked foot was brought to him wrapped in banana leaves. 'It was discoloured,' he commented, 'and the nails had fallen off in cooking. Human flesh is always cooked with the skin after the hair is singed off.' Later, after 'some Negro heads, already in an incipient putrid state', had been presented to him for his collection of skulls, a number of natives 'hastened up to remove the flesh from the bones and eat it'.

Mambanga's uncle, King Munza, was now dead, and when Junker went to look for his capital with its large assembly hall which Schweinfurth had described he could find no trace of it remaining. As with his own settlement at Ndorama's and Ndorama's itself, which were both entirely to disappear within three years, and as with so many other African towns, King Munza's capital had vanished. Not a vestige of it was to be seen; and Junker's glance wandered in vain over the 'grassy surface in search of some slight traces of this former busy centre'.

Returning to Ndorama's, where Bohndorff had enjoyed vegetables from the garden which had never been grown in Central Africa before and where, although it was December, tomatoes continued to ripen and red cabbages and swedes still grew in well-filled rows, Junker left for a tour through the lands of the A-Madi north of the Albert Nyanza; and at the end of 1881 he attained the goal for which he 'had been aiming for a year, the domain of Prince Bakangai'.

Bakangai, a chief of the A-Barmto, was 'one of the most interesting personalities' Junker had met anywhere in Africa. Very short and fat, he was extremely acute with a quick piercing glance and 'a craving for knowledge'. He displayed the deepest interest in all the European objects which were shown to him and delighted in explaining their uses to his court. He also took the keenest pleasure in performing mischievous demonstrations with them, in using a burning-glass to scorch the hands of his attendants or a pair of scissors to cut their clothes in half, and even to cut their hair 'with such effect that some of them were presently quite bald, to the huge delight of the ruler and his suite'.

From Bakangai's, which he left on 14 January 1882, Junker travelled north to the Kibbi river, then south towards the Nepoko, encountering the pygmy tribe whom Schweinfurth had seen. He remarked upon their sharp powers of observation, their extraordinary memories, their astonishing talent for mimicry, their artful, suspicious and revengeful character and their unrivalled marksmanship which was such that, on the rare occasions when they missed their target, they flew 'into a violent passion, breaking bows and arrows and all'. Although he had always prided himself on his good health and his freedom from fever, Junker now began to suffer from a most painful skin complaint. Sores broke out on his hands and legs as well as an abscess on his back, and he felt 'so weary and exhausted' that for long periods he had to be carried in a kind of makeshift sedan chair. By day he was plagued also by 'bloodthirsty mosquitoes' and 'the most ferocious species of ants' which 'tortured [him] pitilessly'. At night his people's huts swarmed with rats which devoured all his leather straps, carried off the greasy hairpins from the heads of the women and, fastening on the neck of a servant, marked him deeply with their teeth. Once he discovered a cobra, six and a half feet long, coiled round the pole of his tent to which he transfixed it with a lance. On 6 May, however, his 'wishes were at last gratified by the sight of the Nepoko whose name had haunted [him] throughout [his] southern wanderings' since he felt sure it 'must be identified with the Aruwimi effluent of the Congo'.

For the next four years Junker travelled about in the Nile-Congo watershed, drawing maps and collecting specimens, moving west from Zemio's to Bagbinne's, and to Ali Kobbo's on the Uele-Makua, east to Lado, then south to Wadelai, making careful records of his observations which he later published in his invaluable *Reisen in Afrika*. Towards the end of 1888, he made his way to Zanzibar by way of Lakes Albert and Victoria, and in April the next year he arrived in St Petersburg where he died five years later at the age of fifty-seven, 'a victim to the insidious disease, the germs of which had been sown during his long wanderings in Central Africa'.

10

NORTH FROM THE CAPE

KARL MAUCH · HIS EXPLORATIONS IN THE
TRANSVAAL, MATABELELAND AND SWAZILAND AND
DISCOVERY OF THE HARTLEY GOLDFIELDS · HIS QUEST
FOR THE BIBLICAL CITY OF OPHIR, CAPITAL OF
THE QUEEN OF SHEBA · HIS DISCOVERY OF THE
RUINS OF ZIMBABWE AND OF THE MAKAHA GOLDFIELD
IN 1872 · DAVID LIVINGSTONE · HIS EARLY LIFE
AND ARRIVAL IN CAPE TOWN · HIS MISSIONARY
ACTIVITIES · HE CROSSES THE KALAHARI DESERT AND
DISCOVERS LAKE NGAMI · HE COMES UPON THE
ZAMBEZI 'IN THE CENTRE OF THE CONTINENT' · HIS LIFE
WITH THE MAKOLOLO · HIS ADVENTURES DURING
HIS JOURNEY TO LUANDA TO OPEN UP A ROUTE TO THE
COAST · HE RETURNS TO THE MAKOLOLO IN SEPTEMBER 1854

Almost five thousand miles south of Tripoli, where so many African explorers had begun their journeys, lies the port of Cape Town which, founded by Dutch settlers in 1652, had been taken over by the British during the Napoleonic Wars. From here and from Natal, where British merchants from Cape Town had established themselves in the 1820s, other men had set out to explore the continent from the south. Among these were Karl Mauch and David Livingstone.

Mauch spent almost a quarter of his short life in continuous travel in Southern Africa. Largely self-trained, he was nevertheless an expert observer and he made important contributions to geological and botanical knowledge. The son of a poor carpenter from a village near Stuttgart, he had from an early age conceived an irrepressible urge to go out to Africa and had spent hours poring over an atlas which he had been given when he was ten. The little money that his father could spare, after the bare necessities of life had been paid for, was spent upon the education of the sons of the family. Karl received

251

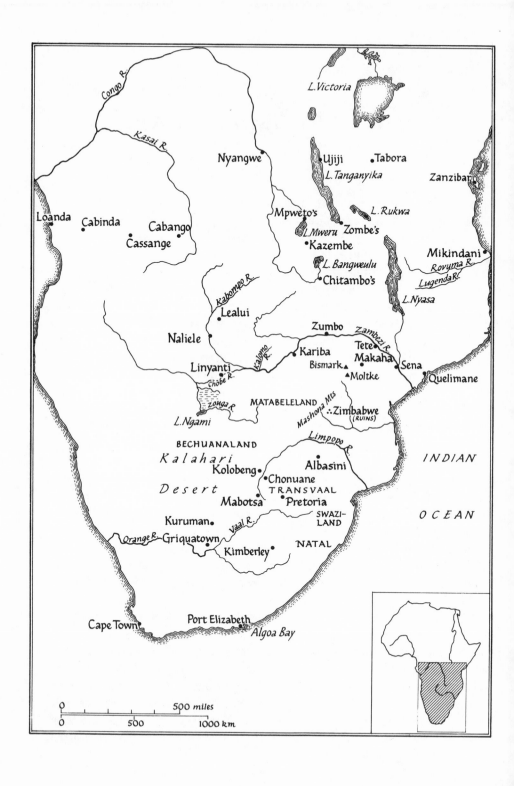

L.Victoria

Congo R.

Kasai R.

Nyangwe

Ujiji   Tabora

L.Tanganyika   Zanzibar

Loanda   Cabinda   Cabango

Cassange

Mpweto's

L.Mweru   Zombe's

Kazembe

Mikindani

Rovuma R.

L.Bangweulu

Chitambo's   Lugenda R.

L.Nyasa

Kabompo R.

Lealui

Zumbo   Zambezi R.

Naliele   Kariba   Tete

Makaha

Linyanti   Bismark.   Sena

Kalomo R.   ▲ Moltke   Quelimane

Chobe R.

Zonga R.   MATABELELAND

L.Ngami   Mashona Mts   ∴Zimbabwe

(RUINS)

BECHUANALAND   Limpopo R.

Kalahari   Albasini   INDIAN

Kolobeng   Chonuane

Desert   TRANSVAAL   OCEAN

Mabotsa   Pretoria

SWAZI-

Kuruman   Vaal R.   LAND

Orange R. Griquatown   NATAL

Kimberley

Cape Town   Port Elizabeth

Algoa Bay

0

500 miles

0

500   1000 km

his due share and was consequently able to obtain a place at a teachers' training school and then to become first a schoolmaster, then a private tutor. But all the while he continued to study such subjects as Arabic, natural history, geology and astronomy which would help him become the explorer he had never ceased longing to be. At last in January 1865, at the age of twenty-seven, having saved enough money to embark upon his adventures, he joined the crew of a boat bound for Natal. At Potchefstroom he obtained financial backing for preliminary explorations in the Transvaal where he met the elephant hunter, Henry Hartley, with whom he travelled north beyond the Limpopo in the lands of Mzilikazi, the paramount chief of the Matabele. In the course of these travels in 1867 Mauch discovered goldfields; and as the months passed and he made further journeys in Matabeleland, the Transvaal and Swaziland, he became convinced that the gold which he had seen in the interior was associated in some way with stories he had heard of massive ruins beyond the Lundi river. He became equally convinced that these ruins were those of the biblical city of Ophir, capital of the Queen of Sheba. This belief was shared and fostered by a missionary named Merensky who had fruitlessly searched for them himself and who encouraged Mauch in his own enthusiasms.

Mauch set out on his quest on 9 May 1871 and towards the end of June arrived at the heavily fortified settlement of Joao Albasini, an Italian adventurer, who lived some two hundred miles north of Pretoria beyond the effective jurisdiction of the Transvaal government. By dint of 'a great deal of labour, persuasion, blows and threats', Albasini managed to obtain six porters for Mauch, and with these he advanced towards the Limpopo through fields where women, planting sweet potatoes and groundnuts, repeatedly asked him, 'Where to? Where to?'

The next day Mauch reached the kraal of a chief called Lomondo, a cruel-looking man with 'an uncouth appearance and a face almost animal-like whose behaviour fully matched one's expectations: crude talk in a shrill voice'. 'I believe he would make a perfect character to portray a cannibal,' Mauch recorded, 'and I can hardly doubt the pronouncement of one of my companions to the effect that he actually is one. In fact all the Berg Kaffirs are such. But he quickly changed his attitude towards me on learning that I was not a Boer ... He even deigned to present me with a goat ... to which he helped himself with gusto.'

The chief of the neighbouring territories, Sewaas, was equally unpre-possessing but also quite friendly. He sat on a pile of dung in his cattle kraal wearing a soldier's cap adorned with feathers beneath which hung long locks of greasy, artificially curled hair. He repeatedly offered his guest pinches of snuff from a box which had originally contained firing-caps and, although Mauch preferred to smoke his pipe, he rather regretted not accepting the snuff as well since it might have made the smell of the chief's sweat less intolerable. Between offers of snuff Sewaas begged for presents, particularly for powder and lead, for a bull's-eye lantern which had caught his fancy and a multi-coloured shawl which he declared would look most splendid upon him.

Mauch was thankful to escape to his hut which had been smeared afresh for him with cattle dung. But he was soon driven out of it by a 'hell of vermin', flies, lice, fleas, cockroaches, spiders and sand-fleas, which compelled him to transfer his bed to the open air. Here, before sunrise, Sewaas joined him and remained there all morning, giving audience to submissive subjects who, 'with their faces to the ground, addressed him with the names of noble beasts'.

He has been well endowed with his tongue which never rests [Mauch wrote in his journal] and only hoarse laughter caused by his own wit interrupts his animated chatter. Having allowed himself to be washed by a girl of about thirteen, he ordered beer which he shared with me. Later he ordered a small ox as a present ... It was killed slowly with an assegai thrust into its flank so that much blood was shed internally, and after the victim had grown weak it was pushed to the ground and had its throat cut. Naturally I immediately had some chunks of meat cooked and ate them with Sewaas. He wanted us to eat more and by nightfall, with the help of his followers, all the meat had been consumed.

The next day, and for days after that, Mauch was compelled to spend his mornings sitting with Sewaas. Whenever he left him for a moment he was pestered by girls and other 'greasy, unclean, chattering, begging creatures' who wanted him to give them beads. One of them crawled into his hut when he was asleep to pull a needle she fancied out of his shirt. 'I am constantly plagued by the black, two-legged rabble that in its proud stupidity thinks itself superior to the whites,' Mauch complained. 'They beg for anything they see and if it is not given them voluntarily, they just grab it. Outside there is rain which does not even permit some fresh air to be let into the hut. When will this end? ... The continuation of the march is very desirable.'

He was permitted to leave at last on 7 August. But before the end of the month he was in trouble again. His bearers deserted him, robbing him of many of his possessions, more of which disappeared when he went to fetch water for the night from a spring. In this predicament he sought shelter from a local chief, Mapansule, who seemed prepared to treat him considerately provided he agreed to remain with him indefinitely as his 'white captive'. Fortunately Mapansule, a little old man almost hidden under a home-made bark cloth, 'a picture of ruin and misery', was not a character capable of inspiring awe; and he could do no more than protest when Mauch moved away to stay with another chief, Pika, whose daughter was married to a German trader and elephant hunter, Adam Renders.

On the three-hour march to Pika's, Mauch heard news which made him forget all the hardships he had recently suffered: 'This most exciting news was that, according to the natives, white people had once lived in this country and that when they themselves had taken possession of it they had occasionally picked up iron tools while working in their gardens ... They affirmed with conviction that they were quite incapable of manufacturing such things.' Mauch heard reports also of a mysterious pot with four legs which walked about upon a high hill only a short distance away. No one knew what was in the pot. Once, a man had put his hand inside to discover its secret and the sides had snapped together and cut the hand off. Nor had any of Mauch's informants climbed to the top of the hill; those who had done so had gone mad or died or had all their hair shaved off by invisible hands. But more thrilling to Mauch than stories of the magic pot and hill were accounts of 'quite large ruins which could never have been built by blacks'.

Excited beyond measure by reports of these ruins, Mauch set off as soon as he could in search of them. And on 5 September he came to the foot of a hill, about 400 feet high, which was 'regarded by all with great awe'. There, in a long line of tumbled-down stones he recognized the remains of a huge wall. He saw other 'extensive stone ruins' and 'a tower-like structure' about thirty feet high, apparently quite undamaged. He saw corridors and what may once have been temples; evidence of buildings, massively constructed of smoothly cut granite blocks; and cross-beams of trimmed stone, some intricately decorated. He came to the 'quite definite conclusion that these ruins must be the fallen remains of a very strong fortification of earlier times'. He had, in fact, found the ruins of Zimbabwe. They were not, as he thought, the remains of the Queen of Sheba's capital but ruins of African origin and medieval date. His letters describing them, which were published in the *Geographischen Mitteilungen*, were, however, the first authentic accounts of them to appear in Europe.

Mauch had ample opportunity of making further visits to the ruins for he was delayed at Pika's for nearly nine months; first, replacing the goods which had been stolen from him, then waiting for the end of the rainy season, and finally held back by reports of a Matabele raiding party moving across his intended route. By the end of the first week in May he was close to despair. Food was so scarce that it could 'hardly be had even for the highest prices'. His trade goods had 'shrunk to almost nothing' and his contempt for the 'bestial race' among whom he was forced to linger had 'almost turned into hate'. But on 26 May 1872 he was at last able to leave; and a month later all his frustrations were dissipated when he made another important discovery, the Makaha goldfield at Samali's. He proudly gave it the name of the Kaiser Wilhelm Field. A nearby 'big mountain range of granite' he called the Bismarck, and to a 'similar, mighty range' he gave the name Moltke, asking himself in his diary,

'If all travellers give names to suitable as well as unsuitable places why then should not I, for once, give a name to a very important site to show that a German had found it?'

Proud as he felt of his achievements, they were not accorded the acclaim in Europe which he believed to be their due. Having reached Quelimane in tattered, dirty clothes on 27 July, he was treated with some disdain by the Portuguese authorities there who listened without interest to his proposals for further explorations at the expense of their government. So at the end of October he returned home, disappointed and embittered, in a French schooner. In Germany he endeavoured to find employment in a university or museum but his lack of formal training and qualifications seems to have told against him; and, after a brief excursion to the West Indies, he was obliged to accept a post in a cement works at Blauberen in Württemberg where he lived alone and in poor health in a room above the railway station. Soon after he had taken up this appointment he was found one night lying on the cobblestones beneath his window with a fractured skull.

Some thirty-five years earlier, in March 1841, David Livingstone had arrived in Cape Town. His forebears had been farmers in the Hebrides; but his grandfather, finding it impossible to support a large family on their smallholding, had gone to work in a cotton mill on the Clyde where David himself was taken on as a piecer when he was ten years old. He worked hard from six in the morning until eight at night, yet attended an evening school for two hours after work and then read in the small overcrowded family tenement until midnight, or even later, if his mother did not snatch the books from him and send him to bed. He read everything he could lay his hands on, studying with particular care scientific works and books of travels, and rejecting nothing except novels and, in those early years, the books of religious instruction which his strict and pious father considered so essential to his proper education that he once beat him for declining to study Wilberforce's *Practical Christianity*. Earnest, self-absorbed and remote, David made few friends: a boy who also worked in the hot and noisy mill, where the children were beaten or plunged into cold water to keep them awake at night, described him as quiet and sulky and unremarkable, by no means a 'by-ordinar laddie'. Yet his tireless industry did set him apart from other boys; and no one in the family was surprised when he announced that he would one day distinguish himself by leaving the mill and becoming a doctor. His father, however, refused to consider any such idea unless it had a religious purpose; so the boy suggested that he should train himself for work as a medical missionary in China. To this his father agreed once David's promotion to a better-paid appointment as a cotton-spinner in the factory had enabled him to afford the necessary lessons in divinity and

49. A page from Samuel Baker's diary giving 'a revised list of Copper and Beads on board for the White Nile'.

40. Florence and Samuel
Baker. A photograph from
the archives of the Royal
Geographical Society.

41. An officer of the King
of Dahomey's army of
Amazons, from Burton's
Mission to Gelele. 'The
army consisted of about
2,500 elderly, hideous women,
most of whom had been
discovered in adultery and
handed over to the King as a
punishment'. Burton
thought that the officers
were 'chosen for the size of
their bottoms'.

42. **King Munza** of the Monbutto, 'an alarming ruler who was said to have a baby roasted for his table every day', as he appeared when granting audience to Georg Schweinfurth.

43. **King Munza** dancing before his wives, from Schweinfurth's *The Heart of Africa*: 'Within the hall there was a spacious square left free, around which the 80 royal wives were seated in a single line upon their little stools, having painted themselves in honour of the occasion with the most elaborate care. They were applauding most vigorously . . . In the midst of all, a wondrous sight, was the King himself.'

44. Schweinfurth's impression of a Dinka village: 'It depicts the scene at about five o'clock in the afternoon. In the foreground there are specimens of the cattle of the country. The men in charge are busy collecting up into heaps the dung that has been exposed during the day to be dried in the sun. Clouds of reeking vapour fill the cattle-park throughout the night and drive away the pestiferous insects. Each animal is fastened by a leather collar to its own wooden peg.'

45. 'Special arrangements had to be made [for my travelling when I was incapable of walking myself],' wrote Wilhelm Junker in his *Travels in Africa*. 'In Egyptian Sudan invalids are carried, couch and all, on the heads of two negroes; and the reader may well fancy how pleasant this primitive means of transport must be ∴ . .[So] I devised the arrangement here illustrated to carry me through.'

46. Gerhard Rohlfs, who had 'an uncomplaining resignation in adversity, an adaptability and a determination which were to redeem many faults'.

47. Women of the Kalahari filling their egg-shells and water-skins at a pool in the desert, from Livingstone's *Missionary Travels*.

48. Livingstone received by Shinte, the greatest of the Balonda chiefs: 'I stated briefly the object of my journey and mission and to all I said the old gentleman, who seems to be about 60 years of age, responded by clapping the hands. His attendants replied, and then all clapped their hands again. I asked if he had seen a white man before. He replied, "Never." '

49. A Lovalé riverside village, from Cameron's *Across Africa*.

50. Fort Dinah, from Cameron's *Across Africa*. 'Four huts in the centre of the village, forming an imperfect square, I had loop-holed as block houses and between them built a barricade of doors and poles from the remaining huts which were either torn down or burnt to prevent them providing cover for our enemies . . . We were constantly shot at and some half dozen of my men were wounded whilst fetching water from the stream.'

51. Choice bits of elephant, the feet and the trunk, by Thomas Baines in 1862.

52. 'Some of the Zanzibar and other natives of Mr H. M. Stanley's Party Nov. 1 1877' sketched after their arrival in Cape Town from Luanda.

53. Fort Bodo, from Stanley's *In Darkest Africa*. 'Ten scouts patrol the plantations every morning, that the mischievous pigmies may not destroy the supplies of the garrison and that no sudden onsets of natives may be made . . . Boys have been instructed in the art of bathing the sores with lotions of carbolic acid and water.'

54. Stanley and his men firing on war canoes in the Congo, from Stanley's *Through the Dark Continent*. Burton condemned Stanley for being 'as ready to shoot Negroes as if they were monkeys'.

medicine. He was looking forward to going out to China when the outbreak of the Opium War forced him to alter his plans. He continued with his lessons, however, a dogged and steady rather than a bright student; and, having eventually been admitted a licentiate of the Faculty of Physicians and Surgeons at Glasgow University, he offered his services to the London Missionary Society. Soon after he had been accepted, Livingstone sailed for the Cape, taking the opportunity on the way to hand out temperance tracts to drunken sailors far from disposed to accept them.

He was now twenty-seven, a rather prudish, narrow-minded and opinionated young man, highly conscious of his own capabilities and ill-prepared to tolerate the weaknesses of those less high-minded and less courageous than himself.

After spending a month in Cape Town with the South African secretary of the London Missionary Society, Livingstone sailed to Algoa Bay whence he trekked by ox-wagon to Kuruman, some 125 miles north-west of Kimberley. It was at that time the most northerly station of the Society, and there he was to wait for the return from Europe of Dr Robert Moffat, the Scottish missionary, who had worked there for twenty years. Livingstone was deeply disappointed by Kuruman, a small, arid village where, despite Moffat's long and unremitting labours, only a few of the native people had been converted to Christianity and most, even of these, seemed to have been drawn to conversion by the material benefits it had to offer.

The prospect of working for so many years and so unrewardingly in the same place dismayed Livingstone who wrote of his desire to 'preach the gospel beyond every other man's line of things'. And he took the earliest opportunity he could of making excursions to the north, at first in company with another missionary who had received instructions to find a site for a new mission in Bechuanaland, and subsequently by himself. By August 1843 he had his own station at Mabotsa where, finding the Bakhatla people unresponsive to Christian teaching, he began to realize the appalling difficulties of missionary work in Africa and to accept that, while Moffat and his colleagues might have preached the gospel in ways quite unintelligible to Africans, the limited success which they had achieved was not to be derided.

After being attacked near Mabotsa by a lion which brought him to the ground and, crushing his shoulder, inflicted a wound that was to trouble him for the rest of his life, Livingstone returned to the station at Kuruman; and there he married the Moffats' eldest daughter, Mary. He did so without apparent enthusiasm, announcing to the Directors of the London Missionary Society that he had made 'the necessary arrangements for union', having been led to the conclusion that his new sphere of labour entailed the duty of entering 'into the marriage relation'. He said privately that his bride had 'a stout stumpy body' and was 'a good deal of an African in complexion'. But although undoubtedly plain, sallow and fat, Mary Livingstone deserved a more commendatory description than that. She was a competent, frugal and highly adaptable young woman, as capable of teaching in a mission school as of making clothes, candles and soap. At first she and her husband lived in Mabotsa, then, after he had quarrelled bitterly with a colleague, at Chonuane, some forty miles further north, where their first son was born, and finally at Kolobeng, where, displaying his acquired skills as smith, carpenter and gardener, he built his family their third primitive home. Here he was busily occupied, teaching, preaching, making a grammar of the Sichuana language and carrying out all those other duties which occupied a missionary's days while his family grew in size, lived in poverty and were often hungry. Hard as he worked, however, he found the Bakwains no readier to listen to the gospel than the Bakhatla. In all his time at Kolobeng he made but one convert, the only one he was ever to make, and even he relapsed. Slowly Livingstone persuaded himself that he must not settle down in any one place. He became increasingly convinced that he ought to move north to 'extend the gospel to all the surrounding tribes', that it was his duty to explore the vast continent of which he had as yet seen so little and 'open it out to the teaching of Christ'. And he must do it on his own. For, although a man of limited self-knowledge, he had already recognized that he must always be the master in any human relationship. He found it difficult and often impossible to work agreeably with others, and he never cared to share with them the recognition to which he felt himself entitled.

For a long time now he had harboured an ambition of crossing the Kalahari Desert in search of the almost legendary Lake Ngami which even the Griquas, half-caste Dutch and Hottentots, who were more capable of enduring thirst than Europeans, had failed to reach. The cost of such an expedition had previously obliged Livingstone to consider it an impractical undertaking but, having met a young English sportsman, Captain Thomas Steele, on one of his previous expeditions, he now approached him with his proposal. Steele, who was to distinguish himself in the Crimean War, readily agreed to help. He talked to a rich young friend of his, an enthusiastic big-game hunter, William Colton Oswell, who, having left Arnold's Rugby and joined the East India Company at Madras, had come out to Africa for health reasons. Oswell was also enthusiastic. So was Oswell's friend, another sportsman, Mungo Murray who, like Oswell, was not to be troubled by any thoughts that Livingstone would wish to arrogate to himself most of the credit for what they were to do.

On 1 June 1849 Livingstone, Oswell and Murray set out together with a guide named Ramotobi, who had spent all his youth in the Kalahari, travelling along the north-east border of the great desert in their search for Lake Ngami.

Although there was no running water in the desert and very little in wells, the soft pale sand was not devoid of vegetation: the quantity of grass was, indeed, remarkable; a plant with a deep tuber which was often as large as the head of a small child and contained a cool fluid like that of a young turnip was often to be found; and sometimes vast tracts of the country were covered with water-melons. Yet water was only to be found with difficulty; and the Bakalahari tribes of the desert, whose women collected the precious fluid by sucking it up through reeds from deep holes dug in the sand and carrying it home in ostrich shells, buried their supplies in secret hiding places. One of their chiefs warned Livingstone of the perils of the expedition. 'You will be killed by the sun and the thirst,' he told him. 'And then all the white men will blame me for not saving you.' And certainly without Ramotobi's knowledge of the area Livingstone and his companions could not have survived. Every clump of bushes looked the same to them; but Ramotobi knew them all and by which of them water was to be found. Even so, the oxen came close to death. The sun was so hot that it was impossible to travel during the day, and the going was painfully slow. 'The second night showed that we had made only twenty-five miles,' Livingstone recorded. 'Ramotobi was angry at the slowness of our progress, and told us that as the next water was three days in front, we should never get there at all. The utmost endeavours of the servants, cracking their whips, screaming and beating, got only nineteen miles out of the poor beasts which were ... exhausted by the sandy ground and by thirst ... At this season the grass becomes so dry as to crumble to powder in the hands. Without a single mouthful the oxen stood wearily chewing, and lowing painfully at the smell of water in the wagons.'

At length water was reached and the oxen rushed into it to drink until their collapsed sides distended as though they would burst. Thus refreshed, the travellers continued their march at a rather quicker pace towards Nchokotsa when Oswell suddenly threw his hat in the air and shouted in triumph as he pointed to a vast shimmering expanse in which the shadows of trees were reflected. The whole party rushed forward to what they felt sure was the lake; but as they approached it the illusion was gradually dispelled: the impression of glittering water was caused by the light of the setting sun on extensive salt pans covered with an efflorescence of lime. The travellers still had more than three hundred miles to go.

Again and again thereafter they thought they saw the lake. But on 4 July when they reached the banks of the Zouga they knew the mirages would soon become reality. For the meek, unwarlike people who lived by the river – spending all their days in crude canoes hollowed out of single trees and rarely venturing ashore for fear of wild beasts, serpents and human enemies – assured the white men that by following the Zouga's course they would reach Ngami.

And so they did. On 1 August 1849 this 'fine sheet of water,' in Livingstone's words, 'was beheld by Europeans for the first time'. He could not judge its extent, since it stretched as far as the eye could see. But the local people told him it took three days to go round it; and so he judged it to be seventy miles in circumference. At this time of year it was shallow and animals found it difficult to approach through the boggy, reedy banks. Yet when the rains came, he was told, not only trees of great size but antelope were swept down into it by the rushing waters.

Gratified as he was that he and his companions had discovered Lake Ngami, Livingstone was disappointed that he was not able to fulfil the other object of his journey which was to meet Sebituane, the great chief of the Makololo tribe. Sebituane lived some two hundred miles beyond the lake and, Livingstone had good cause to believe, would grant permission for the establishment of a Christian mission in his territories. The reason for this disappointment was the young chief of a tribe who held the lands between those of the Makololo and the River Zouga, and who – fearful lest contact with Europeans would result in his rival, Sebituane, obtaining guns – refused to provide guides and ordered the river people not to let the strangers pass.

So Livingstone, having failed to make a raft with the worm-eaten wood which was all that he could find by the banks of the alligator-infested Zouga, was forced to turn back. He made another attempt to reach the Makololo the next year, but on this occasion was defeated by fever and the tsetse fly. In April 1851, however, he set out yet again, once more accompanied by Oswell. He was also, to the Moffats' distress, to be accompanied by his wife and children. Mrs Moffat pleaded with him not to take the family: the proposal was 'preposterous'. Mary, when pregnant, had already made a fearful journey in a rattling wagon after which her baby had died. She and the children should not be required to go with him again. But Livingstone was insistent: all of them must go, he told his mother-in-law; he would send out men in advance to deepen the wells along the desert route. Despite this precaution they all nearly died of thirst in the dreary country south of the River Chobe. Through the carelessness of a servant, the water in the wagons was lost. Their incompetent guide took them wandering off in every direction through sandy landscapes of low scrub, in which there was not a bird or insect to be seen, and then, 'after professing ignorance of everything, vanished altogether'. After four days of terrible suffering, the River Mababe was at last reached; but in approaching it the oxen were bitten by the dreaded tsetse fly and no less than forty-three of them perished.

Sebituane, however, was now close at hand. This renowned warrior, the 'best specimen of a native chief' that Livingstone had ever met, proved as helpful and sympathetic as the missionaries in the south had been led to believe. About forty-five years old, tall and strong, with a palish brown skin, he had travelled some hundred miles down the Chobe to greet the white men from whom he hoped to obtain guns. And when Livingstone and Oswell landed on the island where the meeting was to take place, they found him and his companions singing together. They continued their song for some time after the visitors' approach. Sebituane then greeted them warmly, promised to replace all their oxen, presented them with an ox and a jar of honey, had a fire lit for them, and gave them skins as soft as cloth for their night coverings.

But, to Livingstone's great grief, this powerful friend died shortly afterwards from an infection in an old wound; and, although his daughter, whom he had named as his successor, gave the strangers permission to visit any part of the Makololos' territories they wished, Livingstone failed to find a site suitable for the residence of a European family. Also he had cause to fear that the country would not now be as stable as it had been in Sebituane's day. In his exploration of this country, however, towards the end of June at Sesheke not far from the spot where Silva Porto, a Portuguese trader, had reached the river before them, he and Oswell were 'rewarded by the discovery of the Zambezi in the centre of the continent'. 'This was a most important point,' Livingstone observed, 'for the river was not previously known to exist there at all. We saw it in the dry season, yet there was a breadth of three hundred to six hundred yards of deep flowing water. Mr Oswell said he had never seen so fine a river, not even in India. At the period of the annual inundation it rises fully twenty feet in perpendicular height, and floods fifteen to twenty miles of lands adjacent to the banks.'

This discovery made a profound impression upon Livingstone. He had long believed that if there existed a navigable waterway from the coast to the heart of Africa his dream of 'Christianity and commerce' might be realized. The Africans' demand for European manufactures, already stimulated by foreign merchants, mostly Arabs, might be increased as the exchange of goods for slaves diminished; and trade might be conducted not only to the profit of the outsider but to the benefit also of the African. And as this honest trade prospered and as tribalism, which he had previously defended, began to break up, the work of the Christian missions would prosper, too. The more he considered the matter, the clearer it became to Livingstone that it was his duty to open up that essential trading route between central Africa and the sea. He had once written that native customs and institutions must be respected, that the African character was impaired rather than improved by contact with European traders. Now he insisted that Africans could be civilized only 'by a long-continued discipline and contact with superior races by commerce'. So, returning to Cape Town whence he sent his family home in the hope that the London Missionary Society would look after them, he made preparations for that great trans-African expedition which was to consolidate his reputation.

By the middle of May 1853 he was once more among the Makololo. He was pitifully ill-equipped for the long and dangerous journey upon which he was to embark. He had found it difficult to obtain supplies, particularly of ammunition, in Cape Town where he was accused of being far too partial to the African tribes of the north to whom, it was rumoured, he was in the habit of selling guns; and when he had arrived at his house at Kolobeng he found it had been looted and wrecked by a band of vindictive Boers who distrusted the activities of all missionaries. But he was not much downcast. He had always thought it a mistake to travel with heavy and conspicuous baggage in unknown parts of Africa where the advantages of having the equipment were outweighed not only by its inconvenience but also by the probability of losing it to avaricious natives. Besides, he had no need of the comforts that other Europeans deemed essential to life in Africa. He was perfectly content to eat the food upon which the natives existed, and he took pride in drinking without ill effects copious draughts of water 'swarming with insects, thick with mud, putrid with rhinoceroses' urine and buffalo dung'. He never disguised his contempt for those who could not endure what he endured. Having no pity for himself in his adversities, he had none to spare for others. So, when he arrived in Linyanti, the capital of the Makololo, on 23 May 1853 to be welcomed by its seven thousand inhabitants and by their eighteen-year-old king, Sekelutu, Sebituane's son, who had succeeded to the throne on his sister's abdication, Livingstone was as little concerned by the paucity of his supplies as by the arduous task he had set himself.

His pleasure at his greeting was enhanced when Sekelutu offered to accompany him on a preliminary journey to discover a suitable site for a mission station upstream from Sesheke and asked him to name anything he required. Livingstone's reply that his only wish was to make Sekelutu's people Christians seems to have disconcerted the young king who said that he did not wish to study the Bible himself since it might induce him to accept only one wife, whereas he wanted five at least. For the moment Livingstone, who had long advocated patient forbearance in missionary activities, left the matter there. He accepted the canoe which Sekelutu offered him, gave the ten fine elephant tusks with which he had also been presented to some of the king's subjects to sell on their own behalf, and expressed the hope that one day their ruler would recognize the error of his ways and turn to Christ. Certainly in the meantime, although he was forced to conclude that the Makololo never visited 'anywhere but for the purpose of plunder and oppression', the company of Sekelutu and his entourage of young warriors was a great advantage; and Livingstone, having been delayed for some time by a severe attack of malaria,

262

left for Sesheke towards the end of June. At every village they came to, the people met them singing the praises of King Sekelutu, who accepted their salutations with 'lordly indifference'. They offered their distinguished and feared guests pots of beer and bowls of thick milk. Calabashes, Livingstone noted, were used as cups for drinking the beer, but the milk was scooped up by hand. He presented some of the party with iron spoons, 'which pleased them exceedingly'; but, being unused to them, the 'old habit of hand-eating prevailed; they lifted out a little with the spoon, then put the milk into the left hand and drank from that'. As well as with drink, the villagers supplied their visitors with oxen which were killed with the thrust of a javelin to the heart. The meat was then cut into long strips so many of which were thrown into the fire at once that they nearly extinguished it. Half broiled and burning hot, the strips were then passed round; but no one other than the king spared time to chew the flesh, the aim of the Makololo being to get as much food as possible into the stomach in the short time allowed, rather than to enjoy its flavour.

To vary the diet Livingstone went out into the surrounding country where, in the fine open glades, scores of buffalo, zebra and antelope grazed undisturbed. Even so, hunting them on foot was hard work as the heat was so great; and Livingstone would willingly have forgone the sport if there had been anyone amongst the Makololo whom he could have trusted not to waste his precious powder.

When they gained the upper reaches of the Zambezi near Sesheke, the Makololo collected a fleet of thirty-three flat-bottomed canoes in which to ascend the river. The canoe which Livingstone selected was thirty feet long and was propelled by six men who stood and kept stroke with the utmost precision, using their long paddles as punting poles in shallow water and, where the river was deeper, racing against the other craft at such speed that there was always a danger of their capsizing when the wind whipped up the waves. 'The magnificent stream', as Livingstone called the Zambezi, was over a mile wide and adorned with many islands over whose banks dipped the gracefully curved light-green fronds of date palms above which the feathery foliage of tall palmyras fluttered against the cloudless sky. Sometimes huge herds of buffalo and antelope could be seen and the roar of lions heard. One lion stood on the opposite shore roaring as loud as he could, 'putting his mouth to the ground, as is usual on such occasions, to make the sound reverberate'. Occasionally a village was glimpsed, its huts clustered on mounds which became islands in the rainy season when the valley took on the appearance of a huge lake. In one of these villages lived the father of a rival of Sekelutu who had plotted to kill him and usurp the chieftainship. The rival had already been executed. Now his father and a fellow-conspirator were brought out, killed and tossed into the river. When Livingstone protested, Sekelutu's counsellors justified their acts and calmly added, 'But you see, we are still Boers. We are not taught yet how to behave.'

When they came to Naliele, the capital of the Barotse tribe, Livingstone began his search for a suitable site for a mission station. He went from village to village with a herald provided by Sekelutu to whom the Barotse owed allegiance. But he could find nowhere that he judged sufficiently healthy or free from the tsetse fly; and, abandoning the search, he returned to Linyanti to make preparations for his great journey to the coast.

Sekelutu appointed twenty-seven men to accompany him, only two of them Makololo, the rest Barotse or from other tribes from the banks of the Zambezi. They were not hired, since their people were as eager to trade with the white men of the coast as Livingstone was to establish the commerce without which he regularly maintained 'no permanent elevation of a people could be effected'. Nor did they have much to carry: a few beads for presents; some medicines; a small supply of biscuits, sugar, tea and coffee; a tent, a sheepskin cloak and a horse-rug; guns and ammunition for shooting game to eat; one or two articles of clothing for when they reached civilized life; a magic-lantern; a thermometer and compasses; a Bible and a few other books such as Thomson's logarithm tables; and instruments for making astronomical observations, in the uses of which Livingstone had been trained by Thomas Maclear, Astronomer Royal at the Cape.

The long journey began on 11 November 1853. By the 19th the travellers were back at Sesheke and soon paddling up the Zambezi once more. Where passage upriver was impeded by falls the local people willingly slung the canoes on poles and carried them overland, filling them with meat and meal, butter and milk and asking the strangers to accept the gifts with graceful diffidence.

At Naliele the rains began and Livingstone was again attacked by fever. But his men cared for him tenderly, cutting grass for his bed when they stopped for the night, arranging his boxes on either side, pitching the tent over all, and lighting the principal fire outside the opening. They cooked his food, carefully washing their hands before touching it; they also washed his shirts. Day after day as they followed the course of the river, whose rising waters were now filled with vast shoals of fish, Livingstone grew as attached to his companions as they seemed devoted to him. As they entered the dense and gloomy tropical forests, the local people became ever more friendly and liberal, taking the roofs off their huts to provide shelter for the strangers, so that Livingstone's hopes of a successful outcome of his mission grew day by day. These hopes were enhanced by the welcome accorded him by the local chiefs, by Manenko, a tall, strapping young female chief whose body, smeared with a mixture of fat and red ochre, was, apart from a profusion of ornaments and charms, 'in a state of frightful nudity', and by her uncle, Shinte, the greatest of the Balonda chiefs. Seated on a throne covered with a leopard skin and surrounded by women, Shinte greeted the strangers wearing a checked jacket, a kilt of scarlet baize, a helmet of beads and many strings of beads and iron and copper bracelets.

Shinte had never before seen a man with white skin and straight hair. But he was evidently pleased to have this new experience, particularly when Livingstone presented him with an ox which, however, his niece Manenko appropriated, claiming that the white man belonged to her and, therefore, so did the ox. She had the beast slaughtered and sent her uncle a leg. The good-tempered fellow 'did not seem to be at all annoyed' by his niece's rapacity. He presented Livingstone with a little slave, a girl about ten years old, whom Livingstone declined, explaining his reluctance, as the father of four children, to take the girl from her mother. But Shinte thought that Livingstone was displeased with the girl's size and sent him another slave of about the same age but a head taller. Nor did Shinte appear to understand when Livingstone spoke of God's purpose and of his own mission, though he politely clapped his hands in approbation. He was much more interested in Livingstone's magic-lantern and the shows that he gave with it, watching with calm interest while his women, horrified by the sight of a picture of Abraham about to kill Isaac, fled screaming from the exhibition, shouting, 'Mother! Mother!'

Delayed by the frequent rains and by Shinte's reluctance to part with his interesting visitor, Livingstone at last left on 26 January 1854 taking with him, as proof of the old chief's friendship, a 'string of beads and the end of a conical shell which [was] considered, in regions so far from the sea, of as great value as the Lord Mayor's badge in London'. With the help of this talisman and of the guides whom Shinte ordered to accompany him to the sea, Livingstone reached in safety the territories of the neighbouring chief, Katema, a vainglorious man but both amiable and generous with presents of food. Indeed, it was not until the end of February 1854 when he had traversed a swampy plain, the watershed between the Congo and the Zambezi, and had crossed the Kasai that he came upon people who refused to part with food until they were paid for it, and paid far more than it was worth. Having been forced to part with a quantity of his dwindling stock of beads, Livingstone was then faced with a demand from their chief, Katende, for 'a man, a tusk, beads, copper rings, or a shell' in exchange for permission to pass through his country. After lengthy discussion with one of Katende's servants, it was, however, agreed that one of the white man's shirts would suffice as payment. But a few days later in the country of the Chiboque, whose countenances 'by no means handsome, [were] not improved by their practice of filing their teeth to a point', Livingstone not only had to part with another shirt but also with some more beads, and then with a handkerchief. 'The more I yielded,' Livingstone recorded, 'the more unreasonable their demands became, and at every fresh demand a shout was raised by the armed party and a rush made around us with brandishing of arms. One young man made a charge at my head from behind, but I quickly brought round the muzzle of my gun to his mouth and he retreated.' It was, in fact, only his evident determination to fire the gun if necessary that enabled Livingstone to pass without further molestation from these disagreeable people.

From now on the journey was one of prolonged misery. Tolls were demanded by surly, self-appointed gatekeepers; hostile tribesmen dogged the travellers, looking for opportunities to attack them when they were off their guard; rain poured steadily down. Livingstone felt desperately ill and weak, his incessant attacks of fever culminating in periods of semiconsciousness. Giddy and dazed, he was unable to discern the low creeping plants which hung over the gloomy paths in the dark forests and often fell off his intractable ox, Sinbad, who seemed to take a perverse pleasure in walking into them and then kicking the thin figure of his master as he lay on the ground.

'We were all becoming exhausted,' wrote Livingstone in his account of the last days of this wretched journey. 'And my people [who had been obliged to part with nearly all their ornaments by the grasping Chiboque] were now so much discouraged that some proposed to return home ... After using all my powers of persuasion I declared that I would go on alone, and went into my tent ... I was soon followed by [one of the men who said], "We will never leave you. Do not be disheartened. Wherever you lead we will follow." Others with the most artless simplicity of manner told me to be comforted: they were all my children ... they would die for me.'

A few days later some natives were found who were willing to act as guides on the last stages of the journey but who demanded as their reward the shell that Shinte had given to Livingstone. Livingstone, unwilling to part with it, yielded reluctantly when pressed to do so by his men, and soon regretted that he had done so, for next morning the guides slipped away one by one into the forest. Their assistance, however, was not much missed as the travellers were now approaching the Portuguese territories of the coastal regions. On 30 March they came to a sudden descent from the high land, so steep that Livingstone was obliged to dismount and to stagger down weakly on foot, held up by his companions and angry with himself for being so helpless since he 'never liked to see a man, either sick or well, giving in effeminately'.

Abruptly they came out of the gloom of the trees and the 'glorious sight' of the Quango valley lay spread beneath them. It was a hundred miles broad, entirely clothed with dark forest except for the light-green grass of the meadow-lands beside the banks of the river whose waters, as it wound its way north, could be seen sparkling in the sun. But the troubles of the travellers were not yet over. The people of the valley were quite as unhelpful as the Chiboque, refusing to sell food for the poor old ornaments which were all that Livingstone's men now had to offer, and pestering them for the presents they did not possess. Their chief demanded 'a red jacket and one of the men as a slave', adding that if he did not receive them the party might just as well turn back. The men took off the last of their copper rings and surrendered them to the chief who took them without abating his original demands. While everyone grew 'savage and sulky', Livingstone tried in vain to lie down out of sight of his persecutors but his little tent was in tatters with a wider hole behind than the opening in front. Finding rest impossible, he dragged himself to his feet again and tried to persuade his men to move on despite the natives' objections. At that moment a young half-caste Portuguese sergeant of militia, who had come across the Quango in search of beeswax, made his appearance and encouraged the men to follow Livingstone's advice. Apprehensively they did so, frightened that they would be shot in the back; but when the natives did open fire the bullets fell short, and the travellers succeeded in reaching the river where the ferryman, who demanded Livingstone's blanket as his price for taking them across, was induced by the sergeant to accept a lesser price.

At last Livingstone's trials were over. At the Portuguese militia station, which was manned by neatly uniformed half-caste soldiers, female slaves poured water on the hands of Livingstone and his men who were then invited to 'a magnificent breakfast of ground nuts and roasted maize, then boiled manioc roots, and concluding with guavas and honey as a dessert'. At Cassange, the farthest inland station of the Portuguese in Western Africa, they were treated with equally generous hospitality by the Portuguese officers who fed them well, gave Livingstone new clothes and upon their departure provided them with a guide to conduct them to the coast, a black corporal who was carried by three slaves in a hammock slung from a pole. Livingstone, indeed, was profoundly impressed by the courtesy and magnanimity of the Portuguese at Cassange who not only cared for him with extreme kindness but also treated the Africans with 'far greater impartiality' than they were treated by the British in the south. 'Instances, so common in the south, of half-caste children being abandoned, are here extremely rare,' he commented. 'They are acknowledged at table and provided for by their fathers. The coloured clerks of the merchants sit at the same table as their employers without embarrassment. Nowhere in Africa is there so much goodwill between Europeans and natives as here.'

Even so, Livingstone's men were frightened of what would happen to them when they reached the coast at Luanda. They were proud of having come so far; and afterwards, on describing their feelings at the sight of the boundless ocean, they said, 'We marched along with our father, believing that what the ancients had always told us was true, that the world had no end. But all at once the world said to us, "I am finished; there is no more of me." ' Yet they feared that at Luanda they would be kidnapped, taken on board a ship, fattened and eaten by white cannibals. Livingstone tried to reassure them. 'I am as ignorant of Luanda as you are,' he told them. 'But nothing will happen to you that does not happen to me.' They trusted him and went on with him, fearful though they were. And at Luanda all their fears were dispelled. They were found work in the port at wages which were a marvel to them. They were shown over a frigate which was more like a town, so they exclaimed to the good-natured sailors, than a canoe; and one of them was given the great pleasure of firing a cannon. They were, above all, gratified to discover that their journey had not been in vain: the Portuguese in Luanda were evidently prepared to pay much higher prices for ivory than were traders from the Cape.

Livingstone himself had everything he could desire. Prostrated by his frequent attacks of malaria and dysentery he was given a comfortable bed, a luxury of infinite delight, by the British Consul in Luanda and treated by the surgeon of the *Polyphemus*, a frigate employed in the blockade of the slave traffic. And when he was well enough to consider returning to Linyanti he was far better equipped than he had been on the outward journey. He was provided with, among other things, a good new tent, plenty of guns and generous presents for Sekelutu, including a splendid uniform. Yet, while he assured others that the path he had opened to the coast had many advantages, he could not hide from himself the disappointing fact that his journey had not achieved what he had hoped it would: he had failed to find a fever-free area for a trading and missionary station in the Barotse valley and he had discovered that the route to the interior from the west coast was beset with difficulties and peopled by unwelcoming tribes. Refusing in his proud, stubborn and courageous way to countenance failure, he decided, therefore, to go back to Linyanti and from there to find an easier route inland from the east. So, ignoring suggestions that he might return home by sea from Luanda fully to recruit his health in England or Scotland, he told his men that he would fulfil his promise by taking them home to their country. He set out accordingly on 20 September 1854, declining to accept the company of a Portuguese-German botanist who, so he said, might take the 'opportunity of availing himself of all my previous labours ... without acknowledging his obligations to me in Europe'. And he arrived in the country of the Makololo a year later. He had again been ill on the way, suffering as he recorded in his journal his twenty-seventh attack of fever after crossing the Kasai, about which he had collected a considerable amount of accurate information about the river and its tributaries. He had also been chagrined to learn that the mail steamer by which he had sent home his dispatches and maps had sunk off Madeira, a loss which necessitated his writing out everything again from his notes and memory. When he reached Linyanti he was utterly exhausted. But both he and his men were delighted with the affectionate reception everywhere accorded them, particularly from Sekelutu who was so entranced by his uniform that on Sunday he wore it to come to church, presenting so magnificent a sight, Livingstone ruefully noted, that he attracted much more attention than the sermon.

11

'DRIPPING FORESTS
AND OOZING BOGS'

LIVINGSTONE SETS OUT ONCE MORE FOR THE ZAMBEZI ·
DISCOVERS THE VICTORIA FALLS · TRAVELS DOWN THE
ZAMBEZI WITH HIS MAKOLOLO COMPANIONS · HIS
ADVENTURES ON THE JOURNEY · HIS ARRIVAL AT
QUELIMANE, MAY 1856 · RETURNS TO ENGLAND A
HERO · THE ILL-FATED ZAMBEZI EXPEDITION, ITS
TRIBULATIONS, QUARRELS AND DISASTERS · DEATH
OF THE MAKOLOLO CHIEF, SEKELUTU · BISHOP
MACKENZIE AND THE UNIVERSITIES MISSION ·
TROUBLES WITH THE AJAWA WARRIORS · DEATHS OF
MACKENZIE AND MARY LIVINGSTONE · FURTHER
DISASTERS AND DISINTEGRATION OF THE ZAMBEZI
EXPEDITION · LIVINGSTONE IN ENGLAND AGAIN ·
HIS RETURN TO AFRICA TO SOLVE THE PROBLEM
OF THE NILE BASIN · SUFFERINGS ON THE WAY TO
LAKE TANGANYIKA · LAKES MWERU AND BANGWEULU ·
LIVINGSTONE REACHES THE LUALABA · MASSACRE AT
NYANGWE · 'REDUCED TO A SKELETON' · HIS RESCUE
BY THE RELIEF EXPEDITION

Livingstone spent two months in Linyanti, writing letters and making a record of his discoveries, asking questions, gathering information which would help him decide his future route, and vainly endeavouring to make converts among the Makololo who reduced each other to helpless laughter by imitating his preaching and singing of the psalms. Then, on 3 November 1855, he set out once more for the Zambezi, this time with the intention of following the course of the river eastwards. On the way he came upon the cataract which was called by the natives Mosi-oa-tunya and which he named the Victoria Falls. The scene was one of dramatic beauty as columns of vapour rose above the tumbling waters and were imbued by the sun with the colours of the rainbow. The banks and islands were covered with trees of different colour

270

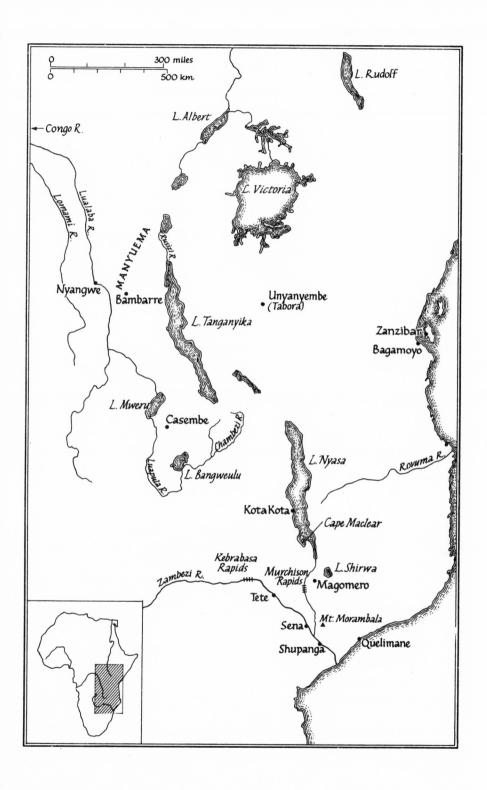

L. Rudolf

300 miles

500 km

Congo R.

L. Albert

L. Victoria

Lomami R.

Lualaba R.

Rusizi R.

MANYUEMA

Nyangwe

Bambarre

Unyanyembe
(Tabora)

L. Tanganyika

Zanzibar

Bagamoyo

L. Mweru

Casembe

Chambezi R.

L. Nyasa

Rovuma R.

Luapula R.

L. Bangweulu

Kota Kota

Cape Maclear

Kebrabasa
Rapids

Murchison
Rapids

L. Shirwa

Zambezi R.

Magomero

Tete

Mt. Morambala

Sena

Shupanga

Quelimane

and form and were perpetually showered by a fine spray; cormorants and plotuses dived for small fish in the calm waters beyond the ceaseless roar of the cataract.

Bidding farewell to Sekelutu who had accompanied him thus far, Livingstone resumed his journey down the Zambezi Valley on 20 November 1855, accompanied by 114 Makololo carrying elephants' tusks to the coast. He passed through the country of the Batoka, a tribe dark of skin and very degraded in appearance, who were addicted to smoking muto kwane (*Cannabis sativa*) which had an extremely strong effect upon them, causing 'a kind of frenzy' after 'the violent fits of coughing that follow a couple of puffs'. Then, after leaving Kaonka, he travelled across a gently undulating countryside, 'the border country between those who accepted and those who rejected the sway of the Makololo'. Here large game abounded: buffaloes, elands, hartebeests, gnus and elephants roamed about, 'all very tame' as no one disturbed them. Crossing the Kalomo river on 30 November, the travellers came on 4 December to the first village of those whom the Makololo deemed rebels. One of the villagers dashed forward 'howling at the top of his voice in the most hideous manner', his eyeballs protruding, his lips covered with foam, his muscles quivering, brandishing a battleaxe over the white man's head. 'I felt a little alarmed,' Livingstone admitted, 'but would not show fear before my own people or strangers, and kept a sharp look-out on the little battle-axe ... I felt it would be a sorry way to leave the world, to get my head chopped off by a mad savage.' After his courage had been sufficiently tested, however, the village headman called the man off; but Livingstone still felt uneasy. The tribesmen did not trouble to conceal their contempt for the Makololo who were travelling without shields, as Sekelutu had ordered them to do, and murmured, 'They have wandered in order to be destroyed.' So, to display a readiness to defend themselves, the Makololo fired their guns and reloaded them in camp that night. After that they were not molested.

The further the travellers advanced, the more the country was found to be 'swarming with inhabitants'. Great numbers came to see the white man, a sight quite new to them; and, in accordance with their custom, they threw themselves to the ground on their backs, rolling from side to side, slapping their thighs, and uttering the words, '*Kina bomba! Kina bomba!*' Disliking this form of salutation, particularly as the men were 'totally unclothed', Livingstone asked them to desist; but they, imagining him to be dissatisfied with their performance, threw themselves about all the more furiously.

The more warlike people beyond the confluence of the Loangwa and the Zambezi accorded the travellers no such welcome. They had been fighting the Portuguese settlers at Tete for the past two years and had come to distrust all white men. Their chief, Mpende, sent two old men to inquire who

Livingstone was. 'I am a *Lekoa*, an Englishman,' Livingstone told them.

'We do not know that tribe. We thought you were Portuguese.'

Livingstone showed them his hair and skin.

'No, we never saw skin as white as that,' one of the old men said, adding, 'You must be one of that tribe that loves the black men.'

Livingstone gladly agreed, and was much gratified that Mpende let his party travel on without further interruption. So they passed safely through Tete and, having missed the Kebrabasa rapids by cutting across a loop in the Zambezi, he arrived at Quelimane on 20 May 1856, the first European to have crossed the African continent from coast to coast.

Livingstone found that the Portuguese in these parts treated the Africans far less well than they did on the west coast. 'Slavery and immorality have done their work,' he commented. 'Nowhere else does the European name stand at so low an ebb ... Here I did not notice the honourable regard for offspring which I noticed in Angola. The son of a late governor of Tete was pointed out to me in the condition and habit of a slave.' Depressed by these observations, by yet another severe attack of fever and by a letter from the London Missionary Society which implied that, while his journeys were, indeed, remarkable, exploration was not the real province of a missionary, Livingstone was also worried that the Portuguese might have been deterred from making use of the Zambezi as a commercial waterway by the difficulties of passage. For the moment, however, ignorant of the Kebrabasa rapids, he was to insist that the Portuguese could have made profitable use of the Zambezi had their faults of character not prevented them. This was the proposition he was to advance in England.

On his arrival in England in December 1856 he found that he had become a widely celebrated and universally popular figure. There could be no question of a quiet rest for a man who had, in Sir Roderick Murchison's words, achieved 'the greatest triumph in geographical research ... in our times'. There were speeches to be made, honours to be received, interviews to be granted, a royal summons to obey. There was also an account of his travels to be written, and he discovered this to be quite as much of an ordeal for him as speaking in public. He used to say, when he had finished it, that he would much rather cross Africa again than write another book. He was not, however, altogether averse to publicity. He protested that the extravagance of his reception embarrassed him, but whenever he appeared in public he was immediately recognized by the unusual peaked cap he always wore. He undertook so many engagements that he could not find time to see much of his family.

To Africa his thoughts constantly returned. He was convinced that his work there was far from complete, though he was not yet sure how that work should be continued. He resigned from the London Missionary Society which had tactlessly indicated their disapproval of his long journeys as being 'only remotely connected with the spread of the gospel', but he still considered himself a missionary. In a speech at Cambridge University which was largely instrumental in establishing the Universities Mission for Christian Work in Africa, he spoke again of opening up 'a path to Commerce and Christianity'. With this end in view he sailed back to Africa on 10 March 1858.

Appointed Her Majesty's Consul for the East Coast of Africa, Livingstone was instructed by the Government to 'extend the knowledge already attained of the geography and mineral and agricultural resources of Eastern and Central Africa' and to 'improve our acquaintance with the inhabitants' who were to be treated with kindness, given instruction in agriculture and 'the more simple arts', set an example of consistent moral conduct and taught Christianity 'as far as they are capable of receiving it'. Although he would have preferred to pursue these objects alone and in his own way, Livingstone was provided with six British assistants, including his younger brother, Charles, who was to act as photographer and secretary. His other assistants were Dr John Kirk, an industrious young Scottish botanist and physician; Commander N. B. Beding-field, a talented and cantankerous officer who had twice been court-martialled; Thomas Baines, the likeable and talented artist and store-keeper; Richard Thornton, a geologist; and George Rae, an engineer. Livingstone was also provided with adequate funds and a small steam-launch which, taken out in sections and reassembled on arrival, was to be used in the exploration of the Zambezi, its mouth and tributaries. But from the beginning the mission was dogged by disagreements and difficulties. Although unusually patient in the past with Africans, Livingstone was never an easy man for others to work for. At once demanding and highly sensitive to criticism, he not only expected more from men than they were able to give but also declined to discuss with his subordinates the formulation of his plans. He would remain silent for days on end, harbouring grievances to which he would suddenly and unexpectedly give vent. Baines was blamed for mistakes which he did not consider his fault and was eventually forbidden by Livingstone to have his meals with the rest of the party. Both he and Thornton thoroughly disliked the priggish, complain-ing and censorious Charles Livingstone whom even his brother eventually decided was 'useless'. Charles Livingstone wholeheartedly returned the dislike of his companions, denigrated Baines for being stupid, lax in his morals and for drinking too much, and attacked Thornton for his disrespectful attitude towards religion and for sneering at Scotsmen. David Livingstone decided that Thornton was quite as untrustworthy as Baines, accused him of being 'insufferably lazy' and finally dismissed him. Kirk found Dr Livingstone's morose moods intolerable. 'He knows how to come round niggers very well,' Kirk wrote in his journal, 'but if his digestive system don't go all right, he loses his diplomatic power wonderfully.' Having heard so much about Livingstone's patience, Kirk was astonished to see him lose his temper with his men more than once and to be advised to break their necks if they did not do as they were told. A missionary was later equally astounded to hear him shouting angrily at his crew and calling them 'useless trash'. Livingstone's relationship with Commander Bedingfield was particularly strained and, after heated quarrels, Bedingfield resigned and left.

Personal disagreements were exacerbated by practical problems. The steam launch was called the *Ma-Robert* in honour of Mrs Livingstone who was so known to the Africans in accordance with their custom of referring to mothers by the name of their first-born sons. But it was more commonly known as 'The Asthmatic' because of the laborious puffing noises it made when, consuming 'a frightful amount of wood', it chugged upstream, easily overtaken by all but the most heavily laden canoes.

Disappointed in his craft, Livingstone was even more frustrated by the Kebrabasa rapids which appeared to constitute an insuperable barrier to the navigation of the Zambezi. He had set so much store by the conviction that the river would be navigable – and would both enable Christian missions to be supported in the healthy uplands of its upper reaches and a fair and honest trade to be established in place of the slave trade – that he refused at first to face the reality that it was not. He obstinately returned time after time to the rapids in his determination to find a way through, exhausting his white companions and the Makololo bearers alike.

Livingstone was equally frustrated by the Shire, a northern tributary of the Zambezi. He had been warned that the river was impenetrable because of duckweed; but he found this less of a problem than the hostile natives who threatened the steamer with their poisoned arrows, and by a magnificent yet impassable cataract to which Livingstone gave the name Murchison Rapids after Sir Roderick Murchison. Deeming it imprudent to risk a land journey beyond these rapids while the natives were so unfriendly and the weather so unfavourable, Livingstone sent presents to the chiefs and returned to Tete, the panting and puffing *Ma-Robert* pursued by crocodiles which evidently mistook it for some huge animal.

In the middle of March a second attempt was made upon the Shire. The natives on this occasion appeared less antagonistic, readily selling rice and fowls; but at night the intimidating sound of drums could be heard from the villages and the travellers were, as Livingstone recorded, 'in constant expectation of attack'. 'Our perseverance, however, was rewarded on 18th April,' he added, 'when we discovered Lake Shirwa, a body of bitter water containing leeches, fishes, crocodiles and hippopotami.' He estimated the extent of the lake as being no more than about seventy miles by twenty; but he was told that there was a far larger lake further north separated from Lake Shirwa only by a tongue of land, a lake about which Livingstone had been told by a Portuguese trader from Tete, Candido José da Costa Cardoso, who had reached it some years before. And it was in search of this great lake that Livingstone and his brother, John Kirk and the expedition's engineer, George Rae, set out in August 1859, accompanied by thirty-six Makololo armed with muskets, a precaution, so Livingstone explained, 'which gave us influence rather than strength, as most of the men had never drawn a trigger and, in any conflict, would have been more dangerous to us than to the enemy'.

The precaution was not, however, necessary. The people of the upper Shire valley, the Makanga, turned out to be a friendly, industrious race, working hard in the fields and digging iron ore out of the hills for making spears, axes, needles, arrow-heads and the numerous ornaments with which they adorned their faces and bodies. These people placed no difficulties in the way of the explorers' passage through their country to the vast lake, Lake Nyasa (now the Malawi), which they discovered a little before noon on 16 September 1859. They did not remain here long for Livingstone, in a sour mood, having found that the area was not only being convulsed by slave raids but also by tribal wars, was anxious to get back to the men they had left in the steamer. So they returned almost immediately, declining to purchase several little children offered them for sale by a party of villainous-looking Arab traders, and left the exploration of the lake to another year.

In the meantime Livingstone took the opportunity to escort the Makololo – who had been his faithful companions in 1856 and had been left at Tete when he sailed for England – back home to their own country. Several of them were not at all willing to leave as they were living with slave-women by whom they had had children; and, although most eventually agreed to return with Livingstone, two or three left the party every night and by the time they had reached the Kebrabasa hills another had run back to Tete. With the remainder Livingstone reached Sesheke where he found his friend, Sekelutu, suffering from leprosy and living in gloomy seclusion in a covered wagon enclosed by a high wall of close-set reeds. Believing himself to be bewitched, he had had a number of his chief men and their families put to death. Other leading families had fled to distant tribes with whom they were living in exile. The great empire which Sekelutu had inherited from his father, Sebituane, was consequently crumbling to pieces, and Sekelutu was dying with it. Livingstone and Kirk did what they could for him; but he did not long survive their departure on 17 September 1860 and, with his death, his empire disintegrated.

Soon after Livingstone's return to Tete a new ship, the *Pioneer*, arrived from England to replace the *Ma-Robert*. This was shortly followed by the arrival of six missionaries sent out by the Universities Mission under Charles Mackenzie, a cheerful, outgoing Scottish bishop of thirty-five whom Kirk pronounced 'a trump of a fellow'. Mackenzie had thought of taking his mission up the Shire and establishing it at Chibisa; but Livingstone, who by now knew only too well the difficulties of the Shire, suggested that the bishop would be better advised to sail in the *Pioneer* up the Rovuma and to found the mission near Lake Nyasa. To this Mackenzie agreed. Yet Livingstone's hopes of discovering in the Rovuma that waterway into the interior which neither the Zambezi nor the Shire could provide were not to be realized. He and Mackenzie were able to ascend no more than thirty miles up the Rovuma whose waters were rapidly falling as the rainy season ceased. They had, therefore, to return to the Shire after all. The *Pioneer* drew too much water for the Shire, however, and it was only with extreme difficulty that they managed to reach Chibisa. Here their troubles increased, for the Makanga people were being attacked by the Ajawa, a tribe employed by the Portuguese and Arabs to capture slaves.

While exploring the country for a suitable mission site, Livingstone's party came upon a long line of manacled men, women and children under the command of black drivers who, they later learned, had shot two women for trying to untie their thongs, knocked out the brains of a baby whose weight prevented its mother carrying her load, and dispatched with an axe a man who had collapsed with fatigue. At Livingstone's approach the black drivers, who had been marching jauntily along as though triumphantly leading captives of war, fled headlong into the forest. The captives were freed, the ropes cut off the women and children, and the men released from the long sticks which were fastened with an iron clasp round their throats.

This humane action almost led to war with the Ajawa warriors who, provoked by the boasts of the Makanga that they now had powerful forces on their side, closed upon the missionaries 'in bloodthirsty fury. Some came within fifty yards, dancing hideously'. Others quite surrounded the white men who 'were obliged, in self-defence, to return their fire and drive them off. When they saw the range of the rifles they very soon desisted and ran away.' After this the missionaries were in constant trouble with the Ajawa and became involved in the tribal wars of the area, much to the dismay of Livingstone who, worried by the effect that this would have upon his own reputation, wrote in his journal, 'People will not approve of men coming out to convert people shooting them. I am sorry that I am mixed up with it, as they will not care what view of my character is given at home.' He did not have cause to worry for long, however: on 31 January 1862 Mackenzie died of fever and soon afterwards the mission withdrew to Zanzibar.

Before Mackenzie's death, Livingstone, his brother and Dr Kirk began their exploration of Lake Nyasa, paying the local people with lengths of cloth to carry their boat, a light, four-oared gig, across the Murchison Rapids. Then, on 2 September 1861, they sailed into the enormous lake, the second largest in Africa. Refreshed by the sudden coolness of the air as they rounded the 'grand mountainous promontory', they named it Cape Maclear after the astronomer at the Cape. Soon they were being borne swiftly across the dark blue waters which were full of fish, most of them unknown to the explorers, and of crocodiles which, having so much else to eat, rarely attacked the native fishermen. Above the surface of the water 'countless millions of minute midges' were collected by night and boiled into dark thick cakes, tasting 'not unlike caviare or salted locusts'.

Around the lake there was an 'almost unbroken chain of villages'. Never before in Africa had Livingstone seen so dense a mass of people. 'On the beach of wellnigh every little sandy bay, dark crowds were standing gazing at the novel sight of a boat under sail.' And whenever the explorers landed they were immediately surrounded 'in a few seconds by hundreds of men, women and children, who hastened to stare at the *chirombo* [wild animals]', yet who politely remained beyond the line which was drawn in the sand to indicate a boundary which they must not cross.

Having spent nearly two months touring the lake, Livingstone and his companions sailed back into the Shire and, returning to the *Pioneer*, steamed back down the Zambesi to the coast. Here, on 30 January 1862, H.M.S. *Gorgon* arrived, towing the sections of a new iron steamer, the *Lady Nyasa*, which had been built for navigation on Lake Nyasa with some of the large profits of Livingstone's *Missionary Travels*. With the *Lady Nyasa* came a brig which had brought out Mrs Livingstone and various ladies for the Universities Mission. One of the ladies was Jessie Lennox who later became a nurse under Florence Nightingale and lived to an even greater age than Miss Nightingale herself. Mary Livingstone, however, who had taken to drink and had become in Kirk's opinion a 'coarse vulgar woman', was not so sturdy. Soon after her arrival she fell ill with fever and died at the end of April.

Her death, coming so soon after that of Bishop Mackenzie, overwhelmed Livingstone with remorse. And, as though to overcome his grief in ceaseless activity, he threw himself back into his work with renewed vigour, driving his men as hard as he drove himself until Kirk decided that he was 'out of his mind', a 'most unsafe leader' to whom it was quite 'useless making any remark'. 'The officers are all but in rebellion,' concluded an assistant of Bishop Mackenzie who had not yet gone to Zanzibar, 'and the Doctor daily becomes more incapable of self control. A catastrophe, or tragedy, I fear is not far off.'

One disaster now followed another. A further attempt upon the Rovuma proved after 160 miles that it was not navigable in its higher reaches; another voyage up the Shire in the *Lady Nyasa* provided only too painful proof that the slave trade was as rife as ever: the villages on the banks stood silent and deserted with skeletons lying beside the paths, and the 'ghastly living forms of boys and girls with dull, dead eyes crouching beside some of the huts'. Dead bodies floating past the steamer were fought over by crocodiles and in the morning the paddles had to be cleared of mangled corpses. A diet of salt provisions and preserved meats further depressed the spirits of the party and brought on attacks of dysentery from which the Livingstones and Dr Kirk all suffered severely. Thornton died in April, having made an exhausting journey to Tete to buy goats and sheep to replenish the dwindling stocks of the mission's food; and Livingstone condemned him as a fool for having done so: 'folly killed him'. Soon after Thornton's death both Charles Livingstone and Kirk sought permission to go home. Livingstone was only too thankful to be rid of them. All his assistants had been 'a complete nuisance'. When Kirk left without a word of thanks for all his help over many years he decided that Dr Livingstone was 'about as ungrateful and slippery a mortal' as he had ever come into contact with ... 'one of those sanguine enthusiasts wrapped up in their own schemes whose reason and better judgement is blinded by headstrong passion'.

In July 1863 a dispatch was received from Lord Russell ordering the expedition home. A year later Livingstone arrived in England having unsuccessfully tried to sell the *Lady Nyasa* first in Zanzibar and then in Bombay. To the public he was still a hero. But the Government were dissatisfied with the results of his mission. Lord Russell received him without warmth; and Prince Albert, a cousin of King Pedro of Portugal, expressed his displeasure at the blunt condemnation of the Portuguese connection with the slave trade which Livingstone made in a speech to the British Association in Bath.

Livingstone was thankful to escape to Newstead Abbey, once Byron's home and now that of a rich big-game hunter whom he had met in Bechuanaland, and here he settled down to write an account of his recent adventures. As he wrote, so he confessed, he felt increasingly ill-at-ease in England, aware of the lure of Africa. And so, when the Royal Geographical Society proposed that he should return to explore the sources of the great African rivers, to solve the problem of the Nile basin and to investigate the relation between Lakes Nyasa and Tanganyika, he prepared to leave Britain once again without regret.

He had already come to the conclusion that both Burton and Speke were wrong about the Nile. Naturally predisposed to dislike Burton, 'a beastly fellow' and 'moral idiot' whose 'bestial immorality' and disgraceful conduct in Africa could not 'be spoken of without disgust', he was not much better disposed towards Speke whom he came to consider 'a poor misguided thing' of 'slender mental abilities'. While, as for Grant, he was a mere cypher who had managed to get a 'good wife, £2,000 a year and a London house' because of the association of his name with the Nile sources which, in fact, he 'never saw'.

The more he considered the matter the more firmly Livingstone became convinced that neither Burton, Speke nor Baker had seen the Nile sources either. He declined to believe that the great river began in Lake Victoria – as Speke was right in claiming – and then flowed into and out of Lake Albert – as Baker had discovered – but he became obsessed with the idea that it originated much further south, probably in Lake Bangweulu from which, as he hoped to show, it flowed north through Lake Mweru into Lake Tanganyika and thence north again into Lake Albert. Anxious as he was to establish this, however, Livingstone did not want to return to Africa simply as an explorer, nor could he afford to do so on the £500 which was all that the Royal Geographical Society were prepared to allow him. But once it had been agreed that he would also report upon the 'enormous evil' of the slave trade in the area of these lakes, and a further £1,000 had been promised by James Young, the industrial chemist, Livingstone was prepared to go to Africa for the last time.

He went by way of Bombay where he sold the *Lady Nyasa* which had cost £6,000 for £2,300, investing the money in shares in an Indian bank that failed soon afterwards. While in India he employed some freed Negro slaves from a government school at Nasik as bearers, and thirteen sepoys to look after the animals. To these he later added ten men from Anjouan (then called Johanna) Island in the Comoros and four or five servants who had been with him on previous expeditions, including Chuma, a freed slave, and Susi, a faithful Yao servant, who were to remain with him to the end. He also bought six camels, three buffaloes and a calf, two mules and four donkeys; and, taking with him letters of recommendation from the Sultan of Zanzibar, he began yet another exploration of the Rovuma River on 9 March 1866. It was a miserable journey during which Livingstone was to show that he could no longer exercise his former mastery over his servants. The sepoys were lazy, incompetent and 'made themselves utterly useless', ill-treating the animals which were also attacked by the tsetse fly; the Somali guide was unreliable; the jungle was so dense that it could be penetrated only by laborious cutting of the bush, and the going was consequently very slow. The 'steaming, smothery air' and 'dank, rank, luxurious vegetation' made Livingstone feel as though he were struggling for his very existence. Everywhere there were distressing indications of a still flourishing slave trade, heaps of human bones and wooden collars, dead bodies tied by their necks to trees as punishment inflicted upon them by the Arab dealers for their inability to keep up with the rest of the caravan. As day followed exhausting day Livingstone was forced to acknowledge that the Rovuma was not the waterway to the interior that he had determined against all odds to prove it.

Having paid off the sepoys, whose behaviour had become insupportable, Livingstone reached Lake Nyasa on 8 August. Soon afterwards he was deserted by the Johanna men who, abandoning their loads on the ground, returned to Zanzibar to spread a story, which was widely believed, that Livingstone and the rest of the party had been murdered. By the time he had crossed the Kirk Mountains, which he named in honour of his erstwhile friend with whom he had become reconciled in England, and had come down to the Loangwa River in the middle of December, only a few of the Nasik men and the two servants, Chuma and Susi, remained with him. The countryside was delightful, but Livingstone was now ill and weak. The rain poured down, and food was hard to find. He was obliged to take in his belt three holes. By the end of January 1867 he and all his party were suffering from 'real biting hunger and faintness'. By the middle of February he had contracted rheumatic fever, for which there were no medicines since the bearer carrying them had run off. 'Every step jars on the chest,' he recorded in his journal, 'and I am very weak. I can hardly keep up with the march, though formerly I was always first.' He struggled on, crossing the Chambezi river which flows into Lake Bangweulu, and made his slow way through 'dripping forests and oozing bogs' into Chitapangwa, the town of the chief of the Ba-bemba. Here, by means of a party of Swahili slave traders, he sent letters to Zanzibar, asking for stores and medicines to be sent to him at Ujiji.

At Chitapangwa he rested for three weeks, then resuming his journey through lovely country which his long-continued fever ill-disposed him to enjoy, he came within sight of Lake Tanganyika, an expanse of blue water of 'surpassing loveliness'. But by now he was so ill that he could go no further. One day he had 'a fit of insensibility' and found himself floundering outside his hut unable to get in. He tried to raise himself up by means of the posts at the entrance, lost hold of them and fell heavily on his head on a box. His servants hung a blanket over the entrance so that no strangers should see his pitiable state.

He longed to reach Ujiji where he could dose himself with medicines, but the peoples of the intervening lands were at war and he was advised that it would be impossible to cross them. So he was obliged to wait for three months until the war was over. Then, on 22 September, he set out for Lake Mweru with a caravan of Arab slave merchants whose company he naturally did not relish but whose leader, a skilful practitioner of Arab medicine, was of great service to him in his ever-deteriorating state of health.

On 8 November 1867 he came to Lake Mweru near which the Portuguese explorer, Francisco José de Lacerda, had died in 1799, and then turned south to find the nearby Lake Bangweulu. Between the two lakes were the territories of Casembe, an evil-looking, squint-eyed tyrant, the gateway to whose house was ornamented with human skulls. His entourage included an executioner with a broadsword for cutting off the heads of subjects who had displeased Casembe and, at his neck, 'a curious scissor-like instrument' for cropping their ears. On Livingstone remarking that the executioner's was 'nasty work' – and it seemed to have been frequently employed – the chief merely smiled, as did many of his companions who 'were not sure of their own ears for a moment'.

Casembe raised no positive objections to Livingstone's proceeding to Bangweulu; but the Arabs, reluctant to allow strangers into one of their most profitable trading areas, did their best to dissuade him and induced the remaining Nasik men, long since weary of their wanderings, to refuse to accompany him. Undeterred by their desertion, by the Arabs' objections, by depleted stores, by the frailty of his health, and by the prospect of having to wade through floods and black tenacious mud, Livingstone continued his journey. Passing on the way a gang of slaves who explained their cheerful songs by telling him that they were rejoicing at the thought of coming back after death to haunt and kill those who had sold them into captivity, he was rewarded on 18 July by seeing the shores of Lake Bangweulu for the first time. From this lake the river Luapula flowed north into Lake Mweru, and out of Mweru flowed the Lualaba which, Livingstone felt sure, was the Nile. He comforted himself with the delusion that he had at last solved the great river's mystery.

He did not remain at Bangweulu long. Concerned that the Arabs might leave for Ujiji without him, he began his return journey to them at the end of the month after the briefest exploration of the lake. But, delayed by another war, it was not until the end of October that he rejoined the Arabs; and not until 11 December that he set out with them and their strings of slaves, yoked together and burdened with provisions, copper and ivory.

On the march Livingstone became seriously ill again. He contracted pneumonia of the right lung. He could scarcely speak and suffered great distress in coughing, his feet were swollen and sore, and he began to suffer from hallucinations, seeing figures and the faces of men in the bark of trees. When at last he reached Ujiji on 14 March 1869 he discovered that the stores sent for him had been plundered and the medicines had not arrived.

Ujiji was a hateful place frequented by the worst kind of slave dealer, 'the vilest of the vile', to whom slaving was not so much a trade as 'a system of consecutive murders'. And he was only too thankful to escape when, having written forty-two letters – only one of which reached the coast – the Arab traders with whom he had travelled from Casembe's offered to escort him across the country of the Manyuema towards the Lualaba river. He was reluctant to travel with such companions again; but the Manyuema were a savage people, reputed to be cannibals, whose practice it was to place a parrot's tail on the ground and challenge those near to pick it up and stick it in their hair, an act which placed upon them an obligation to kill a man or a woman. It would be dangerous to travel through their territories without protection. Besides, Livingstone still had no medicines and the Arabs were skilful doctors. So, suppressing his distaste for their company, he left with them for the 'surpassingly beautiful' land of the Manyuema whom he found quite as bloodthirsty as he had been led to expect. They were not, however, unduly aggressive towards strangers. Although they inspected Livingstone with such rough and unrestrained curiosity that he felt like a wild beast in a cage, he came to no harm at their hands. Yet, during the next unhappy year, he often felt that death was close. He was frequently ill with fever or the symptoms of cholera, while ulcers on his feet compelled him to spend long periods taking shelter from the heavy rains. For over six months he was to remain at Bambarre, halfway between Lake Tanganyika and the Lualaba. Here he read the whole Bible four times and had to satisfy the curiosity of the natives by eating in a roped-off enclosure where the astonished onlookers watched him as he wrote in his journal and occasionally washed his hair, explaining awesomely to each other, as the lather rose between his fingers, that this was the way in which white men cleaned their brains. Most of his servants became mutinous during this long wait, and he was unable to control them. Eventually all of them, apart from the loyal Susi and Chuma and one other, a Nasik boy whom he called Gardner, deserted him. The prayers he wrote at this time in his journal seem almost to be cries of despair; and once, though he had previously always regarded himself as 'the channel of the Divine Power', he recorded his doubt that God looked with favour on his mission after all.

At last in March 1871 he came down to the banks of the Lualaba River at Nyangwe, but after weeks of waiting, of patient negotiations, of promises received and broken, he was unable to persuade the distrustful natives to bring him canoes in which to cross it. His despair deepened. 'I am distressed and perplexed,' he wrote on 14 July. 'All seems against me.' One day in the market he came upon a man with ten human jawbones hung by a string over his shoulder. 'He claimed to have killed and eaten the owners and showed with his knife how he had cut up his victims.' Livingstone expressed his disgust, at which the man and his companions all laughed. Some weeks later a petty quarrel between Swahili merchants and natives provoked a fight which developed into a massacre. Some four hundred people were slaughtered in the marketplace or in the river into which they had jumped for safety. 'As I write,' Livingstone recorded, 'I hear loud wails over those who were slain ... The chief perpetrators continued to fire on the people and fire on their villages ... I counted seventeen villages in flames ... It gave me the impression of being in hell ... I tried to go down the Lualaba, then up it and west, but with blood-hounds it is out of the question ... I see nothing but to go back to Ujiji.'

On the way he was ambushed by the Manyuema. A large spear was hurled at him and almost grazed his back before plunging into the earth beyond him. Another spear followed it, missing him almost as narrowly. 'Guns were fired into the dense mass of forest,' he wrote, 'but with no effect, for nothing could be seen, but we heard men jeering and denouncing us close by. Two of our party were slain. Coming to a part of the forest cleared for cultivation, I noticed a gigantic tree, made higher still by growing on an ant-hill, twenty feet high. It had fire applied near its roots, and I heard a crack that told the fire had done its work, but felt no alarm till I saw it come straight for me. I ran a few paces back, and down it came to the ground one yard behind me, and breaking into several lengths, covered me with a cloud of dust. Three times in one day was I delivered from impending death.'

'Reduced to a skeleton', as he put it himself, Livingstone arrived back in Ujiji on 23 October 1871. He had hoped to recover his strength here with the help of the stores which had been sent for him; but soon after his arrival he was told that they had all been sold off by the leading Arab of the place, a 'moral idiot', as Livingstone called him, who came to shake hands with him and who, when his greeting was spurned, 'assumed an air of displeasure at having been badly treated'.

Livingstone's spirits now sank to 'their lowest ebb' and he 'felt miserable' as he realized he would have to 'wait in beggary' for help to reach him. But help was already closer at hand than he knew. A day's march away a caravan was approaching through the forest. At its head fluttered the stars and stripes of the American flag.

12

'FIND LIVINGSTONE'

H. M. STANLEY · HIS ADVENTUROUS LIFE ·
ARRIVAL IN ZANZIBAR · SETS OUT FOR THE INTERIOR,
FEBRUARY 1871 · HIS RUTHLESS METHODS · HIS ENCOUNTER
WITH LIVINGSTONE · THEIR FRIENDSHIP · THEY EXPLORE
LAKE TANGANYIKA TOGETHER · LIVINGSTONE RETURNS TO
THE INTERIOR WHILE STANLEY SAILS FOR LONDON ·
LIVINGSTONE'S LAST WANDERINGS · HIS DEATH

Stanley's instructions to find Livingstone had been given to him over two years before in the Grand Hotel in Paris in a conversation with James Gordon Bennett, the son of the publisher of the *New York Herald*.

'Go and find him wherever you may hear that he is, and get what news you can of him,' Bennett had said. 'And perhaps the old man may be in want; take enough with you to help him should he require it. Of course, you will act according to your own plans, and do what you think best – *but find Livingstone!*'

'Have you considered seriously the great expense you are likely to incur on account of this little journey?'

'What will it cost?'

'Burton and Speke's journey to Central Africa cost between £3,000 and £5,000 and I fear it cannot be done under £2,500.'

'Well, I will tell you what you will do. Draw £1,000 now; and when you have gone through that, draw another £1,000, and when you have finished that draw another; and so on; but find Livingstone.'

Stanley, a short, thickset man of twenty-seven with abundant dark hair and a big black moustache, had recently returned from Spain where he had been reporting the rebellion for the *Herald*. He had already led an extremely adventurous life. The illegitimate son of a Welshwoman who had gone to live in London after his birth, he had been sent to the St Asaph Union Workhouse where, after years of ill-treatment by a bullying schoolmaster, a former miner who had lost a hand in an accident, Stanley had lashed out at him in furious retaliation, kicked him over a bench and belaboured him with his own birch before running away. He had subsequently found employment as a pupil-teacher in a Welsh village school, then as a shop assistant in Liverpool and finally as a butcher's errand boy before sailing to America as a deck-hand aboard a packet bound for New Orleans. Jumping ship on arrival, he had found employment with a kindly merchant, Henry Morton Stanley, who treated him as his son and gave him his name. Under the merchant's tutelage, the young H. M. Stanley began to dress and talk less roughly, to eat in a more mannerly way, to fill the gaps in a haphazard education and to display a remarkable memory for facts and figures. He still tended to be touchy and socially ill-at-ease, as those who have been denied early love are inclined to be; but he began to lose his uncouthness and to develop a character at once forceful and attractive. When the Civil War came he enlisted as a private in the Confederate Army, was taken prisoner and, persuaded of the errors of its cause, enrolled in the Union artillery. Discharged from that, he went to sea again, first on merchant ships, then in the United States Navy from which he deserted in January 1865. Soon afterwards he began to write stories for newspapers, and in 1867 was appointed to the staff of the *Missouri Democrat*. Having covered an expedition into Indian territory for the *Democrat*, he went out to report the war in Abyssinia for the *New York Herald*. It was thus that he met J. G. Bennett, the sponsor of his African journey.

It was fortunate that Bennett was rich, for on his arrival in Zanzibar with less than a hundred dollars in his pocket, Stanley had borrowed enough in his employer's name to equip one of the most lavishly supplied and well-armed caravans that had ever left the island along the Arab route to Tabora. He bought tens of thousands of beads, yard upon yard of cloth and wire, scores of weapons, including two dozen each of muskets, hatchets and long knives as well as daggers, axes, two carbines, four rifles and eight pistols; he also purchased twenty donkeys, two horses, two boats, and so much food, ammunition, medicine, tenting and clothing that his baggage was eventually to weigh six tons. The *pagazis* he hired to carry the numerous loads were eventually to number 157. In addition to these bearers there were 23 *askaris*, commanded by Sidi Bombay; five other black men; an Arab interpreter named Selim; a Scottish ship's mate, William Farquhar, whom Stanley had hired on a barque sailing from India to Mauritius; and John Shaw, an English sailor, who had been serving aboard an American ship. Later, Stanley was to acquire a little black slave boy, known as Kalulu, who was given to him by an Arab merchant and who served the expedition as servant and mascot. Neither of the white assistants was to prove much use: both were drunk at the time of their departure; Farquhar died soon afterwards of elephantiasis; Shaw, having shown far more interest in making love to native girls than in the search for Livingstone and having repeatedly urged Stanley to turn back, died of fever in Unyanyembe.

From the outset of his journey on 6 February 1871 Stanley was to realize how difficult an assignment he had undertaken. At Bagamoyo there was a fortnight's enforced delay while more *pagazis* were hired to carry the baggage of the first of the six caravans into which Stanley divided the expedition, having been warned that big, slow-moving parties invited attack. Then, as he crossed the humid savannah into Usagara, behind the fluttering American flag which was borne by his huge guide, Asmani, the temperature rose to almost 130°. The rains came; the rivers swelled and in places burst their banks; and many *pagazis* deserted, taking their loads with them. Stanley suffered the first of his recurrent bouts of fever. Sometimes he lost consciousness, and when he recovered he had to face the ordeal of bargaining with chiefs over *hongo*, learning by experience that it was a cardinal error to fly into a rage with them, for only by patient negotiation could a reasonable payment be agreed.

By the time he reached Tabora, after covering 212 miles in just over two months, he prided himself on having so soon become a seasoned African traveller. Certainly he was as imperious as he was decisive, already convinced that Livingstone's methods would not be his methods. 'Each man,' he wrote, 'has his own way'; and, in his opinion, Africa required 'mastering, as well as loving charity'. He did not hesitate to flog the 'lazily inclined' and even, later, to hang miscreants. Nor did he attempt to hide the fact that he had done so. He found ready explanations for the severity of his punishments, just as he found reasons for allowing his men to plunder the fields around villages which had been deserted at his approach. 'It seemed to me an excellent arrangement,' he wrote. 'It saved trouble of speech, exerted possibly in useless efforts for peace and tedious chatter.' When he found his westward route blocked by a rebel chief, Mirambo, who had threatened to destroy all caravans making for Ujiji, he joined forces with the Arabs of Tabora in making war upon him. And when the Arab's army was defeated by Mirambo, he decided to make a detour to the south, taking with him the few *pagazis* who had not fled in terror from the field of battle together with new men whom he had with great difficulty succeeded in hiring at Tabora. Several of these men soon deserted, but Stanley made it clear that he would not stand for such behaviour by taking pains to recapture them and then chaining the ringleaders together so that they could not escape again. At the beginning of October he made another convincing display of his authority by quelling an incipient mutiny. Some of his men were reluctant to depart from the rich grasslands for the desolate country beyond, and Stanley threatened to shoot the gigantic Asmani whom he had overheard grumbling that he ought never to have left Zanzibar.

Despite his domineering and confident manner Stanley, too, was beginning to regret that he had ever left home. 'I do not think I was made for an African explorer,' he wrote, 'for I detest the land most heartily.' By the end of the month it seemed likely that he would perish of hunger or thirst before he reached Lake Tanganyika, and one day he carved in the bark of a tree: 'Starving: H.M.S.' At the beginning of November, however, to his infinite relief and excitement, he was told by a caravan coming from Ujiji of an old white man who was living there. Ujiji was but a few days' march away now and Stanley urged his men on with promises of extra allowances of cloth. They tramped on bare-footed behind the American flag, Stanley himself now wearing a new flannel suit, brightly polished boots and a freshly chalked topee. Selim, the Arab interpreter, was the first to see the man they had travelled so far to find.

'I see the Doctor, Sir,' he said. 'Oh, what an old man! He has got a white beard.'

Stanley admitted that he had an almost uncontrollable urge to turn a somersault, slash a tree or bite his hand, but determined not to let his face betray his emotions 'lest it should detract from the dignity of a white man appearing under such extraordinary circumstances'. He behaved in a manner so self-consciously dignified as to become a classic example of bathos:

> I pushed back the crowds, and passing from the rear walked down a living avenue of people, till I came in front of the semicircle of Arabs, in front of which stood a white man ... As I advanced slowly towards him I noticed he was pale, looked weary, had a grey beard, wore a bluish cap with a faded gold band round it, and had on a red-sleeved waistcoat and a pair of grey tweed trousers. I would have run to him, only I was a coward in the presence of such a mob – would have embraced him, only, he being an Englishman, I did not know how he would receive me; so I did what cowardice and false pride suggested was the best thing – walked deliberately to him, took off my hat, and said:
> 'Dr Livingstone, I presume?'
> 'Yes,' said he, with a kind smile, lifting his cap slightly.

It was the beginning of an unlikely but unaffected friendship. Stanley, warned by John Kirk, now British Consul in Zanzibar, had expected to find a difficult, cantankerous, eccentric old man, impatient of outside interference and unwilling to talk of past discoveries or future plans. The Englishmen Stanley had met, particularly in the army in Abyssinia, had been only too ready to rebuff him, and he feared that this dour Scotsman would be even more off-handedly reserved. But, on the contrary, so Stanley said, Livingstone was friendly and open, as well as 'consistently noble, upright, pious and manly'. After longer acquaintance Stanley confided to his journal 'some intrusive, suspicious thoughts that he was not of such an angelic temper' as he had at first supposed him, that in reiterating complaints about people who had offended him in the past, he showed plainly how his 'strong nature was opposed to forgiveness'. He was, in particular, prepared to believe the worst of John Kirk, whom Stanley had disliked and whom Livingstone came to suspect of being anxious to gain the credit for solving the problem of the Nile sources himself. Yet, the reservations Stanley felt about Livingstone did not undermine the fondness and regard he had for him. Nor were the hyperbolic encomia he lavished upon the heroic figure, whose fame would now ensure his own renown, written without justification. The pain and adversities of the past few years seemed to have purged Livingstone of much of his former vindictiveness and rancour. If scarcely a saint, he was surely now a man to be held in affectionate respect. And Stanley, so insecure behind his often blustering manner, cannot but have been deeply moved when Livingstone, whose own childhood had left ineradicable scars upon his nature, said to him warmly, 'You have brought me new life.'

He put aside the letters Stanley had brought for him and, inviting him to sit in his own chair, asked for 'general news', listening with interest to what his visitor had to tell him. And he seemed not at all put out when Stanley confessed that he had come to Ujiji not as the representative of a government or of a learned society but of a popular New York newspaper. Indeed, far from being annoyed, Livingstone, as he put it himself, was 'extremely grateful'. 'Mr Stanley,' he wrote in his journal, 'has done his part with untiring energy [and] good judgement, in the teeth of very serious obstacles.'

Livingstone immediately took to his tough young admirer. He willingly allowed him to accompany him on an exploratory trip to the northern shores of Lake Tanganyika where they established that the Rusizi did not flow out of the lake, as Burton had always liked to suppose, but into it. When Stanley suggested that the two men should return home together, that Livingstone should have a rest before continuing his exploration and that he should get himself some false teeth, Livingstone demurred. His work was not yet finished. He had become convinced that the Lualaba River was the Nile and he wanted to prove it before he died, before Kirk or someone else forestalled him. So, returning with Stanley to Tabora, he parted from him there and returned into the heart of Africa; while Stanley, who felt he had found and lost another father, went on towards Zanzibar.

On the way, Stanley met the Livingstone Search and Relief Expedition commanded by Lieutenant William Henn, R.N., who promptly resigned when he heard that Livingstone had already been found. W. Oswell Livingstone, the missionary's youngest son, who was with Lieutenant Henn, considered taking the supplies to his father. But, much to Dr Livingstone's distress at the lack of resolution of 'as poor a specimen of a son as Africa ever produced', this plan was abandoned, and the expedition disintegrated. Stanley sailed for Europe on 29 May 1872 to reap the rewards of his success.

Three months later Livingstone left Tabora in his misguided search for the sources of the Nile in those of the Lualaba. 'All your friends', he told himself, 'will wish you to make a complete work of the exploration of the Nile before you retire.' And to his daughter, Agnes, he wrote, 'To return unsuccessful [would mean] going abroad to an unhealthy consulate to which no public sympathy would ever be drawn.' She supported him: 'Much as I wish you to come home,' she told him, 'I would rather have you finish your work to your own satisfaction, than return merely to gratify me.'

But he was in no fit state to embark upon another demanding journey, and was soon suffering from dysentery and losing quantities of blood from haemorrhoids. Yet day after day he doggedly kept on. He managed to reach Lake Tanganyika and, crossing the Kalongosi river which flows into Lake Mweru, to climb the high mountains beyond. He then descended into the country north of Lake Bangweulu, and crossing the Chambezi, explored the swampy shores of the lake where swarms of mosquitoes, stinging ants and poisonous spiders tormented his every step. He was growing weaker day by day. 'I am pale and weak from bleeding profusely ever since 31st March,' he wrote in his journal on 10 April 1873. 'Oh, how I long to be permitted by the Over Power to finish my work.' Occasionally he felt that he might not be near the upper Nile at all, but – as, indeed he was – wandering beside the Congo. Yet he was resolved never to give in, so long as his strength held out. 'Nothing earthly will make me give up my work in despair,' he wrote. 'I encourage myself in the Lord my God, and go forward.'

His strength, however, failed him. By 22 April, in great pain and suffering from violent dysentery, he was being carried in a litter. Five days later he made the last entry in his notebook. On the night of the 30th he asked Susi how many days they still had to travel before reaching the Luapula and when told about three he sighed and murmured, 'Oh dear, dear.' At about midnight he sent again for Susi who helped him take a dose of calomel. 'All right,' he said when he had with difficulty swallowed it, 'you can go now.'

During the night a boy, who had been left to sleep by the door of the hut, looked inside and saw his master kneeling by the bed as though in prayer. He was in the same posture in the morning, his head buried in his hands upon the pillow. He was dead.

His servants allowed the body to dry in the sun for a fortnight. Then, having buried the heart and viscera, they embalmed it and, wrapping it in sailcloth and enclosing it in a cylinder of bark, they lashed it to a pole and began the long journey to the coast. Five months later they carried it into Tabora and there they met another Livingstone Relief Party commanded by a naval officer, Verney Lovett Cameron.

13

ACROSS THE CONTINENT

V. L. CAMERON · HE VOLUNTEERS TO GO OUT TO AFRICA IN
SEARCH OF LIVINGSTONE · HE HEARS OF LIVINGSTONE'S
DEATH BUT DETERMINES TO 'FOLLOW UP THE DOCTOR'S
EXPLORATIONS' · HIS COMPANION COMMITS SUICIDE ·
CAMERON SETS OUT ALONE FOR LAKE TANGANYIKA ·
CROSSES THE LANDS OF THE MANYUEMA AND ARRIVES AT
NYANGWE, AUGUST 1874 · MEETS TIPPU TIB AND JOSÉ
ANTONIO ALVEZ · CUSTOMS OF THE WARUA · WITCH
DOCTORS · KING KASONGO · WITH A SLAVE CARAVAN ·
CAMERON ARRIVES AT KAGNOMBÉ'S · THE MOUNTAINS OF
BAILUNDA · CAMERON CONTRACTS SCURVY BUT REACHES
THE COAST · SAILS HOME TO ENGLAND, MARCH 1876

Three years before, Cameron, a clergyman's son who had served in the Abyssinian campaign of 1868 and on the east coast of Africa in the suppression of the slave trade, had been languishing on the steam reserve at Sheerness, wasting what he considered to be his not inconsiderable talents. He was brave, persevering and industrious, a good writer, an excellent linguist and – though some thought him opinionated – enlightened and unselfish. His experiences in Africa, where he had witnessed the suffering on board the slave dhows, had already awoken in him 'a strong desire to take some further part in the suppression of the inhuman traffic', and had convinced him that it could only be abolished by attacking it at its source in the interior of the continent. Burton's adventures had excited his 'aspirations for travel and discovery', and he had become 'still more anxious to undertake some exploration in Africa on hearing that Arab merchants from Zanzibar had reached the West Coast', for he was convinced that 'what had been accomplished by an Arab trader was equally possible to an English naval officer'.

He had accordingly volunteered to go out in search of Dr Livingstone. The Royal Geographical Society having made other arrangements, however, it was not until 1872 that his offer was accepted and he was commissioned to lead

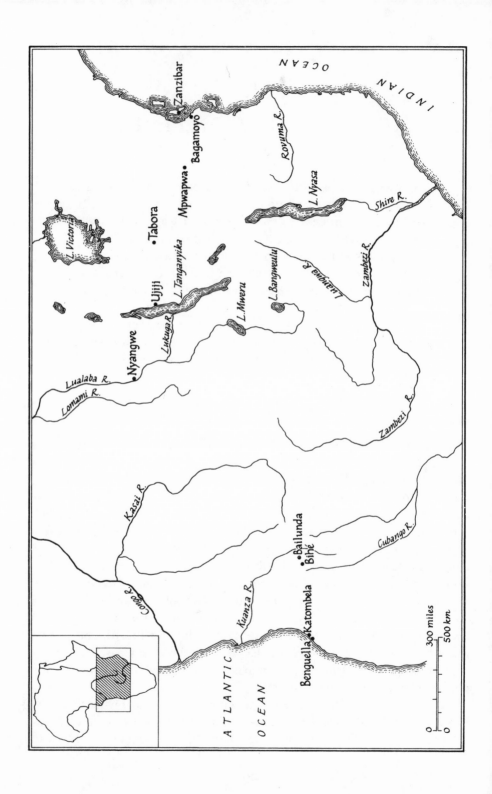

an expedition to find Livingstone and then to undertake some exploration of his own with the help of Livingstone's advice. One of his closest friends, a naval surgeon, W. E. Dillon, was appointed to accompany him; and Cecil Murphy, a lieutenant in the Royal Artillery, subsequently also joined the expedition. At Zanzibar the services of the experienced Sidi Bombay were secured, and with his help donkeys were bought and men were hired as drivers, servants, *pagazis* and *askaris*, the soldiers being smartly uniformed in red patrol jackets, red fezzes, white shirts and cummerbunds. The smartness of their appearance was unfortunately belied by their behaviour. Bombay had not troubled himself to find good men, picking up whatever riff-raff he came across in the bazaar. Before long, several of them had deserted and most of the rest had proved lazy and recalcitrant. The bearers were equally tiresome, quarrelling with each other over the loads, shirking the heavy ones and struggling to possess those which contained the tents and which entitled the men who carried them to the more dignified places at the front of the caravan. To add to their difficulties, Cameron, Dillon and Murphy all fell ill with fever, as, later, did Robert Moffat, Dr Livingstone's nephew who, learning of the expedition, had sold his sugar plantation at Natal and, hastening to join the expedition, had died soon afterwards. There were extortionate chiefs to bribe with *hongo*, the amount of which could often not be determined for some time – occasionally for days on end – because the headmen were too drunk to consider the matter. There were further delays when chiefs insisted on inspecting the contents of the porters' bags, examining minutely every novelty, or when they required the caravan to wait for two or three days for the benefit of their people who had never yet seen a white man. There were difficulties in obtaining provisions which Bombay urged should always be bought in advance because, as he said, sometimes without justification, the country was 'very hungry in front'. The country was certainly difficult to traverse. The route lay through Rahenneko, Mpwapwa, Ugogo, Kanyenye, the Mgunda Mkali and Tabora; over rivers swollen by the heavy rains; across bridges of fallen trees; through the clayey mud of the dreaded Makata swamp and the country of the Wagogo. These people pierced and enlarged the lobes of their ears to such a monstrous extent that they could wear not only huge rings and pieces of wood in them, but also snuff boxes. They worked their hair up with copper wire from their otherwise shaven scalps into stiff prongs decorated with brass bells and beads, and anointed their bodies with red earth and rancid ghee.

By the time he reached Unyanyembe, Cameron was seriously ill. In a letter written on 23 August 1873 Dillon recorded that his friend, delirious with fever, was complaining that he had been blocked inside his hut with drawing-room furniture, and that the leg of a grand piano had been placed on one of his two heads. When he recovered from the fever his mind was still dazed and his sight had been so badly affected by ophthalmia that he was unable to read a letter which was brought to him by one of his servants who came running into his tent. He took it to Dillon who had also been delirious and was equally incapable of comprehending the letter until its bearer, Chuma, was brought into the presence of the white men to announce that his master, Dr Livingstone, was dead.

A few days later Livingstone's body was brought into Tabora. Murphy declared that he would accompany it to the coast; but Cameron and Dillon decided to go on to Ujiji to find a box, to which the Doctor had referred in his dying moments, and then to 'push on towards Nyangwe to follow up the doctor's explorations'. On 18 November, however, in the delirium of a fresh attack of fever, Dillon shot himself; and Cameron, with his eyesight still impaired, in great pain from a back injury caused by a fall from a donkey, and with his weight reduced by fever to little more than seven stone, was left to continue the journey alone.

He had not proceeded far when his path was closed by a quarrel between a local chief and some Arab merchants, and he was forced to spend Christmas 1873 at a village called Hisinene where his nights were disturbed by the people dancing 'round and round for hours at a time yelling and shouting'. 'The women never mingle with the men on these occasions,' he noticed, 'but sometimes engage in a dance by themselves, when the gestures and actions are even more immoral and indecent than those of the men ... Neither men nor women have any objection to be gazed on by the opposite sex whilst going through these antics, but as in most other tribes they never mix or dance together.' These people, the Wanyamwesi, whose customs Cameron had ample leisure to study, came out of their huts every morning at dawn to sit smoking around the fires; then all of them, except the old women and children, the chief and a few elders, would go out to work in the plantations until noon when they returned for their meal of *ugali*, a kind of porridge made with flour and boiling water. Their distinguishing tribal marks were three lines tattooed down their foreheads and a chevron-shaped gap made by chipping the edges of the two upper front teeth. They wore triangular pieces of hippopotamus ivory or shell round their necks and fibres of dark cloth plaited in twisted shapes into their hair which, once arranged after two or three days of elaborate manipulation, remained undisturbed for six months or longer. Their headmen wore in addition enormous cylindrical bracelets of ivory extending from wrist to elbow which, struck together, were used for signalling in battle.

Leaving these people without regret when the road was clear, Cameron set out for Lake Tanganyika at the end of December. The journey through Ugara was painfully slow and became even more so when Cameron, whose donkey had quite broken down through want of corn, and whose leg had been painfully crippled by the bite of a centipede, had to be carried in a litter. There were delays when detours had to be made to avoid gangs of armed slaves who had escaped from their Arab owners and had become marauders. There were further delays when the rain fell so heavily that movement across the swampy ground was impossible and, after the rain had stopped, when Cameron's men clambered up the trees after bees' nests. There were delays, too, when the porters, seeing a herd of buffalo, dropped their loads and ran away. Once they dropped Cameron himself when a solitary buffalo charged through the trees, causing a general stampede. It was not until 2 February 1874 that the Sindi was crossed on a mass of floating vegetation; and not until 18 February, 'fifteen years and five days from the time Burton discovered it', that Cameron's eyes 'rested on the vast Tanganyika'. He spent some time exploring the southern part of the lake, taking random shots at elephants and gorillas, describing and sketching both the people of Kitata, whose hair was anointed with oil mixed in red earth which 'gave them the appearance of having dipped their heads in blood', and the women of Kasangalowa 'who had not even the usual negro apology of a nipple to their breasts, but only a hole' into which they inserted ornaments.

Having found ninety-six rivers flowing into the lake and a large one, the Lukuga, flowing out of it, Cameron left for Ujiji where he arrived on 9 May. From there he set off for Nyangwe, hoping to get boats 'to float down the unknown waters of the Kongo' to the sea. He crossed the beautiful Lugungwa River, on whose 'cliff-like sides most lovely ferns and mosses grew'; and beyond it he first saw the *mpafu*, a magnificent tree which rose to a hundred feet in height and whose olive-like fruit was used by the natives in the manufacture of an agreeably scented oil. He passed villages in which fetish huts with carved idols occupied the places of honour, and fields in which larger, rougher idols stood guard over the crops. And in June he came to Pakwanywa's where the chief, having supervised the laborious painting of his wife's forehead, invited Cameron into his hut whose plastered walls had been decorated with painted patterns executed with equal care. Here, after an exchange of presents, the chief entertained his guest with a tune on a musical instrument which, for want of a better term, Cameron called a harmonium. This performance was a prelude to the ceremony of 'making brothers', a ritual involving one of the chief's headmen smearing blood from an incision in his wrist into a similar wound cut in the wrist of one of Cameron's servants and then rubbing in gunpowder. The chief's wife, 'a merry sort of person and really ladylike in her manners', watched the performance wearing a leopardskin apron at the front and a coloured grass one at the back. She was covered in cowrie shells as well as copper, iron and ivory ornaments, tassels of beads, necklaces of shells, and she had iron rings round her ankles and copper and ivory bracelets on her arms. Her hair was shaved a little back from her forehead the better to display the freshly painted red, black and white lines; and her body, newly anointed with *mpafu* oil, looked 'sleek and shiny'. Cameron thought it 'great fun showing her a looking-glass. She had never seen one before, and was half-afraid of it and ashamed to show she was afraid.'

Refreshed by this pleasant episode at Pakwanywa's, Cameron prepared himself for the journey across the country of the Manyuema, a journey he was dreading since the people, so he was told, were voracious cannibals. 'Not only do they eat the bodies of enemies killed in battle,' he wrote, when he had satisfied himself that the stories about the Manyuema were true, 'but also of people who die of disease. They prepare the corpses by leaving them in running water until they are nearly putrid, and then devour them without any further cooking. They also eat all sorts of carrion, and their odour is very foul and revolting. I was entertained with a song setting forth the delights of cannibalism, in which the flesh of men was said to be good but that of women was bad and only to be eaten in time of scarcity; nevertheless, it was not to be despised when man meat was unobtainable.'

Having passed through the lands of the Manyuema without harm, Cameron reached the Lualaba at Nyangwe in August. But his hopes of floating down the river to the sea were dashed; for, like Livingstone before him, he was unable to find anyone prepared to let him have a canoe, though he offered 'anything within reason'. Cameron was wondering how best to proceed and even contemplated turning back when the celebrated half-Arab, half-Negro trader, Hamed ibn Hamed, arrived in Nyangwe. This man, later to be known to the British as Tippu Tib, was 'a good-looking man and the greatest dandy' that Cameron had seen among the traders. 'Notwithstanding his being perfectly black, he was a thorough Arab, for curiously enough, the admixture of Negro blood had not rendered him less of an Arab in his ideas and manners.' Tippu Tib suggested that Cameron should return with him to his camp beyond the Rovubu river, and then, since the Lualaba route was impossible, proceed to the African coast by a more southerly path. Cameron, who formed a high opinion of Tippu Tib, accepted this advice. But soon after leaving he was once again attacked by fever and 'reeled like a drunken man, scarcely able to drag one foot after another'. In his delirium each large, white pyramidal ant-hill beside the path appeared to him to be a tent, and it was only the hope that the next one might actually prove to be so that kept him moving. The following day he felt a little better, though his feet were so blistered he was obliged to slit open his boots. And on 29 August he managed to stagger into the village of a chief named Russuna where he rested for two days. Russuna came to see him frequently, bringing with him each time a different beautiful wife who offered her thighs as a footstool. Having paid their formal visits with the king, the wives, of whom there were about 160, all came together to look at the stranger's belongings and, losing all shyness, turned up the legs and sleeves of his clothes to discover whether or not it was his face alone that was white. Fearing they would undress him altogether, Cameron threw beads and cowries on the floor to divert their attention from his 'personal peculiarities'.

After leaving Russuna's for Tippu Tib's camp, Cameron received a visit from the most powerful king of the district of whom all lesser chieftains were in awe. Preceded by drummers, some forty spearmen and six female warriors carrying shields, the great man approached, accompanied by various members of his family and officials. He was strangely dressed in a jacket and kilt of red and yellow woollen cloth trimmed with long-haired monkey skins, and wore a greasy handkerchief tied round his head. At the door of Cameron's hut his attendants formed a ring, inside which he performed a kind of jigging dance with two of his daughters. He then entered the hut where he and Cameron had a long and friendly conversation during which permission was readily given for the white man to pass through his domains.

When Cameron continued his journey on 12 September he found the people in the large, neat villages as friendly as Russuna's had been. They brought him presents of corn and dried white ants which were considered by them a great delicacy. Their huts were wonderfully clean and neat, equipped with elaborately carved wooden doors beneath porches of well-trimmed thatch. Cameron was invited to enter one of these huts at Kifuma and found it as neat inside as out. The high dome-like roof was constructed of slender rods fitting at the apex into a round piece of wood carved in concentric circles and painted black and white. The clay floor was raised eighteen inches above the ground and polished until quite slippery. The chief, whose hut this was, offered it to Cameron as a resting-place, and was so thankful not to have his whole village burned down because a rifle was stolen from his guest during the night that the next morning he presented him with two goats. Afterwards he covered himself with mud as a token of gratitude when Cameron returned one of the goats together with a small gift. Cameron explained that the British did not punish indiscriminately for theft and, even if he had caught the thief, he 'should only have compelled him to return the stolen rifle and have given him a sound flogging'. The chief 'had never before heard of such merciful treatment, and said the inhabitants of villages usually fled on the approach of caravans, because the only strangers they had any previous knowledge of were those who came slave-hunting and who seized the slightest pretext to make war and destroy villages for the sake of obtaining slaves and plunder'.

As he progressed, however, beyond the Lukazi river, a branch of the Lomami, Cameron found the people less meek and amenable than they were around Tippu Tib's camp. Once some arrows were shot at his men as they passed through a narrow strip of jungle; and later, in a village where his goat was stolen, a crowd of natives hurled spears at them. 'As matters were now becoming rather serious,' Cameron reluctantly 'allowed a few shots to be fired'. One of these 'fortunately took effect in the leg of a native who happened to be a person of consideration and ... this ... made such an impression that a parley was proposed by the chief of the village'.

An agreement was eventually negotiated, but, on the arrival of another chief with more armed men, arrows soon started flying again. 'Determined to make some show of retaliation', Cameron burned down a hut and threatened that if not allowed to leave peaceably he would let the natives know 'what bullets really were'. This firm stand resulted in permission being given for his departure, but on approaching another village Cameron was met by a fresh volley of arrows. Calling on his men to follow him, a summons which only a few of them obeyed, he dashed forward through the forest, firing his gun as he entered the village at one side while its inhabitants ran away from it at the other end. Joined now by the rest of his men who, 'Falstaff-like, began to boast of their great deeds and of the still greater performances they intended in future', Cameron set about turning the village into a fortress which he named Fort Dinah in memory of his stolen goat. For three days he held out there, constantly shot at by the villagers who succeeded in wounding five or six of his men when they went to fetch water from a stream. But their arrows were no match for his guns and after several natives had been killed, others wounded and two had been taken as hostages, peace was concluded and Fort Dinah evacuated on 6 October.

Soon afterwards Cameron came across a half-caste slave dealer who, although he was quite black, wore European clothes, spoke Portuguese and called himself by a Portuguese name, José Antonio Alvez. This old rogue declared that Cameron's party was 'far too small to travel through the intervening countries in safety' and he offered to conduct him to the coast on condition that, on arrival there, he would receive 'a present proportionate to the value of his services'. This offer Cameron felt obliged to accept.

While waiting for Alvez to complete his preparations for departure, Cameron left to explore Lake Mohrya which he reached on 1 November. He discovered it to be inhabited by a people who occupied huts built on platforms which were raised about six feet above the surface of the water. Beneath the platforms canoes were moored, and fishing nets hung out to dry. Occasionally the lake people went ashore to graze their goats or tend their fields, but otherwise they lived entirely in these huts with their animals, swimming about from one dwelling to the next, apparently unconcerned by the enormous poisonous snakes which, so Cameron learned, were to be found in the lake in large quantities.

On his return from Lake Mohrya, Cameron found that Alvez was still not ready to depart. Nor, indeed, could departure take place until permission had been received from the tyrant who ruled over the people of these regions, the great King Kasongo. And, since Kasongo was away and no one knew or dared to divulge where he had gone, Cameron was obliged to settle down, using his time to study the Warua people over whom Kasongo ruled. He witnessed a wedding ceremony whose celebrations continued for days and nights on end, involving what seemed to him continuous shouting, dancing, drumming, the playing of rude pan-pipes and the clapping of hands. 'On the afternoon of the second day the bridegroom made his appearance and executed a *pas seul* which lasted about half an hour, and on its termination the bride – a girl of nine or ten years of age and dressed in all the finery the village could produce – was brought in by [two women] who jumped her up and down most vigorously whilst she allowed her body and arms to sway about uncontrolled. The bridegroom gave her fragments of tobacco-leaves and quantities of beads, which she, keeping her eyes shut, scattered indiscriminately amongst the dancers ... After this the bride was set down and danced with the bridegroom, going through most obscene gestures for about ten minutes, when he picked her up, and tucking her under his arm walked her off to his hut. The dancing, drumming and yelling was still continued, and, indeed, had not ceased when we left on the following day.'

Cameron also witnessed the performances of medicine men who, with faces whitened with pipeclay and necks ornamented with necklaces of birds' skulls, pranced through villages accompanied by attendants carrying their mats and idols. When they sat down they were surrounded by devout women who bent down, moaned, clapped their hands and offered them fowls. These were accepted, with a spit in the face of the donors, in exchange for 'a ball of beastliness as a charm'.

Wherever he went Cameron was regaled with stories of the great Kasongo, a king with magical powers who claimed that he did not have to eat and drink to live but did so purely for the pleasure it afforded him. Several of his wives came to see Cameron. They were usually drunk and occasionally in a mood to dance before him, when 'their looseness of gesture and extraordinary throwing about of their limbs certainly exceeded anything [he] had ever seen before'. He was told that Kasongo, in addition to the pleasures of his harem, had a right to enjoy any woman who pleased his fancy throughout his dominions. If any gave birth to a male baby, the child was given a monkey skin to wear when he grew up and this gave him authority to commandeer provisions and cloth from anyone not of royal blood. In his harem, which incestuously included sisters and daughters as well as wives, no male was allowed between sunset and sunrise on pain of death. Should a woman give birth there to a male child during the night both mother and baby were hustled out immediately. When Kasongo slept at home he had no bedroom furniture other than that afforded him by female flesh: some women, on hands and knees, formed a couch with their backs, while others, lying on the ground, provided a carpet.

On their master's death many of them could expect to die themselves. For custom required the king to be buried on the bodies of living women in an enormous pit dug in the bed of a diverted stream. After the earth had been shovelled over them all, it was further required that a number of male slaves, sometimes forty or fifty, should also be killed and their blood poured over the grave. Then the river was allowed to resume its course. It was said that on the death of Kasongo's father no less than a hundred women had been buried alive with him.

Kasongo himself returned at last from his plundering raids on 21 January 1875. He received Cameron in his enclosure which was guarded by sentries, by women carrying his shields and by an official wearing a huge leopard skin and carrying an immense crooked stick in his hand. Among his courtiers were a large number of men whom the king had mutilated 'simply for caprice or as an instance of his power'. Many of them had lost hands and ears and even lips and nose in consequence of a fit of temper on their master's part, yet they all displayed the utmost reverence for him, seeming to 'worship the ground he stood upon'. He was a tall young man of outlandish vanity who evidently considered himself one of the greatest rulers of the earth, more powerful than the sovereign of England whom he instructed, through Cameron, to pay him tribute. And, as though in demonstration of his power, he commanded Cameron to attend a levee on 10 February when lesser chiefs were coming to pay him homage.

Cameron accordingly attended on the appointed day when he witnessed these chiefs making their obeisances in turn before Kasongo, daubing themselves with powdered pipeclay as a token of their submission and shouting the king's titles at the tops of their voices. Each then ran forward, sword in hand, as though intent upon cutting Kasongo down, but just before reaching him they stopped dead in their tracks, fell to their knees, drove the sword into the ground and rubbed their foreheads in the dust. When the last chief had performed this ritual, Kasongo delivered a long speech in which he elaborated upon his bravery, greatness, power and his divine right to rule.

Cameron had hoped to get away after this levee but Alvez decided that they ought not to leave until Kasongo had completed the prescribed period of mourning for a wife who had just died. And when this period was over Kasongo, 'looking very seedy and dirty' – as well he might, since custom had required him to spend every night for a week sleeping with the corpse –

decreed that the strangers could not now depart until Alvez had completed a house which he had promised to build for him. This house was at length finished at the beginning of April but by then a large number of the men who were to accompany the caravan to the coast had gone off to Kanyoka and it was considered impossible to set out until they returned. Then, one of Cameron's men who had 'smoked himself stupid with bhang' set fire to his hut. The fire spread rapidly, destroying several other huts and a good deal of property for which Cameron was required to pay compensation. And it was not until the last claim had been settled that Cameron was finally able to leave on 10 June.

He soon found into what evil company he had fallen. The conduct of Alvez's people on the road was 'disgraceful'. They attacked all the small parties of natives whom they chanced to meet and plundered their loads. 'Any cultivated spot they at once fell on like a swarm of locusts, and, throwing down their loads, rooted up ground nuts and sweet potatoes, and laid waste fields of unripe corn out of sheer wantonness. In the villages where they camped they cut down bananas and stripped oil-palms of their fronds for building their huts, thus doing irreparable injury to the unfortunate inhabitants.'

On Cameron's remonstrating with them he was merely told that they had permission from Kasongo to take whatever they required; and, while he was able to keep his own men from following their example, he could not prevent them buying food from Alvez's thieves who were thus encouraged to rob the more. Cameron's shame at being associated with such men was much increased when one of Kasongo's lieutenants joined the caravan with fifty-two female slaves, tied together in lots, some of them carrying children, others pregnant, all heavily laden and displaying the weals and scars of savage whippings. On the appearance of these slaves the dreadful Alvez immediately demanded some of them to add to his own stock which was already distressingly large, the mournful procession taking two hours to pass through the smallest village.

Women and children, footsore and over-burtherned, were urged on unremittingly by their barbarous masters; and even when they reached their camp it was no haven of rest for the poor creatures [Cameron recorded]. They were compelled to fetch water, cook, build huts, and collect firewood for those who owned them ... The loss of labour entailed by working gangs of slaves tied together is monstrous; for if one pot of water is wanted twenty people are obliged to fetch it from the stream, and for one bundle of grass to thatch a hut the whole string must be employed. On the road, too, if one of a gang requires to halt the whole must follow motions, and when one falls five or six are dragged down.

Across the Njivi valley the long human cargo marched, waist-deep in stagnant water clogged with rotting vegetation; through swamps and bogs; beneath wooded sandstone hills; past vast ant-hills, fifty feet in height; over the Lovoi; into stockaded villages; across open plains, destitute of trees or shade; into

Kawala and on to Angolo and Lupanda; through the marshes beyond Lupanda and across streams covered with foliage; beside lagoons and into long grass so thick and strong it had to be burned before it could be penetrated, until, on 27 July 1875, the weary travellers crossed the Lubiranzi river and entered Ulunda.

Here the villages were small and the country largely primeval forest. The Walunta people, 'a dirty, wild-looking race', were scantily clothed in skin aprons and bark cloth. They wore no ornaments of any kind, and their hair was 'not worked up into any fashion but simply matted with dirt and grease'. They seemed to have had no dealings with caravans for not one of them possessed a bead or a piece of cloth. Cameron spent a whole day out with his gun, looking for an animal or bird to shoot but 'returned unsuccessful, not having seen either hoof or feather'. Alvez's men, however, shot two small elephants on whose carcasses they fell, hacking and tearing them to pieces, fighting and quarrelling with each other in a scene of 'disgusting confusion'. Cameron managed to secure a piece of the trunk, knowing it to be considered a great delicacy, but the dish that his cook served up was not at all to his liking. He returned to his monotonous diet of rice and beans without relish but without regret.

On 5 August he crossed the Lukoji river and on the 28th arrived at the village of Katendé in the country of the Lovalé. There were numerous fetishes in all the villages, crude wooden figures of men and women, or clay representations of wild beasts painted with red and white spots. Grotesquely attired fetish men appeared in the camp, wearing net suits with horizontal black and white stripes and huge feathered or horned masks. These were 'sham devils' who were paid to frighten away the real devils who inhabited the forest.

The Lovalé had guns and Alvez's people were consequently much more wary of them and treated them with a great deal more deference than they had those tribes further inland who were armed only with bows and arrows. They continued, though, to treat the slaves with unremitting savagery. These poor creatures, Cameron noticed, were now half starved and their bodies were covered with large sores occasioned by the heavy loads they had to carry and the perpetual blows and cuts they received. One woman, the ropes that bound her eating into her flesh, struggled along, still carrying a baby who had died in her arms. Another, a discarded member of Alvez's harem, was exchanged with a local headman for a bullock. Cameron was relieved whenever a string of slaves managed to escape, though he had reason to fear that 'numbers of them died of starvation in their endeavours to reach home, or fell into the hands of Lovalé men, who [were] reported to be harsh task-masters'.

At the beginning of October 1875 the caravan crossed the Kuanza river and at last reached Alvez's settlement in Bihé, an untidy collection of large huts surrounded by rough land which, although he had lived there for over thirty years, Alvez had made no attempt to cultivate. The arrival of the caravan was greeted by shrieking women who pelted Alvez with flour, served out unlimited quantities of *pombe*, and, when comparative quiet had been restored, took charge of the slaves which their menfolk had brought home with them. In front of Alvez's hut half-a-dozen men kept up a rapid fire with their guns in honour of their master's arrival. Among them were 'a civilized black man named Manoel' and a white man, commonly known as Chico, who had escaped from a penal settlement on the coast. Chico was told to act as guide to take Cameron on to Kagnombé's; but objecting that he might be recognized, he asked Alvez to send Manoel instead.

Kagnombé's proved to be the largest town Cameron had seen in his entire journey. But Kagnombe himself, the chief of the Bihé, for all his pretensions, numerous scarlet-waistcoated attendants, including a secretary (who could not write), and the evidence of his power, provided by a collection of skulls of conquered chiefs, turned out to be a drunken figure in an ancient black suit, a large grey plaid, the ends of which were held up by a naked little boy, and a dirty old wideawake hat. Hearing that his visitor had been a long time on the road he graciously consented to accept the presents which were offered but remarked that next time he would expect gifts more suitable to his greatness. Then, taking an enormous swig from a bottle of *aguardiente*, he began 'swaggering and dancing about in the most extraordinary manner, occupying intervals in his performance by further pulls at the bottle'.

Cameron was thankful to escape to the nearby settlement of one Señor Gonçalves, a trader in ivory and beeswax. Having been master of a ship and spent thirty years in Africa, Gonçalves had retired to Lisbon where, failing to settle down, he had decided to return to the country where he had been happy. He, his two sons and another white man who had been boatswain of a Portuguese man-of-war, were having breakfast when Cameron arrived and was shown into a comfortable room with a boarded floor, a ceiling of white cloth, plastered and neatly painted walls, and green jalousies at the windows. He was invited to sit down and enjoyed the best meal he had tasted for 'many a long day'. That night, for the first time since he had disembarked from the *Punjab*, Cameron enjoyed the exquisite pleasure of sleeping between sheets; and the next morning he parted from Gonçalves as though from an old friend, with a bottle of brandy and several tins of meat for his journey to the coast.

A few days later he crossed the Kutato river which formed the boundary between Bihé and Bailunda, and as he went forward towards the mountains of Bailunda he thought that he had never before seen a landscape of such surpassing beauty. It was 'a glimpse of paradise'. In the foreground were glades in the woodland and knolls crowned by groves of splendid trees beneath which sheltered villages with yellow-thatched roofs; the sunlight flashed upon streams running through fields of green crops and bright red, newly hoed earth; in the far distance were 'mountains of endless and pleasing variety of form, gradually fading away until they blended with the blue of the sky. Overhead there drifted fleecy white clouds; and the hum of bees, the bleating of goats, and crowing of cocks broke the stillness of the air.'

The journey to the sea was, however, far less pleasant than this paradisal vision had encouraged Cameron to hope. Indeed, after passing through Kambala and crossing the Kukewi in heavy rain, many of his men were in so sorry a plight that they could not carry on. So Cameron, his tongue swollen and his mouth bleeding, decided that he would have to throw away all his baggage, apart from his instruments, journals and books, and with a few picked men make a forced march to Benguella. From there he would send back assistance to the rest. On through jungle, across torrent beds and streams they went; passing caravans bearing bags of salt and bottles of *aguardiente* from the coast to the interior, skeletons and slave sticks testifying to the traffic that went the opposite way; clambering over huge masses of stone on their hands and knees; descending into gorges and struggling up the heights beyond with the help of the creepers that grew in the crevices of the rock; dragging their way through pools whose slimy, stagnant water reached their shoulders; slipping and bruising themselves in the dark of the dry ravines. And then, at last, they glimpsed the sea at Katombela.

Cameron, swinging his rifle round his head, almost hysterical with relief, ran on towards the town, followed by his men as excited as himself. Then, controlling himself, he unfurled the British flag and walked on in a manner which he considered more befitting an officer who had once served under it. As he approached the town he came across a former naval officer, now a merchant, 'a jolly-looking little Frenchman' who jumped out of a hammock and 'instantly opened a bottle to drink "to the honour of the first European who had ever succeeded in crossing tropical Africa from east to west" '.

This Frenchman took Cameron and his men to his house at Katombela where they were all found accommodation and food; but realizing that Cameron's bleeding mouth and swollen tongue were caused by scurvy he soon had him hurried away to a doctor at Benguella. After treatment there he was well enough to sail to Luanda where he immediately went to see the British Consul to whom he said dramatically, 'I have come to report myself from Zanzibar – overland.'

At the mention of the word 'Zanzibar', the Consul stared at his visitor; at the word 'overland' he stepped back a pace. Then coming forward and placing both his hands on his visitor's shoulders, he cried out with reciprocal theatricality, 'Cameron! My God!'

Sending his men back to Zanzibar by sea, Cameron himself sailed for Liverpool in the steamship *Congo*, arriving in the Mersey on 2 April 1876. His great achievement in being the first European to cross the African continent from east to west and in suggesting the probable course of the Congo, over whose basin he declared a British protectorate, led to Cameron's being received in England as an explorer whose name was worthy to be ranked with Livingstone's. He was promoted Commander, created a Companion of the Bath, given an honorary doctorate at Oxford and awarded the Founder's Medal by the Royal Geographical Society. He came to be considered a leading expert on African affairs and an influential advocate of Livingstone's view that 'commercial enterprise and missionary effort' must do their best to assist each other. 'Wherever commerce finds its way,' so he maintained, 'there missionaries will follow; and wherever missionaries prove that white men can live and travel, there trade is certain to be established.' Having retired from the Navy, he became a director of numerous companies with African interests, always insisting that the welfare of the Africans was quite as important as financial profit. When he died in a hunting accident in 1894 he was considered to be one of the most gentlemanly heroes of the late Victorian age, a man whom the readers of the boys' magazines for which he wrote adventure stories might justly revere.

14

'IN DARKEST AFRICA'

Before Stanley sailed for England in 1872 he had been warned by a member of the Livingstone Search and Relief Expedition that, as an American, he could not expect the kind of reception which would have been accorded to an Englishman. Nor did he get it.

In some quarters he was welcomed as a hero, but in others accused of being a charlatan. Several newspapers echoed the *Standard*'s 'suspicions and misgivings' about Stanley's story. Sir Henry Creswicke Rawlinson, the Assyriologist who had become President of the Royal Geographical Society after Murchison's death the year before, commented slightingly on the American's achievement in a letter to *The Times*. Others went so far as to suggest that Stanley had never been in Africa at all. Queen Victoria granted him an audience but, although she behaved with regal graciousness, she was not impressed by him – 'a determined, ugly little man – with a strong American twang'. An ill-constructed and ill-delivered talk which he gave to the Geographical Section of the British Association for the Advancement of Science was received with a marked lack of enthusiasm, while his reception at a subsequent dinner was, in his opinion, so discourteous that he 'withdrew from the room in great indignation'. Deeply wounded by these affronts, Stanley wrote many years later that all his thoughts since 1872 had been 'strongly coloured by the storm of abuse and the wholly unjustifiable reports' that had circulated about him at

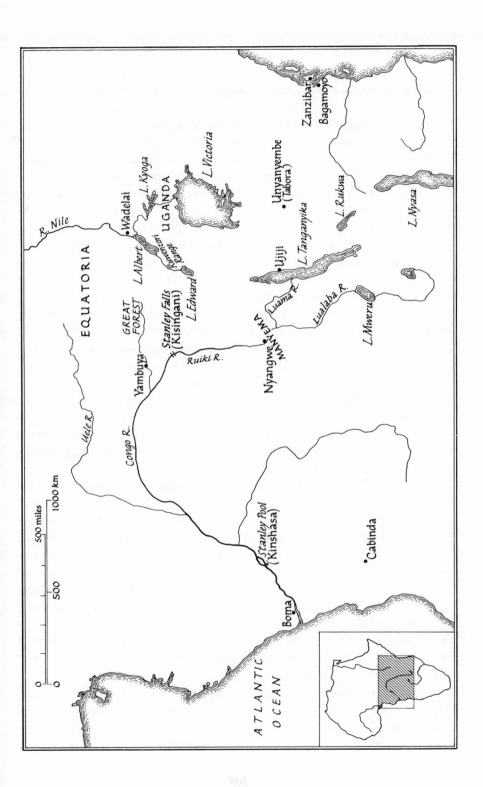

ATLANTIC OCEAN

Boma

Stanley Pool
(Kinshasa)

•Cabinda

Congo R.

Uele R.

EQUATORIA

Yambuya

GREAT FOREST

Stanley Falls
(Kisingani)

Ruiki R.

R. Nile

•Wadelai

L. Albert

Ruwenzori Range

L. Edward

UGANDA

L. Kyoga

L. Victoria

Nyangwe

MANYEMA

Luama R.

Lualaba R.

•Ujiji

L. Tanganyika

L. Mweru

Unyanyembe
(Tabora)

L. Rukwa

L. Nyasa

Zanzibar•
•Bagamoyo

500 miles

1000 km

500

500

0

this time. Even when the authenticity of the letters he had brought back with him was confirmed by Livingstone's family, and he was awarded the Victoria Medal of the Royal Geographical Society, the resentment still festered. Nor was he much soothed by his reception in America. He was greeted in New York with enthusiasm, except by James Gordon Bennett who considered that his employee was getting far too big for his boots; but, while he was gratified by such compliments as those of Mark Twain who compared his triumph to that of Columbus, he was angered by newspaper reports which, repeating the slurs of the English press, dismissed his story as a 'monstrous sell', a 'humbug' and 'a hoax' and which revealed that far from being a patriotic American he was an illegitimate Welshman who had deserted from the United States Navy. Determined to achieve lasting fame rather than transient notoriety, and the respect of those who had insulted him, Stanley constantly thought of returning to Africa, feeling, as he wrote, that 'when a man returns home and finds for the moment nothing to struggle against, the vast resolve, which has sustained him through a long and difficult enterprise, dies away, burning as it sinks in the heart'. So, when he heard that Livingstone was dead, he made up his mind to complete the work which his old friend had begun. Having returned to England, he went to the offices of the *Daily Telegraph* to put his proposition to the proprietor. He was told that the *Telegraph* would back him if the *New York Herald* would also. Bennett immediately agreed. And so, on 15 August 1874, Stanley set sail once again for Zanzibar.

He was accompanied by Kalulu, the little black boy he had brought back with him in 1872, by two mastiffs, and three white companions whom he had selected from the hundreds who had offered to go with him, Frederick Barker, a clerk from the Langham Hotel, and two young brothers experienced in the management of small boats, Francis and Edward Pocock. All of them, humans and animals, black and white alike, were soon to perish in Africa. At Zanzibar Stanley experienced the usual difficulty in hiring reliable men, and several of those whom he did collect caused an uproar in Bagamoyo where they plundered the inhabitants and carried off some of their women. West of Bagamoyo, Stanley's difficulties multiplied: porters and guides deserted; fever struck; food ran short; hostile tribes attacked the caravan and were dispersed with heavy loss of life on both sides. And this open warfare with uncooperative natives, which was to characterize the expedition, led to far more serious questioning of Stanley's methods than any he had yet had to face.

Having reached Lake Victoria at Kagehyi on 27 February 1875, he set out to explore it a week or so later in a boat, the *Lady Alice*, which he had designed himself and had had carried from Zanzibar in five sections. Initially he had avoided conflict, sitting quietly beneath the awning of the *Lady Alice*. But at Bumbire island by the south-western shore of the lake he was so provoked by the king's warriors that he opened fire on them, first with a rifle then with a shotgun. Having held them back on that occasion and completed his circumnavigation of the lake, he was drawn into battle with them again when he took his people north to explore Lake Albert.

In his efforts to reach Lake Albert he had hoped to secure the help of Mutesa, the *kabaka* of Uganda with whom Speke had spent so long. He established the most friendly relations with Mutesa and soon after his visit the *kabaka*, more interested than ever in what the admired Europeans could do for him, welcomed missionaries to his country. But Mutesa, who was preparing to make war against a rebellious tribe, had been unable to spare Stanley sufficient warriors as an escort and, when the war was over, the men he was allocated, although two thousand strong, proved unwilling to face the warlike tribes of the lake regions. So, turning his back on Lake Albert, Stanley made south for Lake Tanganyika which he circumnavigated with the same thorough attention he had given to Lake Victoria.

He now had even more important work to do: the exploration of the Lualaba River which flowed northwards from Nyangwe and which Livingstone had so fervently hoped would prove to be the Nile. With the intention of establishing whether or not Livingstone's hopes were justified, Stanley arrived in Nyangwe on 27 October 1876.

Like Livingstone and Cameron before him, Stanley was unable to obtain a single canoe at Nyangwe; but he had the *Lady Alice* and, after prolonged negotiations, he managed to persuade the Arab trader, Tippu Tib, to accompany him for sixty marches down the river with some 700 of his men for a fee of $5,000. So, on 5 November 1876, Stanley set out with almost a thousand followers, including women and children, on his momentous and dangerous journey.

After the first day's pleasant march the country became increasingly unwelcoming: the open plain gave way to dense and steamy jungle so dark and airless that the travellers seemed to be struggling through a miasmal fog. Carrying the sections of the *Lady Alice* proved intolerably difficult, and Stanley was obliged to divide the expedition, leaving Tippu Tib, who had frequently expressed a desire to turn back, to command the land party while he continued the journey by boat. At least Stanley could comfort himself that the native tribes were not nearly as ferocious as their reputation at Nyangwe had suggested. The villages were deserted and had evidently been abandoned in haste, for the inhabitants had left their possessions behind. As the days passed, however, dark figures could be seen watching the intruders through the foliage, and drums could be heard rhythmically beating in the distance. And then on 24 November, at a point where the Ruiki River turns and then narrows, the expedition was suddenly attacked by natives in war canoes, hurling spears, shooting arrows and intoning an incessant war cry, '*Ooh-hu-hu, ooh-hu-hu-hu, ooh-hu-hu!*' Stanley and his men opened fire and put them to flight. But thereafter few days passed without a battle with the warriors of the river regions whose ivory war horns rent the stillness of the humid air and whose poisoned arrows whistled through the vegetation by the river's banks. After beating off repeated attacks in the country known as Vinja-Njara, Stanley counter-attacked, captured and occupied a village. And one dark night, when the splash of rain and the howl of wind deadened other sounds, he and a party of trusted companions succeeded in capturing nearly all the natives' canoes. With as many boats now as he needed to get all his men on the river, Stanley could more willingly dispense with the help of Tippu Tib whose followers, tired, ill and dispirited, were all demanding to go home. Several of Stanley's men were also ill, others badly wounded, and he had to let these return to Nyangwe with Tippu Tib.

With the expedition thus depleted, Stanley moved on again on 27 December. Attacks by natives covered in war paint and hurling spears from canoes almost a hundred feet long became more frequent than ever. At every curve and bend of the river, so Stanley said, savages could be heard passing to each other their warning signals. 'The forests on either bank flung hither and thither the strange echoes; huge war drums sounded the muster.' Reed arrows, tipped with poison, flew out of the forest as the canoes glided by. One day Stanley awoke in his riverside camp to find the entire expedition had been enclosed on the land side by a high net beyond which sharp cane splinters had been buried in the earth to cut his men's bare feet. On another occasion they were attacked by some two thousand warriors, chanting war cries as, standing up in cascades of foam, they paddled furiously towards the *Lady Alice* in immense canoes each containing eighty men, parrots' feathers in their hair, ivory bangles around their arms, spears and poisoned arrows at their feet. Yet in every encounter the native forces, however strong, were eventually driven back by Stanley's rifles and muskets. There were killed and wounded on both sides, but it was always the tribesmen who suffered the worse. Even when the expedition entered the territory of the brave and fierce Bangala who possessed muskets, Stanley's fire power ensured his victory, for the Bangala had no musket balls and the bits of iron and copper with which they loaded their guns did not have the velocity to penetrate the shields of the Zanzibari. So the Bangala were forced to let the white man's little army pass.

Hostile natives, indeed, were less a problem to Stanley than the passage of the river itself. Some 150 miles beyond Vinja-Njara he encountered the first of the seven roaring cataracts which were to be known as the Stanley Falls. There could be no question of negotiating these cataracts in the canoes which consequently had to be carried past them by land. By day and by night the men struggled with the heavy boats through the jungle by the river's bank, their labours in the hours of darkness being illuminated by flaring lights from palm branches and bundles of cane soaked in gum. In daylight their ordeal was aggravated by the swarms of red ants which settled in millions upon their bodies, biting and blistering their skins. These seven cataracts were but a fore-taste of what was yet to come. Beyond the point where the river widened into what was to be known as Stanley Pool there were thirty-two more cataracts to be negotiated – the cataracts which Stanley was to call the Livingstone Falls. Here the expedition suffered grievous losses. Stanley himself, who at-tributed his apparent immunity in his fights with the natives to their surprise and consequent hesitation on coming face to face with a white man in battle, escaped with slight injuries when he fell thirty feet into a chasm. But later he was nearly drowned; and seven men, as well as the little boy Kalulu, did lose their lives when their canoe was swept over one of the cataracts. In attempting to shoot another, three more men were lost including the former bargeman, Frank Pocock, apart from Stanley the sole white survivor of the expedition, who had proved himself a cheerful, brave and resourceful assistant and had become known to the men as the 'Little Master'.

After Pocock's death, which profoundly grieved Stanley and increased his sense of loneliness and isolation, a deep gloom settled over the entire expedi-tion. The Zanzibari became sullen and mutinous, and thirty-one deserted in a single day. They were eventually persuaded to return, but one of them was soon afterwards captured by the natives while stealing food and had to be ransomed with a large consignment of cloth. The expedition's supply of food was now running dangerously low. The prices demanded by the natives were so high that they could not be met, and in trying to steal what could not be bought several men were wounded and two others were captured and had to be left behind as slaves since Stanley was unable to pay the ransom demanded.

The survivors went on, many of them ill and all emaciated. One became insane and ran off into the jungle shouting, 'Ah, Master! We are home! We have reached the sea.' And then at last, after journeying almost five thousand miles, they were, indeed, near the sea. Satisfied now that the river was the Congo, Stanley made up his mind to complete the last stages of the journey by land. So, abandoning the *Lady Alice* on a rock, he led his hungry people towards Boma. Here they found food and rest.

Some few weeks later, Stanley and those who had survived the rigours of the long journey sailed for Luanda and thence to Cape Town and Zanzibar. Eight-two people landed at Zanzibar, 277 less than had started out three years before. Amongst them were twelve of the original thirty-six women, and with these were four babies who had been born on their travels. All of them disappeared into obscurity; while Stanley left for Europe, his reputation assured as one of the greatest if most ruthless of all the explorers of Africa.

As on his arrival in England in 1877, Stanley was again subjected to censure for the manner in which he had conducted the expedition. In Parliament and in several newspapers he was condemned for being readier to shoot natives than to negotiate with them; and the Aborigines Protection Society reprimanded him for having allowed his men to loot a *meskiti* in which, beneath thirty-three tusks of ivory, they had discovered a painted idol. But open to censure as his methods were, it was impossible to deny their success; and when in 1886 there was talk of sending out a mission to rescue the Governor of Equatoria, the southernmost province of the Sudan, Stanley was immediately suggested as the man to lead it. The Governor was a Prussian doctor of Jewish descent, Eduard Schnitzer, who had been tutor to the children of a Turkish pasha, had had an affair with their mother and, after his employer's death, had become head of the family. Leaving them all behind, he had gone out to Khartoum where his many talents had recommended him to General Gordon, Governor General of the Sudan. After Gordon's death at the hands of the followers of Mohammed Ahmed, the self-styled Mahdi or Messiah of Islam, the Sudan was evacuated and Schnitzer, who now called himself Mohammed Emin, had, in his own words, been 'cut off from all communication with the world ... forgotten and abandoned by the Government'. 'If our ammunition holds out for some time longer,' Emin had added in a letter to a missionary friend, 'I mean to ... remain here until help comes to us from some quarter.'

Over £20,000 was accordingly raised to provide Emin with the help he needed, and Stanley was appointed leader of the relief expedition. He arrived at the mouth of the Congo on 18 March 1887. With him were eight white subordinates, nearly 700 Africans, mostly Zanzibari, and about a hundred people, including thirty-five wives belonging to Tippu Tib who had been promised the governorship of the Stanley Falls area so that his presence there would protect the Emin Pasha Expedition from attacks by other Arab dealers.

Stanley's plan was to follow the Congo as far as its confluence with the Aruwimi River, from there go up the Aruwimi to the Yambuya – where the rear column was to be left – march through the region known as the Great Forest towards Lake Albert, and then to sail up the lake towards Emin Pasha's headquarters at Wadelai. Although there were occasional quarrels between Stanley and his white officers who found him, so they variously declared, arrogant, impatient, boastful, intolerant, self-righteous, tetchy and unwilling to delegate authority; and although the men had often had to go hungry, the first part of the journey to Yambuya was achieved without excessive losses of men or equipment. The march through the Great Forest, however, was an appalling ordeal. No white man had been that way before, and no man would wish to go again. A gloomy, dank, steaming, primeval rain forest, it was for Stanley 'a region of horrors'. Trees smothered in creepers, rising two hundred feet above the dense, wet vegetation, obscured the light of the sun; huge snakes coiled menacingly round overhanging boughs; all kinds of loathsome insects buzzed, crawled and flitted between the fungus and the leaves; primitive tribesmen kept strangers at bay with spears and arrows and poisoned skewers which they buried in the ground beneath the rotting leaves. Men fell ill and died of fevers and lockjaw; there was little to eat but bananas and plantains, fungus and wild fruit, slugs and ants. One of Stanley's officers, a 'decrepit skeleton' covered in a 'mass of blisters', as the expedition's surgeon described him, had to be left behind with fifty-two men all ill and starving. Within three days forty-seven of these were dead. Stanley struggled on, maintaining the harshest discipline, hanging a man for stealing a rifle, until, on 2 December in a village deserted by pygmies, the edge of the forest could be seen and beyond it the grasslands of Equatoria.

The countryside, into which Stanley's men ran excitedly, looked welcoming, but the natives were not. More battles had to be fought and so much ammunition was expended that Stanley felt obliged to retreat and to build a fortified camp. Here the supplies that had been left behind, including the iron boat, could be brought up; and here the rear column, which was presumably by now on its way from Yambuya, could be established.

When the boat arrived Stanley left for Lake Albert with his sadly depleted advance column. Fortunately the natives were now more friendly, explaining that their previous hostility had been occasioned by their belief that Stanley's force was a raiding party from a neighbouring tribe. The advance column was consequently able to reach the lake without further mishap. Here in a steamer, accompanied by the Italian explorer, Gaetano Casati, who had become his adviser, they found Emin Pasha. Far from being the harassed, imperilled Governor of the European press, he was fit, neatly dressed, affable and un-ruffled. He read the letters which Stanley had brought for him and declared that it was difficult for him to decide what to do: while the Egyptian government had indicated that he ought to leave his province and that they would not be responsible for him if he stayed, he was evidently reluctant to go. Leaving the mysterious little man to make up his mind, Stanley returned to his fortified camp, hoping to find the rear column there and, if it were not, intending to go back through the rain forest to Yambuya to find out the reason why. On his way back to the camp Stanley caught an exhilarating glimpse of snow-capped mountains. Two of his officers had told him the previous month that they had seen these mountains, but he had declared that their eyes must have deceived them. He had seen nothing when he had passed that way himself in 1876; nor had Baker seen the range when he had discovered Lake Albert in 1864. But now the mountains were clearly to be seen behind the drifting mist. He knew that they must be the Ruwenzori, Ptolemy's Mountains of the Moon.

Excited by this discovery Stanley went on to the fort and, finding that the rear column had still not arrived there, he faced once again the dreaded Great Forest. And, in the forest, some ninety miles from Yambuya, he came across the demoralized remnants of the column. Slowly, and with mounting dismay and anger, he learned how the white officers, faced by Tippu Tib's failure to supply them with porters, had lost all authority. Their commander, having conceived a fierce hatred of all blacks, had been shot while shouting at a native woman whose drum beating had infuriated him; and the numbers of the column had been gradually reduced from 258 men to 98, including but a single white man.

As he made his way back through the jungle, enduring its horrors yet again, Stanley's losses were also severe. Scarcely a day passed without the death of a man killed by smallpox, by some other disease or by the poisoned darts and arrows of the pygmies. When he arrived once more in the country of the lake he found that a rebellion had broken out amongst Emin Pasha's troops. Yet Emin could still not make up his mind whether to leave the province. Irritated beyond endurance by the vacillation of the man for whom he had risked so much and for whom so many lives had been wasted, Stanley lost his temper, furiously abused Emin and everyone with him. 'I leave you to God,' he shouted, 'and the blood which will now flow must fall upon your own head!'

Eventually about 1,500 people including Emin Pasha, the 'utterly worthless' Egyptian officers and clerks who had been working in Equatoria under him, and numerous natives acting as bearers of their heavy loads, left for Zanzibar. The long straggling column, from which men frequently deserted, passed beneath the Ruwenzori. Here it halted for a time while one of Stanley's officers tried to scale the highest peak but could get less than two-thirds the way up its 16,795 feet. To make up for this disappointment the size of Lake Albert was correctly estimated; and the Semliki river which flowed out of it to the south was traced towards a new lake which Stanley called Lake Edward. From here the column made its weary way south of Lake Victoria and eastwards to the sea. There was only one more battle to be fought with hostile natives; yet by the time Zanzibar came into view at the beginning of December 1889 most of Emin Pasha's people had disappeared, and of Stanley's original expedition almost three-quarters had not returned. It had been a dreadful experience. But, against all the odds, Stanley had succeeded in his mission once again; and the map of Central Africa was almost complete.

Stanley lived on for another fifteen years, a misunderstood and often mis-represented figure, still masking a fundamental insecurity behind a bombastic and aggressive manner. When he died in 1904 the Africa whose secrets he had done so much to reveal had already become a European empire.

EPILOGUE

Before the great age of exploration in Africa was over the scramble for colonies had begun, and the explorers themselves had made their various contributions to the expansion of imperialism. As early as the 1850s Livingstone – who had told his assistants in the Zambezi expedition to remember that they went among the river's tribes 'as members of a superior race and servants of a Government that desires to elevate the more degraded portions of the human family' – had been strongly urging the colonization of Central Africa by his countrymen. Speke, who had shared that scorn of Africans which nearly all European explorers displayed, with the notable exceptions of Barth and Livingstone, had often spoken of his desire to see British rule triumphant in the backward and degraded continent. Lovett Cameron had persuaded several chiefs to form treaties which were intended to secure a kind of colonial authority for England. Pierre-Paul-François-Camille Savorgnan de Brazza, the Italian count who became an officer in the French navy and explored the Ogowé river from the coast of Gabon to the interior, had entered into treaties with local chiefs which resulted in a French protectorate over the area that became the French Congo. Joseph Thomson, the romantic, adaptable and adventurous Scotsman who hurriedly travelled across the plateau between Lakes Nyasa and Tanganyika, discovered Lake Rukwa, solved the problems of the Lukuga river and in 1883–4 crossed the unknown lands of the Masai to Lake Victoria, also played an important part in the establishment of African colonies by his work for the National African and British South Africa Companies. And Stanley, after his exploration of the Congo, had written, 'I had hoped to have inspired Englishmen with something of my own belief in the future of the Congo. I delivered addresses, after-dinner speeches, and in private have spoken earnestly to try and raise them to adopt early means to secure the Congo basin for England.' Disappointed in this hope for his adopted country, Stanley had turned to King Leopold II of Belgium whose exploitation of the region became notorious.

Although the colonization of Africa had been slow to begin, once it had started it progressed at such a rate that within twenty years almost the entire continent had been divided up between the European powers. Before 1880 their colonial possessions had been few and were nearly all limited to coastal regions.

316

A few years later national rivalries, the need for African raw materials for European industries, and genuine belief in the virtues of bringing civilization and Christianity to the backward and the heathen, had brought about the scramble for Africa. The French had driven eastwards from their base in Senegal and northwards from the Congo in an attempt to prevent the British – who had already assumed authority under Lord Lugard in what is now Nigeria – from taking too much of West Africa. The British meanwhile, urged on by the financier, Cecil Rhodes, had pushed outwards from Cape Colony, taken over territories between the Portuguese colonies of Angola and Mozambique, established protectorates over the present-day Kenya and Uganda, and moved into the Sudan. The Germans, whose Chancellor, Bismarck, had acted as host in 1884–5 at the Congress of Berlin which had been called to settle the peaceful partition of Africa and decide upon the future of the Congo, had entered the contest late, but had then quickly acquired the territories of South West Africa, German East Africa, Togoland and Cameroon. Indeed, by 1900 there were only a very few independent countries left in Africa: Liberia, which had been declared an independent republic in 1847; Libya, which was to be occupied by Italy in 1911; Morocco, which was to be taken over by France and Spain in 1912; Egypt, which was to become a British protectorate in 1914; and Ethiopia, which was to be invaded by Italy in 1935.

The map of Africa, partially shattered by the First World War, after which Germany was deprived of all her colonies, survived thereafter almost unchanged until 1960. But since then there has been an upheaval as sudden and as widespread as the scramble which brought the African empires into existence. One old name after another has been revived as former colonies have achieved nationhood; and only in the south has the struggle for independence yet to be resolved. In looking at the map of modern Africa – at such names as Zaire, Zimbabwe, Guinea, Angola, Uganda, Niger, Chad – the adventures of the explorers who first traversed these countries are vividly recalled.

GLOSSARY

The spelling of the vernacular words listed here has followed that of the original texts. Where the word is still in current usage in a major African language, this has been indicated by Ar. = Arabic; H. = Hausa; Kan. = Kanuri; Sw. = Swahili.

Aendi	thieves
Aguardiente	strong Portuguese brandy
Almamy	title of local chief in the Gambia
Askari (Sw.)	soldier, armed policeman or escort
Babbar Salla (H.)	Id-el-Kabir, the major Muslim festival held on the tenth day of Muharram to mark the Pilgrimage rites in Mecca
Barka (Ar.)	a blessing, also used for 'thank you' (also *berka*)
Bambarnia	a kind of bush
Bazeen (Ar.)	coarse kind of *couscous* (*q.v.*), usually made from millet
Begos	heavy wooden collars fastened tightly round the neck of slaves or criminals
Bentang	raised platform under shady tree used as a village public meeting place
Beredi (Sw.)	cold; ice; hence snow (Sw. : *baridi*)
Bint-el-re (Ar.)	princess (Ar. : *bint*)
Blaqua	a mantrap, consisting of a deep hole dug into a path with sharp stakes at the bottom, the whole covered over with grass
Booza	an intoxicating drink made from corn, honey, peppers and the root of a certain grass generally fed to cattle
Burnous	Arab dress consisting of hooded cloak, usually made from wool or from wool and camel-hair
Caboceer	headman of a town
Caffas	balls of porridge made from corn, boiled to the consistency of thick paste
Caftan	*see* kaftan
Celane	kind of spurge found on sandy soil in the Western Sudan
Coffle	a gang or caravan of roped slaves on the march (? corruption of *kafila*, *q.v.*) Also *gafflie*
Coozies	circular, grass-roofed dwelling huts (Kan. : *kasi*)
Couscous (Ar.)	stew of granulated wheat, barley or flour cooked over steaming broth, generally containing vegetables and sometimes meat (Ar. : *kuskus*)
Coussabes (Ar.)	a sort of shirt embroidered with gold
Dum palm	kind of palm with forked stems, commonly found in the Western Sudan, also known as 'Gingerbread Palm', *Hyphaene thebaica*; H. : *goruba*
Durra (Ar.)	sorghum grass of the sugarcane family; Indian millet, *Sorghum vulgare*
Fighi (Ar.)	writer of protective charms; scribe or jurisconsult (Ar. : *faqih*)

Fsug	market (corruption of Ar. *suq*)
Gafooly	parched beans or barley (also *gufally*)
Gerbas	waterskins (Ar. : *qirba*)
Gombo	a soup made of okra or 'lady's fingers', *Hibiscus esculentus* (also *gumbo*)
Goorgee	kind of tree with dark red flowers
Goora (H.)	*kola* nut(s) (*q.v.*), used throughout West Africa for ceremonial courtesies as well as for sustenance (also *goro*)
Grisgris	magic or *juju*; charm, amulet (also *greegree*)
Gussub	porridge made from grain or millet, often mixed with onions, peppers and hot fat
Hongo	a toll, or payment to a chief to ensure safe passage through his territory; hence often a bribe, extortion
Jellaba	loose cloak with hood worn by Arab men
Kabaka	traditional title of the king of Buganda
Kadi (Ar.)	Islamic judge
Kaffir (Ar.)	Muslim term of contempt for an infidel
Kaftan	long-sleeved outer garment open in front, made of wool or camel-hair, originally from Turkey often used as a present to a favourite in north Africa
Kafila (Ar.)	caravan or camel-train
Kaid (Ar.)	Islamic governor of a province
Kalgo (H.)	shrub commonly found on uncultivated land, whose bark is used for cordage (also *kargo*); *Bauhinia reticulata*
Kirdi	generic term used to describe certain 'pagan' (animist) peoples in the western Sudan and north Africa (also *kerdy*)
Kohl (Ar.)	antimony, used in Africa and Asia for adornment of the eyelids
Kola	the bitter seed of the *Cola acuminata*, with renowned stimulant properties. *c.f. goora*
K(o)uka (H.)	the baobab or 'monkey-bread' tree, *Adansonia digitata*, found in west, east and central Africa
Kouskous	*c.f. couscous*
Liffa	a deadly snake found in the western Sudan
Litham (Ar.)	muslin veil, pulled up protectively over the mouth or nose
Magaria (H.)	a thorny shrub, with pale brown edible berries; *Zizyphus jujuba*
Manioc	cassava, a staple foodstuff in parts of Africa
Marabout	Muslim religious teacher, often a hermit; such a holy man's tomb
Merissa	alcoholic drink generally brewed from corn
Meskiti	temple
Mosi-oa-tunya	'The Smoke that Thunders', local name for the Victoria Falls
Mpafu	a tall tree, whose olive-like fruit is used as a scented oil for self-adornment
Muansa	hollowed-out piece of wood which when rubbed emits a strange noise
Mumbo-jumbo	west African fetish; a bugbear
Muto kwane	narcotic (*Cannabis sativa*) widely smoked by those living in the Zambezi valley
Neema-tuba	a kind of tree
Néoe	pulpy white fruit, used for quenching thirst
Pacotille	small stock of cheap goods used by travellers as presents to sweeten local officials
Pagazi (Sw.)	carriers or porters hired to headload goods and baggage on the march

Pombe (Sw.)	beer
Ramadan (Ar.)	the Moslem fast month, calling for abstinence from food or drink throughout the daylight hours
Riga (H.)	characteristic large gown, often embroidered, worn by Hausa men (*c.f. burnous, tobe*)
Saphie	written charm, amulet
Seriba (Ar.)	protective stockade to keep out enemies or wild animals; fortified encampment (also *zareba, zeriba*)
Sherif	descendant of the Prophet Mohammed through his daughter Fatima; a noble, illustrious person
Simoom (Ar.)	a burning, suffocating desert wind (Ar. : *samum*). Also *simoon*
Sinkatoo	dish made from meal mixed with sour milk
Skiffa (Ar.)	entrance-hut or hall, porch, portico (Ar. : *saqifa*)
Suag	kind of bush found in the desert, on which camels can feed
Talha	tree of the acacia family
Tobe (Ar.)	kind of loose-fitting shirt or gown, often dyed blue (Kan. : *kulgo*)
Tulloh	prickly tree found in the western Sudan
Ugali (Sw.)	staple east African foodstuff, being a porridge made with flour and water
Wadads	Moslem holy men, often itinerant, purveying charms and cures
Wadi (Ar.)	dry bed of a torrent; dried-up gorge
Waki (H.)	kind of porridge made from boiled beans (H. : *wake*)
Zeriba (Ar.)	*see* seriba

BIBLIOGRAPHY

ANSTRUTHER, IAN, *I Presume: Stanley's Triumph and Disaster*, London, 1956
AXELDON, ERIC, *Congo to Cape: Early Portuguese Explorers*, London, 1973

BAKER, JOHN NORMAN LEONARD, 'Sir Richard Burton and the Nile Sources', *English Historical Review*, LIX, 1944; 'John Hanning Speke', *Geographical Journal*, CXXVIII, 1962
BAKER, SIR SAMUEL W., *Ismailïa: A Narrative of the Expedition to Central Africa for the Suppression of the Slave Trade*, London, 1895
—— *The Albert N'yanza*, London, 1866
BARTH, HEINRICH, *Travels and Discoveries in North and Central Africa*, London, 1857–8
BARTTELOT, WALTER GEORGE (ed.), *The Life of Edmund Musgrave Barttelot*, London, 1890
BLAIKIE, W. G., *The Personal Life of David Livingstone*, London, 1894
BOVILL, E. W. (ed.), *Missions to the Niger*, 4 vols, Cambridge University Press, 1966
—— *Caravans of the Old Sahara*, London, 1933
—— 'Henry Barth', *Journal of the African Society*, XXV, 1926
—— *The Golden Trade of the Moors*, London, 1958
—— *The Niger Explored*, London, 1968
BRADNUM, FREDERICK, *The Long Walks: Journeys to the Sources of the White Nile*, London, 1969
BRIDGES, ROY CHARLES, 'Explorers and East African History', *Proceedings of the East African Academy*, I, 1963
BRODIE, FAWN, *The Devil Drives: A Life of Sir Richard Burton*, London, 1967
BROWNE, W. G., *Travels in Africa, Egypt and Syria*, London, 1806
BRUCE, JAMES, *Travels to Discover the Sources of the Nile in ... 1768 ... 1773*, 5 vols, London, 1790
BURCHELL, WILLIAM, *Travels in the Interior of Southern Africa*, London, 1822
BURCKHARDT, J. L., *Travels in Nubia*, London, 1822
BURKE, E. E. (ed.), *The Journal of Carl Mauch: His Travels in the Transvaal and Rhodesia, 1869–1872* (trans. F. O. Bernhard), Salisbury, Rhodesia, 1969
BURTON, ISABEL, *The Life of Captain Sir Richard F. Burton*, London, 1893
BURTON, RICHARD F., *Zanzibar*, London, 1872
—— *The Lake Regions of Central Africa*, London, 1860
—— *Abeokuta and the Cameroon Mountains*, London, 1863
—— *The Lands of Cazembs*, London, 1873
—— *Wanderings in West Africa*, London, 1863
—— *A Mission to Gele, King of Dahome*, London, 1864
BURTON, RICHARD F., and JAMES M'QUEEN, *The Nile Basin*, London, 1964
BURTON, RICHARD F., and VERNEY LOVETT CAMERON, *To the Gold Coast for Gold: A Personal Narrative*, London, 1883

321

CAILLIÉ RENÉ, *Journal d'un Voyage à Temboctou et à Jenne dans l'Afrique Centrale*, Paris, 1830

CAMERON, VERNEY LOVETT, *Across Africa*, 2 vols, London, 1877

CASATI, GAETANO, *Ten Years in Equatoria*, 2 vols, London, 1891

CHEESMAN, R. E., *Lake Tana and the Blue Nile*, London, 1936

CLAPPERTON, HUGH, *Narrative of Travels and Discoveries in Northern and Central Africa in 1822–4 and 1825–7*, London, 1831

—— *Journal of a Second Expedition into the Interior of Africa from the Bight of Benin to Saccato*, London, 1829

COUPLAND, REGINALD, *Kirk on the Zambezi*, Oxford, 1928

—— *The Exploitation of East Africa, 1856–1890*, London, 1939

—— *Livingstone's Last Journey*, London, 1945

DAVIDSON, BASIL, *Old Africa Rediscovered*, London, 1959

DEBENHAM, FRANK, *The Way to Ilala: David Livingstone's Pilgrimage*, London, 1955

DENHAM, DIXON, *Narrative of Travels and Discoveries in Northern and Central Africa*, London, 1826

DESCHAMPS, HUBERT, *L'Europe découvre l'Afrique*, Paris, 1967

DU CHAILLU, PAUL BELLONI, *A Journey to Ashango-Land and Further Penetration into Equatorial Africa*, New York, 1867

—— *Explorations and Adventures in Equatorial Africa*, London, 1861

DUPUIS, JOSEPH, *Journal of a Residence in Ashantee*, London, 1824

FARWELL, BYRON, *The Man Who Presumed: A Biography of Henry M. Stanley*, London, 1957

—— *Burton*, London, 1963

FISHER, ALLAN G. B., and HUMPHREY J. FISHER (eds.), *Gustav Nachtigal, Sahara and Sudan*, 3 vols, London, 1971–4

FISHER, RUTH H., *Twilight Tales of the Black Baganda*, London, 1912

FLINT, JOHN E. (ed.), *The Cambridge History of Africa*, vol. 5, Cambridge, 1976

FORAN, W. ROBERT, *African Odyssey: The Life of Verney Lovett–Cameron*, London, 1937

FORBATH, PETER, *The River Congo*, London, 1978

FOSKETT, REGINALD (ed.), *The Zambezi Journal and Letters of Dr John Kirk 1858–1863*, 2 vols, London, 1965

FOX BOURNE, H. R., *The Other Side of the Emin Pasha Relief Expedition*, London, 1891

GARDINER, A. F., *A Narrative of a Journey to the Zooloo Country*, London, 1836

GARDNER, BRIAN, *The Quest for Timbuctoo*, London, 1968

GELFAND, MICHAEL, *Livingstone the Doctor*, Oxford, 1957

GIBBON, LEWIS GRASSIC, *Niger: The Life of Mungo Park*, Edinburgh, 1934

GLADSTONE, PENELOPE, *Travels of Alexine*, London, 1970

GRANT, JAMES AUGUSTUS, *A Walk Across Africa*, Edinburgh, 1864

GRAY, JOHN MILNER, 'Mutesa of Buganda', *Uganda Journal*, I, 1934

GRAY, RICHARD, *A History of the Southern Sudan, 1839–1889*, London, 1961

GUENTHER, KONRAD, *Georg Schweinfurth*, Stuttgart, 1954

—— *Gerhard Rohlfs*, Freiburg, 1912

GWYN, STEPHEN, *Mungo Park and the Quest of the Niger*, London, 1934

HALL, RICHARD, *Lovers on the Nile*, London, 1980

—— *Stanley: An Adventurer Explored*, London, 1974

HALLETT, ROBIN, *The Penetration of Africa: European Enterprise and Exploitation, Principally in Northern and Western Africa*, London, 1965

—— *Records of the African Association, 1783–1831*, London, 1964

—— (ed.) *R. L. and J. Lander's Niger Journal*, London, 1965

HEAD, F. B., *The Life of Bruce, the Abyssinian Traveller*, London, 1830

HEUSS, THEODOR, HERBERT GANSLMAYR, and HEINRICH SCHIFFERS, *Gustav Nachtigal, 1869–1969*, Bad Godesberg, 1969

HIRD, FRANK, *H. M. Stanley: The Authorized Life*, London, 1935

HOWARD, C., and J. H. PLUMB, *West African Explorers*, London, 1951

HUXLEY, ELSPETH, *Livingstone and His African Journeys*, London, 1974

ITALIANDER, ROLF, *Heinrich Barth: Im Sattel durch Nord- und Zentral-afrika*, Wiesbaden, 1967

JEAL, TIM, *Livingstone*, London, 1973

JOHNSTON, HARRY HAMILTON, *The Nile Quest*, London, 1903

JONES, ROGER, *The Rescue of Emin Pasha*, London, 1972

Journal of African History

The Journal of Frederick Hornemann's Travels from Cairo to Mourzouk ... in 1797–8, London, 1902

Journal of the Royal Geographical Society

JUNKER, WILHELM (trans. A. H. KEANE), *Travels in Africa during the Years 1876–1886*, 4 vols, London, 1890–92

KAMM, JOSEPHINE, *Explorers into Africa*, London, 1970

KIRK-GREENE, A. H. M., *Barth's Travels in Nigeria*, London, 1962

—— 'West African Exploration: Africans, Auxiliaries and Also-Rans', in Shepperton, *op. cit.*

KRAPF, JOHANN LUDWIG, *Travels, Researches, and Missionary Labours During an Eighteen Years' Residence in Eastern Africa* (with an introduction by Roy C. Bridges), London, 1968

LAING, ALEXANDER GORDON, *Travels in Timmannee, Kooranko, and Soolima, Countries of West Africa*, London, 1825

LANDER, RICHARD, *Records of Captain Clapperton's Last Expedition to Africa*, 2 vols, London, 1830

LANDER, RICHARD, and JOHN LANDER, *Journal of an Expedition to Explore the Course and Termination of the Niger*, 3 vols, London, 1832

LISTOWEL, JUDITH, *The Other Livingstone*, 1974

LIVINGSTONE, DAVID, *Missionary Travels and Researches in South Africa*, London, 1857

LIVINGSTONE, DAVID, and CHARLES LIVINGSTONE, *Narrative of an Expedition to the Zambezi and its Tributaries*, London, 1865

LLOYD, CHRISTOPHER, *The Search for the Niger*, London, 1973

LUPTON, KENNETH, *Mungo Park: The African Traveller*, London, 1979

LYON, G. F., *A Narrative of Travels in Northern Africa, 1818–20*, London, 1821

MACKAY, MERCEDES, *The Indomitable Servant*, London, 1978

MACNAIR, JAMES I., *Livingstone's Travels*, London, 1954

MARTELLI, GEORGE, *Livingstone's River*, London, 1970

MAURICE, ALBERT (ed.), *H. M. Stanley: Unpublished Letters*, London, 1957

MIDDLETON, DOROTHY, *Baker of the Nile*, London, 1949

—— *Victorian Lady Travellers*, London, 1964

MOOEHEAD, ALAN, *The Blue Nile*, London, 1962

—— *The White Nile*, London, 1960

MUKASA, HAM, 'Speke at the Court of Mutesa I', *Uganda Journal*, XXVI, 1962

MURRAY, ALEXANDER, *Account of the Life and Writings of James Bruce*, Edinburgh, 1808
MURRAY, T. D., and A. S. WHITE, *Sir Samuel Baker: A Memoir*, London, 1895

NACHTIGAL, GUSTAV, *Sahara und Sadan. Ergebrisse Sechsjähriger Reisen in Afrika*, Berlin, 1879, 1889
NEWBURY, C. W. (ed.), *Richard F. Burton, Mission to King Gelele of Dahome*, London, 1966
NEWSON-SMITH, S. (ed.), *Quest: The Story of Stanley and Livingstone Told in their own Words*, London, 1978

OLIVER, ROLAND, and ANTHONY ATMORE, *Africa Since 1800*, 2nd edn, London, 1972
OSWELL, W. E., *William Cotton Oswell*, 2 vols, London, 1900
OWEN, RICHARD, *Saga of the Niger*, London, 1961

PARK, MUNGO, *Travels in the Interior Districts of Africa in the Years 1795, 1796 and 1797*, London, 1799
PARKE, THOMAS HEAZLE, *My Personal Experiences in Equatorial Africa*, London, 1891
PERHAM, MARGERY, and JACK SIMMONS (eds.), *African Discovery: An Anthology of Exploration*, London, 1942
PETERS, CARL (trans. H. W. DULCKEN), *New Light on Dark Africa: Being the Narrative of the Emin Pasha Expedition*, New York, 1891
PETHERICK, JOHN and KATHARINE, *Travels in Central Africa*, 2 vols, London, 1869
PLACE, JAMES, and RICHARDS, CHARLES, *East African Explorers*, London, 1960
PLUMB, J. H., *Men and Places*, London, 1966 (see also HOWARD)
—— *West African Explorers*, with C. Howard, London, 1951

RAVENSTEIN, ERNST GEORG, 'Verney Lovett Cameron', *Geographical Journal*, III, 1894
REID, J. M., *Traveller Extraordinary: The Life of James Bruce of Kinnaird*, London, 1868
RICHARD, CHARLES, see PLACE
RICHARDSON, JAMES, *Narrative of a Mission to Central Africa*, 2 vols, London, 1853
—— *Travels in the Great Desert of Sahara*, 2 vols, London, 1848
ROBINSON, RONALD E., JOHN GALLAGHER and A. DENNY, *Africa and the Victorians*, London, 1961
RODD, F. R., *People of the Veil*, London, 1926
ROHLFS, GERHARD, *Adventures in Morocco and Journey through the Oases of Draa and Trafilet*, London, 1874
—— *Reise durch Marokko*, Norden, 1884
—— *Quer durch Afrika*, Leipzig, 1874–5
—— *Land und Volk in Afrika*, Bremen, 1870
ROTBERG, ROBERT I. (ed.), *Africa and its Explorers: Motives, Methods and Impact*, Harvard University Press, 1970
—— *Joseph Thomson and the Exploration of Africa*, London, 1970

SCHAPERA, I. (ed.), *David Livingstone: Family Letters, 1841–1856*, London, 1959
—— *Livingstone's Missionary Correspondence, 1841–1856*, Berkeley, 1961
—— *Livingstone's Private Journals, 1851–3*, London, 1960
SCHIFFERS, HEINRICH (ed.), *Heinrich Barth: Ein Forscher in Afrika*, Wiesbaden, 1967
—— (trans. DIANA PYKE), *The Quest for Africa*, London, 1957

SCHUBERT, GUSTAV VON, *Heinrich Barth, der Bahnbrecher der deutschen Afrika-forschung*, Berlin, 1897

SCHWEINFURTH, GEORG (trans. ELLEN E. FREWER), *The Heart of Africa*, 2 vols, London, 1873

SEAVER, GEORGE, *David Livingstone: His Life and Letters*, New York, 1957

SELIGMAN, C. G., *Races of Africa*, London, 1930

SELOUS, F. C., *Travel and Adventure in South-East Africa*, London, 1893

SEVERIN, TIMOTHY, *The African Adventure*, London, 1973

SHEPPERSON, GEORGE (ed.), *David Livingstone and the Rovuma*, Edinburgh, 1965

—— *The Exploration of Africa in the Eighteenth and Nineteenth Centuries*, Edinburgh, 1971

SIMMONS, JACK, *Livingstone and Africa*, London, 1955

SIMPSON, D. H., *The Dark Companions*, London, 1976

SMITH, IAIN R., *The Emin Pasha Relief Expedition*, Oxford, 1972

SPEKE, JOHN HANNING, *What Led to the Discovery of the Source of the Nile*, Edinburgh, 1864

—— 'The Supposed Source of the Nile', *Blackwood's Magazine*, October 1859

—— *Journal of the Discovery of the Source of the Nile*, Edinburgh, 1863

—— 'The Upper Basin of the Nile', *Journal of the Royal Geographical Society*, XXXIII, 1863

STANLEY, LADY DOROTHY (ed.), *The Autobiography of Sir Henry Morton Stanley*, London, 1909

STANLEY, HENRY MORTON, *In Darkest Africa*, London, 1890

—— *How I Found Livingstone*, London, 1862

—— *Through the Dark Continent*, London, 1878

STANLEY, RICHARD, and ALAN NEAME (eds.), *The Exploration Diaries of H. M. Stanley*, London, 1961

SYMONS, A. J. A., *H. M. Stanley*, London, 1933

TABLER, E. C. (ed.), *The Zambezi Papers of Richard Thornton*, 2 vols, London, 1963

THOMSON, JAMES B., *Joseph Thomson, African Explorer*, London, 1896

THOMSON, JOSEPH, *To the Central African Lakes and Back*, London, 1881

—— *Through Masai Land: A Journey of Exploration among the Snowclad Volcanic Mountains and Strange Tribes of Eastern Equatorial Africa*, London, 1883

TROUP, J. ROSE, *With Stanley's Rear Column*, London, 1890

TUCKEY, JAMES KINGSTON, *Narrative of an Expedition to Explore the River Zaire . . . in 1816*, London, 1818

WALLER, HORACE (ed.), *The Last Journals of David Livingstone*, London, 1874

WALLIS, J. P. R. (ed.), *The Zambezi Expedition of David Livingstone, 1858–1863*, London, 1956

—— (ed.), *The Matabele Mission*, London, 1945

WARD, HERBERT, *My Life with Stanley's Rear Guard*, London, 1890

—— *A Voice from the Congo*, London, 1910

WASSERMAN, J., *H. M. Stanley, Explorer*, London, 1932

WATERFIELD, GORDON (ed.), *Richard F. Burton, First Footsteps in East Africa*, London, 1966

WELBOURN, FREDERICK B., 'Speke and Stanley at the Court of Mutesa', *Uganda Journal*, XXV, 1961

WELCH, G., *The Unveiling of Timbuctoo*, London, 1938

WELLARD, JAMES, *The Great Sahara*, London, 1964

WEST, RICHARD, *Brazza of the Congo: European Exploration and Exploitation in French Equatorial Africa*, London, 1972

INDEX

Abai River, *see* Nile, White
Abakah people, 246
A-Banga people, 243
Abeokuta, 223
Aboh, 149, 150, 152
Aboudah, Lander's slave, 126, 127, 128
Abyssinia, *see* Ethiopia
Achmet, nephew of Naib of Massawa, 25, 27
Addis Ababa, 32
Adelan, Sheikh, 48
Adele, chief of Badagry, 133, 134–5
Aden, 193, 205, 212
Adishen, chief of Mandara, 185
Adowa, 30, 193
Affadai, 99
Affagay, 90
African Association: formed, 13, 18; aims of, 19; proposed expeditions, 19; and exploration of R. Niger, 53, 55; Park, 55–6, 72, 74; Edwards, 73; Hornemann, 79; and Geographical Society, 130; Burckhardt, 228
African Inland Commercial Company, 152
Agades, 180–81
Agau people, 41, 42, 44
Ajawa people, 277
Akka people, 242–3, 249
Albasini, Joao, 253
Albert, Lake: Luta N'zigé, 217, 220; Baker, 220–21; Gessi, 245; Livingstone, 280; Stanley, 309, 313, 314
Albert, Mount, Krapf names, 201

Albert, Prince (1819–61), 279
Alburkah, 152
Alexander Bay, 18
Alexandria, 13, 24, 50, 226, 244
Algiers, 23
Ali, ruler of Ludamar, 65–6, 67
Almeida, Lourenço de (d.1508), *History of High Ethiopia*, 24
Alvarez, Francisco, 24
Alvarez, José Antonio, 298, 299, 300, 301, 302
Amadi Fatouma, Park's guide, 77, 78
Amoul-Gragrin, 175
Anderson, Alexander, 73, 75, 77
Angala, 99
Angola, 17
Angornu, 89, 99
Antonio, son of chief of Bonny, 135
Arabs: invasions of Africa by, 15; on slaving expedition, 89, 90, 93–4; killed and wounded, 95; accompany Clapperton and Oudney 104; Shuwa, 106; armed escorts for caravans, 106; and the English, 110, 182–3; widow of Wawa, 118; Lander and, 125; robbers, 184; location of dagger, 206; slave trade, 276, 277, 281, 295; Livingstone and, 281, 282–3; medical skill, 283; Livingstone's stores sold, 284; Cameron and, 291; Tippu Tib, 296
Arami, Tubu chieftain, 234–5, 236

Arguin archipelago, 17
Arouane, 175
Aruwimi River, 312
Asongho, 77
Assoudo, 115
Aswan, 49, 50, 226
Aswan cataract, 13
Ato Aylo, chief adviser of the Iteghe, 32–3
Atoopa, 138
Axum, ruins of, 30

Baba, Caillié's host, 168, 169
Babani, the sheikh, 161, 162
Ba-bemba people, 281
Badagry, 113, 127–9, 132–135, 136
Baga people, 167
Bagamoyo, 287, 308
Bagirmi, 89, 98, 100–101, 103, 186
Bailunda, mountains of, 303–4
Baines, Thomas, 274
Bakalahari people, 259
Bakangai, a chief of the A-Barmto, 249
Bakel, 165
Baker, Florence, 218, 220, 221, 222
Baker, Samuel, 217–18, 220–22, 280, 314
Bakhatla people, 257
Bakongo people, 17
Bakwain people, 258
Balugani, Luigi (d. 1771): and Bruce, 23, 39, 50; in Ethiopia, 27, 30; death of, 38, 45; crosses Nile, 42
Bamako, 77
Bamba, 77
Bambara, 69, 188
Bambarre, 283
Bangala people, 310